A Strictly Biblical PERSPECTIVE MINISTRIES

ONE STEP WITH JESUS RESTORATION PROGRAM

WHAT GOD'S WORD SAYS ABOUT ADDICTION AND RELAPSE PREVENTION

A Biblical Cognitive Relapse Prevention
Support Group
Participant Guide

Robert F. Vann

Forewords by Jorge Valdes, PhD;
and Reverend Joseph Williams

ISBN 978-1-64471-596-3 (Paperback)
ISBN 978-1-64471-597-0 (Digital)

First Edition

Covenant Books, Inc.
11661 Hwy 707
Murrells Inlet, SC 29576
www.covenantbooks.com

DEDICATION

This workbook is dedicated to every individual that has been called by God to minister to individuals addicted to alcohol and other drugs. This workbook will equip them with the biblical insight necessary to complete the task God has set before them.

This workbook is likewise dedicated to thousands of Christians participating in the world's recovery system, unaware of its high recidivism rate, through little knowledge of the spiritual battles that shall confront them.

We also dedicate this manual to the millions of individuals who are seeking to enter into an intimate relationship with the God of the Bible. It is written and dedicated to those searching to find true deliverance from addiction, rather than accepting a counterfeit god of the world's recovery system by settling for merely arresting their addiction.

Furthermore, this workbook is dedicated to the thousands of Christians struggling with relapsing, who have a desire to please God, but need practical biblical know–how to avoid yielding to their old sinful and fleshly cravings.

Finally, this workbook is dedicated to millions of nonbelievers who are bound in sin and addictive behavior, being alienated from God, but searching for a true solution. This workbook was designed so that they would look for the answer to their addiction within the "Body of Christ," by accepting Jesus Christ, the only true solution to sin and addiction.

TABLE OF CONTENTS

List of Illustrations

FOREWORD

Jorge Valdes, PhD
(Former kingpin in the Medellin Drug Cartel of Columbia)

Dr. Jorge Valdes, founder of Coming Clean Ministries, Inc., provides the following insight into the enormous problem of drug addiction in America. As we look around us, it seems that our country is totally consumed with what we have come to call the "War on Terrorism." It seems that this "war" is mainly focused on fighting a foreign enemy who is located somewhere in the Middle East. This terrorist, by most accounts, is responsible for taking the lives of approximately 5,000 Americans. The senseless death of even one American should be enough to alarm our nation, and especially our churches. Yet, what amazes me is how we have been so blinded into not seeing that the greatest terror America faces are the drugs and addictions that are claiming the lives of so many Americans each year. The biggest tragedy is that over 27,500 of these victims are teenagers!

I have known Bob Vann to be not only an authority and great resource in the field of addiction and relapse prevention, but also a man with a passion for his work. Thus, it is refreshing to see him design The One Step with Jesus Restoration Program and author *A biblical Perspective of Addiction and Relapse Prevention*; a book that offers great insight into fighting a war which cannot be won by law enforcement, no matter what resources are allocated to it. This is a war that will not be fought on some foreign soil but in our blessed land. And a war where the greatest cost is the blood of our youth. If Abraham Lincoln is correct in his assessment that the future of mankind lies in the hands of our youth, Bob's contribution to fighting this war will be to aid us in assuring that there will be a future.

Reverend Joseph Williams

The abuse of drugs and alcohol is a tremendous blight on our country and many cultures around the world in this current age. Millions of souls have been greatly marred or totally destroyed over the past several decades by this insidious bondage. Unfortunately, Christians have not been immune to this terrible plague. Church leaders too often find themselves in a quandary as to how to help church members, their families, or members of their community in finding relief from bondage to drugs and/or alcohol.

As a former drug and alcohol abuser for thirteen years and having worked directly and indirectly in this field now for over twenty years, I am naturally more sensitive to this issue than many others in our society. Like many others who have worked in this field, I have met with a great deal of frustration due to the lack of success and progress we have made in learning to help people get off and stay off drugs permanently. Many related theories have been advanced over the years that have promised to increase success in this area, only to meet with meager or no success.

Ever since I have worked in this field, it has commonly been accepted that substance abuse is a spiritual problem. Alcohol Anonymous (AA) related programs have done much to advance this idea.

Their advancement of the belief that submission to a "higher power" being crucial to one's success in getting off and staying off drugs is widely known and practiced in substance abuse treatment circles. To them, however, "higher power" does not necessarily refer to the God of the Bible. In fact, it has been my observation that strong Christian convictions by those seeking treatment and bringing Bibles to "meetings" have been often ridiculed.

Like the aforementioned groups, I too believe that substance abuse is a spiritual problem; therefore, a spiritual solution is crucial to overcoming it successful. In fact, I have had the privilege over the years to become a part of a wonderful fraternity of men and women, including Robert Vann, whose lives have been dramatically transformed by the power of God. Some like me have experienced dramatic deliverance from drugs and alcohol through a miraculous event. Others have experienced deliverance and restoration through a process. The thing we have in common is that we all acknowledge that it was the power of God and not a program that ultimately helped us to achieve wholeness in our lives.

It is my firm conviction that it is the church that truly possesses the answer to the daunting challenge we face related to helping people overcome this devastating bondage. So why it is that many church leaders shrink away from direct ministry to those bound by substance abuse, opting to refer them to professionals outside of the church? Many pastors have referred church members to secular counselors and programs for substance "treatment." Many of these counselors and agencies do not see the church, the scriptures, or the God of the Bible as being relevant to the "recovery process." This is tragic!

Church leaders engage in this unfortunate practice simply because they do not know how to work with substance abusers. These kinds of courses are not offered in most Bible colleges and seminaries. And counseling professionals have done an effective job in convincing the clergy to stay out of this work, that they should leave it to the "professionals." As a result, too many Christians and their families continue to suffer through this cruel bondage, believing that they can never be truly free by the power of God.

Thank God for brothers like Robert Vann! I had the privilege of working shoulder to shoulder with Bob in ministry to prisoners, ex–prisoners, and their families for many years. Nearly 90 percent of those we have worked with have at one time been in bondage to substance abuse. Together, we rejoiced over victories and wept over apparent tragedies in the lives of those we served. We learned by suffering through the failure of the secular substance abuse treatment community, by searching the scriptures, and by hearing the testimonies of other victorious Christians that the answer to this dilemma lies in the Word of God.

Bob has allowed God to use his education, training, and own personal experience (past bondage to addiction) to establish an effective biblical approach to overcoming the ravages of substance abuse. Bob has done the difficult work of laboring in the Word, day and night, to find biblical principles related to helping anyone, Christian and non–Christian, find true freedom from addiction.

Pastors and other church leaders will find Bob's work tremendously helpful in first understanding the spiritual dynamics of addiction from a biblical perspective and to implement these principles to effectively minister to members of their congregation and their community. It will help them to reclaim ground that has been lost to the enemy of our souls. It is true that substance abuse is a spiritual issue that calls for a spiritual response. Who better to address these spiritual issues than the Church of Jesus Christ? This is the time for the church to rise up and confront and overcome this great challenge through God's power.

By allowing God to use his gifts, Bob has provided us with a great teaching tool that will help us to more effectively wield the very powerful spiritual weapons at our disposal. You will be tremendously helped and encouraged as you feast on this bountiful spiritual banquet our brother Bob Vann has prepared for us. Oh, taste and see that the Lord is good!

PREFACE

WELCOME
TO THE
ONE STEP WITH JESUS
RESTORATION PROGRAM.
WHY ONE STEP WITH JESUS?
BECAUSE ONLY HE
COULD HAVE
PAID THE
PRICE,
AND
HE
DID!

The world's recovery system relies on 12 steps, therapeutic change, behavioral modification and sin management as a solution to the issue of addiction. God's solution to addiction is experienced through one step–that is, accepting Jesus Christ as Lord and Savior (salvation). Salvation provides spiritual transformation and the potential and power to address all sin not just addiction. The foundation of the "One Step With Jesus Restoration Program" is based salvation and restoration of the soul. "I am the way, the truth, and the life: no man cometh unto the Father, but by me. The Son therefore shall make you free, ye shall be free indeed." (John 8:26)

> "If ye continue in my word, then are ye my disciples indeed; And ye shall know the truth, and the truth shall make you free. (John 8:31, 32)"

What Did Salvation Cost God? And Who Paid the Price?

> For by grace are ye saved through faith; and that not of yourselves: it is the gift of God: Not of works, lest any man should boast. (Ephesians 2:8–9)

Yes, salvation is free and available to all mankind; yet, it cost God His most precious possession. Victory over every type of bondage to sin is included in salvation through Christ Jesus. Jesus has paid the price and obtained a victory for those who accept Him as Lord in every area of their lives, including being set free from the bondage of alcohol and other drugs.

The solution to every issue in life is found in a relationship with God through Jesus Christ, His Son. Christians are commanded to love God with all their heart, soul, and mind. In order to do this, we must first experience the love of God. The Father's love is demonstrated through His grace by supplying mankind with all they need to enter into a loving relationship with Him.

The Greatest Commandment

> Jesus said unto him, "Thou shalt love the Lord thy God with all thy heart, and with all thy soul, and with all thy mind." (Matthew 22:37)

Learning to love God with all our heart begins with understanding what it cost God to enter into a relationship with fallen man; it cost Him His most precious possession, His Son.

God demonstrated His great love for all of mankind by sacrificing, His only begotten Son, in order that mankind might enter into a relationship with Him.

Every Christian must accept and learn to experience His great love demonstrated on Calvary by understanding their position in Christ and thereby exercising faith in that position.

True love for God comes from experiencing His love: a love demonstrated by Him sacrificing His most precious possession, Jesus Christ.

Understanding all that Christ endured emotionally, spiritually, and physically—prior to and during His crucifixion—will help every Christian apprehend how great God's love for them truly is. Subsequently, it will foster in them a genuine love for God.

> We love him, because he first loved us. (1 John 4:19)

> What? Know ye not that your body is the temple of the Holy Ghost which is in you, which ye have of God, and ye are not your own? For ye are bought with a price: therefore, glorify God in your body, and in your spirit, which are God's. (1 Corinthians 6:19–20)

The Price Jesus Paid Emotionally in the Battle of the Will: Agony in the Garden

Jesus experiences the darkest night of His Life.

> Then cometh Jesus with them unto a place called Gethsemane, and saith unto the disciples, "Sit ye here, while I go and pray yonder." And he took with him Peter and the two sons of Zebedee, and began to be sorrowful and very heavy. Then saith he unto them, "My soul is exceeding sorrowful, even unto death: tarry ye here, and watch with me. And he went a little further, and fell on his face, and prayed, saying, O my Father, if it be possible, let this cup pass from me: nevertheless, not as I will, but as thou wilt." And he cometh unto the disciples, and findeth them asleep, and saith unto Peter, "What, could ye not watch with me one hour? Watch and pray, that ye enter not into temptation: the spirit indeed is willing, but the flesh is weak." He went away again the second time, and prayed, saying, "O my Father, if this cup may not pass away from me, except I drink it, thy will be done." (Matthew 26:36–42)

Listen to Jesus's remarks as He struggles with His emotions leading up to His crucifixion: "My soul is exceeding sorrowful, even unto death." He requested the support of His closest friends during that time, "Tarry ye here, and watch with me."

Listen as He prays during that time of emotional distress: "Father, if it be possible, let this cup pass from me: nevertheless, not as I will, but as thou wilt." Here, Jesus battles against His own will through prayer. Jesus's intense emotional struggle against His will continues through three consecutive prayer sessions.

In anticipation of what's to come, He cries out in the midst of His emotional struggle, in essence saying, "Father, if it is at all possible that I don't have to endure what's ahead, allow it not to happen." However, after His final prayer session, Jesus submits His will to the Father's by completing His mission and work on Calvary's cross.

Jesus acknowledges the weakness of His humanity (flesh) and its unwillingness to experience the cross. He tells that the spirit is indeed willing, but the flesh is weak. However, through prayer, His spirit wins out in the midst of the emotional struggle enabling Him, even through angelic empowerment to endure the cross.

> And he came out, and went, as he was wont, to the Mount of Olives; and his disciples also followed him. And when he was at the place, he said unto them, "Pray that ye enter not into temptation." And he was withdrawn from them about a stone's cast, and kneeled down, and prayed, saying, "Father, if thou be willing, remove this cup from me: nevertheless, not my will, but thine, be done." And there appeared an angel unto him from heaven, strengthening him. And being in an agony he prayed more earnestly: and his sweat was as it were great drops of blood falling down to the ground. And when he rose up from prayer, and was come to his disciples, he found them sleeping for sorrow, and said unto them, "Why sleep ye? rise and pray, lest ye enter into temptation." (Luke 22:39–46)

The gospel of Luke provides an even clearer picture of the emotional struggle the savior experienced, declaring, "And there appeared an angel unto him from heaven, strengthening him."

Furthermore, the intensified emotional struggle is clearly seen and expressed by this statement, "And being in agony he prayed more earnestly: and his sweat was as it were great drops of blood falling down to the ground."

Agony refers to tension before combat, fight, or a wrestling match. It involves a type of fear that trembles in the face of an issue, yet allows one to remain to face it.

What was causing such emotional and mental anguish? Jesus was anticipating the ordeal He had ahead of Him, which wasn't only physical, but spiritual as well. He was anticipating:

The agony of being spiritually separated from His Father, knowing that His Father, God is holy and cannot look upon sin.

In His Holiness, never having sinned, He was contemplating having to experience the burden of shouldering the sins of the world.

Being taunted by Satan, all his principalities, and the intense spiritual warfare he would endure.

The physical pain of the scourging and the crucifixion that would accompany His fulfilling the Father's mission.

The Price Jesus Paid Spiritually

> Hereafter I will not talk much with you: for the prince of this world cometh, and hath nothing in me. (John 14:30)

Christ was totally aware of the intense spiritual warfare that lay ahead of Him as He prepared to fulfill the Father's mission on earth.

> Then Jesus said unto the chief priests, and captains of the temple, and the elders, which were come to him, "Be ye come out, as against a thief, with swords and staves? When I was daily with you in the temple, ye stretched forth no hands against me: but this is your hour, and the power of darkness." (John 14:30)

Christ knew that those who came to crucify Him were under demonic influence, being led by Satan and his cohorts.

> Howbeit we speak wisdom among them that are perfect: yet not the wisdom of this world, nor of the princes of this world, that come to nought: But we speak the wisdom of God in a mystery, even the hidden wisdom, which God ordained before the world unto our glory: Which none of the princes of this world knew: for had they known it, they would not have crucified the Lord of glory. But as it is written, Eye hath not seen, nor ear heard, neither have entered into the heart of man, the things which God hath prepared for them that love him. (1 Corinthians 2:6–9)

What Satan and his demonic forces didn't know was that in their attempt to destroy Jesus by putting Him to death on the cross, they were actually assisting Him in fulfilling the Father's mission of redemption.

The Price Jesus Paid Physically

> I am poured out like water, and all my bones are out of joint: my heart is like wax; it is melted in the midst of my bowels. My strength is dried up like a potsherd; and my tongue cleaveth to my jaws; and thou hast brought me into the dust of death. For dogs have compassed me: the assembly of the wicked have enclosed me: they pierced my hands and my feet. I may tell all my bones: they look and stare upon me. They part my garments among them, and cast lots upon my vesture. (Psalm 22:14–18)
>
> He was oppressed, and he was afflicted, yet he opened not his mouth: he is brought as a lamb to the slaughter, and as a sheep before her shearers is dumb, so he openeth not his mouth. (Isaiah 53:7)
>
> And so Pilate, willing to content the people, released Barabbas unto them, and delivered Jesus, when he had scourged him, to be crucified. (Mark 15:15)

A Careful Examination of the Procedure

Step by agonizing step, we'll walk with Jesus through the last of His momentous earthly life.

The Scourging

After Jesus's final trial before Pilate, the Roman governor had Jesus scourged (Matthew 27:26; Mark 15:15)—a cruel act that was completely unwarranted and unnecessary. Unlike Jewish scourging, in which the victim could not receive more than forty lashes (Deuteronomy 25:1–3), Roman law was not so humane. Jim Bishop, from his text, *The Day Christ Died*, provides a descriptive narrative of what was necessary for the scourging:

> A lictor, trained in the ghoulish art of torture, administered the scourging with an instrument called a flagellum. This had a round, wooden handle that had strips of leather attached to it. Into the ends of these strips were sown pieces of bone or small iron chains. The lictor had no limit to the lashes he could deliver, and no part of the body was off-limits.

Jesus was stripped and then tied to a low stone column. In vivid detail, modern-day medical doctors recreate the gruesome event as *The Journal of American Medical Association*, in its article, "On the Physical Death of Jesus Christ," states:

> As the Roman soldiers repeatedly struck the victim's back with full force, the iron balls would cause deep contusions, and the leather thongs and sheep bones would cut into the skin and subcutaneous tissues. Then, as the flogging continued, the lacerations would tear into the underlying skeletal muscles and produce quivering ribbons of bleeding flesh. Pain and blood loss generally set the stage for circulatory shock. The extent of blood loss may well have determined how long the victim would survive on the cross…
>
> The severe scourging, with its intense pain and appreciable blood loss, most probably left Jesus in a pre-shock state. Moreover, hematidrosis had rendered his skin particularly tender. The physical and mental abuse meted out by the Jews and the Romans, as well as the lack of food, water, and sleep also contributed to his generally weakened state. Therefore, even before the actual crucifixion, Jesus's physical condition was at least serious and possibly critical.

The Robe

But Jesus's suffering was far from over. The cruel soldiers, who had circled around Christ's bloody body like vultures, now moved in to pick at the remains.

> Then the soldiers of the governor took Jesus into the Praetorium and gathered the whole Roman cohort around Him. They stripped Him and put a scarlet robe on Him. (Matt. 27:27–28)

This was not a long flowing robe. The Greek term *chlamus* indicates a short cloak worn over the shoulders. Standing there, naked from the waist down, Jesus became the object of their vulgar remarks.

The Crown

Then came more violence.

> And after twisting together a crown of thorns, they put it on His head, and a reed in His right hand; and they knelt down before Him and mocked Him, saying, "Hail, King of the Jews!" They spat on Him, and took the reed and began to beat Him on the head. After they had mocked Him, they took the scarlet robe off Him and put His own garments back on Him, and led Him away to crucify Him. (Matthew 27:29–31)

Mocking, jeering, abusing—it's as if each soldier was trying to top the other's joke. Each took his turn spitting on Jesus...cursing His name...slapping and jabbing Him with the reed...punching His chest with their fists. Jesus, upon whom God would soon bestow a name that was above every other name, Jesus, at whose name every knee would someday bow. Jesus, before whom every tongue would someday confess, "He is Lord" (Phil. 2:9–11). But for now, humanity offered this king only spit, expletives, and fists. And Jesus bore it all with silent patient dignity (see 1 Pet. 2:23).

The Cross

After dressing Jesus, the soldiers followed their usual course with criminals. Such a victim was surrounded by four Roman soldiers and led by a centurion, all the while struggling to carry the six-foot crossbeam that would later be attached to the larger vertical post of the cross. And so it was with Jesus. After the scourging and beating, however, He was too weak to carry the beam Himself; Matthew tells us that Simon of Cyrene was pressed into the service to help Him (Matt. 27:37).

Above Jesus's head would hang a twelve-by-twenty-four-inch placard declaring His "crime:" This Is Jesus the King of the Jews (v. 37). Pilate had it written not only in Hebrew so the Jews could read it, but also in Latin for the Romans, and in Greek for the more educated and sophisticated in the crowd (John 19:20). No one was going to miss the meaning of what was about to happen. It was meant as a mockery...yet, it said more than anyone could realize (see Matt. 27:37).

The Gall

> They gave him vinegar to drink mingled with gall: and when he had tasted thereof, he would not drink. (Matthew 27:34, KJV)

The use of drugs and alcohol (sorcery) are cited in both the Old and New Testaments. In New Testament times, it was customary for criminals to be administered a potion called gall which was a mixture of old wine (alcohol), an unused herb referred to as a poisonous plant bitter in taste.

Both the Greek and Hebrew dictionaries state the plant was probably poppy, so this potion was a sedative mixed with alcohol to ease the pain of crucifixion.

The NIV Study Bible states, "Traditions says that the women of Jerusalem customarily furnished this pain-killing narcotic to prisoners who were crucified. Jesus refused to drink it because he wanted to be fully conscious until his death."

If Jesus had drank the potion, the redemption of mankind would have spoiled. Christ would have taken a worldly solution to alleviate His emotional, mental, and physical anguish.

Satan uses a strategy today in our culture that has led to us readily accepting the legalization and use of drugs such as alcohol, nicotine, and caffeine, and the widespread use of illegal drugs such as cocaine, marijuana, heroin, etc.

This incident should provide believers who are in restoration from addiction with practical biblical insight into Christ's victory over alcohol and other drugs and should provide them with inspiration during their own restoration from bondage to alcohol and other drugs.

We could never imagine the physical pain and emotional and spiritual anguish Christ experienced, and nothing that you have had to endure compares to His ordeal. However, just knowing His physical, emotional, and mental state as a man, and His refusing to accept the world's way out to alleviate his condition by sedating Himself should provide us with the courage to follow His example and resist the enemy and endure without using alcohol and other drugs.

The Crucifixion

Crucifixion was a barbaric form of capital punishment that originated in Persia. The Persians believed that the earth was sacred to Ormazd, the earth god, so death should not contaminate the earth. Criminals, therefore, were fastened to vertical shafts of wood by iron spikes and hung above the earth to die from exposure, exhaustion, or suffocation. Death was painfully slow and publicly humiliating. Jim Bishop, from his text, *The Day Christ Died*, again conveys the horror.

> The executioner laid the crossbeam behind Jesus and brought him to the ground quickly by grasping his arm and pulling him backward. As soon as Jesus fell, the beam was fitted under the back of his neck, and on each side, soldiers quickly knelt on the inside of the elbows. The thorns pressed against his torn scalp. With his right hand, the executioner probed the wrist of Jesus to find the little hollow spot. When he found it, he took one of the square-cup iron nails...raised the hammer over the nail head and brought it down with force...
>
> Two soldiers grabbed each side of the crossbeam and lifted. As they pulled up; they dragged Jesus by the wrists. With every breath, he groaned. When the soldiers reached the upright, the four of them began to lift the crossbeam higher until the feet of Jesus were off the ground. The body must have writhed with pain...
>
> When the crossbeam was set firmly, the executioner...knelt before the cross. Two soldiers hurried to help, and each one took hold of a leg at the calf. The ritual was to nail the right foot over the left, and this was probably the most difficult part of the work. If the feet were pulled downward and nailed close to the foot of the cross, the prisoner always died quickly. Over the years, the Romans learned to push the feet upward on the cross, so that the condemned man could lean on the nails and stretch himself upward (to breathe).

The Agony and Death

Excruciating pain stabbed Christ's body as He hung on unbending nails. Jim Bishop concludes:

> The pain in his wrists was beyond bearing, and...muscle cramps knotted his forearms and upper arms and the pads of his shoulders...his pectoral muscles at the sides of his chest were momentarily paralyzed. This induced in him an involuntary panic; for he found that while he could draw air into his lungs, he was powerless to exhale. At once, Jesus raised himself on his bleeding feet. As the weight of his body came down on the insteps, the single nail pressed hard against the top of the wound. Slowly, steadily, Jesus was forced to raise himself higher until, for the moment, his head hid the sign which told of his crime. When his shoulders were on a level with his hands, breathing was rapid and easier... He fought the pain in his feet in order to breathe rapidly for a few moments. Then, unable to bear the pain below, which cramped legs and thighs and wrung moans from the strongest, he let his torso sag lower and lower, and his knees projected a little at a time until, with a deep sigh, he felt himself to be hanging by the wrists. And this process must have been repeated again and again.

In every crucifixion, fever would inevitably set in, inflaming the wounds and creating an insatiable thirst. Waves of hallucinations would drift the victim in and out of consciousness. In time, flies and other insects would find their way to the open wounds.

To speed up death, soldiers would break the victims' legs so they could no longer raise themselves to breathe. But with Jesus, that wouldn't be necessary. He was already dead.

So the soldiers came and broke the legs of the first man and of the other who was crucified with Him, but coming to Jesus, when they saw that He was already dead, they did not break His legs. But one of the soldiers pierced His side with a spear, and immediately, blood and water came out (John 19:32–34)

One sign of death is the quick separation of dark red corpuscles from the thin, whitish serum of the blood, here called water. Normally, the dead do not bleed. But after death, the right auricle of the human heart fills with blood, and the membrane surrounding the heart, the pericardium, holds the watery serum. Jesus's heart must have been punctured with the spear, causing both fluids to flow from His side.

> And about the ninth hour Jesus cried with a loud voice, saying, "Eli, Eli, lama sabachthani?" that is to say, "My God, my God, why hast thou forsaken me?" (Matthew 27:46)

Jesus's spiritual separation from His Father was so devastating that the moment it occurred, Jesus cried out in a loud voice, "My God, my God, why hast thou forsaken me?"

The scene was so gruesome, the Father turned out the lights!

> And it was about the sixth hour, and there was a darkness over all the earth until the ninth hour. And the sun was darkened, and the veil of the temple was rent in the midst. And when Jesus had cried with a loud voice, he said, Father, into thy hands I commend my spirit: and having said thus, he gave up the ghost. (Luke 23:44–46)
>
> For even hereunto were ye called: because Christ also suffered for us, leaving us an example, that ye should follow his steps: Who did no sin, neither was guile found in his mouth: Who, when he was reviled, reviled not again; when he suffered, he threatened not; but committed himself to him that judgeth righteously: Who his own self bare our

> sins in his own body on the tree, that we, being dead to sins, should live unto righteousness: by whose stripes ye were healed. (1 Peter 2:21–24)
>
> And having spoiled principalities and powers, he made a shew of them openly, triumphing over them in it. (Colossians 2:15)

Jesus conquered and disabled them, stripping them of their weapons and power.

> Forasmuch then as the children are partakers of flesh and blood, he also himself likewise took part of the same; that through death he might destroy him that had the power of death, that is, the devil. (Hebrews 2:14)

ACKNOWLEDGEMENTS

Maria and I would like to acknowledge my brother, Michael D. Vann, and mother, Gladys Wilson, for their contributions to this workbook. We would also like to acknowledge our Grace Community of Detroit family, where our spiritual journey began, and our mentors, Pastor William and Dorothy Harris.

We would like to acknowledge the Detroit Rescue Mission Ministries, Prison Fellowship Ministries, and Transition of Prisoner's Inc. staff, where we were privileged to serve in full-time ministry for ten years. We would also like to acknowledge the ministries who allowed ASBP Ministries to use their materials in writing this workbook: Insight for Living; The Majesty of God's Son, by Charles R. Swindoll; The Unger Bible Book, by Merrill F. Unger; Effective biblical Counseling, by Lawrence J. Crabb, Jr.; Prison Fellowship Ministries; Effective Principles for Mentoring Ex–Offenders, by Robert Vann; Discover Your God-Given Gifts, by Don & Katie Fortune; and The Foundations of Christian Doctrine, by Kevin J. Conner.

A special thanks to The Atlanta Mission and Dunklin Memorial Church for allowing ASBP Ministries Inc. to use their Christ-centered materials on tools for recovery in this workbook (*Daily Attitude Inventory, Journaling and Body Ministry*).

The Last Mile

He'd reached the city just about dawn,
Had been mocked scorned and spat upon,
His earthly goal was now in sight,
On that day to become dark as night.
He had come too close to miss;
He must accept the Judas kiss.
A promise to His Father He had made,
For unbelievers the debt would be paid.
In exalted reverence it would be kept,
'though in anguish, tears would be wept.
His steps in blessedness had been taken,
He'd kept His followers from being shaken.
He taught prayers and songs to sing,
In their belief in God as King.
His heavenly bond could not be broken,
To all He met His words were spoken.
With love, as the Lord God saith,
Welded together as he taught faith.
His stride was forward as He bid God–speed,
Showed there is hope when there is need.
To all whom He met along the way,
He promised an answer for those who'd pray.
With gentle touch, this Son of God,
Wrought His miracles with a saintly nod.
Tarried on this earth only awhile,
Saved the world, then walked His last mile.
His back was bowed as our burdens He bore,
His brow bled from the thorny crown He wore.
He hung and died on the cross He drug up Calvary,
He asked His Father that forgiveness be.
His low beloved voice was quiet, was stilled,
The prophecy of Isaiah was then fulfilled…

—Gladys L. Wilson

BIBLICAL REFERENCES FOR PERPLEXING PROBLEMS

Alcoholism (See Drunkenness)

Anger
Gen. 4:5–7
Pro. 14:17, 29;
15:1, 18; 19:11, 19;
20:3, 22; 22:24; 24:29;
25:15, 28; 29:11, 22
Mark 3:5
Eph. 4:26–32
Jam. 1:19, 20

Adultery
Ex. 20:14
11 Sam. 11:2
Pro. 2:16–18, 5:1–23,
6:23–35; 7:5–27; 9:13–16
Hosea, book of,
Mal. 2:13–16
Mat. 5:28; 15:19; 19:9
1 Co. 6:9–11

Anxiety (See Worry)

Associations (bad/good)
Pro. 9:6; 13:20; 14:9;

Body

Ro. 12:1, 2
1 Co. 3:16, 17;
6:18–20; 15
11 Co. 5:1–4

Change
Eze. 36:25–27
Mt. 16:24
Eph. 4:17–32
Col. 3:1–14
1 Thes. 1:9
11 Tim. 3:17
Heb. 10:25
Jam. 1:14, 15
1 Pet. 3:9

Children (See Family)

Church
Eph. 4:1–16
Heb. 10:25
Rev. 2, 3

Commandment
Ex. 20
Pro. 13:13
Lk. 17:3–10
John 13:34; 15:12

Death

Psalm 23:6
Pro. 3:21–26; 14:32
1 Co. 15:54–58
Phil. 1:21, 23
Heb. 2:14, 15

Decision Making
11 Te. 3:15–18
Heb. 11:23–27

Depression
Gen. 4:6, 71 Pet. 2:1
Psa. 32, 38, 51
Pro. 18:14
11 Co. 4:8, 9

Desire
Gen. 3:6
Ex. 20:17
Pro. 10:3, 24;
11:6; 28:25
Mt. 6:21
Lk. 12:31–34
Ro. 13:14
Gal. 5:16
Eph. 2:3
Tit. 2:12; 3:3

Doubt

Jam. 1:6–8

Drunkenness
Pro. 20:1; 23:29
30; 31:4–6; 23:20
Eph. 5:18

Envy
Titus 3:3
Jam. 3:14–16

Family
Gen. 2:18, 24
Ex. 20:12

Husband/Wife
Gen. 2:18, 24
Eph. 5:22–33
Col. 3:18–21
1 Pet. 3: 1–17
1 Tim. 2:11–15

Parent/Child
Gen. 2:24
11 Co. 12:14

22:24; 23:20, 21; 29:24
Ro. 16:17, 18
1 Co. 5:9–13
11 Co. 6:14–18
11 Tim. 3:5

Assurance
Heb. 4:16; 6:11
1 Pet. 1:3–5

11 Pet. 1:10
1 John 5:13, 18, 19

Avoidance
Gen. 3:8
Pro. 18:1
1 Tim. 6:11
11 Tim. 2:22

Bitterness (See Resentment)

Blame Shifting

Gen. 3:12, 13
Pro. 19:3

1 John 5:2, 3
1 John 2:16

Communication
Eph. 4:25–32

Confession
Pro. 28: 13
Jam. 5:16

1 John 1:9

Conscience
Mat. 6:19
Acts. 24:16
Ro. 2:15
1 Co. 8:10, 12
1 Tim. 1:3
Heb. 13:18
1 Peter 3:16, 21

Conviction

John 16: 7–11
11 Tim. 3:17

Jude 15

Jam. 1:13–16; 4:2, 3
1 Pet. 1:14; 4: 2, 3
Jude 18

Discipline
Pro. 3:11, 12; 13: 24;
19:18; 22:6,
15; 23: 13;
29:15
1 Co. 5:1–13;
11:29–34
11 Co. 2:1–11
Eph. 6:1–4
1 Tim. 4:7
Heb. 12:7–11

Divorce
Gen. 2:24
Deut. 24:1–4
Isa. 50:1

Jer. 3:1

Mal. 2:16
Matt. 5:31,
32; 19:3–8
Mark 10:3–5
1 Co. 7:10–24,
33–34,
39–40

Eph. 6: 1–4
1 Tim. 3: 4, 5

Father
(See Family)

Fear
Gen. 3:10
Pro. 10:24;

29:25
Mat. 10:26–31

11 Tim. 1:7
Heb. 2:14, 15
1 Pet. 3:6, 13, 14
1 John 4:18

Forgiveness
Pro. 17:9
Mat. 6:14, 15;
18:15–17

Mark. 11:25

Luke 17: 3–10
Eph. 4:32

Col. 3:13
Jam. 5:15

1 John1: 8–10

Friendship
Pro. 27:6, 10; 17:9, 17
John 15: 13–15

Lying
Ex. 20:16
Pro. 12:19, 22

Eph. 4:25

Repentance
Luke 3:8–14; 24:47
Acts. 3:19; 5:31;
17:30; 26:20
11 Co. 7:10; 12:21

Gifts
Ro. 12:3–8
1 Co. 12–14
1 Pet. 4:10, 11

Gossip
Pro. 18:10; 11:13;
18:8; 20:19; 26: 20–22
Jam. 4:11

Grief
Pro. 14:13; 15:13
Isa. 1:10–17
Jer. 13:23; 22:21
Ro. 6–7
Gal. 5:16–21
Heb. 5:13ff
1 Pet. 2:14, 19

Homosexuality
Gen. 19
Lev. 18:22; 20:13
Ro. 1:26–32
1 Co. 6:9–11
1 Tim. 1:10

Hope
Pro. 10:28; 13:12
Ro. 15:4, 5
1 Thes. 1:3; 4:13–18
Heb. 6:11, 18, 19

Humility
Pro. 13:34; 15:33;
16:19; 22:4; 29:23
Gal. 6:1, 2
Phil. 2:1–11
Jam. 4:6, 10

Life–dominating Problems

1 Co. 6:9–12; 21:8
Eph. 5:18
Rev. 21:8; 22:18

Listening
Pro. 5:1, 2, 13; 13–18;
15:31; 18:13

Love
Pro. 10:12; 17:19
Mat. 5:44; 22:39, 40
Ro. 13:10
1 Co. 13
1 Pet. 1:22
1 John 4:10, 19; 5:2, 3
11 John 5, 6

Mother (See Family)

Obedience
1 Sam. 15:22
Luke 17:9, 10
Acts 4:19; 5:29
Eph. 6:1
Heb. 5:8; 13:17
1 Pet. 1:22

Peace
Pro. 3:1, 2; 16:7
John 14:27
Ro. 5:1; 12:18; 14:19
Phil. 4:6–9
Col. 3:15
Heb. 12:14

Pride

Resentment
Pro. 26:24–26
Heb. 12:15

Reward/Punishment
Pro. 13:24; 22:15; 29:15

11 Co. 2:6; 10:6
Heb. 10:35; 11:26
11 John 8

Sexuality
Gen. 2:25
1 Co. 7:1–5

Shame
Gen. 2:25
Pro. 11:2; 13:18
1 Co. 4:14

Stealing
Ex. 20:15
Pro. 20:10, 22; 29:24; 30:7–9
Eph. 4:28

Work
Gen. 2:5, 15; 3:17–19
Pro. 14:23; 18:9; 21:5; 22:29;
24:27; 31:10–31
1 Co. 15:58
Col. 3:22–24
1 Thes. 4:11
11 Thes. 3:6–15

Worry
Pro. 12:25; 14:30; 17:22
Matt. 6:24–34

Jealousy (See Envy)

Laziness
Pro. 12:24, 27; 13:4;
15:19; 18:9; 26:13–16
Matt. 25:26

Pro. 8:13; 11:2; 13:10;
16:18; 18:12; 21:24;
27:1; 29:23

Reconciliation
Matt. 5:23, 24; 18:15–17
Luke 17:3–10

Phil. 4:6, 7
1 Pet. 5:6, 7

Emergency Numbers May Be Dialed Direct

No Operator Assistance is Necessary

When in sorrow,	call John 14
When men fail you,	call Psalm 27
If you want to be fruitful,	call John 15
When you have sinned,	call Psalm 51
When you worry,	call Matthew 6:19–34
When you are in danger,	call Psalm 91
When God seems far away,	call Psalm 139
When your faith needs stirring,	call Hebrews 11
When you are lonely and fearful,	call Psalm 23
When you grow bitter and critical,	call 1 Corinthians 13
For Paul's secret to happiness	call Colossians 3:1–17
For understanding of Christianity,	call 2 Corinthians 5:15, 19
When you feel down and out,	call Romans 8:31
When you want peace and rest,	call Matthew 11:25–30
When the world seems bigger than God,	call Psalm 90
When you want Christian assurance,	call Romans 8:1–30
When you leave home for labor or travel,	call Psalm 121
When your prayers grow narrow or selfish,	call Psalm 67
For great invention/opportunity,	call Isaiah 55
When you want courage for a task,	call Joshua 1
For how to get along with fellow men,	call Romans 12
When you think of investments and returns,	call Mark 10
If you are depressed,	call Psalm 27
If your pocket book is empty,	call Psalm 37
If you are losing confidence in people,	call 1 Corinthians 13
If people seem unkind,	call John 15
If discouraged about your work,	call Psalm 126
If you find the world growing small and yourself great	call Psalm 19

Alternate numbers:

For dealing with fear,	call Psalm 34:7
For security,	call Psalm 121:3
For assurance,	call Mark 8:35
For reassurance,	call Psalm 145:18

All lines to heaven are open, twenty-four hours a day!
Feed your faith, and doubt will starve to death.

MENTORING: A KEY COMPONENT IN RESTORATION

Mentoring is a biblically based relational learning process where you are befriended by a mature believer who has been successfully involved in the restoration process for the purpose of assisting you in reaching your full potential in Christ Jesus, through using God's resources.

> As iron sharpens iron, so one man sharpens another. (Proverbs 24:17, NIV)

1. Mentoring is a relationship based on a common desire for spiritual growth on the part of both the mentor and you, resulting in the reaping of mutual benefits. Study Proverbs 27:17.
2. The focus of the mentoring relationship is for you to learn the practical application of biblical principles in daily life by entering into a relationship with someone who is actively practicing the principles.
3. There are three factors necessary for the mentoring relationship to be successful:
   - ☐ *Attraction:* common ground (interest) on which to bond.
   - ☐ *Responsiveness:* the willingness of both you and mentor to interact with one another.
   - ☐ *Accountability:* the willingness of both you and your mentor to submit your lives to each other for inspection (being transparent), evaluation, and for the purpose of gaining spiritual growth and development.
4. The mentoring relationship will provide relational support for both your mentor and yourself in all aspects of your Christian walk as needed.

How to Select a Good Mentor

- ☐ A born-again believer who has actively been involved in the restoration process within their own lives for at least two years if they were in bondage to an addiction.
- ☐ Someone who accepts you knowing your past and does not hold it against you.
- ☐ Someone who is understanding and willing to listen and provide you with spiritual, mental, and emotional support.
- ☐ Someone you will allow to keep you accountable regarding your relationship with the Lord.
- ☐ Someone who is loyal and willing to keep your innermost secrets without ever violating your confidences by sharing them with others.
- ☐ Someone who is willing to share with you their experiences, feelings, insight, wisdom, and successes concerning their walk with the Lord as well as their failures.
- ☐ Someone who will be available for you night and day, even at an inconvenient time (3:00 a.m.).

- ☐ Someone who is genuine, living a consistent lifestyle walking with the Lord, who is who they say they are.

What Should You Expect from a Mentor

> Faithful are the wounds of a friend; but the kisses of an enemy are deceitful. (Proverbs 27:26)

1. To monitor your spiritual activities, church, Bible study, and Word-focused Fellowship Group attendance (for accountability).

> He who conceals his sins does not prosper, but whoever confesses and renounces them finds mercy. (Proverbs 28:13, NIV)

2. To inform you if you begin to lose focus during your restoration process and begin walking in the flesh (providing corrective feedback).
3. To share practical spiritual insights with you regarding their own restoration from a lifestyle in bondage to drugs/alcohol.
4. To spend time with you in leisure activities within the community.
5. To be a resource guide, informing you of available resources within the church community.

Prayer for a Mentor

Dear heavenly Father,

I understand that I need a godly person in my life: someone who has spent some time with You and understands You. I need someone to help keep me accountable to You, to walk with me during difficult times, to challenge me to grow and reach my full potential in Christ Jesus. Father, please bring such a person into my life as You restore me from the effects of addiction. I ask this in Jesus's name… Amen.

Laying the Foundation

Understanding the Problem: Spiritual Disorder

For the word of God is *living* and *active.* Sharper than any double–edged sword, it *penetrates even to dividing soul and spirit,* joints and marrow; it *judges the thoughts and attitudes of the heart.* Nothing in all creation is hidden from God's sight. Everything is uncovered and laid bare before the eyes of him to whom we must give account.

—Hebrews 4:12–13, NIV

UNDERSTANDING THE PROBLEM: SPIRITUAL DISORDER

Learning Objectives

Group Participants will be able to:

- Describe the make-up or composition of man.
- Distinguish the difference between the *spirit* and the *soul* of man.
- Explain the origin of man's problems.
- Describe the solution to man's problems.

Key Biblical Concepts and Definitions

(1) Inner Man: Man's *spirit,* his new nature created in God's image and likeness, located in man's heart where the Holy Spirit resides; is how man interacts with God (Gen. 1:27).

(2) Outer Man: Man's soul consists of his mental (mind), volitional (will), and emotional (emotions) capacity to interact with others (Genesis 2:7).

(3) Heart: The *heart* is the seat or center of a believer's soul (thoughts, reasoning, understanding), will (judgments, decisions), and emotions (love, hatred, fear, joy, sorrow, anger) where it converges with their inner being, his spirit (Proverbs 4:20–23). By definition, the heart in also the inner man; it is the hidden man.

(4) Restoration issue: Man's soul (Outer Man) being restored back to its original position as a servant to man's spirit (Inner Man) rather than continuing to live independent of God. The original spiritual order being restored (James 1:21)

(5) Developmental Issue: The maturing of man's spirit (Inner Man) enabling it to maintain the authority of God assuming its original role as master (1 Peter 2:2).

The Composition of Man before His Fall: Spiritual Order (Relational Harmony—No Problems)

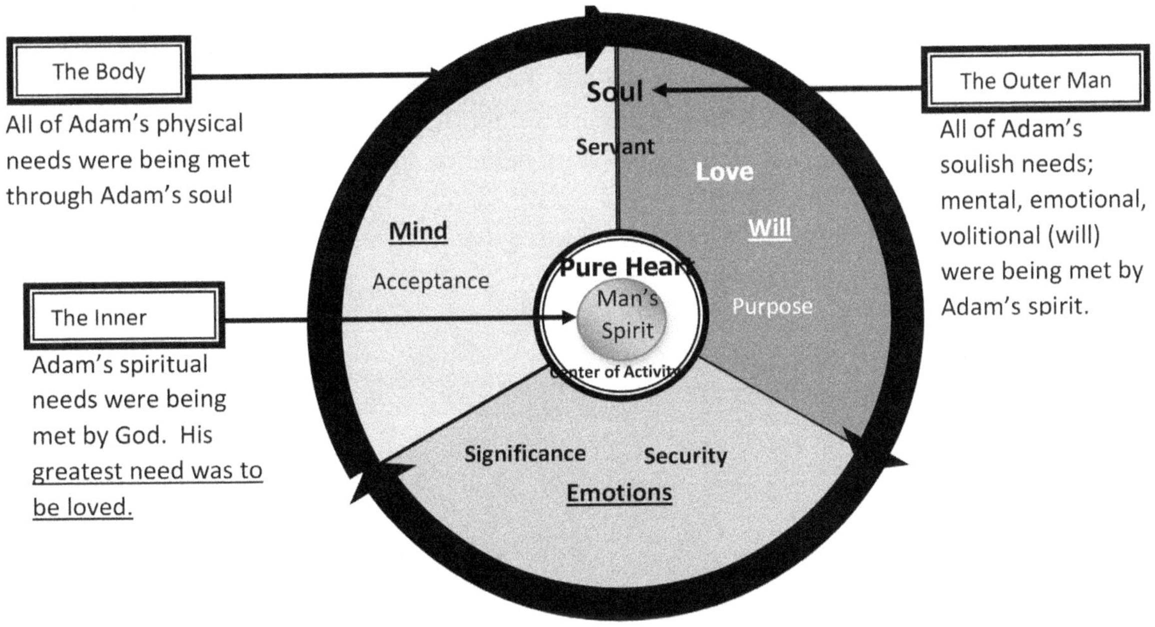

Figure 1: Relational Harmony

This diagram represents Adam's Divine Design (body, soul, and spirit) and the *relational harmony* that Adam experienced prior to the fall. You can see that he was spiritually minded and emotionally stable and his decisions were made based on the condition of his mind and emotions. He had security, significance, acceptance, and purpose; and he experienced God's love. He had no problems due to relational harmony and spiritual order.

As a believer, it is important to understand God's solution to problems and life controlling issues. This requires that you first understand God's view of how man's problems began. They began in the Garden of Eden with our spiritual parents, Adam and Eve.

- And God said, "Let us make man in our own image, after our own likeness:" (Genesis 1:26a). So God created man in His own image, in the image of God created He him; male and female created He them (Genesis 1:27a).
- And the Lord God formed man of the dust of the ground and breathed into his nostrils the breath of life; and man became a living soul (Genesis 2:7).

> The first reason God created man was for the purpose of relationship. God the Father wanted a family of children to share life with to get to know in a personal way. Throughout Scriptures God's desire for *fellowship* and *communion* with man is revealed. From the time that God sought Adam "in the garden in the cool of the day" God has been seeking *fellowship* with man (Genesis 3:8).
>
> —Kevin J. Conner

Adam was a spiritual being who had a soul and lived in a physical body. Through his *spirit, he interacted with God;* and via his *soul, he interacted with Eve and others.* Through his physical *body, Adam interacted with his environment.* Adam's heart was pure prior to the fall because he had no knowledge of "good and evil." Adam's life was governed by his relationship with God, centered on obedience. All of Adam's spiritual needs, including his greatest need, *being loved,* were met through his relationship with God.

Adam's spirit (Inner Man) was in charge; Adam's soul (Outer Man) found its greatest reward as a *servant* of Adam's spirit. Adam's identity was based on being created in God's image; he found his *significance* and *security* in his relationship with God. Adam had no problems, because there was *"spiritual order."* However, *spiritual order was disrupted by Adam and Eve's disobedience, leading to their fall in the garden.* They decided to live independent of God.

The Composition of Man Following the Fall: Spiritual Disorder (The Origin of All Man's Problems—Relational Poverty)

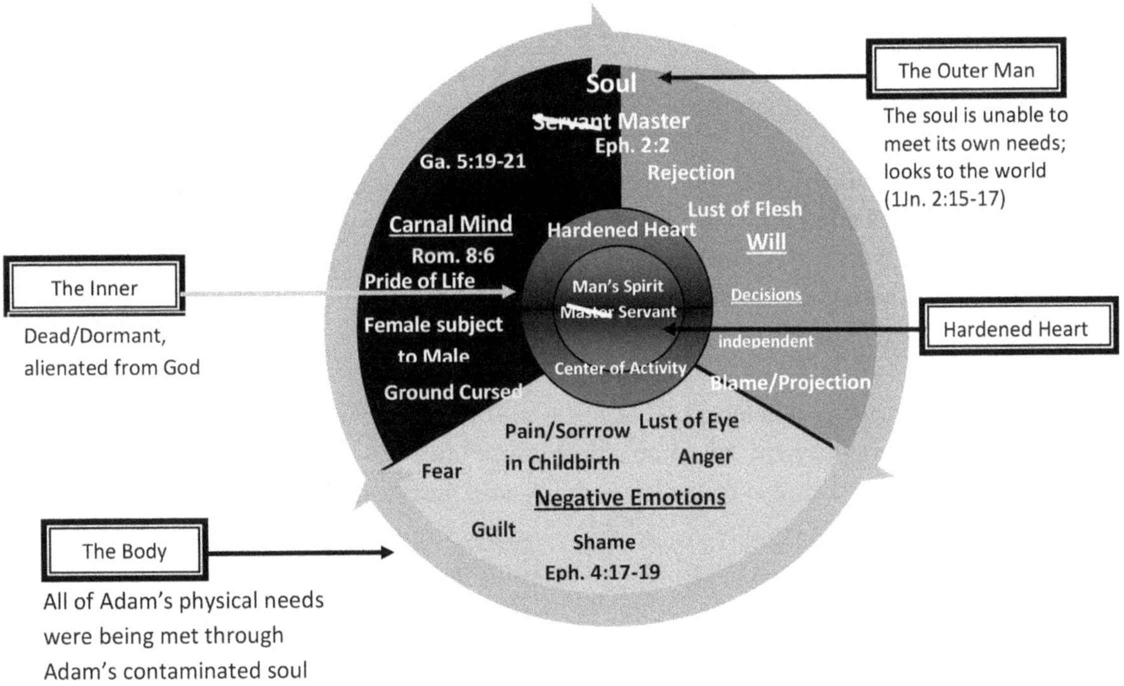

Figure 2: Relational Poverty

This diagram represents the condition of man's Soul & Spirit and the *relational poverty* that Adam and Eve experienced following the fall. You can see that they were carnal minded and emotionally unstable due to sin.

> The sin which caused Adam to hide from God has been hindering man's relationship with God ever since (Isaiah 59:1,2). It is only through the New Covenant that God's purpose of a relationship with man is fully accomplished. Now God indwells each believer making *fellowship* constantly available (John 14:16–20,23).
>
> —Kevin Conner

Man's greatest need, *being love,* is unfulfilled, and man enters the world a *soulish being* due to spiritual death. The *roles of the "inner man" and "outer man" are reversed; the soul becomes master and the human spirit becomes servant to the soul.* The soul was not designed by God to be master, but to be subordinate to man's spirit. Prior to Adam's fall, the soul's needs were met by his spirit, which depended on a proper relationship with God for fulfillment. Without a proper relationship with God, man looks to the world to find fulfillment. Consequently, God warns mankind about loving the world.

Steve Corbett and Brian Fikkert best describe *relational poverty* in their text *When Helping Hurts*:

> Of course, the grand story of scripture does not the end with creation. Adam and Eve disobeyed God, and their hearts were darkened. The Genesis account records that all four of Adam and Eve relationships became distorted: Their relationship with God was damaged, as their intimacy with Him was replaced with fear; their relationship with self was marred, as Adam and Eve developed a sense of shame; their relationship with others was broke, as Adam quickly blamed Eve for their sin; and their relationship to the rest of creation became distorted, as God cursed the ground and childbearing process.
>
> Love not the world, neither the things that are in the world. If any man love world, the love of the Father is not in him. For all that is in the world, the lust of the flesh, and the lust of the eyes, and the pride of life, is not of the Father, but is of the world. And the world passeth away, and the lust thereof: but he who doeth the will of God abideth forever. (1 John 2:15–17)

Satan, who in scripture, is referred to as the *god of this world* and perverted God's world order into an atmospheric environment for man's flesh—to fulfill its ungodly appetites, passions, and desires. Satan's diabolical scheme is to infiltrate man's soul and to deceive man into worshiping him. Attempting to fulfill his greatest desire, to be loved, and to meet other various needs through the lures of worldly attractions; man develops mental and emotional strongholds, making wrong decisions based on worldly perspectives, resulting in bondages, including drugs and alcohol.

Our spiritual parents, Adam and Eve, decided *to live independently of God by yielding to the lust of the flesh, the lust of the eyes, and the pride of life. As we harbor sin in our heart, the old nature rebounds in opposition to the will of God.* Spiritual death not only affected man's soul and spirit, but also his heart, causing it to become desperately wicked (Jeremiah 17:9–10). The heart is the seat or *center* of a believer's mind, will, and emotions, where it converges with our spirit or innermost being. The mind consists of one's thoughts, reasoning, and understanding. The will involves one's judgments and decisions. From our emotions stem love, hatred, fear, joy, sorrow, anger, etc. The change in the condition of the heart leads to the birth and origin of a *depraved nature* a nature opposed to God controlled by ungodly appetites and desires.

Due to the spiritual condition of our spiritual parents, Adam and Eve (Genesis 2:17), every human being enters the world spiritually dead, alienated from God. Therefore, spiritual disorder and a poor relationship with God and man's depraved nature are the *original causes of man's problems.*

CHRIST RESTORED SPIRITUAL ORDER: PROVIDING A SOLUTION TO ALL MAN'S PROBLEMS (POTENTIAL FOR RELATION HARMONY TO BE RESTORED)

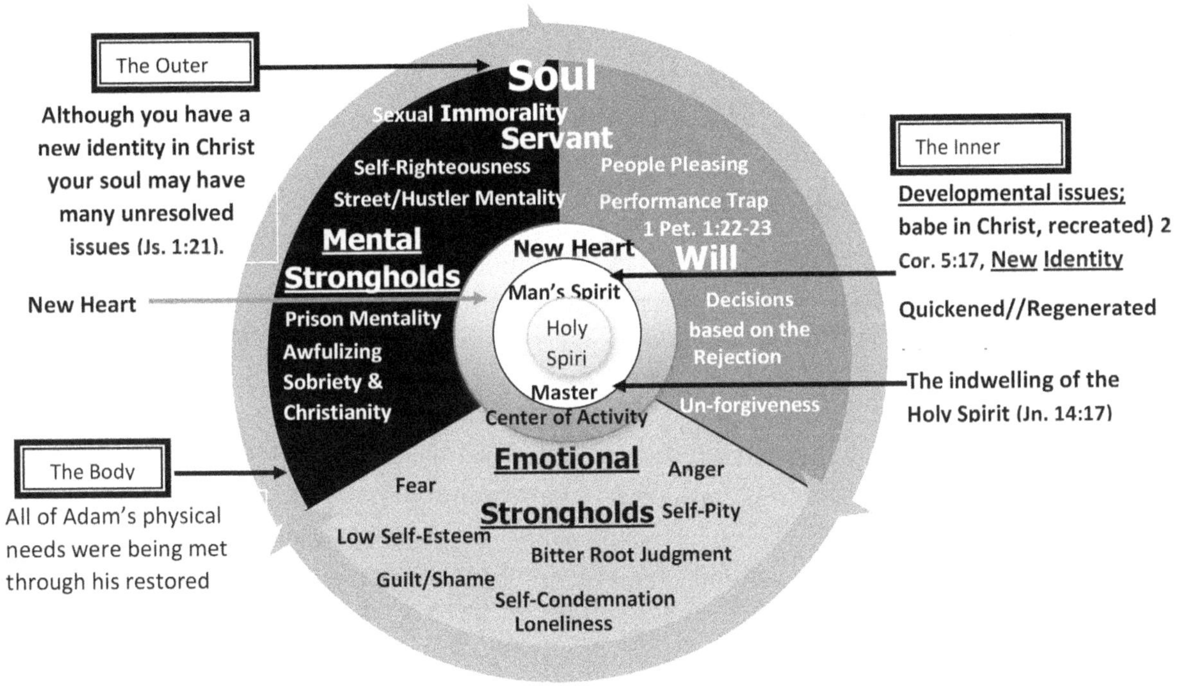

Figure 3: Salvation the Potential for Relational Harmony to Be Restored

This figure represents the condition of an individual's soul and spirit after being in bondage to crime/addiction following salvation. It also represents the potential for relational harmony to be restored through salvation with new birth as a believer is given a new nature and heart and the Holy Spirit comes to reside in that individual.

> You have been regenerated (born again), not from a mortal *(corruptible seed),* origin (seed, sperm), but from one that is immortal by the ever living and lasting Word of God. (1 Peter 1:23)

Salvation is the only way that *spiritual order can be restored.* Through salvation, God provided a solution to the origin of problems, a new identity in Christ, and restores man's original relationship with Him. Yet, there remain two major issues.

1. *a developmental issue* due to spiritual immaturity. Man's human spirit strives to maintain the authority of God; however, his spirit is only a "babe" at birth and must be developed.
2. *a restoration issue* attributable to a soul that has been polluted by the flesh and trained to live independently of God. As a result, it developed its own worldly and devilish wisdom and power. Being indoctrinated by the world, it strives to maintain its own independence and authority. The soul of man must be taught to cooperate and submit to the Spirit of God. The *Word of God is the key* to overcoming both the *developmental issue* of the human spirit and *restoring the soul.*

A Developmental Issue

> As newborn babes, *desire the sincere milk of the word*, that ye may grow thereby: 3If so be ye have tasted that the Lord is gracious. (1 Peter 2:2)
>
> However, Brethren, I could not talk to you as to spiritual [men], but as to nonspiritual [men of the flesh, in whom the carnal nature predominates], *as to mere infants [in the new life] in Christ [unable to talk yet!]* (1 Corinthians 3:1, AMP)
>
> For everyone who continues to feed on milk is obviously inexperienced and unskilled in the doctrine of righteousness *(of conformity to the divine will in purpose, thought, and action)*, for he is a mere infant [not able to talk yet]! (Hebrews 5:13, AMP)

As a believer, you need to understand the key to the spiritual development for a "babe" in Christ is *receiving a steady diet of the Word of God.* A believer must develop the spiritual maturity necessary to gain spiritual ascendency over the flesh and soul to cast down imaginations and capture and bring every thought in to obedience of God's Word. This takes more than a mere head knowledge of the Word or mental assent to obtain the spiritual maturity necessary to *conform to God's will and purpose in thought and action; it involves an experiential knowledge of the Word within one's everyday relationships and lifestyle.*

A Restoration Issue

> Wherefore lay apart all filthiness and superfluity of naughtiness, and receive with meekness the *engrafted word, which is able to save your soul.* (James 1:21)
>
> Since you have *purified your souls in obeying the truth* through the Spirit in sincere love of the brethren, love one another fervently with a pure heart. (1 Peter 1:22)
>
> (For the weapons of our warfare are not carnal, but mighty through God to the pulling down of strongholds;) *Casting down imaginations*, and every high thing that exalteth itself against the knowledge of God, and *bringing into captivity every thought to the obedience of Christ.* (2 Corinthians 10:4–5)

As a believer, you also need to understand the key to the restoration of the soul is in *digesting a study diet of God's word.* The Word is the weapon that the Holy Spirit uses in the *pulling down of the mental and emotional strongholds* that contaminate the soul. The word purifies (decontaminates) the soul, and the individual begins the process of being transformed through the renewing of the mind (Rom. 12:10). The process of the soul being saved (restored) is the end the faith process (1 Peter 1:9).

Every believer—not just believers being restored from crime, drugs/alcohol addiction—is faced with these two issues of *spiritual development* and *restoration of the soul.* God doesn't have a different plan for those in bondage to addictions. His plan for all His children is the same. God's children have different "besetting sins," however; His process for all His children is the same.

> During the years you spent separated from God, your worldly experiences thoroughly programmed your brain with thought patterns, memory traces, responses and habits which are alien to God. So even though your old skipper (nature) is gone, your flesh remains in opposition to God as a preprogrammed propensity for sin, which is living independent of God.
>
> —Neil Anderson

SMALL GROUP EXERCISE (15 MINUTES)

Each group will select a *recorder* to take notes, and a *reporter* to present information for their group.
Review the diagrams located in this section and discuss the following question within your group:

- ☐ What was Adam's make–up in the garden prior to his fall? How does this affect all of mankind? Please explain.
- ☐ What is the function of the soul & spirit and heart? Please explain.
- ☐ How was God's spiritual order restored?
- ☐ What two issues does every believer face, following salvation?
- ☐ What role does God's Word play in restoring spiritual order?

UNDERSTANDING THE SOLUTION: SALVATION

Learning Objectives

Group Participants will be able to:

- Identify God's threefold provision for Christian Recovery (restoration).
- Describe the three stages of Spiritual Progress.
- Identify the barriers that can hinder the ministry of the Word.
- Describe three factors that hinder the ministry of the Holy Spirit.
- Identify what causes the ministry of the Body of Christ to be ineffective in Christian recovery (restoration).

Key Biblical concepts & Definitions

1. God's threefold provision for Christian Recovery: The ministry of the Holy Spirit, the ministry of the Word, and the Ministry of the Body of Christ (church).
2. Three stages of Spiritual Progress: (a) Truth-Cause, receiving the Word, attending local church sermons, Bibles studies (Ro. 10:17; Eph. 4:11–12); (b) Faith-Process, discipline/training of the Holy Spirit, test, trials, temptations and relationships within the Body of Christ (1 Pt. 1:6; He. 12: 5–11); (c) Experience-Effect results—learning to walk in the Spirit, experiencing the Fruit of the Spirit (Ga. 5:22).

God's Threefold Provision for Christian Recovery

> According to the grace of God which is given unto me, as a *wise master builder*, I have laid the foundation, and another buildeth thereon. *But let every man take heed how he buildeth thereupon.* For other foundation can no man lay than that is laid, which is Jesus Christ. Now if any man build upon this foundation *gold, silver, precious stones,* wood, hay, stubble. (1 Corinthians 3:10–12)

Figure 4: God's Threefold Provision for Restoration/Recovery

As a believer being restored from alcohol/drug addiction, you should desire to become a "wise master-builder," and to do so, it is important that you understand the *necessity of using recovery strategies and tools based on God's threefold provision.* It's common for Christians in recovery to be *influenced more by the world's methods to recovery than to use God's threefold provision,* building on "gold, silver, and precious stone." What you must understand is that if you omit God's threefold provision, your tools become ineffective because they are no longer joining God in what He desires to do in your life; they are building on "wood, hay, and stubble."

Understanding Roles & Functions of the Holy Spirit

Understanding God's perspective of addiction begins with understanding how *His spiritual order was disrupted and how He restored His order through Jesus Christ.* The key to understanding God's solution is in not only understanding and accepting Jesus's role but, likewise, the role of the Holy Spirit who is every Christians' spiritual mentor. Every Christian is involved in a relational learning process with the Holy Spirit.

As a believer, you must understand that the primary method of change in your life is your relationship with the Holy Spirit. Matthew Henry's Commentary clearly defines the role of the believers' spiritual sponsor, the Holy Spirit.

> In the economy of our salvation, the *applying* and *effecting part* is especially attributed to the Holy Spirit. We are said to be *born of the Spirit,* to be *quickened and sanctified* by the Spirit, to be *led and guided, strengthened and helped, by the Spirit.* Through Him we *mortify sin, perform duty, walk in God's ways; all the acts and operations of the divine life in us,* the works and fruits of righteousness without us, all are *through this blessed and Holy Spirit,* who is therefore *called the Spirit of life, and of grace and holiness;* all grace is from Him. Earnestly therefore is He to be sought and greatly to be heeded by us, that we quench not his holy motions, nor resist and oppose Him in his workings.

Ministry of the Holy Spirit

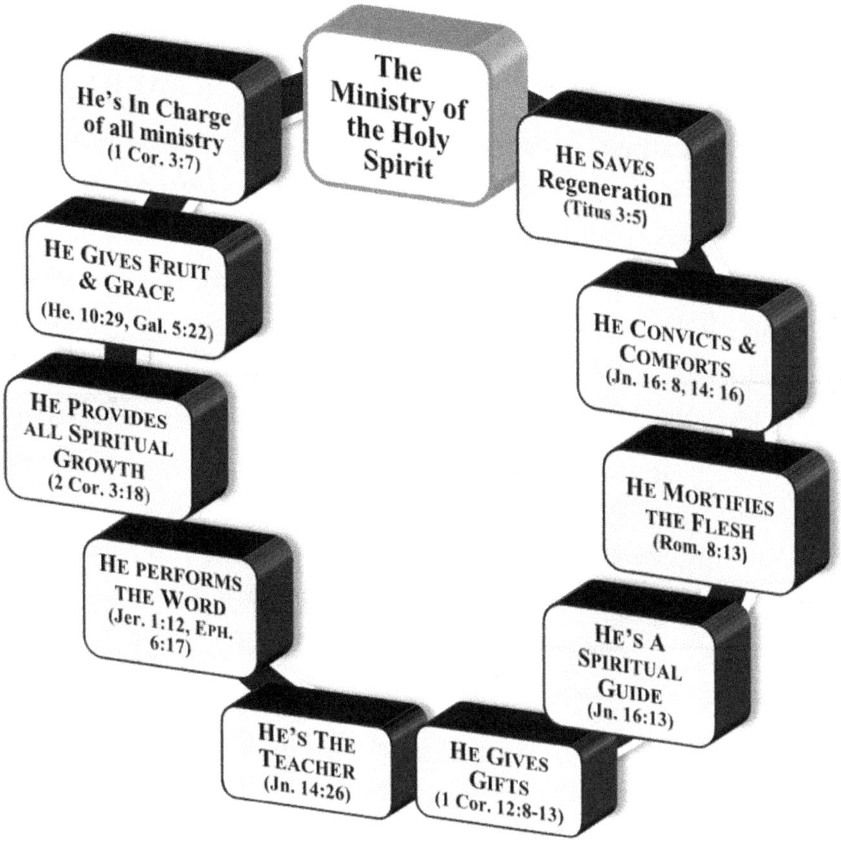

Figure 5: Understanding the Roles/Functions of the Holy Spirit

THE FRUIT OF THE SPIRIT

A Work of the Holy Spirit

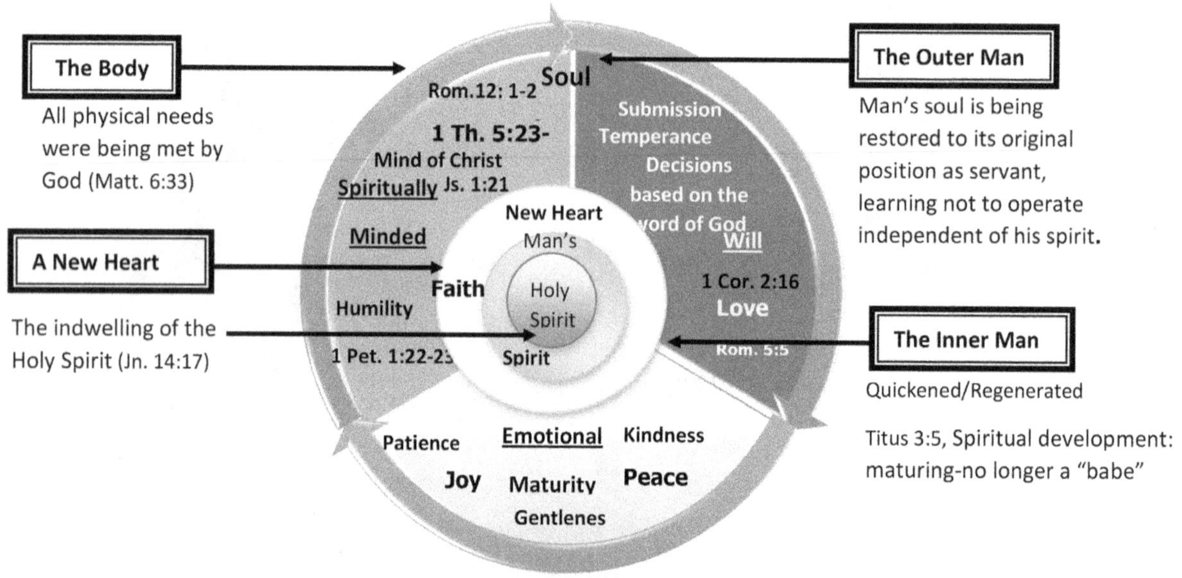

Figure 6: The condition of a mature Christians' soul following restoration

> *This* I say then, "*Walk in the Spirit, and ye shall not fulfill the lust of the flesh.* For the flesh lusteth against the Spirit, and the Spirit against the flesh: and these are contrary the one to the other: so that ye cannot do the things that ye would. But if ye be led of the Spirit, ye are not under the law."
>
> But the fruit of the Spirit is love, joy, peace, longsuffering, gentleness, goodness, faith, 23 Meekness, *temperance (self-control):* against such there is no law. *And they that are Christ's have crucified the flesh with the affections and lusts.* (Galatians 5:16–24)

God has provided the believer, being restored from drug/alcohol addiction, with everything they need to prevent them from relapsing. They have the "fruit of the Spirit" within them which is the key to destroying the "works of the flesh" but they are seeds and need to be developed. *Therefore, relapse prevention for a believer is a developmental issue.* The more spiritually mature a believer becomes, the less likely they will return to their old addictive lifestyles. The "inner man" does not crave or have an appetite for drugs/alcohol (works of the flesh) but strives to maintain the authority of God.

- ☐ All of the "fruit of the Spirit" are equally important, but one component in particular is of great significance when being restored from addiction—*temperance or self-control.*
- ☐ The world's understanding of self-control is centered totally on abstinence through one's own *self-control* and depending on their own strength.
- ☐ The self-control or temperance that is provided by the *Holy Spirit* for believers is much different because it is a part of the "fruit of the Spirit," a quality God provides for His children. Temperance or self-control from the Holy Spirit does not depend on a believer's own personal strength but on their cooperation with the Holy Spirit and it is a Christlike characteristic developed through an active relationship with God.

Ministry of the Word

As a believer, you must also understand that the primary tool that the Holy Spirit uses for change in the life of a believer is the Word of God. The Bible is not an outdated history book or a collection of devotional articles; it is men performing, experiencing, and living out the Word of God. The Bible is a living book, "God-breathed." It is a living book because it is spoken by the living God. The *governing principal* throughout the Bible is *the Word becoming flesh (experiential) in the life of the believer.*

The ministry of the Word is based on the Christ that you know gradually becoming the Word in you. As you progressively experience the reality of Christ through the Word, you will be able to supply Him to others through the Word. By God's grace, once you receive the Word, you will experience the Holy Spirit transforming the Word into Christ in you. This is called the "*supply of Christ.*" You are supplied Christ through the Word of the Bible; you receive Him when you receive the Word.

Ministry of the Word: The Primary Tool of the Holy Spirit

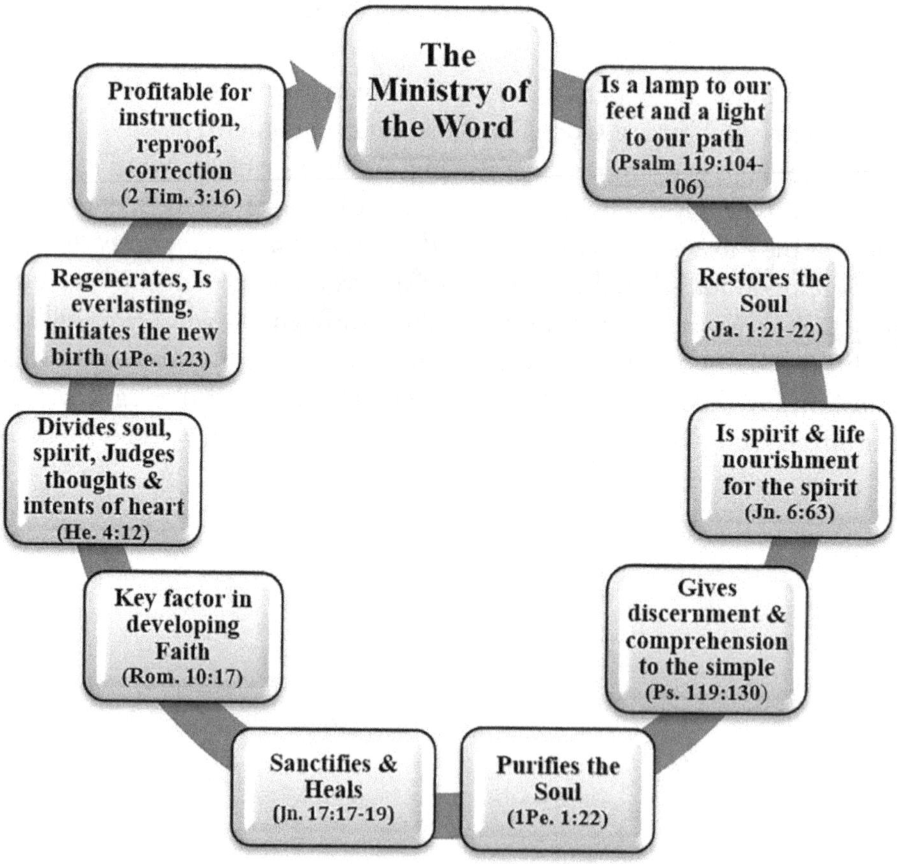

Figure 7: Understanding the Roles/Functions of God's Word

For My thoughts are not your thoughts, neither are your ways My ways, says the Lord.

For as the heavens are higher than the earth, so are *My ways higher than your ways and My thoughts than your thoughts.* For as the rain and snow come down from the heavens, and return not there again, but water the earth and make it bring forth and sprout, that it may give seed to the sower and bread to the eater, So shall My word be that goes forth out of My mouth: *it shall not return to Me void [without producing any effect, useless], but it shall accomplish that which I please and purpose, and it shall prosper in the thing for which I sent it.* (Isaiah 55:8–11)

Understanding the Role & Functions of the Body of Christ (Church)

> And to make all *men* see what *is* the fellowship of the mystery, which from the beginning of the world hath been hid in God, who created all things by Jesus Christ: To the intent that now unto the principalities and powers in heavenly *places* might be *known by the church the manifold wisdom of God, 11 According to the eternal purpose which he purposed in Christ Jesus our Lord.* (Ephesians 3:9–11)

The third method of change which God uses is the Body of Christ, other members of the "household of faith." Fellowship is the key component within the Body of Christ. *A common mistake that many ministry leaders make in working with believers being restored from drug/alcohol is that they better equip them for transition into recovery groups than for transition into the Body of Christ (local church).*

As a believer, you must understand that God's eternal purposes are focused in the "Body of Christ;" God has a divine order here on earth, and it begins with the "Body of Christ." Christ is the Head, and He has delegated His authority to the church. Christ, the Head, has commissioned His Body, the Church, to continue His ministry on earth. The Church has the power delegated by Christ to be victorious over the enemy in every area of life. God has given gifts of pastor, teacher, etc., for the edification or "building up" of the saints (Eph. 4:11–12). Church attendance promotes spiritual growth and development that is necessary for the fulfillment of God's purposes in every Christian's life; gifts are "For the perfecting of the saints, for the work of the ministry, for the edifying of the body of Christ."

Therefore, every Christian needs to be involved in a local church for the purpose of submitting to a pastor who has been called by God as a caretaker of souls with a vision from God. Church attendance will allow each member opportunity to interact with other Christians and mature through a relational learning process and receive the nourishment needed to prepare them for service. Failure to be an active member in a local congregation is harmful to a believer's spiritual well-being and could result in them returning to their old lifestyle. God's purposes are accomplished within the Church.

In *The Father Heart of God*, missionary Floyd McClung Jr. states, "So many people are orphaned, not just from their physical parents, but from any kind of healthy spiritual or emotional heritage." He also discusses how the church is filled with spiritual orphans, not nurtured in their faith. Many have no church home or spiritual families. This is especially true for thousands of men and women who have accepted Christ in prison and are returning to our communities each year. Believers being restored from drug/alcohol addiction face the same issues.

One of greatest challenges they will face is learning to "fit in" and feel accepted into a local church. There is no room for "lone rangers," operating outside the Body of Christ. Jesus is the Head, and the Church is the Body of Christ, and every believer is a vital part of that membership.

In an essay "Strong Mentoring Relationships" in the *Seven Promises of a Promise Keeper*, Glen Wagner clearly states, "In strong mentoring relationships, we obey what God commands us to do within the Body of Christ. *All issues of spiritual growth and maturity are framed in the context of relationships.*" This concept is clearly expressed in the many "one another" passages of the New Testament.

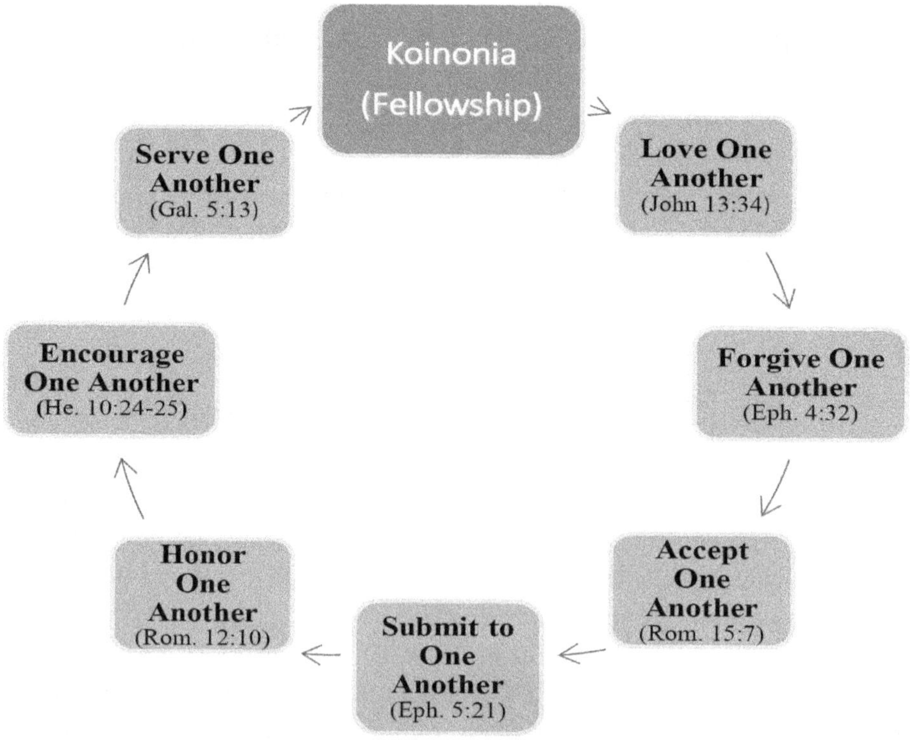

Figure 8: The Role of Fellowship with the Body of Christ

Four Basic Objectives of the Church

Dr. Howard Morgan, in his text, *Leaves from the Olive Tree*, makes an extremely significant statement regarding the biblical Church, the Body of Christ, that impacts understanding ministry. "A study of the Bible reveals to us that the will of God for His Church is accomplished by fulfilling four basic objectives." These four objectives reveal the God-centered focus of all ministry. Dr. Morgan continues by pointing out how "a biblical church" is:

1. *Evangelizing the lost:* Every Church should be actively engaged in local and global evangelism. Every believer is to be an active personal witness of the gospel. Believers should be regularly added to the church. The fulfillment of the great commission is every Christian responsibility. We are either being sent or we are helping to send others.
2. *Maturing the Saints:* In order for people to grow in spiritual health and maturity, they must be in an environment where the Word of and Spirit of God impact their whole life. This environment should provide the necessary nutrition for growth and maturity, including all aspects of the biblical ministry, such as worship, prayer, communion, baptism, study, preaching, teaching healing, spiritual gifts, building quality personal relationships, etc.
3. *Training the mature:* As believers at a certain level of maturity, they are ready for the appropriate kind of disciplining, educating, and equipping needed to fulfill their particular ministry.
4. *Sending the train:* Every trained member is sent out to fulfill their own call and ministry, whether locally as a part of their own congregation or to another place in the world. No one should be burying their talents.

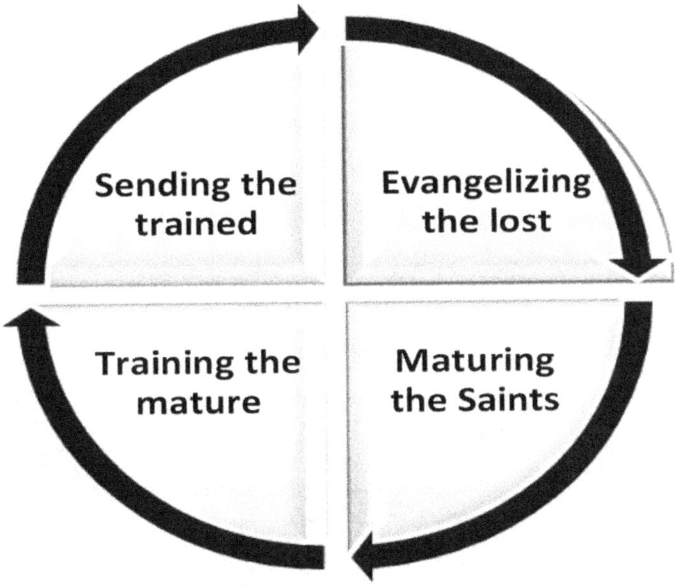

Figure 9: The Four Objectives of the Church

Three Stages of Spiritual Progress: Truth, Faith, and Experience

Wherefore, my beloved, as ye have always obeyed, not as in my presence only, but now much more in my absence, *work out your own salvation with fear and trembling.* For it is God which worketh in you both to will and to do of his good pleasure. (Philippians 2:12–13)

Wisdom is the principal thing therefore get wisdom: and with all thy getting get understanding. (Proverbs 4:7)

THE KEY TO RELAPSE PREVENTION

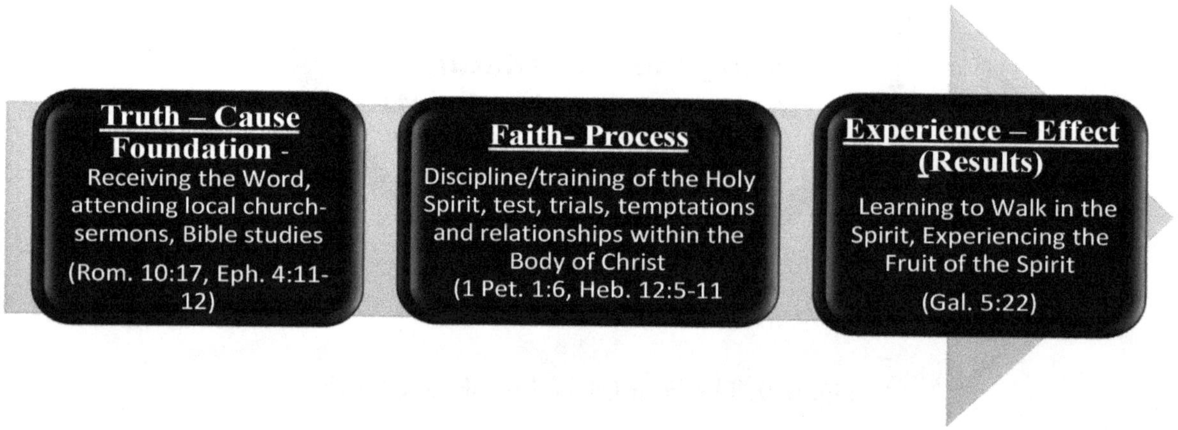

Figure 10: Spiritual Progress

As a believer, you must understand that spiritual progress (maturity) is the key to you not returning to your old addictive lifestyle (sowing to the flesh). The more spiritually mature you become, the less likely you will relapse. *The spiritual person you have become due to your new birth doesn't crave the desires and appetites of the flesh, but strives to maintain the authority of God.*

The more mature you become, the more you will develop a love for God and begin to despise the world and the things in it. *Ultimately, your love for God will be the determining factor that will keep you from relapsing.*

Small Group Exercise (15 Minutes)

Each group will select a recorder to take notes, and a reporter to present information for their group. Review the diagrams located in this section and discuss the following questions within your group:

- ☐ What three components make up God's threefold provision for Christian Recovery (restoration)? Please explain.
- ☐ What are the three stages of Spiritual Progress? Please explain.

Believers have *Christ's nature* and the *"mind of Christ;"* and God's Word provides them with *Christ's perspective* and the *Holy Spirit brings the Word to life,* allowing believers to experience Christ in their everyday lives.

Tools for Christian Restoration

Understand that the tools for Christian restoration have no power within themselves. They are effective only because they are instruments designed to allow you access into God's threefold provision for Christian restoration—the Ministry of the Holy Spirit, the Word of God, and the Body of Christ.

Quiet Time

> Search me, O God, and know my heart; try me and know my anxious thoughts; and see if there be any hurtful way in me, and lead me in the everlasting way. (Psalm 139:23–24)

You must present yourself to God if you want Him to search your heart and reveal your character defects. This is why you need quiet time. You must set a certain time each day, preferably in the morning, for meditation and prayer.

To make this time most meaningful, you need to find a quiet secluded place where you can be completely alone. Jesus often withdrew from the crowds to be alone with His Father. If you want to grow into His likeness, you also must spend time alone with God. Select a place that will be your "prayer closet" where you can shut out the world for a time of communion with Him.

You may begin your quiet time by reading scripture, reading Christian devotional material, or by singing praise songs. If you read scripture, try to visualize yourself in the scene. Each of these ways may help you rid your mind of distractions and center your focus on God. This quiet time is to be your personal time with God. It needs to become a part of your daily schedule.

The goal of quiet time is to enhance your relationship with God. You must present yourself to God in order to have a relationship with Him. It is during your quiet time that you carefully pray over each attitude on your DAI and ask the Lord to show you which of these attitudes caused you a problem the previous day (the last twenty-four hours).

The most important tool in Christian recovery is *journaling*, which requires use of another tool, the *Daily Attitude Inventory (DAI)*. This is an extremely valuable tool, because it allows an individual daily opportunity to develop a closer relationship with God and His Son, Jesus Christ (through the agent of the Holy Spirit). As individuals in recovery learn to identify and discuss their major ungodly attitudes and behaviors with God, they will develop the intimacy with God needed to restore their soul and promote their spiritual growth.

How to Take the DAI

It is a simple process to take our DAI. You do not inventory your life history on the DAI. You simply review the past twenty-four hours and record your negative and positive attitudes.

You prayerfully review the activities of the last twenty-four hours. You think about the day's work, the relationships, and anything troubling your mind. You look beyond the offense of the problems caused by other people to see what attitudes we expressed in your response to their behavior.

Then you look at the DAI sheet. On the left side, you see a list of negative (relapse) attitudes, and on the right, a list of corresponding positive (recovery) attitudes. Along the top, you see numbers for days one through thirty-one that correspond to each day of the month. In the center, a graph of boxes is ready to be filled in.

Beginning with the appropriate day of the month, you move your finger down the list of attitudes, one at a time. Stop at each pair of attitudes and ask God, "God, did I have the attitude of self-pity or the attitude of serenity yesterday?" If I had the attitude of self-pity, I would then blacken that box. If I had the attitude of serenity, I would leave a check mark in that box.

You then move down to the next pair of attitudes and ask the corresponding question. There is a separate handout with definitions for each attitude listed on the DAI.

After completing the DAI, you go to the Lord in prayer. You ask Him to help you with your character defects and thank Him for your positive attitudes.

Prayer—The Inner Journey

Prayer is conversing with God. He is not only your savior but also your counselor and guide. He is delighted to give direction to His children and forgiveness to those who confess their sins.

> If any of you lacks wisdom, let Him ask of God, who gives to all liberally and without reproach, and it will be given to him. (James 1:4)
>
> If my people who are called by my name, shall humble themselves and pray, and seek my face, and turn from their wicked ways; then shall I hear from heaven, and will forgive their sins, and heal their land. (2 Chronicles 7:14)

The following is a suggested method for communing with God in prayer. It is by no means the only way to commune with God. Be sure you have a pen in hand and your journal open to record the impressions the Lord may give you in response to your questions.

1. Close your eyes. This creates immediate privacy and places you in your personal prayer closet.
2. Focus your attention on moving toward the temple of the Holy Spirit in your heart or try to picture yourself sitting or walking with Jesus in a beautiful quiet place (If you have accepted Jesus Christ as your savior, He lives in your heart by His Holy Spirit).
3. Ask Him if He loves you, and possibly sing to Him a song of praise. This may help you focus your mind on Him and enter into His presence.
4. Thank Him for the positive attitudes on your DAI.
5. Confess the negative attitudes of your DAI to the Lord and ask Him, "Do you forgive me? Will you cleanse me?" This simple act of asking is all we need to do. There is no need for punishment to gain forgiveness or cleansing. 1 John 1:19 tells, *"If we confess our sins, He is faithful and just to forgive us our sins and cleanse us from all unrighteousness."*
6. Ask Him what caused each of the negative attitudes and what you should do about them. Also, ask Him what you can do to prevent them from happening again (Write down His response).
7. Ask Him if there is anything else He wants to tell you or to show you (Write down His response).

Journaling: Recording God's Response to Your Prayers

It is important to write down the impressions God gives you in your time of prayer. This is partly because it may mean more to you later than it does now. God often speaks to your true needs rather than to the questions that burn in your mind. He looks beyond your desire to understand everything and speaks to a need you don't realize you have. The words He speaks in your heart begin to work in your mind. Soon you realize what He was conveying and you are comforted.

Your journal becomes a written record of your personal journey with God. You can refer to it when you find yourself struggling in faith. You can refer to it when you forget what He said. You can refer to it to learn more in retrospect than you did at the time you received it.

You can also refer to it when you need the input of the Body of Christ and the Bible to test the word you received. This will help you fine-tune your hearing and teach you how to distinguish between the voice of the Lord, your own thoughts, and Satan's suggestions.

Use your journal to record the impressions you hear from God. This includes descriptions of any visions He may give you. Date each entry for future reference and be as specific as possible when recording the impressions. You should try to differentiate between what you have received from God and how you think and feel about it.

You may also use it to record any personal insights you have gleaned from your quiet time. God is concerned about your recovery. He is more interested in revealing information about your own character development than information about others.

Your Goal: Your goal is to become more like God by allowing Him to transform you into His likeness by the renewing of your mind: Romans 12:1–3, 8:29; 2 Corinthians 3:17,18; Ephesians 5:26; Titus 3:5. Isaiah 26:3 tells that the reward is perfect peace.

Daily Attitude Inventory Definitions

Serenity—being at peace on the inside; shifting the center of your interest from your own selfish wants to concerns for the needs of others around you.

Self-Pity—feeling sorry for yourself; sulking, being moody and silent; strong sense of not being liked; "Poor me."

Humility—honestly accepting your limitations and personal defects without trying to justify them or pretend they are not there; having no false pride.

Self-Righteousness—becoming puffed up (proud) or needing to be right; excusing ourselves of any wrong behavior or attitude while condemning others for the very same things; justifying ourselves or whitewashing one's true character to give people a better impression.

Self-Valuation—is maintaining an honest, realistic, positive self-image, realizing that you are changing and growing. We are unique unrepeatable miracles of God and do not need to continually define ourselves by the mistakes we have made in the past.

Self-Condemnation—is the act of showing a low self-esteem (self-hatred) by succumbing to false guilt and declaring oneself unfit or unworthy of love from God or others. This is false humility.

Being a Giver—having a desire to put in more than you take out; being grateful (genuine appreciation) for what you have received.

Being a Taker—Desiring to take more than you give in relationships and other things; demanding instant gratification for all your needs and wants and whining when others do not meet your expectations; not genuinely appreciating what is given to you or the people through whom God has given it.

Honesty—Being genuine, truthful, open, and frank; accepting responsibility for your actions.

Lying—Not being truthful or trustworthy; cheating, or telling half-truths; not being totally honest with God, ourselves, and others. The two most common behaviors in recovery are denial and projection.

Patience—Demonstrating a quiet, uncomplaining, endurance under distress or annoyance; being tolerant, tender, or forbearing.

Impatience—Annoyance because you don't get what you want when you want it; an unwillingness to wait; not being content with what you have.

Gratitude—is being grateful to God and other people for what you have and where you are; it is being content.

Complaining—is when you continually talk about the negative aspects of something over which you have no control. It is evidence of you neglecting to practice the serenity prayer.

Forgiveness—is the result of giving grace and pardon to someone who has wronged you. It occurs when you give up the right to get even. It is the result of having relinquished negative emotions that plague you in reaction to perceived wrongs. Forgiveness occurs when we surrender our hate and let go of our resentment.

Resentment—having a feeling of bitterness that forms a mental chain that binds you to the person or thing you hate.

Admittance—Accepting ownership and responsibility for your own recovery and accepting the reality of your situation. Recognizing the effects and consequences of your addiction and/or life-controlling problem.

Denial—Blinds you to your own problems and enables you to go through disaster after disaster without learning from your mistakes. Thinking that you are the one exception to the rule. Minimizing the seriousness of your situation.

Trust—Being able to believe and relax in the care of God and the fellowship of others. Not trying to isolate or be a lone ranger.

Worry—Not trusting God or others to do what they have promised. Having your thoughts consumed by the things you cannot change.

Working the Program—realizing the life and death nature (seriousness) of your life; controlling problems and putting forth a determined effort to change. Applying the principles of recovery to all aspects of your life.

Complying—Doing enough to get by but not putting forth any real effort to change. Doing only what is expected or required, but not having self-motivation.

Accepting Responsibility—Being accountable for both my attitudes and actions. Not being a victim of circumstance, environment, or other people's behaviors. Realizing that I will never change by blaming God, other people, places, or things for my faults.

Projection—Excusing your wrong behavior by accusing others of being the source of the problem. Blaming other people, places, and things for the problems you are responsible for.

Doing Things on Time—Actively working to accomplish tasks (large or small) on time. Being punctual and prepared.

Procrastination—Putting things off (large or small), lateness, loafing, shirking responsibility, sloppiness, and apathy.

Being Real—Not worrying about what other people think of you. Being honest and open to expression of inner feelings. Being transparent.

Being Phony—Trying to impress others making people think you are something that you are not, or that you know something that you don't.

Positive Thinking—Choosing to dwell on the positive. Having hope as you see health in others and ourselves as you grow in recovery.

Negative Thinking—Consistently believing that bad things will happen or that people will reject you because of some real or imagined character defects. Dwelling on the negative traits of others or ourselves.

Clean Thinking—Keeping your mind free from lust and dealing in the present, focused on continued growth in your relationship with God.

Vulgar Thinking—Dwelling on memories of past or imagined sexual encounters or fantasies. Allowing lust to control your mind and to hinder your relationship with God, self, and others. Continued use of profanity.

Accepting Forgiveness—Laying down the guilt from your past as you take responsibilities for your wrongs, receive forgiveness, and make amends as needed.

False Guilt About Past—Holding on to guilt even after you have accepted responsibility for your wrongs, received forgiveness, and made amends as needed. Believing that your wrongs are too great for God, self, or others to forgive.

Temperance—Balance in consumption of food, beverage, etc.

Gluttony—Compulsive overeating or overindulging.

Concentration—Keeping your mind and body together in the present and working on the life-controlling problems that have affected you.

Head & Butt—Daydreaming, living in the fantasy world of the future, or reliving the unchangeable events of the past.

Communion with God—Improving your conscious contact with God by being conscious of His presence throughout the day.

Forgetting God—Running on your own steam and best thinking. Going through the day with hardly a thought of God. Not yielding your will and life to the care of God.

MY DAILY ATTITUDE INVENTORY

MY RECOVERY IS MY RESPONSIBILITY

RELAPSE	1	2	3	4	5	6	7	8	9	10	11	12	13	14	15	16	17	18	19	20	21	22	23	24	25	26	27	28	29	30	31	*RECOVERY*
Self-Pity																																**Serenity**
Self-Righteousness																																**Humility**
Self-Condemnation																																**Self-Valuation**
Being a Taker																																**Being a Giver**
Lying																																**Honesty**
Impatience																																**Patience**
Complaining																																**Gratitude**
Resentment																																**Forgiveness**
Denial																																**Admittance**
Worry																																**Trust**
Complying																																**Working the Program**
Projection																																**Accepting Responsibility**
Procrastination																																**Doing Things on Time**
Being Phony																																**Being Real**
Negative Thinking																																**Positive Thinking**
Vulgar Thinking																																**Clean Thinking**
False Guilt About Past																																**Accepting Forgiveness**
Gluttony																																**Temperance**
Head & Butt Disease																																**Concentration**
Forgetting God																																**Communion With God**
Anger																																**Calm**

SERENITY PRAYER

God, give me grace to accept with serenity the things that cannot be changed, Courage to change the things which should be changed, and the wisdom to distinguish the one from the other. Living one day at a time, Enjoying one moment at a time, Accepting hardship as a pathway to peace, Taking, as **Jesus** did, This sinful world as it is, Not as I would have it, Trusting that You will make all things right, If I surrender to Your will, So that I may be reasonably happy in this life, And supremely happy with You forever in the next. Amen.

(Psa 139:23-24 NIV) "Search me, 0 God, and know my heart; test me and know my anxious thoughts. {24} See if there is any offensive way in me, and lead me in the way everlasting."

(Rom 12:2 NIV) "Do not conform any longer to the pattern of this world, but be transformed by the renewing of your mind. Then you will be able to test and approve what God's will is--his good, pleasing and perfect will."

(2 Cor 10:4-5 NJV) "The weapons we fight with are not the weapons of the world. On the contrary, they have divine power to demolish strongholds. {5} We demolish arguments and every pretension that sets itself up against the knowledge of God, & take every thought captive to the obedience of Christ."

THE BOMBSHELL

I CANNOT CHANGE OTHERS
BY DIRECT ACTION,
I CAN ONLY CHANGE MYSELF;
BY THE GRACE OF GOD.
OTHERS HAVE A
TENDENCY TO CHANGE
IN REACTION
TO MY CHANGE.

HOUSES EXERCISE

This is a tool designed to assist a believer in exposing the enemy by *identifying the origin of the emotional and mental strongholds in their life.* This tool allows believers to recall the most important and painful incidents in their lives, opening the door for the healing power of Christ to rest on them.

Believers are asked to divide their lives into six parts, based on their age; next, they record all major events—their negative and positive emotions that were present during these events. After placing the information on paper, they are given a large marker board to divide into six segments, each segment being shaped like a house with stick figures representing each member in the household. A cross is placed inside the home if Christ was in the home.

Then they transfer the information onto the board with different color markers. Once this is complete, they meet with the counselor/group who they trust and present each house on the board. They allow the counselor/group opportunity to relate and identify with their life experiences and challenge them regarding their openness and honesty. The counselor/group assists the individual in exposing any hidden or unseen patterns or trends established in their life that need addressing.

The Home in Divine Order

Study Ephesians 5:21–6:4.

In this home, Christ is the head. He brings light, love, and purpose into it. He dwells in the hearts of the members of His home. Similarly, the father is the spiritual leader, responsible directly to God for the affairs of his home. He leads his home with the same kind of self-sacrificing love that Christ leads the Church. He must be closely related to Christ in order to do this.

The mother respects her husband and is subject to him as she is to the Lord. She is not self-serving but gladly submits her plans to her husband and has the best interest of all members of the family in mind. She assists her husband, encouraging and supporting him as the spiritual leader of the home.

The children are related to the Lord, and by His help, they obey their parents. They are raised in the nurture, affection, training, instruction, and purpose of the Lord. Understanding *The Home in Divine Order* is extremely important for understanding the areas in which you need restoration. Using stick figures, illustrate *Divine Order* in the house below.

Divine Oder

Divine Order

My Childhood Home

Again, using stick figures, draw the order of each member of your childhood home. Do not draw the order by age, but in the order it seemed to be to you at the time. Was Christ the head? Was He present in the hearts of the members? Was the father the spiritual leader? Did he lay down his life for his family? Or did he rule the roost with a strong arm? Who was in control or in charge of this home? Did the mother respect, assist, and submit to the father? Did she only do so while he was present, for fear of him? Did the children relate to the Lord and obey their parents? Try to illustrate the answers to these questions in your stick figure drawing.

Childhood Home

There are imperfections in every home. As painful as it may be to face the losses we experienced in our original home, in order to work through and overcome them during the course of our program, it is important to "tell it like it is." Now, as we leave our childhood home and set out on our own, we must look at our own marriage home or independent home. Using stick figures as before, illustrate what your own personal home looks like in comparison to the "Divine Order."

Marriage or Personal Home

As you progress through their program and witness the presentation of your peers' houses, begin now to list attitudes or emotional reactions to other members of your home and situations that occurred in those homes. We begin these houses from birth to present day.

Different houses can be determined by physical moves to different cities or neighborhoods, by divorce or family separations, or by marriages or independent living. Be sure to include positive and negative reactions to specific incidents or persons throughout each house. It is important to share our story with others, story with others, but not to tell "war stories." We must look at our emotional responses, confessing our faults one to another. Our reactions or actions are the areas we must acknowledge to each other and God.

Body Ministry Exercise

Most of your restoration (recovery) will take place in your relationships and interactions with other believers. Believers working together as a unit have a role to fulfill in Christ's Body. You will play a vital part in the Christian growth and recovery of other believers, and they will play a vital role in yours. If the Body is working together functionally and is getting healthier, all the members will benefit. If it is not functioning well or if there is division, then all the members will be negatively affected.

In order to measure the Body's functionality as a community and ensure an atmosphere of healthy Christ-centered recovery, a relational exercise known as the Body Ministry Group is held each week. The Body Ministry Group is used to give an honest evaluation of how you see other clients working their program of recovery and growing in their Christian faith. It will also help you see yourself as others see you. The Body Ministry Group is designed to teach you how to give and receive correction, constructive criticism, affirmation, and encouragement.

Being a vital contributing part of the Body will require you to do your part in holding it together and helping to make it strong. This will require you to actively participate by practicing certain principles daily in your program. Biblical principles utilized in the Body Ministry Group are listed below:

(Romans 12:9–11) *Love and honor each other.*

We often say, "I love you." But we often fail to show it. Love is an action, not necessarily a feeling. Love is best demonstrated through an active commitment to others, delighting in their successes, and caring enough to give them our personal attention and time. Loving God, by showing love to others, is actually the ministry to which we are all called. Valuing someone as important in your life is the beginning of trust. Trust and faith are essential for the development of a Christian life. These loving relationships enable you to stand for what is right.

(Hebrews 10:24–25) *Motivating others to love and good works.*

Motivating means to move to action and implies genuinely caring for others, allowing them to care for you, and then putting that care into action. As you genuinely care for others, demonstrating that care and concern, you will help both them and yourself. When we speak the truth in love, encourage, and affirm each other out of a motivation of love, care, and concern, the Body is built up in Christ, and its individual members will benefit.

(Galatians 6:1–3) *Help someone in need.*

If we are properly seeking God in our recovery, it is important that we help others in need. By helping each other and being occupied with doing God's will, we are less likely to make a wrong choice. By sharing each other's problems, troubles, and bearing each other's burdens, we are fulfilling God's command to love one another. This keeps us humble and reminds us of our need for God and each other. The Bible says that we should confess our faults to one another and pray for each other.

(1 Corinthians 12:25–27) *Having equal concern for each other.*

You should encourage other believers to do the best they can in the program. This may involve confronting them when they are wrong, pulling them up when they are falling, or affirming them as they make progress. Remember, we desire to build each other up, not tear each other down. Do to others what you would have others do to you.

(Ephesians 4:15–16) *Speaking the truth in love.*

We often tell others what they want to hear to cause them to like us. This is a selfish motivation, not love. You would not expect a doctor to tell you only what you want to hear when you are sick. You would want him to tell you the truth and how to get well. Just the same, you must practice telling others the truth about what you see in them and help them so that they have the opportunity to get well.

Body Ministry Guidelines

Body Ministry should be a continual daily process throughout the week with other clients as you live, work, and recreate together. As the Daily Attitude Inventory is a daily event, the Body Ministry Group is a weekly assessment of one another.

The big question to answer is:

What individual stands out to you as *"Working a Program?"*
This individual displays one or more of the recovery attitudes on the Daily Attitude Inventory as demonstrated through his actions.

What individual stands out to you as *"Needing Improvement?"*
This individual displays one or more of the relapse attitudes on the Daily Attitude Inventory as demonstrated through his actions.

Hint: To help you answer these questions, first look at yourself. Each of us has strengths and each of us has weaknesses. You will likely see similar behaviors and attitudes in others as you get to know other clients in this program. Simply identify the behavior(s) that are strengths or weaknesses and the corresponding attitude(s).

The night prior to the Body Ministry Group, you are asked to:
...pray, asking God who He would have you choose and speak to with encouragement or correction.
...be prepared to speak only to what you have witnessed.
...have a different individual chosen for each category.
...prayerfully write down specifically what you wish to say to each individual looking at their action(s) and their attitude(s) behind it.

During the Body Ministry Group, when asked...
...speak the individual's name clearly for all to hear.
...looking the man in the eye, speak confidently; start with "I love you" and end with "I love you."
...turn in your written choices to the group facilitator.

Following a Body Ministry Group...
...a relational homework assignment will be given by the group facilitator to encourage continued relationship building.

Welcomes You to The One Step with Jesus Restoration Program:
A Biblical Cognitive Approach to Understanding and
Addressing Addiction and Relapse Prevention

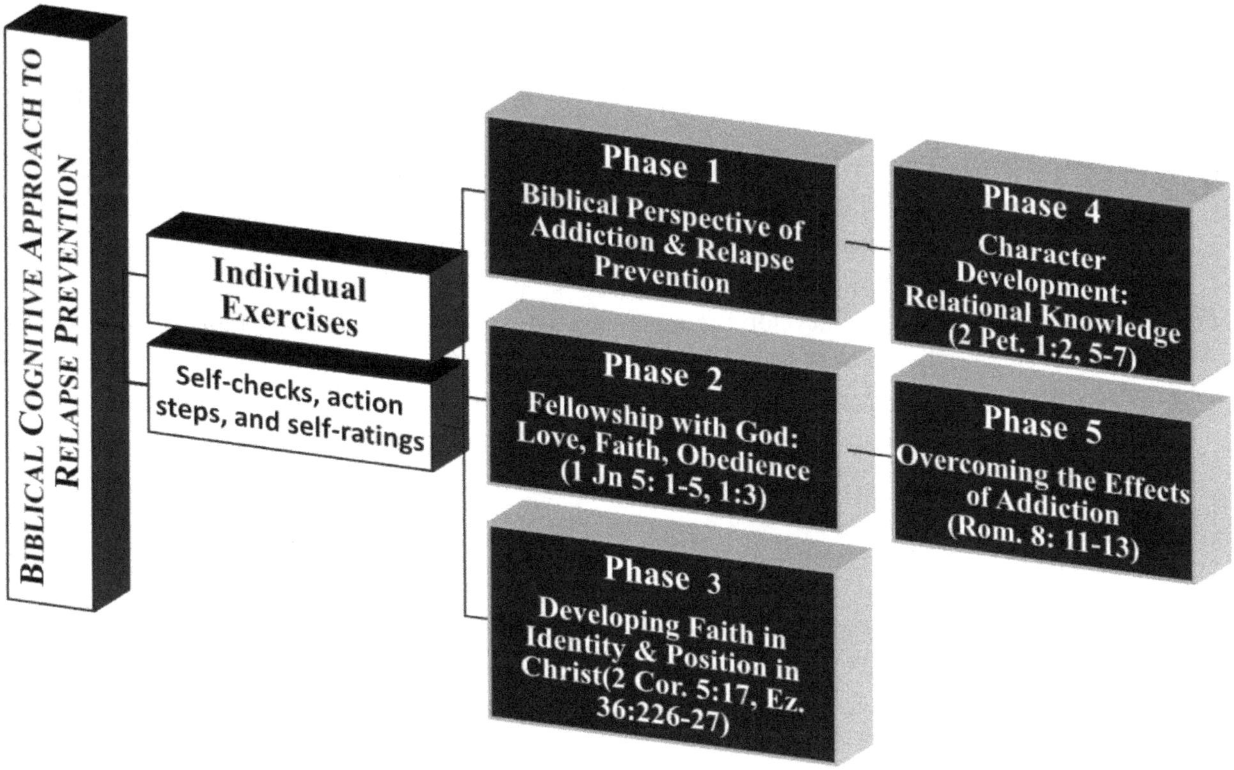

A Biblically Strategic Support Group

ASBP Ministries has developed a biblically strategic support group, A Biblical Cognitive Relapse Prevention Support Group. It was designed to provide Christians being restored from drug/alcohol addictions with a Christ-centered approach to understanding and addressing addiction issues. Because of its biblically strategic design, it can be *easily modified* to equip the Body of Christ with population, such as returning citizens, families/members of returning citizens.

The support group is designed with *five phases* to assist believers in developing a biblical perspective of both addiction and relapse prevention:

Phase 1 provides the believer with God's perspective of addiction and then introduces them to His solution.

Phase 2 is a very crucial phase where believers learn how to cultivate their relationship with God.

Phase 3 gives believers understanding of their *identity* in Christ, and is vital in helping believers view themselves as God sees them. This phase is key to them accepting their rightful places in the Body of Christ, and being comfortable in local churches.

Phase 4 is designed to help them develop the much needed *"self-control"* and other Christlike *characteristics* to overcome the *effects* of their addiction.

Phase 5 presents a *lifelong process* that focuses on cooperating with the Holy Spirit as He identifies the areas in the flesh (cravings, appetites, set-up behaviors) that need to be addressed to mortify the desires and deeds of the flesh.

Believers need intensive *mentoring/discipleship* early in their restoration; if not, they will quickly return to their old lifestyle and former friends.

The support group is designed to *enhance the quality of ministry* to believers being restored from addiction by producing a biblical cognitive approach to understanding and addressing the effects of addiction. The support group has individual exercises designed to provide biblical insight and wisdom into key biblical principles necessary for being restored from alcohol/drug addiction.

This workbook is designed to assist the Christian who is *serious* about being restored from the effects of a lifestyle of addiction to drugs/alcohol. Developing a biblical relapse prevention plan *requires you to be honest with yourself, God, and others.* It also requires that you are *open* and *transparent,* willing to acknowledge your weaknesses, needs, and depend on God and others. In fulfilling these requirements, you will gain the understanding necessary to address the effects of your addiction and avoid relapse.

It will take *commitment* and *hard work* for you to address the issues identified in this book, and in doing so, you will benefit greatly by developing a much closer relationship with God and deeper understanding of His will for your life. *Jesus has already paid the price for your bondage to alcohol and other drugs. Moreover, He has already obtained the victory for you over the root cause and the effects (desire, cravings, and appetite) of your addiction.* This workbook will assist you in *learning to experience* that victory. You will learn to walk in that victory through applying God's Word and learning to walk in the Spirit.

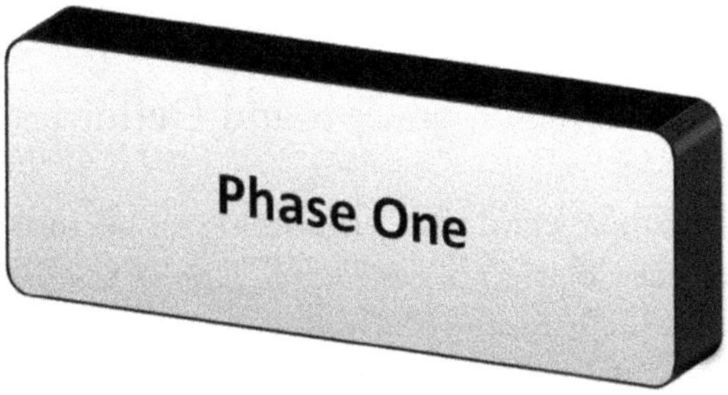

DEVELOPING A BIBLICAL VIEW OF ADDICTION AND RELAPSE PREVENTION

Wisdom *is the* ***principal thing*** *therefore get* ***wisdom****:*
and with all thy getting get ***understanding****.*

—Proverbs 4:7

LEARNING OBJECTIVES

For the group participant to be able to:

- Identify the key components in the Biblical Cognitive Relapse Prevention Model.
- Define relapse prevention from a biblical point of view.
- Identify the most significant factors in relapse prevention.

Key Biblical Concepts and Definitions

(1) *Addiction*: is an effect of a sinful condition originating in an individual's *heart* due to their *old nature*, resulting from a direct violation of *the Divine Law of Sowing and Reaping*. Addiction manifests itself within an individual's soul in the form of a *stronghold*. Following conversion where God crucifies the old nature, the *works of the flesh* remain within the soul and must be addressed through *mortification* by the Holy Spirit.

(2) *Heart*: The heart is the seat or center of a believer's mind (thoughts, reasoning, understanding), will (judgments, decisions), and emotions (love, hatred, fear, joy, sorrow, anger) where it converges with their inner being, spirit (Proverbs 4:20–23).

(3) *Old Nature*: All of mankind is born spiritually dead and alienated from God with a hardened heart (Genesis 2:17; Romans 5:12,19). Consequently, the old (sinful) nature, resulting from Adam's disobedience, comprises man's spiritual condition prior to becoming a new man in Christ.

(4) *Divine Law of Sowing and Reaping*: The spiritual law governing the quality of life a believer or nonbeliever will experience is based on their decision of sowing to the Spirit or sowing to the flesh (Galatians 6:7–10).

(5) *Flesh*: is the residue of sin that still remains in a believer's life (Romans 7:18). Flesh also relates to the *moral spiritual weakness and helplessness* of the *human nature still clinging to saved souls* (Romans 6:19). The flesh functions apart from and against the Spirit. In the believer's soul, the flesh stands against the work of the Spirit.

(6) *Relapse*: Relapse is the process of a believer becoming involved in returning to the *works of the flesh,* those old behaviors and attitudes that were common practices prior to their salvation. Thus, they return to their *besetting sin* of using drugs/alcohol.

(7) *Idolatry*: Idolatry refers to the worship of man-made things, things of the world (money, power, position, relationships, etc.), and material possessions, the "god" of the 12-Step Movement.

(8) *Witchcraft*: Witchcraft is the New Testament translation of the Greek word *pharmakeus* referring to the administering (selling) or use of mood and mind-altering drugs (cocaine, heroin, alcohol, etc.). All sin hinders our relationship with God; but the sin of witchcraft strikes directly at the work of the Holy Spirit.

(9) *Infirmities*: Within the soul, an infirmity or weakness refers to a person's inability or lack of strength to bear a trial, trouble, or restrain from corrupt desires in a particular area of their life (Hebrews 4:14–16; Romans 8:26–28).

(10) *Foothold*: A foothold is established in an individual's life when he or she gives place to Satan by providing an opportunity for entry through sin (Ephesians 4:26–27).

(11) *Stronghold*: A stronghold is a negative pattern of thoughts leading to negative emotions, or attitudes causing behaviors to be burned into the soul either through repetition over time or through a one-time traumatic experience that is contrary to the Word and will of God.

(12) *Mortification*: God's process of addressing the flesh, *"putting to death"* the flesh through the power of the Holy Spirit is mortification (Colossians 3:5; Romans 8:11–13). To mortify the flesh means *to put to death, to destroy the strength, vitality, or sinful functions of flesh.*

(13) *Mentoring*: *Mentoring is a biblically based relational learning process* in which a believer is befriended by a more mature believer who has been successfully involved in the restoration process for the purpose of assisting the believer in reaching their full potential in Christ Jesus through using God's resources.

How Does God View the Use of Alcohol & Other Drugs?

Woe to those who rise early in the morning to run after their drinks, who stay up late at night till they are inflamed with wine. They have harps and lyres at their banquets, tambourines and flutes and wine, *but they have no regard for the deeds of the LORD, no respect for the work of his hands.* Therefore, my people will go into exile for lack of understanding; their men of rank will die of hunger and their masses will be parched with thirst. (Isaiah 5:11–13, NIV)

- ☐ Isaiah states very clearly that those who become addicted to alcohol disregard God and have no respect for His plans for their lives.

The Book of Proverbs cites several important facts regarding the condition of drunkenness:

For they eat the bread of wickedness and drink the wine of violence. (Proverbs 4:17)

- ☐ Violence results from drinking.

Wine *is* a mocker, strong drink *is* raging: and whosoever is deceived thereby is not wise. (Proverbs 20:1)

- ☐ Those who become involved in practicing the works of the flesh, drunkenness, are unwise.

For the drunkard and the glutton shall come to poverty: and drowsiness shall clothe *a man* with rags. (Proverbs 23:21,29–31)

- ☐ Bondage to alcohol leads to poverty and financial ruin.

Who has woe? Who has sorrow? Who has strife? Who has complaints? Who has needless bruises? Who has bloodshot eyes? (Proverbs 23:29, NIV)

☐ Intoxicants produce sorrow, disagreements, arguments, wounds without cause, babbling, redness of eyes.

Those who linger over wine, who go to sample bowls of mixed wine. Do not gaze at wine when it is red, when it sparkles in the cup, when it goes down smoothly! (Proverbs 23:30–31)

☐ Warns you not to allow yourself to be tempted by intoxicants because they are addicting.

What Does the Book of Proverbs Say About Using Intoxicants (Alcohol & Other Drugs)?

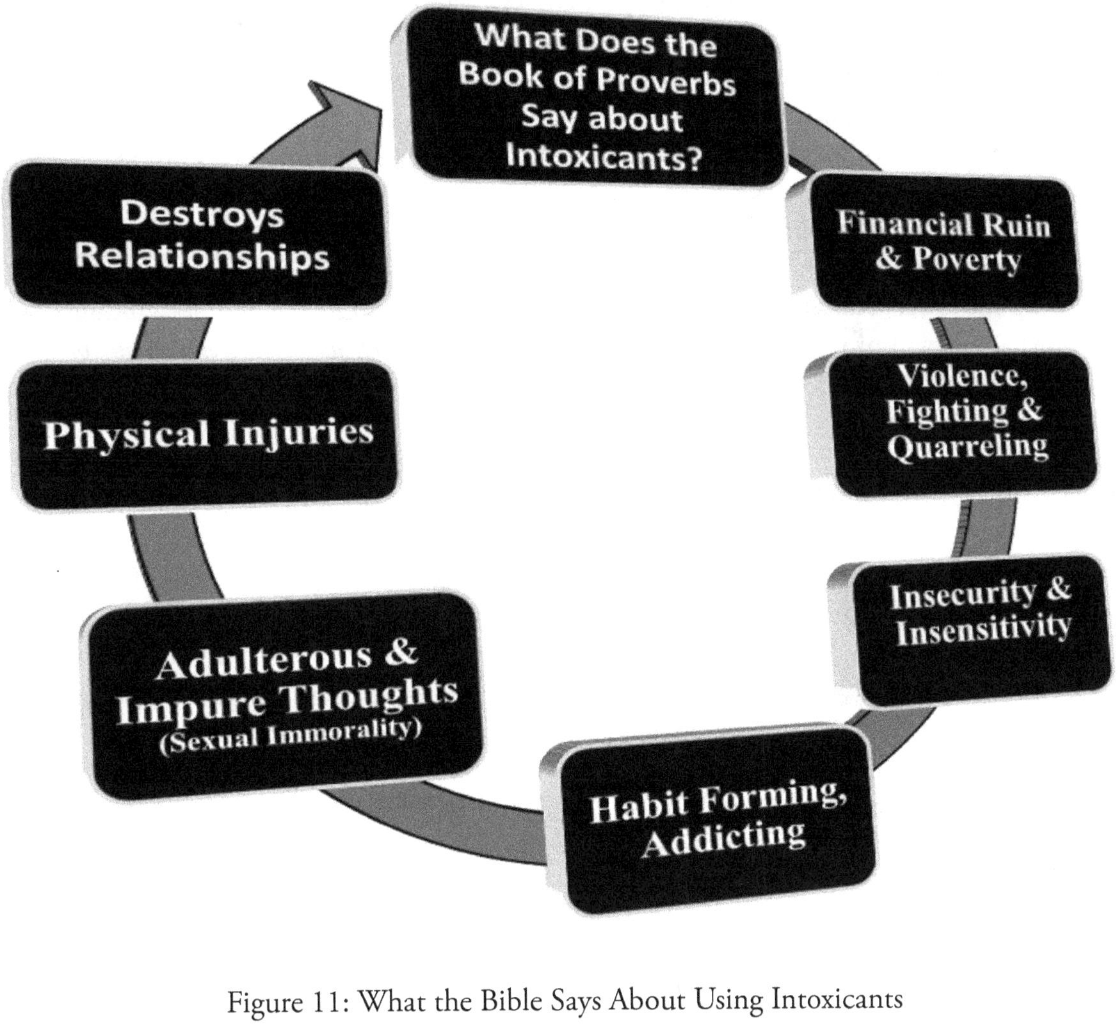

Figure 11: What the Bible Says About Using Intoxicants

At the last it biteth like a serpent and stingeth like an adder. Thine eyes shall behold strange women, and thine heart shall utter perverse things. Yea, thou shalt be as he that lieth down in the midst of the sea, or as he that lieth upon the top of a mast. They have stricken me, *shalt thou say, and* I was not sick; they have

> beaten me, *and* I felt *it* not: when shall I awake? I will seek it yet again. (Proverbs 23:32–35)
>
> *Be careful, or your hearts will be weighed down with dissipation, drunkenness and the anxieties of life,* and that day will close on you unexpectedly like a trap. 35 For it will come upon all those who live on the face of the whole earth. 36 Be always on the watch, and pray that you may be able to escape all that is about to happen, and that you may be able to stand before the Son of Man. (Luke 21:34–36, NIV)

Our Lord Himself informs you to be alert and prayerful in Luke 21:34–36:

- ☐ He warns against drunkenness and the lifestyle that accompanies it of "sowing to the flesh" and the troubles that follow.
- ☐ He cautions you that drunkenness is a trap designed to destroy your relationship with Him.

Apostle Paul in the Book of Ephesians provides tremendous insight regarding the use of *intoxicants* (stimulants, depressants, etc.) This passage of scripture is clearly directed toward the believers instructing them how not to become entangled in alcohol/drugs following regeneration.

> *Wherefore he saith, "Awake thou that sleepest, and arise from the dead, and* Christ shall give thee light. See then that ye walk circumspectly, *not as fools, but as wise,* redeeming the time, *because the days are evil. Wherefore be ye not unwise,* but understanding what the will of the Lord is. *And be not drunk with wine, wherein is excess; but be filled with the Spirit."* (Ephesians 5:14–18)

In this first passage of scripture, Paul clearly expressed that following regeneration through Christ a believer must:

- ☐ *"walk circumspectly,"* meaning to progress accurately, to be intentional about following God's path by living a godly lifestyle.
- ☐ *"redeeming time,"* making wise use of every opportunity for living righteous in evil times. Prior to their salvation, many individuals spent years walking in unrighteousness, and now that they are on the path of righteousness, they must make every effort to remain there by developing and maintaining a godly lifestyle.
- ☐ He also cites that to live such a life, they must be engaged in *"understanding what the will of the Lord is"* and implies that intoxicants *"be not drunk with wine, but be filled with the Spirit,"* striking at the very work of the Holy Spirit.
- ☐ Intoxicants are counterfeits, a strategy devised by the enemy to deceive them into believing that they can find peace within their soul independent of God's grace and forgiveness.

Mark I. Bubeck, in his discussion on how the flesh (drunkenness) works against the spirit man, states in his text, *The Adversary,* "This fleshiness springs from a desire to create a sense of well-being. It strikes at the work of the Holy Spirit who convicts man of his sins and creates guilt and conviction designed to bring man to faith and repentance. Drunkenness seeks by a fleshly stimulation to produce a sense of well-being which in truth and permanency can only be produced by the fullness of the Holy Spirit" (Ephesians 5:18).

UNDERSTANDING THE SPIRITUAL WARFARE INVOLVED THE USING & SELLING OF DRUGS

Apostle Paul in the Book of Galatians 5:19–21 provides believers with a list of sins referred to as the "works or practices of the flesh." It is not an exhaustive list but a list that describes sin in three major areas of a believer's life. All sin affects an individual's relationship with God; however, the sins are placed in three categories. The first group is sexual sin that defiles the human body; the second consists of *idolatry* and *witchcraft*, which directly defiles an individual's relationship with God; and the last group defiles human relationships.

- ☐ The second group of sin—idolatry and witchcraft—relate to man-made religion and like sexual sin; not only do they corrupt man, but they likewise hinder his relationship with God as well. This second category of sin is of particular interest as we address the issue of substance abuse and addiction in this text.

  (1) Idolatry refers to the *worship* of man-made things, things of the world (money, power, position, relationships, etc.), material possessions (car, home, clothing, jewelry) the generic god of the 12 Step Movement, (NA, AA, CA), etc.
  (2) Witchcraft refers to the *administration* (selling) or *use* of mood and mind-altering drugs (cocaine, heroin, alcohol, etc.). All sin hinders our relationship with God, but the sin of witchcraft strikes directly at the work of the Holy Spirit.

With regard to witchcraft, Mark I. Bubeck in his text, *The Adversary*, makes the following statement regarding the use of alcohol and other drugs: "The use of drugs for sensational, mind-expanding experience is a form of sorcery. Drug experimentation is a fleshly sin which leads on into deeper bondage with Satan's kingdom." The Greek interpretation for the work of witchcraft cited in this passage is *pharmakeus* and is defined as the use or the administering of drugs, one who prepares or uses magical remedies derived from *pharmakon*, a drug from which we receive the term *pharmacy*.

Dr. John MacArthur, in his text, *The New Testament Commentary Galatians*, makes the following statement regarding the "work of the flesh," known as witchcraft or sorcery.

> Sorcery translates *pharmakeia*, from which we get pharmacy and pharmaceutical. It was originally used of medicines in general but came to be used primarily of mood–and mind–altering drugs similar to those that create so much havoc in our own day. Many ancient religious ceremonies involved occultic practices in which drugs were used to induce supposed communications with deities and pharmakeia thereby came to be closely related to witchcraft and black magic. Aristotle and other Greek writers used the word as a synonym for witchcraft and black magic, because drugs were so commonly used in their practice.

PART ONE

The Dynamics of Addiction and Relapse Prevention Biblical Cognitive Model of Addiction

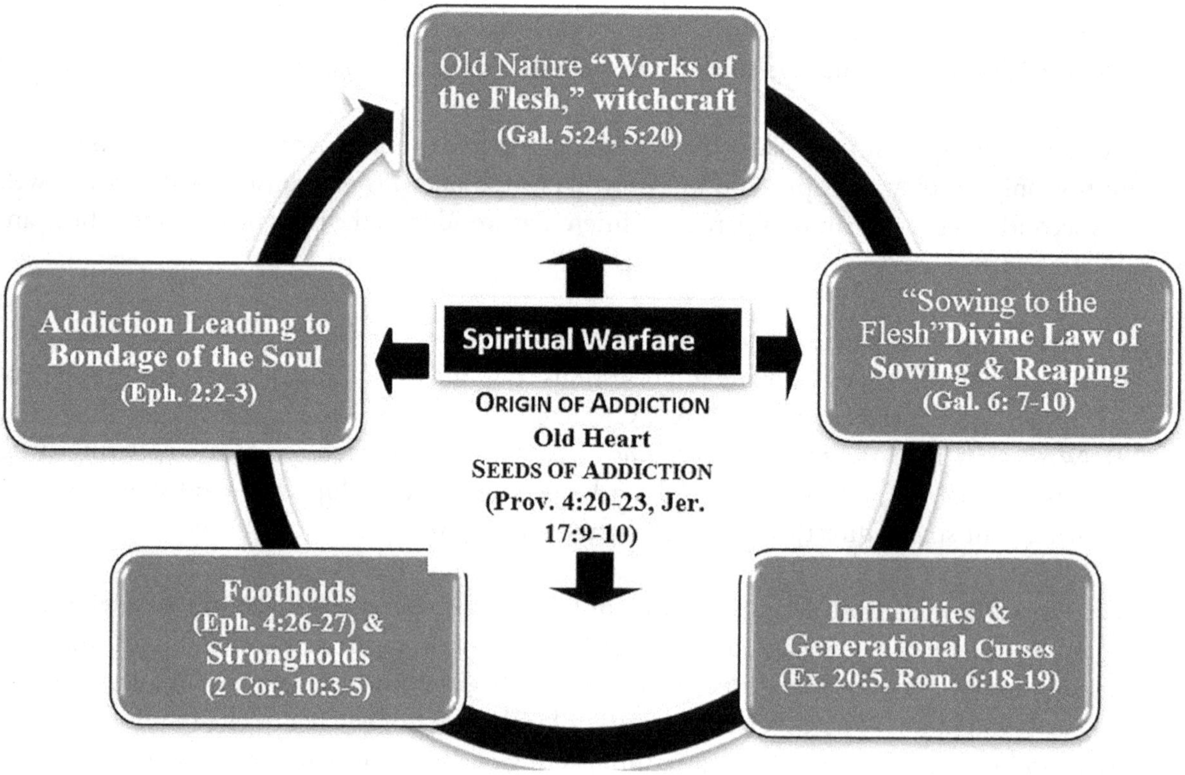

Figure 12: A Biblical Cognitive Model of Addiction

Biblical Definition of Addiction

An addiction is an effect of a sinful condition originating in an individual's *heart* due to their *old nature* being activated by *them yielding to fleshly desires (This is the result of the Divine Law of Sowing and Reaping)*. Addiction manifests itself within an individual's soul in the form of a *stronghold*. Following conversion, when God crucifies the old nature, the "*works of the flesh*" remain within the soul and must be put to death by the Holy Spirit.

Paul tells us in Galatians 2:20 that he is crucified with Christ, which is positional truth. A believer's position has to become experiential. Like Paul, a believer has to walk out and workout the reality of their own salvation, which is accomplished through mortification, sanctification, and identification.

The heart is where addiction has its *origin*. Every human being is born with the *"seeds of addiction"* in their heart, and you were no exception. So addiction is a *spiritual issue* due to *spiritual disorder* that can only be addressed by the *"new birth."*

When you decided to use (sin) drugs/alcohol, you began *sowing to the flesh;* you began cultivating the seeds of addiction in your heart. Two factors came into play that determined the *intensity* of your use; you could have been under the influence of a *generational curse* and/or have had an *infirmity* (weakness) for drugs/alcohol. Regardless why you began using drugs/alcohol, once you began, the enemy (demonic forces) gained a *foothold* (abuse) in your soul (mind, will, emotions) that eventually resulted in a *stronghold*, leading you into bondage—into an addiction to drugs/alcohol.

God's plan of *salvation* provided you with the *only solution* for both the *origin* and the *effects* (desires, passions, cravings) of your addiction (sin) that remain following your "new birth." God handled the *"root cause"* of addiction and requires that you *cooperate* with the Holy Spirit to prevent you from sowing to the flesh and relapsing by experiencing victory over the effects of addiction (trigger, cravings, and set-up behaviors).

BIBLICAL COGNITIVE RELAPSE PREVENTION MODEL

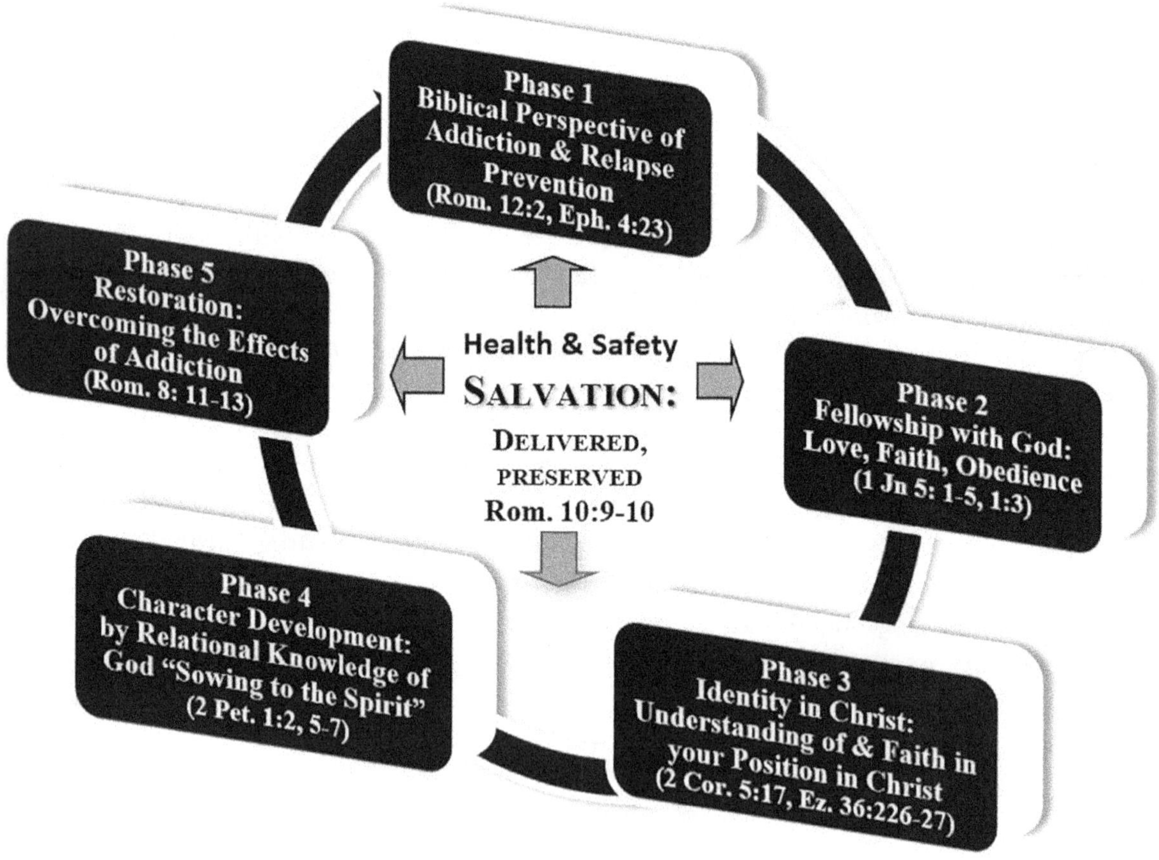

Figure 13: A Biblical Cognitive Model of Relapse Prevention

What Does It Mean to Relapse?

Relapse, from a biblical view, simply means you have become involved in the process of returning to practicing the "works of the flesh," those old behaviors and attitudes that were common practices prior to your salvation, with the end result being that you return to your "besetting sin" of using drugs/alcohol.

Understanding Salvation: God's Plan of Sobriety (Change)

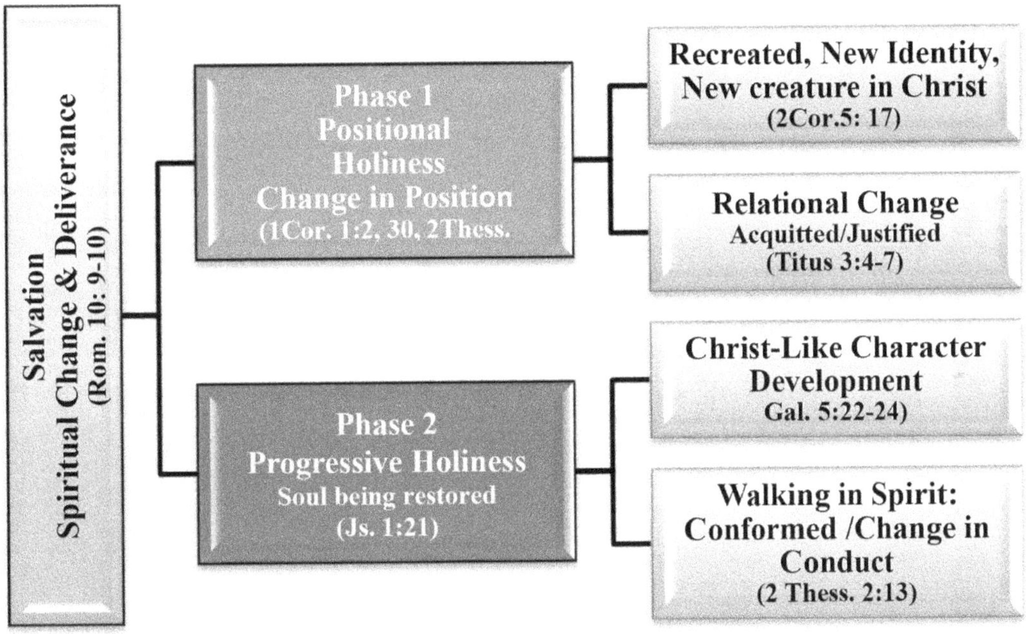

Figure 14: Salvation: God's Plan of Change

Salvation provides believers with every *spiritual* resource needed to prevent relapse. *Being transformed by the "renewing of the mind"* is the *foundation* on which the Biblical Cognitive Relapse Prevention Model is based. "Renewing the mind" must be *progressive* throughout each of the phases of the model.

Phase 1 provides the believer with God's perspective of addiction and relapse prevention, and then introduces them to His solution.

Phase 2 is a very crucial phase where believers learn how to cultivate their relationship with God.

Phase 3 gives believers understanding of their *identity* in Christ and is vital in helping believers view themselves as God sees them. This phase is key to them accepting their rightful place in the "Body of Christ" and being comfortable in local churches.

Phase 4 is designed to help them develop the much needed *"self-control"* and other Christlike *characteristics* to overcome the *effects* of their addiction.

Phase 5 presents a *lifelong process* that focuses on cooperating with the Holy Spirit as He identifies the areas in the flesh (cravings, appetites, set-up behaviors) that need to be addressed to mortify the desires and deeds of the flesh. Believers need intensive *mentoring/discipleship* early in their restoration; if not, they will quickly return to their old lifestyle and former friends.

Spiritual Change Provides the Potential and Power Needed for Relapse Prevention

Relapse prevention is going to require you to make changes in both your lifestyle and behavior. Due to your relationship with God, you will have divine assistance in making those changes. However, the greatest change by far that you will ever experience is *relational and positional change.* This occurred the moment you repented, prayed the sinner's prayer, and acknowledged Christ as Lord. God immediately accepted you into His family. You experienced *a rebirth, being born-again spiritually,* became *a new creature in Christ,* and were given a *new identity.* The *first aspect of change* you experienced began with your *repentance.*

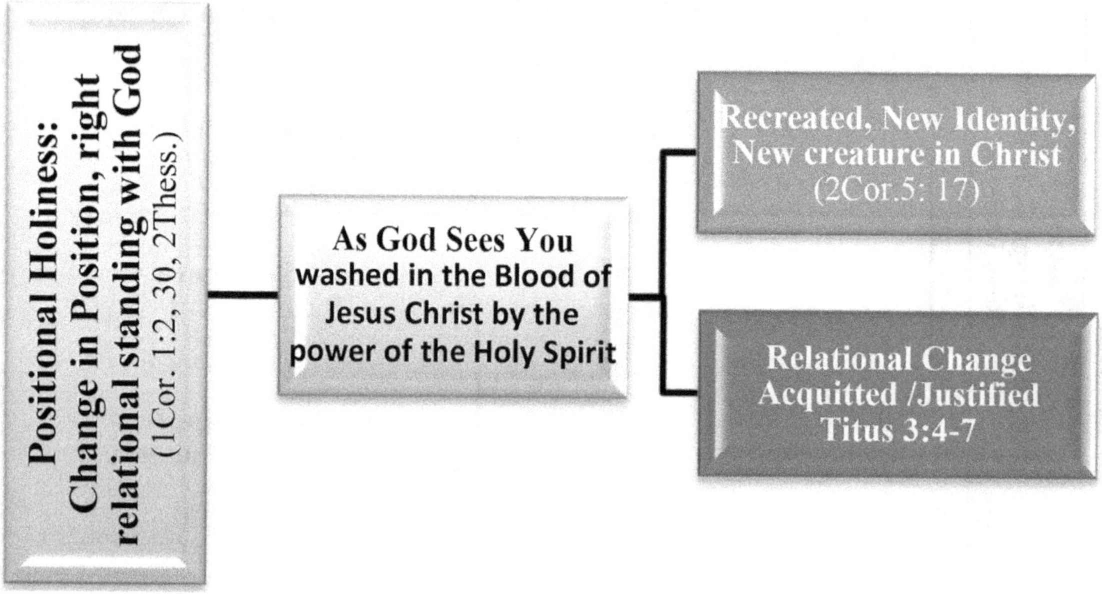

Figure 15: Positional Holiness (sanctification)

> Jesus answered and said unto him, Verily, verily, I say unto thee, *"Except a man be born again, he cannot see the kingdom of God."* Nicodemus saith unto him, "How can a man be born when he is old? can he enter the second time into his mother's womb, and be born?" Jesus answered, "Verily, verily, I say unto thee, except a man be born of water and of the Spirit, he cannot enter into the kingdom of God. That which is born of the flesh is flesh; and that which is born of the Spirit is spirit. Marvel not that I said unto thee, 'Ye must be born again.'" (John 3:3–7)

Relapse prevention is about you making the transition from your old identity to your new identity. This is a necessity in the life of every Christian, and because you made a commitment to Christ, you are no exception. As we have already stated, by far, the greatest change that you experienced is *positional and relational change.*

Understanding and having faith in the spiritual changes God has made in you, and your willingness to continue in fellowship with God, will determine how successful you will be at relapse prevention.

You must clearly understand that salvation is the beginning of your growth process and that you received the *minimum amount of spiritual growth* at the moment of your conversion. With your conversion, there is a great potential for spiritual growth to be changed into the image and likeness of Christ. You must understand that the ultimate source of change is the Holy Spirit and the Word of God. God also uses the human element of change, the Body of Christ (believers in local churches).

During your initial salvation process, you make a decision to receive God's grace, you mostly played a passive role, while the Holy Spirit made the necessary changes. Now you must play an active role: you are required to participate with God's plans for your life by committing to having your way of *thinking changed.* This change occurs through the renewing of your mind by receiving and applying God's Word to your daily life. You must learn to view yourself as God sees you and guard your thinking from anything contrary to God's Word.

Restoring the Soul: The Key to Making the Transition into Your New Identity (Phase 2)

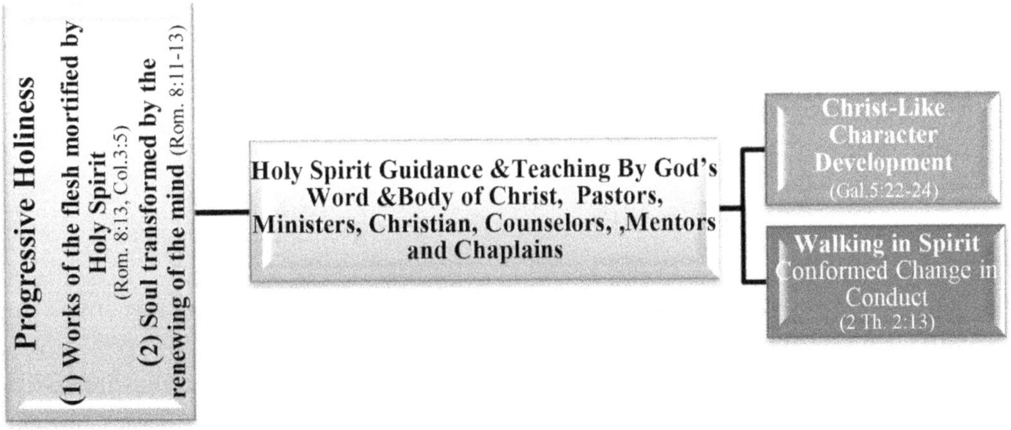

Figure 16: Understanding Progressive Holiness (sanctification)

Sanctification means to be made holy, separated unto God for His service. It is an activity of the Holy Spirit, of setting you apart unto God for salvation, and also enabling you to be holy as God is holy. God has *spiritually transformed* you; this was the *first phase* of change in your life. Now you must advance in your Christian walk with Christ through the grace provided by the Holy Spirit into the *second phase* of change. Holiness in your *conduct* and *character* is the key to overcoming the effects of your addiction as a *result of your cooperation with the Holy Spirit.* Remember that your *role was passive* with regard to your *position of holiness*; however, you are required by God to play *an active role* in *progressive holiness.*

Cooperating with God means you agree to *build boundaries*, agreeing to avoid dangers that will hinder God's plan for your life. You must agree to be highly *selective about who you associate with,* making a conscious decision to avoid certain people, places, and things that will potentially disrupt your relationship with God. You must be willing to *separate yourself from your past*, learning to forgive yourself so that you can accept God's forgiveness and learn to forgive others. You must be *humble, open to correction, teachable*, and willing to *depend on God and other believers for support.*

Understanding the World's Way for Relapse Prevention Self-Rehabilitation

Most likely, you have tried to avoid relapsing in the past. You probably made several unsuccessful attempts at *"self-rehabilitation,"* deciding to quit using drugs/alcohol through abstinence by your own effort, determination or willpower. Individuals attempting to overcome addiction referred to this process as going "cold turkey" when attempting to withdraw from drugs and going on the "water wagon" when referring to attempting to withdraw from alcohol. These methods do not result in freedom from addiction. *Self-rehabilitation* is the least successful form of change, because it doesn't include addressing spiritual needs or assistance of others and is an ineffective attempt at managing sin.

> When an evil spirit comes out of a man, it goes through arid places seeking rest and does not find it. Then it says, "I will return to the house I left." *When it arrives, it finds the house swept clean and put in order.* Then it goes and takes seven other spirits more wicked than itself, and they go in and live there. *And the final condition of that man is worse than the first.* (Luke 11:24–26)

- ☐ *The NIV Study Bible,* states, "The place has been cleaned up but left unoccupied. A life reformed but lacking God's presence is open to re-occupancy by evil."
- ☐ If a person decides to stop using alcohol and other drugs, or finds a means to assist them in quitting some particular sin in their life, that doesn't change the fact that they are still spiritually dead and alienated from God.

Therapeutic Change

You may have also been involved in some form of *therapeutic/clinical change* involving treatment programs with counseling, possibly a 12-Step Recovery program with support groups or a combination of the two. *Therapeutic/clinical change* differs from *self-rehabilitation* in that it's based on secular theories and strategies and focuses on modifying behavior by addressing how an individual thinks, feels, and makes decision. Like *self-rehabilitation,* its goal is also abstinence through an individual's own effort, determination or willpower, but with assistance from others in addressing the condition of the soul. Like *self-rehabilitation, therapeutic/clinical change* is not true freedom from addiction due to not addressing spiritual change which is obtained through salvation.

Both *therapeutic/clinical change* and *self-rehabilitation* are similar in that they do nothing to change an individual's relationship with God; therefore, a nonbeliever involved in either of these two forms of change are missing the most important factor in change—a relationship with God through believing in Jesus Christ.

Some programs refer to a generic god. *Divine assistance* is missing in both these forms of change; therefore, *spiritual change* through being born again is far superior to both *therapeutic/clinical change* and *self-rehabilitation.* This is because it addresses the root cause of the addiction—sin.

Without *spiritual change,* you do not have the potential to free yourself from the effects (cravings, desires, set-up behaviors) of your addiction; at best, you can only hope to manage or arrest them. A believer who becomes involved in *therapeutic/clinical change* or *self-rehabilitation* following salvation has the potential to be set free from the effects of addiction but has chosen the wrong methods to develop their potential and, at best, will experience behavioral modification.

Edward M. Smith sums up the major differences between God's plan and man's plan for addressing addictive behavior. In his text, *Healing Life's Hurts*, he states, "It is not based on my effort, determination, or willpower, but is a natural overflow of His work in me. This does not negate obedience, repentance, discipline, or effort on the part of the believer, but rather puts all of these practices in a divine perspective. *Self-control* that is *provided* and *maintained* as a *by-product of the fruit of the Holy Spirit* (Gal. 5:23) is different from *controlled behavior* that is *a fruit of man's effort.* When I know the truth and reside in the peace that Christ gives, my 'self' is under control as a work of God in me. Controlled behavior is better than sinful choices, but self-control provided by the Holy Spirit is best."

UNDERSTANDING THE WORLD'S WAY OF CHANGE

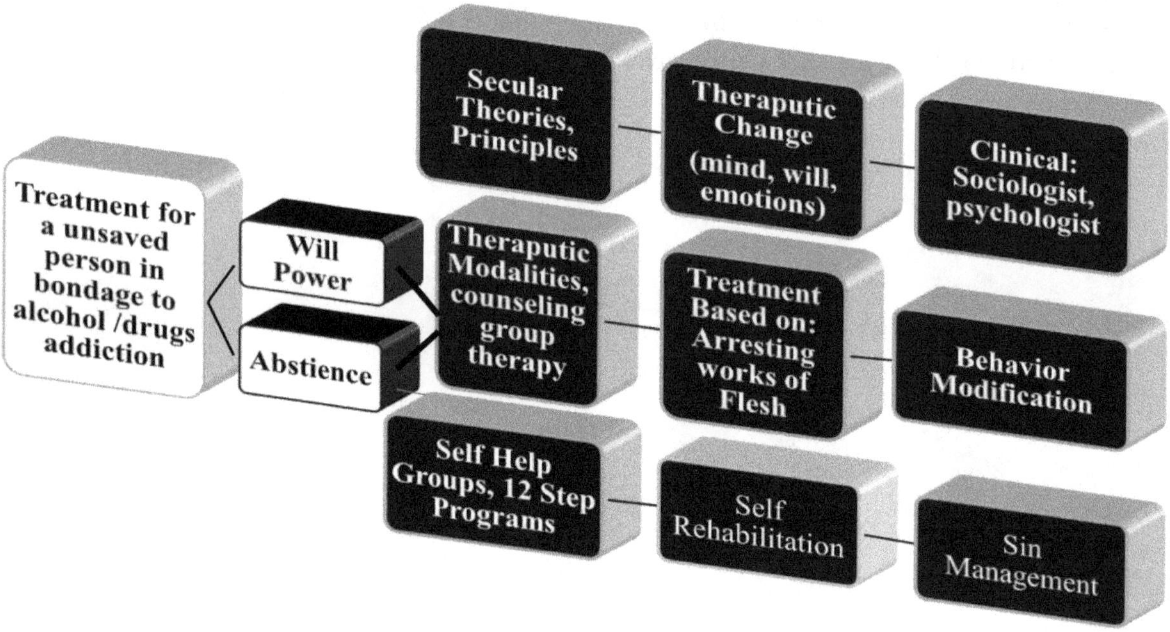

Figure 17: Understanding the World's Way of Addressing Addiction

UNDERSTANDING THE DIFFERENCE BETWEEN SPIRITUAL TRANSFORMATION AND THERAPEUTIC CHANGE AND SELF-REHABILITATION

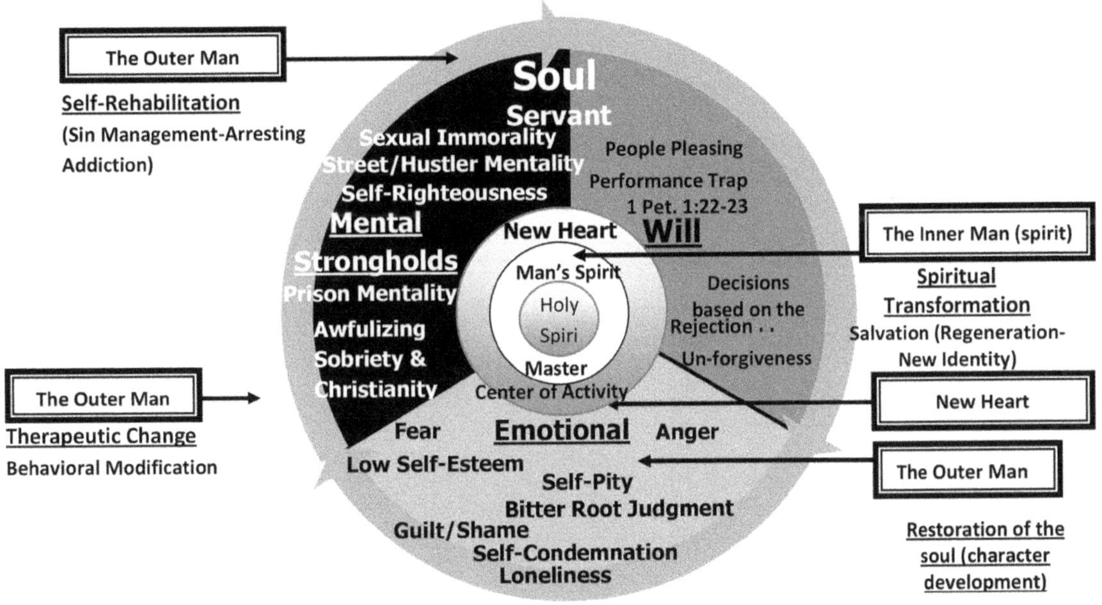

Figure 18: Spiritual Transformation vs. Therapeutic Change and Self-Rehabilitation

In the above diagram, you can clearly see that both *Therapeutic Change* and *Self-Rehabilitation* are limited, focusing exclusively on the condition of the outer man (soul, mind, will, emotions). The most these two forms of change can provide is behavioral modification and sin management, *arresting addiction. Spiritual transformation* not only transforms man's spiritual state of being, *but it changes his heart* and provides the potential/power for *restoration of his soul.* Spiritual transformation addresses the origin of addiction: the old heart/nature and the effects of addiction in the soul, providing the only solution to problem addiction.

Review the above chart, *A Contrasting Overview of Recovery versus Spiritual Change/Restoration.*

Then answer the following questions:

1. What is the difference between therapeutic change and self-rehabilitation?

2. How are therapeutic change and self-rehabilitation similar?
3. What makes spiritual change more effective than both therapeutic change and self-rehabilitation?
4. What key element is missing from both therapeutic change and self-rehabilitation? Which form of change is least successful?

PART TWO

The Role Spiritual Warfare Plays in Addiction and Relapse and Relapse Prevention

Significant Facts Regarding Relapse: "Fallen Nature"

> But of the tree of the knowledge of good and evil, thou shalt not eat of it: *for in the day that thou eatest thereof thou shalt surely die.* (Genesis 2:17)

- ☐ As a result of Adam's disobedience, all of mankind is born spiritually dead and alienated from God with a hardened heart.

> Wherefore, as by one man sin entered into the world, and death by sin; and so death passed upon all men, for that all have sinned. (Romans 5:12)

- ☐ Adam's sin resulted in all of mankind being born with the seeds of addiction in their heart, because of spiritual death.

> For as by one man's disobedience many were made sinners, so by the obedience of one shall many be made righteous. (Romans 5:19)

- ☐ Jesus Christ reversed the curse placed on mankind by God due to his disobedience; therefore, the only true solution to addiction is salvation through Jesus becoming Lord of your life.

The Vital Role the Heart Plays

The heart is the seat or *center* of a believer's mind (thoughts, reasoning, understanding), will (judgments, decisions), and emotions (love, hatred, fear, joy, sorrow, anger) where it converges with their inner being (spirit).

- ☐ The heart contains the sinful desires that lead to bondage of alcohol and other drugs, and only God can change it.
- ☐ God had accomplished something in every believer only He could do; He gave them a new heart. Now they must guard it with His Word.

> *The heart is deceitful above all things, and desperately wicked: who can know it?* I the LORD search the heart, *I* try the reins, even to give every man according to his ways, *and* according to the fruit of his doings. (Jeremiah 17:9–10)

☐ The heart is where the addiction has its *origin* and is the root of the issue. The *seeds* of addiction are planted in every individual's heart at the time of birth due to inheriting an old depraved nature.

> A new heart also will I give you, and a new spirit will I put within you: *and I will take away the stony heart out of your flesh*, and I will give you a heart of flesh. And I will put my spirit within you, and cause you to walk in my statutes, *and ye shall keep my judgments, and do them.* (Ezekiel 36:26–27)
>
> Again, Jesus called the crowd to him and said, *"Listen to me, everyone, and understand this. Nothing outside a man can make him 'unclean' by going into him. Rather, it is what comes out of a man that makes him 'unclean.'"* After he had left the crowd and entered the house, his disciples asked him about this parable. "Are you so dull?" he asked. *"Don't you see that nothing that enters a man from the outside can make him 'unclean'? For it doesn't go into his heart but into his stomach, and then out of his body."* He went on: *"What comes out of a man is what makes him 'unclean.' For from within, out of men's hearts, come evil thoughts, sexual immorality, theft, murder, adultery, greed, malice, deceit, lewdness, envy, slander, arrogance and folly.* All these evils come from inside and make a man unclean. (Mark 7:14–23, NIV).
>
> The good man brings good things out of the good stored up in his heart, and the evil man brings evil things out of the evil stored up in his heart. For out of the overflow of his heart his mouth speaks. (Luke 6:45, NIV)

Anyone could end up in bondage to alcohol or other drugs. Research indicates that individuals who become bound by addiction to alcohol and other drugs come from various backgrounds.

☐ A certain percentage of the individuals who participate in social drinking and recreational use of drugs will end up in bondage to addiction. Many individuals who came from families with excellent backgrounds, with no reported use of alcohol or other drugs, will end up in bondage to addiction. Addiction cannot be predicted in advance. The origin of addiction is found in mankind in their *fallen* nature with its hardened heart.

> My son, attend to my words; incline thine ear unto my sayings. Let them not depart from thine eyes; keep them in the midst of thine heart. *For they are life unto those that find them, and health to all their flesh. Keep thy heart with all diligence; for out of it are the issues of life.* (Proverbs 4:20–23)

☐ *All issues of life, including addictions, are centered* within a person's *heart.* Thus, the heart must be changed through the new birth in order to address the origin of the problem. Once saved, a believer must guard his heart by the Word of God.

Understanding the War Within

> During the years you spent separated from God, your worldly experiences thoroughly programmed your brain with thought patterns, memory traces, responses, and habits which are alien to God. So even though your old skipper (nature) is gone, your flesh remains in opposition to God as a preprogrammed propensity for sin, which is living independent of God.
>
> —Neil Anderson

The Flesh as an enemy

As a believer, you must also understand the corrupt nature of the flesh. It can never be improved. It must die according to the Scriptures. This compulsive inner force inherited from the fall of Adam will continue to express itself in rebellion against God and His holiness (Romans 8:7–8). The flesh is a lifelong opponent that must be dealt with.

As a believer, you need to familiarize yourself with the works of the flesh listed in the fifth chapter of Galatians. This will help you identify temptation in your own life and assist you in applying God's biblical solution in those areas.

The flesh is extremely difficult to address because of its close relationship to personality. Following conversion, there is a constant inner struggle between the "old man" and the "new man." A believer who becomes entangled in the works of the flesh opens a door for the enemy, allowing the compulsive inner desires of the "old man" to be joined by the forces of evil, resulting in a demonic foothold. (Galatians 5:17; Ephesians 4:22–27)

God Provides a New Nature and Heart, but the Flesh Remains

> Those who live according to the sinful nature have their minds set on what that nature desires; but those who live in accordance with the Spirit have their minds set on what the Spirit desires.
>
> *For to be carnally minded is death; but to be spiritually minded is life and peace. Because the carnal mind is enmity against God:* for it is not subject to the law of God, neither indeed can be. *So then they that are in the flesh cannot please God. But ye are not in the flesh, but in the Spirit,* if so be that the Spirit of God dwell in you. Now if any man has not the Spirit of Christ, he is none of his. (Romans 8:5–9, NIV)

- ☐ The term flesh is used to collectively describe the state of the unredeemed, those who are "in the flesh" who are controlled by their sinful passions (Romans 7:5). Generally, it is used in a figurative sense to refer to *man's fallen nature.*
- ☐ Flesh also relates to the *moral, spiritual weakness and helplessness* of the *human nature still clinging to saved souls* (Romans 6:19).
- ☐ The flesh *functions apart from and against the Spirit.* In the believer's heart, the flesh *stands against the work of the Spirit.* The flesh is the residence of sin that still remains in a believer's life (Romans 7:18).
- ☐ The flesh is a difficult enemy to handle because of its *close relationship to the believer's personality.*

The flesh is intimately intertwined with the faculties of the soul (mind, will, and emotions) and *prior to your being "born again,"* it controlled your life.

- ☐ You must understand that you begin the *process* of sowing to the flesh (relapsing) the moment you stop meeting your spiritual needs by sowing to the Spirit.
- ☐ When you stop practicing the spiritual disciplines (praying, praising/worshipping God, reading the Bible, and fellowshipping with other Christians), you are already in the process of returning to practicing the works of the flesh (relapsing).
- ☐ Soon you will begin hanging with old friends/associates from the past, entertaining old thoughts, not addressing negative emotions, etc. Eventually, the desires and cravings will become more and more intense and frequent, and you most likely will return to your besetting sin, using drugs/alcohol.

> *This* I say then, *"Walk in the Spirit, and ye shall not fulfil the lust of the flesh. For the flesh lusteth against the Spirit, and the Spirit against the flesh: and these are contrary the one to the other: so that ye cannot do the things that ye would. But if ye be led of the Spirit, ye are not under the law."* (Galatians 5:16–18)

- ☐ To walk in the Spirit means to walk and govern your life in accordance with the leadership of the Holy Spirit, which results in being delivered from the dictates of sin and made holy—that is, being set apart for an intimate relationship and fellowship with Jesus Christ (Every task that the Holy Spirit has been sent and commissioned to do with, to, and through us is for this purpose—to make ready a people prepared for the Lord and Bridegroom, Jesus Christ!).
- ☐ The moment you acknowledged Jesus as Lord, you entered into a spiritual crisis. You were spiritually born again, and a struggle began between your flesh and spirit. A struggle begins because your spirit now desires the things of God, but your flesh desires the things of the world.
- ☐ You must be aware that even though you are a new creature and God has taken care of the "root cause" of your addiction, the desires, cravings, and passions of the flesh for drugs/alcohol may still remain.

Works of the Flesh (Acts of the Sinful Nature)

> *The acts of the sinful nature are obvious*: sexual immorality, impurity and debauchery; idolatry and witchcraft; hatred, discord, jealousy, fits of rage, selfish ambition, dissensions, factions and envy; drunkenness, orgies, and the like. (Galatians 5:19–21, NIV)

Paul lists three specific groups of sin that relate to man's works of the flesh: sex, religion, and human relationships.

The first group consists of immorality, impurity, and sensuality.

(1) *Sexual immorality* refers to all sexual sin in general, especially, but not limited to adultery, fornication, prostitution, homosexuality, bestiality, and incest.
(2) *Impurity* refers to a moral uncleanness that hinders a person from approaching God (because of impure thoughts).
(3) *Debauchery* refers to a readiness for sexual pleasure and lack of control with regard to sexual activity.

The second group of sin, idolatry and witchcraft, relate to man-made religion. Like sexual sin, not only do they corrupt man, but they also hinder his relationship with God.

(1) *Idolatry* refers to the worship of man-made things, things of the world (money, power, position, relationships, etc.), material possessions (car, home, clothing, and jewelry), 12-Step Movement (Idolatry is not limited to or relegated to only man-made objects. God created the moon and sun; these are not man-made; however, the worship of these is also idolatry).
(2) *Witchcraft or sorcery* refers to the administering (selling) or use of mood and mind-altering drugs (cocaine, heroin, alcohol, etc.). All sin hinders our relationship with God, but the sin of witchcraft involves an active participation in demonic activity.

Witchcraft: The Using and Selling of Drugs

With regard to witchcraft, Mark I. Bubeck makes the following statement, "The use of drugs for sensational, mind-expanding experience is a form of sorcery. Drug experimentation is a fleshly sin which leads on into deeper bondage with Satan's kingdom." The Greek word for the work of witchcraft cited in this passage is *pharmakeus,* and is defined as the use or the administering of drugs. It can refer to one who prepares or uses magical remedies; it is derived from *pharmakon,* a drug, from which we get the word *pharmacy.*

- ☐ Any person who is a believer that once misused drugs must accept that they were actively involved in sorcery or witchcraft.
- ☐ Likewise, anyone who was involved in selling or trafficking drugs was engaged in the works of witchcraft or sorcery.
- ☐ There is definite demonic activity in both the use and sell of drugs. This is why being entangled in the use or trafficking of drugs is such a difficult bondage to overcome.

Note: You must understand that becoming involved in any of the practices or works of the flesh are sinful and displeasing to God and could cause you to relapse.

> Wherefore he saith, "Awake thou that sleepest, and arise from the dead, and Christ shall give thee light. See then that ye walk circumspectly, not as fools, but as wise, Redeeming the time, because the days are evil. Wherefore be ye not unwise, but understanding what the will of the Lord is. *And be not drunk with wine, wherein is excess; but be filled with the Spirit."* (Ephesians 5:14–18)

Mark I. Bubeck, in his discussion on how the flesh (drunkenness) works against the spirit-man states in his text, *The Adversary,* "This fleshiness springs from a desire to create a sense of well-being.

It strikes at the work of the Holy Spirit who convicts man of his sins and creates guilt and conviction designed to bring man to faith and repentance. Drunkenness seeks by a fleshly stimulation to produce a sense of well-being, which in truth and permanency can only be produced by the fullness of the Holy Spirit."

The third group of sin listed in the works of the flesh refers to human relationships and hinders the believer from fulfilling the second greatest commandment.

(1) *Hatred* refers to hateful attitudes resulting in hostility and reason for opposition to others.
(2) *Discord* or variance is a direct result of hatred and results in serious conflicts (quarreling).
(3) *Jealousy* is a dislike for others because they have something you don't.
(4) *Fits of rage* or sudden outbursts of anger toward others for little or no apparent reason, uncontrollable temper.
(5) *Selfish ambitions* being self-willed.
(6) *Dissension* or divisions.
(7) *Factions,* the feeling that everyone else is wrong except those in your own little group.
(8) *Envy* refers to a desire to have what belongs to another, resulting in anger and resentment caused by coveting: these four sins represent long-term disagreements among individual after original conflict has occurred.
(9) *Drunkenness,* affected by alcohol to the extent of losing control of one's faculties or behavior.
(10) *Orgies* or carousing, referring to the behavior that results from living a lifestyle out of control, drinking, partying, etc.

THE DANGER OF PRACTICING THE WORKS OF THE FLESH

Self-Check

Check [√] the box that best answers the questions listed below. Have you experienced problems with any of the following "works of the flesh" in the past?

1. **Sexual immorality**	[ ] yes	[ ] no
2. **Impurity**	[ ] yes	[ ] no
3. **Debauchery**	[ ] yes	[ ] no
4. **Idolatry**	[ ] yes	[ ] no
5. **Witchcraft**	[ ] yes	[ ] no
6. **Hatred**	[ ] yes	[ ] no
7. **Discord**	[ ] yes	[ ] no
8. **Jealousy**	[ ] yes	[ ] no
9. **Fits of Rage**	[ ] yes	[ ] no
10. **Selfish Ambitions**	[ ] yes	[ ] no
11. **Dissension**	[ ] yes	[ ] no
12. **Factions**	[ ] yes	[ ] no
13. **Envy**	[ ] yes	[ ] no
14. **Drunkenness**	[ ] yes	[ ] no
15. **Orgies**	[ ] yes	[ ] no

1. Review the diagram below of the Works (Practices) of the Flesh. Using a scale from 1 to 15, with 1 being the greatest problem and 15 being the least problem, rank the following "works of the flesh" according to the level at which you experienced problems with them in the past.

WORKS OF THE FLESH

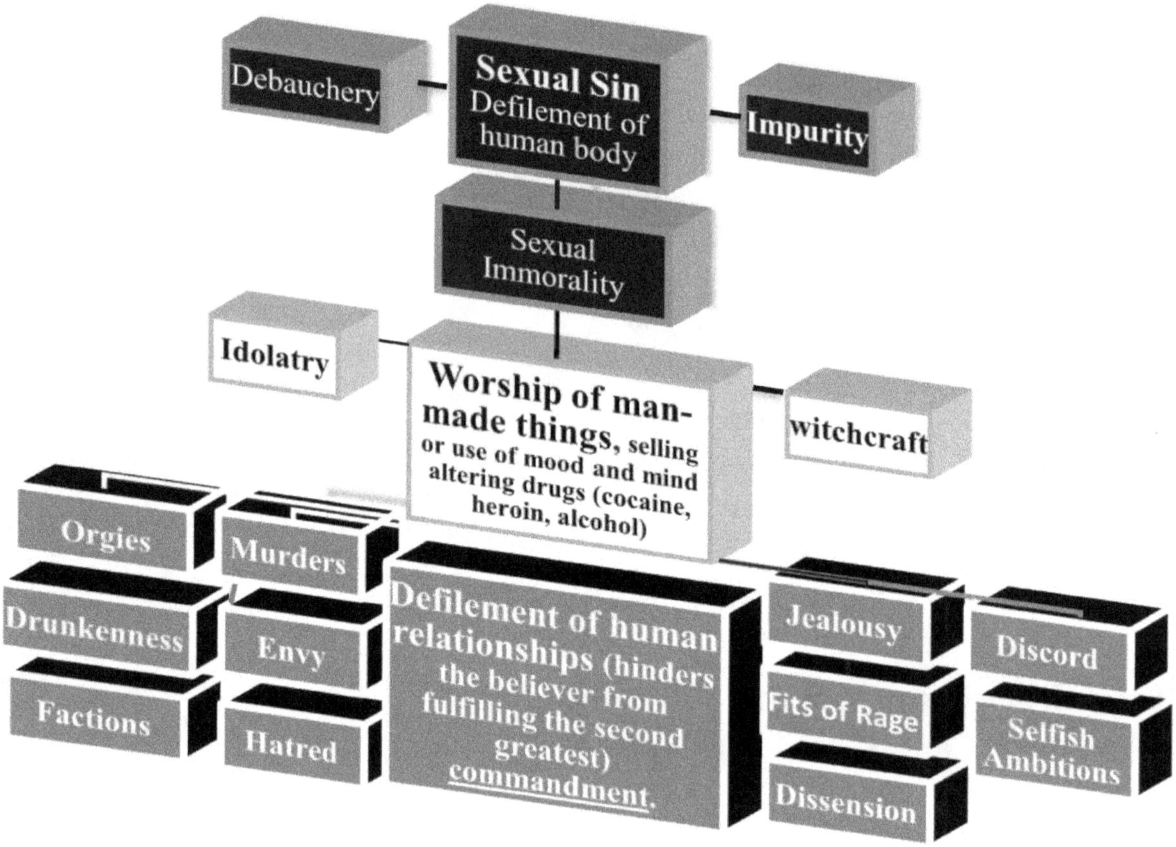

Figure 19: Understanding the Works of the Flesh

You need to understand that the quality of your spiritual life following salvation will depend on what you choose to sow to. If you choose to sow to the flesh, the quality of your spiritual life will be low and your spiritual growth will be hindered; consequently, you will struggle with the works of the flesh. However, if you sow to the Spirit, He will produce His fruit in you, and you will prosper spiritually; you will therefore experience a high quality of spiritual life and grow enormously in Christ.

UNDERSTANDING THE WORKS OF THE FLESH

Self-Rating

> I say then: "*Walk in the Spirit,* and you shall not fulfill the *lust (works) of the flesh.* For the flesh lusts against the Spirit, and the Spirit against the flesh; and these are contrary to one another, so that you do not do the things that you wish.18 But if you are led by the Spirit, you are not under the law." (Galatians 5:16–18)

1. According to this passage of scripture, is God telling you the best way not to live is to fulfill the works of the flesh?
2. What are some examples of how you used to walk in the flesh?
3. What are some examples of how you can walk in the Spirit?

Action Steps

List two things you can do to increase your walk in the Spirit.

1.
2.

Action Steps

List three things you are willing to do to overcome the problems you have experienced in the past fulfilling the works of the flesh.

1.
2.
3.

Paul makes it very clear that these are just some of the sins of the flesh. He tells that we should not continue to practice these once we are saved, because these are the characteristics of an unbeliever.

- The works of the flesh are put to death by sowing to the Spirit; because in doing so, you are blessed with the fruit of the Spirit, which nullifies and defeats the works of the flesh.

Fruit of the Spirit

> But the fruit of the Spirit is love, joy, peace, longsuffering, gentleness, goodness, faith, meekness, *temperance (self-control):* against such there is no law. *And they that are Christ's have crucified the flesh with the affections and lusts.* (Galatians 5:22–24)

- God has provided you with everything you need to prevent you from relapsing. You have the fruit of the Spirit within you, which is the key to destroying the works of the flesh; but they are seed-fruit and need to be developed.
- All the elements of the fruit of the Spirit are equally important, but *temperance or self-control* is of great significance when being restored from addiction.
- The world's understanding of *self-control* is centered totally on *abstinence* through one's own willpower, which depends on their own strength.
- The self-control or temperance that is developed through the Holy Spirit is much different because it is part of the fruit of the Spirit, a Godlike characteristic for developing and molding His children in His likeness. Yes, you practiced abstinence at the beginning of your restoration. However, God's self-control does not depend on your own personal strength; it is empowered by your cooperation with the Holy Spirit, developed through an active relationship with God and His Son.
- Christ provided victory over the "works of the flesh" on the cross, and that victory is part of your inheritance. Now you must learn to experience that victory in your daily life by cooperating with the Holy Spirit.
- If you don't learn to cooperate with the Holy Spirit, you will relapse and become entangled in your old addictive lifestyle.

> Everyone who believes that Jesus is the Christ is born of God, and everyone who loves the father loves his child as well. *This is how we know that we love the children of God: by loving God and carrying out his commands. This is love for God: to obey his commands. And his commands are not burdensome,* for everyone born of God overcomes the world. This is the victory that has overcome the world, even our faith. *Who is it that overcomes the world? Only he who believes that Jesus is the Son of God.* (1 John 5:1–5, NIV)

- Love for God is the key to overcoming all that is in the world, including bondage to drugs/alcohol. Learning to experience God's love demonstrated on Calvary develops your love for God.
- Love for God is demonstrated by your obedience, and obedience is necessary to prevent you from returning to practicing the works of the flesh or relapsing.

Love for God is also demonstrated by your love for other believers, which is extremely important. Lack of fellowship with other Christians and fellowship with old friends are major factors in returning to the old lifestyle of the works of the flesh and relapsing.

FRUIT OF THE SPIRIT

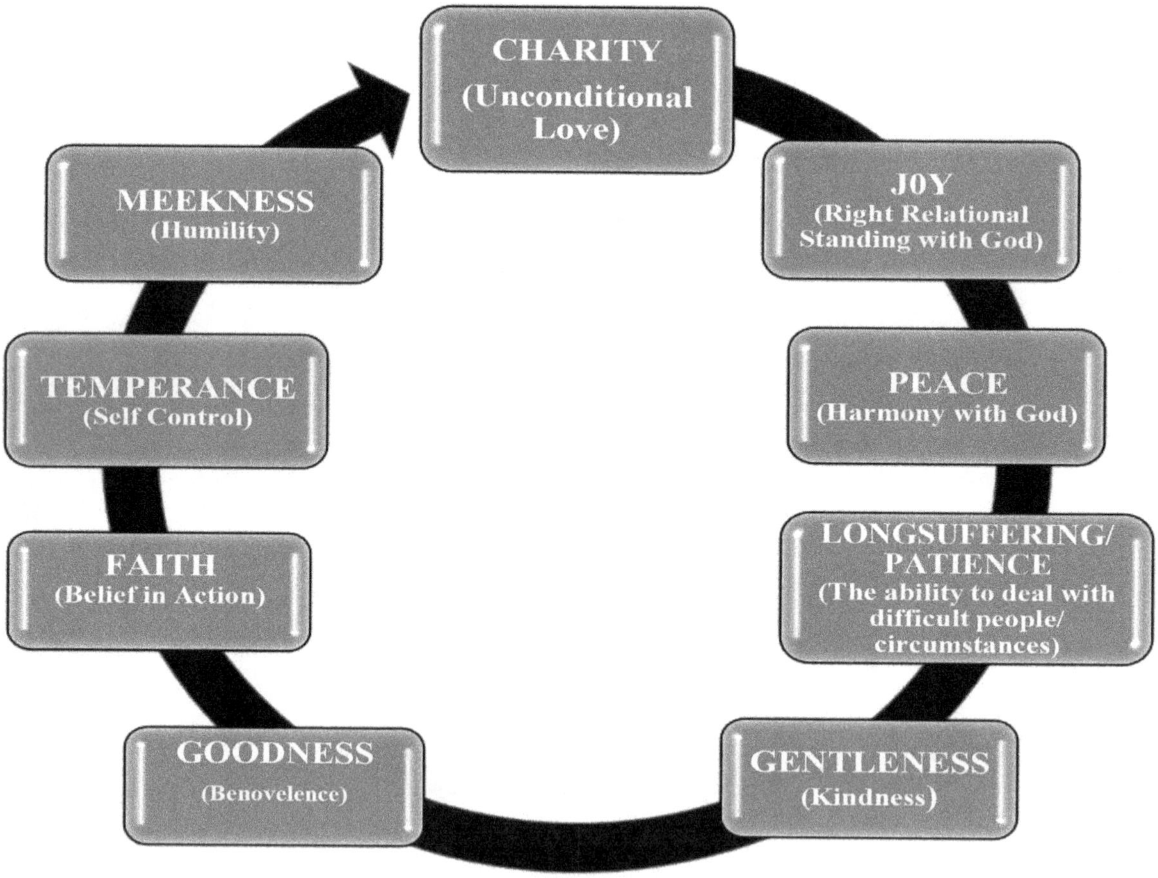

Figure 20: The Fruit of the Spirit

Understanding the Fruit of the Spirit

Self-Rating

> But the fruit of the Spirit is love, joy, peace, longsuffering, gentleness, goodness, faith, meekness, *temperance (self-control):* against such there is no law. *And they that are Christ's have crucified the flesh with the affections and lusts.* (Galatians 5:22–24)

Discuss your answers to the following questions in your group.

1. What role does the "fruit of the spirit" play in preventing you from relapsing?
2. What makes "temperance" or self-control such an important factor in relapse prevention?
3. What role does love play in you overcoming your old lifestyle?

Action Steps

List the three weakest Christlike characteristics you are currently experiencing in the fruit of the spirit.

1.
2.

Action Steps

To develop your Christlike character, list three things you are willing to do to promote an increase in the fruit of the Spirit.

1.
2.
3.

Part Three

The Role that the Divine Law of Sowing & Reaping Plays in Addiction and Relapse and Relapse Prevention

How Can You Avoid Relapsing?

> Be not deceived; God is not mocked: *for whatsoever a man soweth, that shall he also reap. For he that soweth to his flesh shall of the flesh reap corruption; but he that soweth to the Spirit shall of the Spirit reap life everlasting.* And let us not be weary in well doing: for in due season we shall reap, if we faint not. As we have therefore opportunity, let us do good unto all *men*, especially unto them who are of the household of faith. (Galatians 6:7–10)

The Divine Law of Sowing and Reaping not only was key in your understanding how you became addicted, but it also plays an important role in relapse prevention.

In the passage of scripture above, the Apostle Paul warns us not to be deceived into thinking that God does not deal with sin in the lives of His children. There are consequences for the choices we make. The Divine Law of Sowing and Reaping applies to every human being, saved or unsaved.

> *For he that soweth to his flesh shall of the flesh reap corruption.* (Galatians 6:8)

Prior to accepting Christ as Lord, you were involved in a lifestyle of sin, unaware of the consequences, being deceived into believing there are no consequences for your sin. Addiction is one of the numerous consequences you faced when you choose to sow to the flesh.

- ☐ The term *corruption* spoken of here in the first portion of Galatians 6:8 refers to physical death and other earthly consequences (HIV, addictions, lung cancer, disease of liver, incarceration, STD, divorce, financial ruin, etc.).

> *But he that soweth to the Spirit shall of the Spirit reap life everlasting.* (Galatians 6:8)
>
> But the fruit of the Spirit is love, joy, peace, longsuffering, kindness, goodness, faithfulness, gentleness, *self-control.* Against such there is no law. (Galatians 5:22–23)
>
> I say then: "*Walk in the Spirit*, and you shall not fulfill the *lust (works) of the flesh*. For the flesh lusts against the Spirit, and the Spirit against the flesh; and these are contrary to one another, so that you do not do the things that you wish. But if you are led by the Spirit, you are not under the law." (Galatians 5:16–18)
>
> *And let us not be weary in well doing: for in due season we shall reap, if we faint not.* (Galatians 6:9)

Walking in the Spirit, which is conducting your life in union and in agreement with the Holy Spirit and in conjunction with His task to sanctify, lead, and present you as a chaste bride to the One who is Truth, Jesus Christ. Your cooperation with Him in this process is extremely important to keep you from relapsing. Galatians 6:9 encourages us to be persistent in our following the lead of the Spirit; we will reap the glorious rewards if we don't quit.

Infirmities: A Significant Factor in Relapse Prevention

Within the soul, an infirmity or weakness refers to a person's inability or lack of strength to bear a trial, trouble, or restrain from corrupt desires in a particular area of their life.

> You have been set free from sin and have become slaves to righteousness. *I put this in human terms because you are weak in your natural selves.* Just as you used to offer the parts of your body in slavery to impurity and to ever-increasing wickedness, *so now offer them in slavery to righteousness leading to holiness.* (Romans 6:18–19, NIV)

- ☐ You must admit your weakness and your inability to bear trials, trouble, or to restrain from corrupt desires in a particular area of their life.

> Seeing then that we have a great high priest, that is passed into the heavens, Jesus the Son of God, let us hold fast *our* profession. *For we have not a high priest which cannot be touched with the feeling of our infirmities; but was in all points tempted like as we are, yet without sin.* Let us therefore come boldly unto the throne of grace, that we may obtain mercy, and find grace to help in time of need. (Hebrews 4:14–16)

- ☐ You must remember that whatever temptations, trials, and troubles you experience, Jesus is the only one who totally understands and is able to relate to what you are going through. You are instructed to look to Him in time of need: to receive the grace and mercy you need to overcome your situation.

> *Likewise, the Spirit also helpeth our infirmities:* for we know not what we should pray for as we ought: but the Spirit itself maketh intercession for us with groanings which cannot be uttered. And he that searcheth the hearts knoweth what *is* the mind of the Spirit, because he maketh intercession for the saints according to *the will of* God. *And we know that all things work together for good to them that love God, to them who are the called according to his purpose.* (Romans 8:26–28)

- ☐ The Apostle Paul explains how the Holy Spirit assists you with your prayers because of your weakness or infirmity in that area of your life.
- ☐ Notice he states that the Holy Spirit helps you with your weaknesses, not just the weakness in prayer, but with all your weaknesses.
- ☐ Now that you are saved, you must learn to submit your body to a lifestyle of living holy to achieve permanent freedom from bondage to alcohol and other drugs.

> And lest I should be exalted above measure through the abundance of the revelations, there was given to me a thorn in the flesh, the messenger of Satan to buffet me, lest I should be exalted above measure. For this thing I besought the Lord thrice, that it might depart from me. And he said unto me, *"My grace is sufficient*

> *for thee: for my strength is made perfect in weakness. Most gladly therefore will I rather glory in my infirmities, that the power of Christ may rest upon me."* Therefore, I take pleasure in infirmities, in reproaches, in necessities, in persecutions, in distresses for Christ's sake: *for when I am weak, then am I strong.* (2 Corinthians 12:7–10)

- ☐ The Apostle Paul discusses his personal weakness or infirmity in this passage of scripture and shares how the Lord responded to his request for deliverance: "My grace is sufficient for thee: for my strength is made perfect in weakness."
- ☐ Just as the Apostle Paul learned to rely on the Lord's strength by receiving His grace in his area of weakness, you must learn to do the same—because when you are weak, then you can become strong through Christ.

Understanding Your Infirmities (Weaknesses)

Self-Check

> *My grace is sufficient for thee: for my strength is made perfect in weakness. Most gladly therefore will I rather glory in my infirmities, that the power of Christ may rest upon me.* Therefore, I take pleasure in infirmities, in reproaches, in necessities, in persecutions, in distresses for Christ's sake: *for when I am weak, then am I strong.* (2 Corinthians 12:9–10)

According to this scripture, what role does God's grace play in you overcoming your weaknesses?

Can you identify any particular weakness emotional/mental (infirmities) that played a role in you becoming addicted?

1.
2.

Action Steps

List two things you can do to join cooperate with God in overcoming your infirmities or weaknesses.

1.
2.

Foothold: A Significant Factor in Relapse Prevention

> "In your anger do not sin": Do not let the sun go down while you are still angry, *and do not give the devil a foothold.* (Ephesians 4:26–27, NIV)

A foothold is established in an individual's life when they give place to Satan by providing an opportunity for entry through sinning.

Sowing to the flesh led to footholds being formed in your life, and footholds led to strongholds. You may have become involved in the use of alcohol and other drugs for various reasons, unaware of the consequences and the spiritual warfare involved. Not having a relationship with God, you may have viewed the use of alcohol and other drugs as a remedy or solution to some mental, emotional, relational problem, or issue in your life. You never planned on what you viewed as being the solution to your problem becoming an even greater problem or addiction.

Understanding the Foothold Exercise
Self-Rating

According to the passage of scripture on footholds, what is God telling you?

List three ways you allowed the enemy to gain footholds in your life.

1.
2.
3.

Action Steps

Identify three existing footholds in your life that you need to address before they become strongholds.

1.
2.
3.

Strongholds: A Significant Factor in Relapse Prevention

> For though we live in the world, we do not wage war as the world does. *The weapons we fight with are not the weapons of the world.* On the contrary, they have *divine power to demolish strongholds.* We demolish *arguments* and every pretension that sets itself up against the knowledge of God, *and we take captive every thought to make it obedient to Christ.* (2 Corinthians 10:3–5, NIV)

A stronghold is a negative pattern of thoughts, emotions, or attitudes leading to behaviors burned into the soul either through repetition over time or through a one-time traumatic experience that is contrary to the Word and will of God.

> For I know that nothing good lives in me, that is, in my flesh [my human nature, my worldliness—my sinful capacity]. For the willingness [to do good] is present in me, but the doing of good is not. For the good that I want to do, I do not do, but I practice the very evil that I do not want. But if I am doing the very thing I do not want to do, I am no longer the one doing it [that is, it is not me that acts], but the sin [nature] which lives in me. (Romans 7:18–20, AMP)

Strongholds can be identified by several factors in a person's life: cycles, addictions to substance, broken relations, unrealistic expectations, and automatic actions without thinking. Addictions are not in themselves strongholds, but a fruit or results of a stronghold. Strongholds affect a person's *attitude, actions, emotions,* and many problems can be related to strongholds. They can also cause mental health issues, such as anxiety, depression, panic attacks, attitudes of pride, narcissism (everything is about them), worry, need to control, busyness, contention, perfectionism, negativity, and racism are just a few attitudes that can be attributed to strongholds. There are numerous negative emotions related to strongholds; fear, self-pity, anger, loneliness, guilt, shame, rejection, worthlessness, hopelessness are some of the most common. Some actions that have their origin in strongholds are addiction to drugs, alcohol, money, power, pornography, food, shopping, gambling, sex, social media, video games, and exercise.

Demonic forces observed your passion for alcohol and other drugs; and therefore, they took advantage of your weaknesses in the flesh. They gained footholds in your life when you chose to become involved in a sinful lifestyle of using alcohol and other drugs. This gave opportunities to the enemy to enslave you in a much serious condition over a period of time. Satan built strongholds in your soul that only the power of the Holy Spirit and God's Word can destroy.

FOUR STEPS LEADING TO THE STRONGHOLD OF ADDICTION

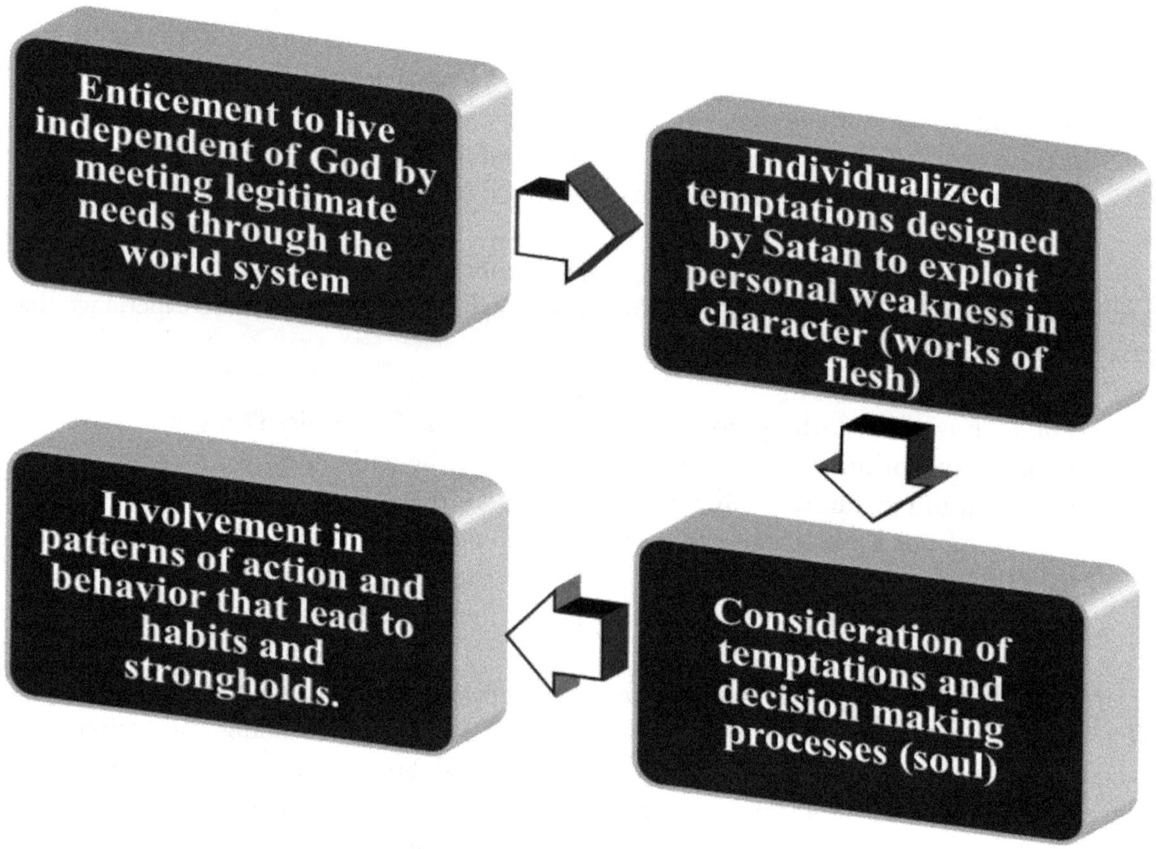

Figure 21: Understanding How Stronghold Are Developed

Dr. Wise in his text, *The Fundamentals of Spiritual Warfare*, cites these four steps leading to strongholds:

- ☐ enticement to live independent of God by meeting legitimate needs through the world system (environmental stimulus)
- ☐ individualized temptations designed by Satan to exploit personal weakness in character (works of flesh)
- ☐ an individual's consideration of temptations and decision-making processes (soul)
- ☐ an individual's involvement in patterns of action and behavior which lead to habits or strongholds.

You may have begun as social or casual users of alcohol and other drugs, or you may have started as a weekend user or on holidays. You may have used alcohol and other drugs because you were in emotional pain from broken relationships; possibly you may have experienced childhood traumas (physical/sexual abuse, verbal abuse, physical/emotional neglect, or abandonment). You may have used drugs/alcohol as a solution to cope with your strongholds. Regardless of the reason why you used your strongholds allowed an opportunity for spiritual forces to exploit you. Your lack of a close relationship with God to assist you with your problems may have caused you to consciously choose a worldly solution to your problems by sowing to your flesh. Regardless of what type of weakness you experienced in the flesh, the enemy took full advantage and caused you to become addicted to alcohol and other drugs, in an effort to control your life.

Many individuals began as social or casual users of alcohol and other drugs; others start as weekend users or on holidays. Some used alcohol and other drugs because they were in emotional pain from broken relationships; some possibly had experienced childhood traumas (physical/sexual abuse, verbal abuse, physical/emotional neglect, or abandonment).

Regardless of the reason why they used, they allowed an opportunity for spiritual forces to enter their lives and exploit them, which led to the stronghold of addiction. Many lacking a relationship with God to assist them with their problems consciously chose "to sow to flesh." Regardless of what type of weakness they experienced in the flesh, the enemy took full advantage and caused them to become addicted to alcohol and other drugs in an effort to control their lives.

Four Steps Leading to the Stronghold that Lead to Addiction

Which of the four steps leading to the development of strongholds resulting in your addiction do you least understand?

Action Steps

List four things you are willing to do to break the cycle of these four steps leading to your addiction.

1.
2.
3.
4.

Self-Rating

According to the scripture on strongholds, what is God's way of overcoming strongholds?

What are the weapons of divine power used to demolish strongholds? What are some of the strategies listed in that passage of scripture to overcome strongholds?

Action Steps

Identify any existing addictions/problems you know that you need to overcome, other than drugs/alcohol.

1.
2.
3.

Four Steps Leading to the Restoration from Addiction

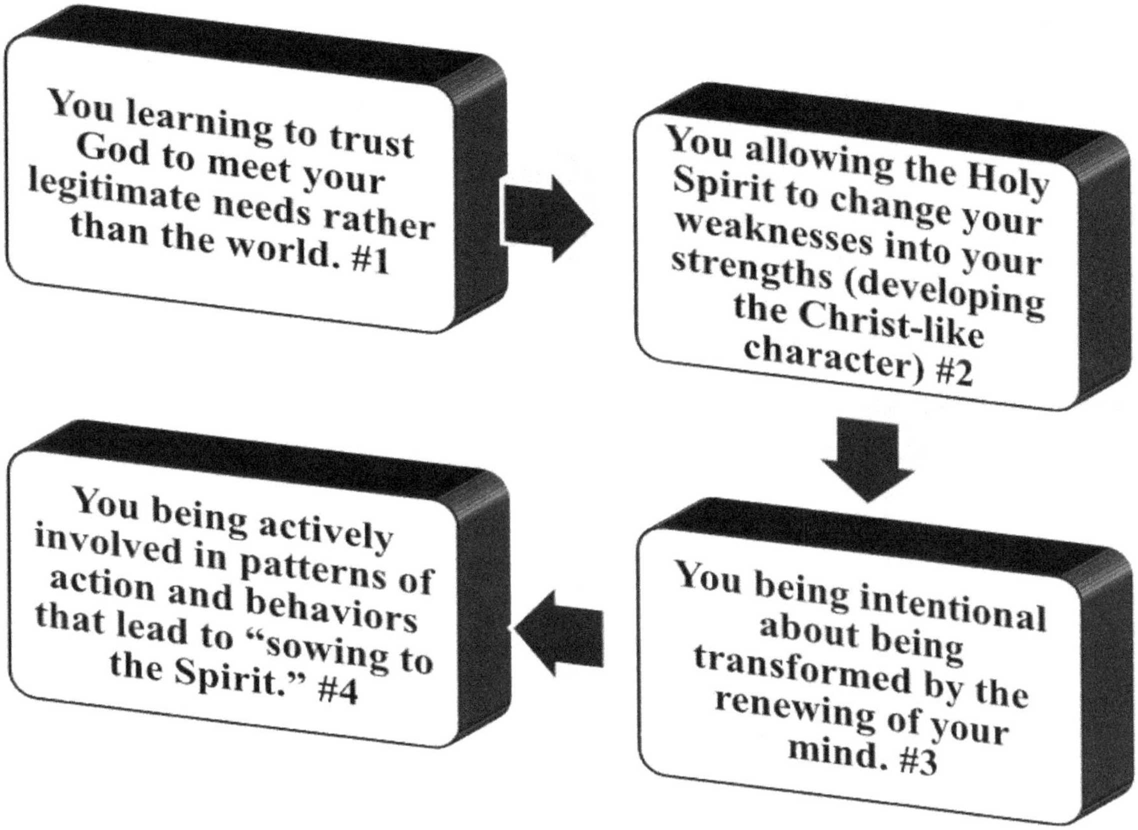

Figure 22: Understanding How to Overcome Drug/Alcohol Addiction

Using a scale from 1 to 4 with the 1 being the easiest step to apply in your life and 4 being the most difficult step to apply, rank the four steps necessary for overcoming drug/alcohol addiction in your life.

1. Step # 1 _____
2. Step # 2 _____
3. Step # 3 _____
4. Step # 4 _____

You need to learn to take your thoughts captives (thinking about what you're thinking) and to identify where you're thought are coming from and recognize any negative patterns of thoughts. You need to replace your negative thought with the Word of God.

Pastor Bruce Rhodes of Lifeway Church cites three positive outcomes that believers experience from overcoming strongholds and experiencing freedom in their minds:

- Developing determination and perseverance.
- Increasing personal trust in God.
- Experiencing visible victory within their soul (mind, emotions, and decision-making).

Self-Check

Which of the four steps leading to overcoming your drug/alcohol addiction do you least understand?

Action Steps

List three things you are willing to do to help you become more involved in applying the four steps in your daily life.

1.
2.
3.

Generational Curses (Ancestral Sin)

Dr. Terry Wise in his text, *The Fundamentals of Spiritual Warfare*, makes the following statement regarding the disbelief of many Christians regarding ancestral sin (generational curses):

> Revealing their scientific worldview, many find it hard to believe that ancestral sin can also be an entry point for Satan's work. However, this reality is based on both theology and experience. If one's parents or ancestors were involved in the occult and experienced demonic activity, then the children and ancestors may also be affected by that experience.

With regard to witchcraft in his text, *The Adversary*, Mark I. Bubeck makes the following statement regarding the use alcohol and other drugs:

> The use of drugs for sensational mind-expanding experience is a form of sorcery. Drug experimentation is a fleshly sin which leads on into deeper bondage with Satan's kingdom.

Dr. John MacArthur, in his text, *The New Testament Commentary Galatians,* makes the following statement regarding the "work of the flesh," known as witchcraft or sorcery.

> Sorcery translates *pharmakeia*, from which we get pharmacy and pharmaceutical. It was originally used of medicines in general but came to be used primarily of mood and mind-altering drugs similar to those that create so much havoc in our own day. Many ancient religious ceremonies involved occultist practices in which drugs were used to induce supposed communications with deities, and pharmakeia thereby came to be closely related to witchcraft and black magic. Aristotle and other Greek writers used the word as a synonym for witchcraft and black magic, because drugs were so commonly used in their practice.

Any person who has become involved in the use of drugs, as a result, has also become actively involved in sorcery or witchcraft. Likewise, anyone who has become involved in selling or trafficking of drugs has fallen into the works of witchcraft or sorcery.

- ☐ There is definite demonic activity in both the use and sell of drugs. This is why being entangled in the use or trafficking of drugs is such a difficult bondage to overcome.

Individuals through habitual practices or experimenting with the occult (witchcraft) automatically allow demonic forces entry into their lives. What many believers fail to understand is that this involvement with demonic forces can become a problem for succeeding generations. When a person who is involved in witchcraft dies, demonic forces continue to live and seek to complete Satan's strategies. They view the deceased person's immediate family as their most direct claim (children, grandchildren, nieces, and nephews). Thus, bondage to alcohol and other drugs become a generational curse. God's Word indicates the consequences of ancestral sin (generational curses): "Thou shall not bow down thyself unto them, nor serve them: for I, the Lord thy God, am a jealous God, visiting the iniquity of the fathers upon the children unto the third and fourth generations of them that hate me" (Deut. 5:9).

Dr. Terry Wise, in his text *The Fundamentals of Spiritual Warfare*, makes the following statement regarding disbelief in ancestral sin (generation curses).

> We have no problem accepting this principle in the physical realm. Why is it so hard to accept in the spiritual realm? A child born to drug addicted parents may come into the world with a chemical dependency on those drugs from which he/she has absolutely no responsibility. The child is a victim of the parents' sin. It is readily accepted that children who are victims of emotional abuse have a greater tendency to become abusive parents themselves.

"Genetic predisposition" is a common term in the field of substance abuse and is readily accepted by professionals in the secular realm as well as by Christians. Authorities state that children of alcoholics and addicts are at a much higher risk of becoming alcoholic/addicts if they choose to use substances than do children who do not have parents that have been addicted to alcohol and other drugs.

Recorded in the *Christian Research Journal,* Kathy McReynolds and Boyd Luter, in their article, "Recovering Through Fully Biblical Recovery," make the following statement regarding *intergenerational sin.*

> Without alleviating personal responsibility, however, it is crucial to acknowledge the profound affect that past experiences can have on the present. To downplay this is to bypass a bedrock scriptural principle: sin is "intergenerational;" that is, the sins of the fathers are passed down to their children (Deut. 5:9). This is why the Israelites were commanded not only to obey the Law, but also to teach it to their children (6:7–9). In this way, the Israelites would "pass down" to their posterity the right ways of the Lord so it might go well with them.
>
> If the children were not taught the ways of the Lord, however, they were being "instructed" in some other way. And this "other" behavior that was passed on had devastating repercussions. This is not to say that they were "locked in" to such behaviors, but that the propensity to repeat such patterns is extremely strong. With the Lord's intervention, however, future generations could break those patterns and learn to walk in truth.
>
> For you know that it was not with perishable things such as silver or gold that you were redeemed from the empty way of life handed down to you from your forefathers, *but with the precious blood of Christ, a lamb without blemish or defect.* He was chosen before the creation of the world, but was revealed in these last times

> for your sake. Through him you believe in God, who raised him from the dead and glorified him, and so your faith and hope are in God. Now that you have purified yourselves by obeying the truth so that you have sincere love for your brothers, love one another deeply, from the heart. (1 Peter 1:18–22, NIV)

As a believer, you must look past the natural and embrace the spiritual truths God has revealed through His Word. Demonic forces make claim to individuals who have given them entry into their lives through involvement in witchcraft and sorcery. If that individual dies without confessing those sins, demonic forces have a right to harass their offspring. Their offspring are not responsible for their parents' sin, because every individual is responsible for their own sins. However, demonic strongholds developed through ancestral sin (generational curses) are real as seen through the scriptures and experienced in the lives of both believers and nonbelievers.

Every believer has been *redeemed from the empty way of life, handed down from their forefathers, through the precious blood of Christ.* Every believer has the solution to overcoming generational curses; this solution is the salvation that Jesus Christ provides. So it's a matter of learning to walk in that victory by allowing the Holy Spirit to assist them in experiencing their victory in their everyday walk. Demonic forces know they are defeated but attempt to hang on until believers learn to exert their authority over them.

Seven Steps to Breaking Generational Curses

Pastor Dennis Rouse in his audio series, "Breaking Generational Curses," cites seven excellent steps designed specifically for breaking generational curses.

Step #1

You must begin the process of breaking the curse by *openly acknowledging and confessing* the iniquities (sins) of your forefathers (use of alcohol and other drugs).

> *If they shall confess their iniquity, and the iniquity of their fathers, with their trespass which they trespassed against me, and that also they have walked contrary unto me*; And *that* I also have walked contrary unto them, and have brought them into the land of their enemies; if then their uncircumcised hearts be humbled, and they then accept of the punishment of their iniquity: Then will I remember my covenant with Jacob, and also my covenant with Isaac, and also my covenant with Abraham will I remember; and I will remember the land. (Leviticus 26:40–42)
>
> And the seed of Israel separated themselves from all strangers, *and stood and confessed their sins, and the iniquities of their fathers.* (Nehemiah 9:2)
>
> O Lord, according to all thy righteousness, I beseech thee, let thine anger and thy fury be turned away from thy city Jerusalem, thy holy mountain: *because for our sins, and for the iniquities of our fathers, Jerusalem and thy people are become a reproach to all that are about us.* (Daniel 9:16)

Step #2

You must *humbly ask God to forgive the iniquities (sins) of your forefathers, and you must forgive your family members for any role they played in your involvement in witchcraft* (using alcohol and other drugs).

> For if ye forgive men their trespasses, your heavenly Father will also forgive you: But if ye forgive not men their trespasses, neither will your Father forgive your trespasses. (Matthew 6:14–15)

Step #3

You must *confess* your personal participation in witchcraft (using alcohol and other drugs) to the Lord.

Step #4

You must now *ask God to forgive you for what you personally did to become involved* in witchcraft (using of alcohol and other drugs).

> *If we confess our sins, he is faithful and just to forgive us our sins, and to cleanse us from all unrighteousness.* (1 John 1:9)

Step #5

You must learn to *submit your will to God and His authorities,* understanding the dangers of rebellion.

> *Submit yourselves therefore to God. Resist the devil, and he will flee from you.* Draw nigh to God, and he will draw nigh to you. Cleanse *your* hands, *ye* sinners; and purify *your* hearts, *ye* double minded. (James 4:7–8)
>
> *For rebellion is as the sin of witchcraft, and stubbornness is as iniquity and idolatry.* Because thou hast rejected the word of the LORD, he hath also rejected thee from *being* king. (1 Samuel 15:23)

Step #6

You must *confess and repent* before another person (significant other, children, siblings, etc.) *who you have sinned against through your involvement in witchcraft* (through using alcohol and other drugs).

> *Confess your faults one to another, and pray one for another, that ye may be healed.* The effectual fervent prayer of a righteous man availeth much. (James 5:16)

Step #7

You must claim your authority over the generational curse, in the name of Jesus, through being washed in His blood.

> Much more then, *being now justified by his blood,* we shall be saved from wrath through him. (Romans 5:9)
>
> In whom we have *redemption through his blood,* the forgiveness of sins, according to the riches of his grace (Ephesians 1:7)
>
> Neither is there salvation in any other: *for there is none other name under heaven given among men, whereby we must be saved.* (Acts 4:12)

Understanding Generational Curses

Self-Check

How do you rate your understanding of generational curses? Discuss your answer within your group. Do you think that during your addiction, you were living under a generational curse?

[ ] not sure [ ] no [ ] yes

How do you rate your understanding of the seven steps to break generational curses? Discuss your answer within your group.

Action Steps

List two things you can do to increase your understanding of generational curses.

1.
2.

List two things you can do to increase your understanding of the seven steps to break generational curses.

1.
2.

"DISTRACTION"

My name is **"DISTRACTION"** and my goal is very clear;
To divert your attention and end your career.
I search for moments to catch your eye,
To change your heart to believe a lie.
Many have fallen by my subtle appeal,
They have knowingly and willingly departed from God's will,
They believe that I am good for them,
and they will argue in my defense,
They will compromise their holy standards for what I say to them makes sense.
You see, my Name is **"DISTRACTION."**
My terms are very simple, it only requires one thing;
That Jesus Christ is made second, and I become your king.
I will hook you by rewarding you – every now and then,
I will keep you so preoccupied that your ways will become your sins.
I will take what God has blessed you with, and keep you in such a daze,
That I will have you talk more about your blessings, instead of giving God the praise.
You see, my Name is **"DISTRACTION."**
I even tried to distract Jesus, as He hung with His blood soaked crown,
I used a thief to try to let himself down.
No doubt you will grow to hate me, and wonder why I am so cruel;
Dear friend, don't you ever forget one thing, I am only Satan's tool.

My name is **"DISTRACTION."**

Relapse Prevention (Reversing the Process Addiction)

Figure 23: Understanding How to Reverse the Process

Mortifying: (Putting to death sinful desires of the flesh)—to mortify the flesh means to put to death, to destroy the strength, vitality, or sinful functions of the flesh.

Once you became a new creature in Christ, God addressed the root cause of your bondage to alcohol and other drugs (addiction) through salvation. You must now learn to address your old desires, appetites, and passions that remain by participating with the Holy Spirit. This will prevent you from relapsing and returning to your old lifestyle.

You must understand the role of the Holy Spirit who is every Christian's spiritual mentor. Every Christian is involved in a relational learning process with the Holy Spirit. Matthew Henry's Commentary clearly defines the role of your spiritual mentor, the Holy Spirit. The world speaks of having a sponsor; well, you have a divine sponsor, the Holy Spirit.

> In the economy of our salvation, the *applying* and *effecting* part is especially attributed to the Holy Spirit. We are said to be born of the Spirit, to be *quickened* and *sanctified* by the Spirit, to *be led and guided, strengthened and helped, by the Spirit. Through him we mortify sin, perform duty, walk in God's ways; all the acts and operations of the divine life in us,* the works and fruits of righteousness without us, all are through this blessed and Holy Spirit, who is therefore called the Spirit of life, and of grace and holiness; *all grace is from him. Earnestly therefore is he to be sought and greatly to be heeded by us, that we quench not his holy motions, nor resist and oppose him in his workings.*

> But if the Spirit of him that raised up Jesus from the dead dwell in you, he that raised up Christ from the dead shall also quicken your mortal bodies by his Spirit that dwelleth in you. Therefore, brethren, we are debtors, not to the flesh, to live after the flesh. *For if ye live after the flesh, ye shall die: but if ye through the Spirit do mortify (put to death) the deeds of the body, ye shall live.* (Romans 8:11–13)

- ☐ You must realize that the Spirit of God who dwells in you will direct your life if you allow Him to. Prior to salvation, the flesh controlled you, but having been set free, you must learn to practice your freedom through Christ.
- ☐ Christ has provided you with the power to overcome your sinful fleshly cravings by destroying them through the power of the Word and by your willingness to apply it daily to your life.
- ☐ If you allow the Spirit to control your life, He will direct and provide you with the power you need to address your cravings for drugs/alcohol in every area of your life.

> Put to death, therefore, whatever belongs to your earthly nature: *sexual immorality, impurity, lust, evil desires and greed, which is idolatry.* (Colossians 3:5, NIV)

- ☐ You are clearly instructed to destroy all the practices that were a part of your old lifestyle, not just the drugs/alcohol.

The Holy Spirit performs *in* us all that the Lord has done *outside* us. Jesus's crucifixion is a finished work; mortification or "putting the flesh to death" is accomplished by the Holy Spirit assisting a believer in experiencing Christ's work (victory) in every area of his/her life.

> *This I say then, "Walk in the Spirit, and ye shall not fulfil the lust of the flesh. For the flesh lusteth against the Spirit, and the Spirit against the flesh: and these are contrary the one to the other: so that ye cannot do the things that ye would. But if ye be led of the Spirit, ye are not under the law."* (Galatians 5:16–18)

- ☐ You are in a spiritual crisis due to your flesh desiring to continue to practice the "works of the flesh" and your new nature desiring to follow the guidance of the Holy Spirit.

Apostle Paul instructs you in the above passage of scripture to allow the Spirit to guide your Christian life by taking every advantage of His divine assistance. He also informs you that the Christian lifestyle is an active lifestyle involving conflict. There is a constant battle as your old ways of the flesh and world continue to tempt and seduce you.

> Those who belong to Christ Jesus *have crucified the sinful nature with its passions and desires.* (Galatians 5:24, NIV)

- ☐ You must understand that because you have been spiritually changed during the salvation process, your old sinful nature was crucified, and you must learn to consider it dead even though the "practices of the flesh" remain; and act accordingly, having faith in your new position in Christ.

> Since, then, you have been raised with Christ, *set your hearts on things above, where Christ is seated at the right hand of God. 2 Set your minds on things above, not on earthly things.* For you died, and your life is now hidden with Christ in God. When Christ, who is your life, appears, then you also will appear with him in glory. (Colossians 3:1–4, NIV)

- ☐ Paul makes it crystal clear that your life is in Christ, not the world; therefore, your relapse prevention plan must be Christ centered.

> *Put to death, therefore, whatever belongs to your earthly nature: sexual immorality, impurity, lust, evil desires and greed, which is idolatry.* Because of these, the wrath of God is coming. (Colossians 3:5–6, NIV)

- ☐ The only method God has for you to address those old desires, appetites, and passions of the flesh is to put them to death through the power of the Holy Spirit as you cooperate with Him during your restoration (recovery).

> *You used to walk in these ways, in the life you once lived. But now you must rid yourselves of all such things as these: anger, rage, malice, slander, and filthy language from your lips.* Do not lie to each other, since you have taken off your old self with its practices *and have put on the new self, which is being renewed in knowledge in the image of its Creator.* (Colossians 3:7–10, NIV)

- ☐ Yes, you once lived according to the ways of the world in the past, but now God instructs you to be willing to change old behaviors, attitudes, and character.
- ☐ You must recognize and accept that you are in the process of being changed into the image and likeness of Jesus Christ.

LEARNING TO DEPEND ON GOD FOR LEGITIMATE NEEDS

Addictions develop in various forms. Gambling, sex, greed, power, alcohol, and other drugs are the most common. The dynamics are universal with the substances being different in form, but all serve to meet a legitimate need that can only be fulfilled by God.

Meeting Basic Humans Needs

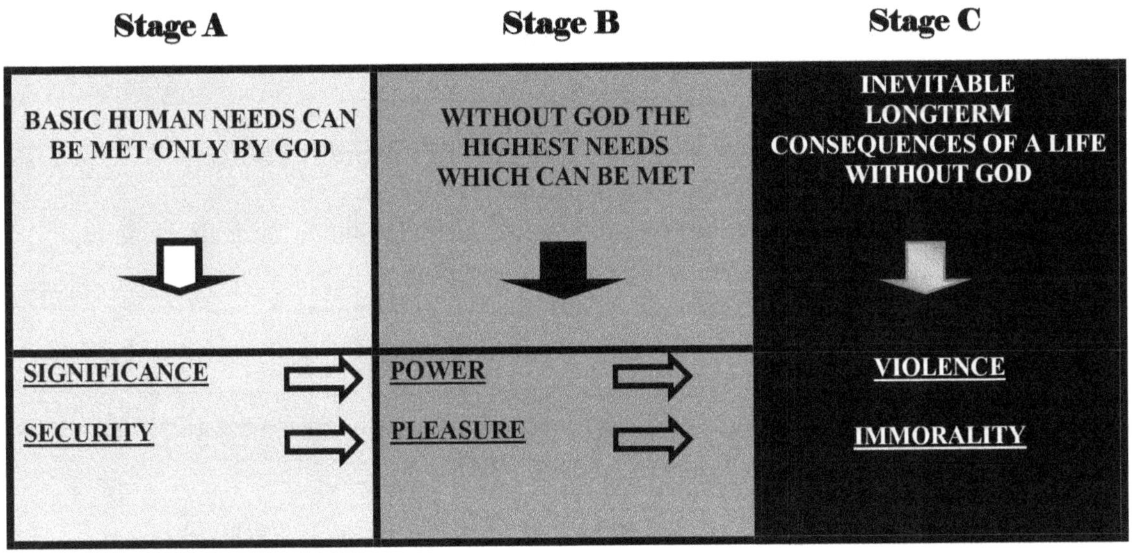

—Dr. Larry Crabb (modified)

Figure 24: Meeting Basic Needs

You have all the resources available to live in Stage A, (with the indwelling of the Holy Spirit, the Word, and Body of Christ). If you choose to turn your back on God and live a life based on the world's value system, (money, desires of flesh, recognition, and pleasure) you will end up in Stage B.

Stage B is marked by hanging out with old friends who are actively involved in your past lifestyle, relapse, selling of drugs, and old criminal behaviors. You can repent and return to Stage A, true significance and security in Christ.

If you continue in this lifestyle of seeking pleasure and power rather than true significance and security through your relationship with Christ, a life of corruption is unavoidable. Addiction, bondage to drugs/alcohol is a consequence that will result.

Yes, as a Christian you can willfully choose to continue to "sow to the flesh" by indulging in drugs/alcohol. If you do, you will live as though you were never delivered; you will live a low quality of spiritual life and face many adverse consequences for your actions. God has made the following promises and He will keep them:

God Promises to Meet Your Physical Needs

> But seek first his kingdom and his righteousness, and all these things (*referring to food, shelter, clothing, and employment*) will be given to you as well. (Matt. 6:33, NIV).

God Has Provided You with Security in Knowing that Your Needs will Be Met

> Therefore, do not worry about tomorrow, for tomorrow will worry about itself. Each day has enough trouble of its own. (Matt. 6:34, NIV).
>
> Do not be anxious about anything, but in everything, by prayer and petition, with thanksgiving, present your requests to God.
>
> And my God will meet all your needs according to his glorious riches in Christ Jesus. (Philippians 4:6,19, NIV).

God Has Met Your Need for Security Through His Love

> Who shall separate us from the love of Christ? Shall trouble or hardship or persecution or famine or nakedness or danger or sword?
>
> Neither height nor depth, nor anything else in all creation, will be able to separate us from the love of God that is in Christ Jesus our Lord. (Romans 8:35,39, NIV).
>
> But God demonstrates his own love for us in this: While we were still sinners, Christ died for us. (Romans 5:8, NIV).

God Had Given You Purpose and Met Your Need for Significance

> For we are God's workmanship, created in Christ Jesus to do good works, which God prepared in advance for us to do. (Ephesians 2:10, NIV).

Identifying Your Needs Exercise

1. Can you identify any need(s) that you attempted to meet by using drugs/alcohol prior to you becoming a Christian, that now you know only God can meet?
2. Can you identify any need(s) that you attempted to meet by using drugs/alcohol since you became a Christian, that you need to be depending on God to meet?

Prayer for Understanding

Dear heavenly Father, help me to view addiction and relapse prevention as You view them so that I can clearly understand and embrace Your solution. Help me to understand that Your ways are different from the world's ways and that You have a purpose and plan for my life in spite of my past lifestyle of addiction to drugs/alcohol. I thank You for Your solution, salvation, and understand that as I submit to You, You will assist me in overcoming the effects of my addiction.

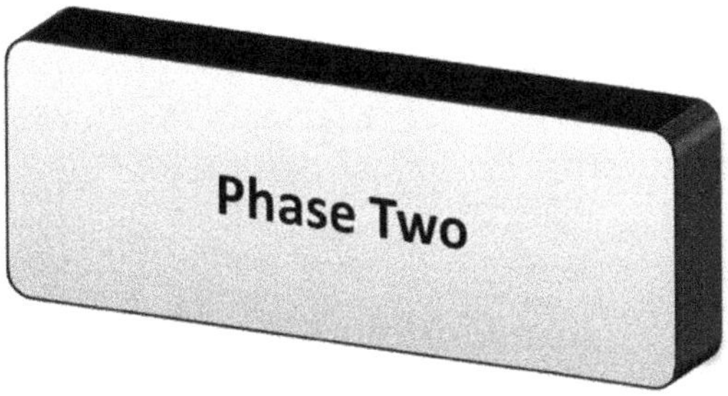

THE MOST SIGNIFICANT FACTOR IN RELAPSE PREVENTION

Fellowship with God

That which we have seen and heard declare we unto you, that ye also may have *fellowship with us: and truly our fellowship is with the Father, and with his Son Jesus Christ.* And these things write we unto you, that your joy may be full.

—1 John 1:3–4

Learning Objectives

For workshop participants to be able to:

- Describe the three key ingredients of fellowship (koinonia).
- Identify the three most significant factors in relapse prevention.
- Identify the five requirements necessary to remain in fellowship with God.
- Identify the five basic spiritual disciplines necessary to cultivate (enrich) your relationship with God.

Key Biblical Concepts and Definitions

(1) *Koinonia or Fellowship*: A partnership between God and a believer requiring *faith* and *obedience* in common participation of a *love* experience.

(2) *Spiritual Disciplines*: God has given us the Disciplines (God's Word, prayer, praise, thanksgiving, fellowship, and fasting) of the spiritual life, as *a means of receiving grace.* The Disciplines allow us to place ourselves before *God so that He can transform us.*

Part One

Koinonia: Fellowship with God
Understanding How God Prepared You for A Relationship with Him

God's Primary Purpose for Mankind

The first reason God created man was for the *purpose of relationship.* God the Father wanted a family of children to share life with to get to know in a personal way. Throughout Scriptures God's desire for *fellowship* and *communion* with man is revealed. From the time that God sought Adam in the garden in the cool of the day.

God has been seeking *fellowship* with man (Genesis 3:8). However, the sin which caused Adam to hide from God has been hindering man's relationship with God ever since (Isaiah 59:1,2). It is only through the New Covenant that God's purpose of a relationship with man is fully accomplished. Now God indwells each believer making *fellowship* constantly available (John 14:16–20, 23).

—Kevin J. Conner

Significant Truths about Your Relationship with God

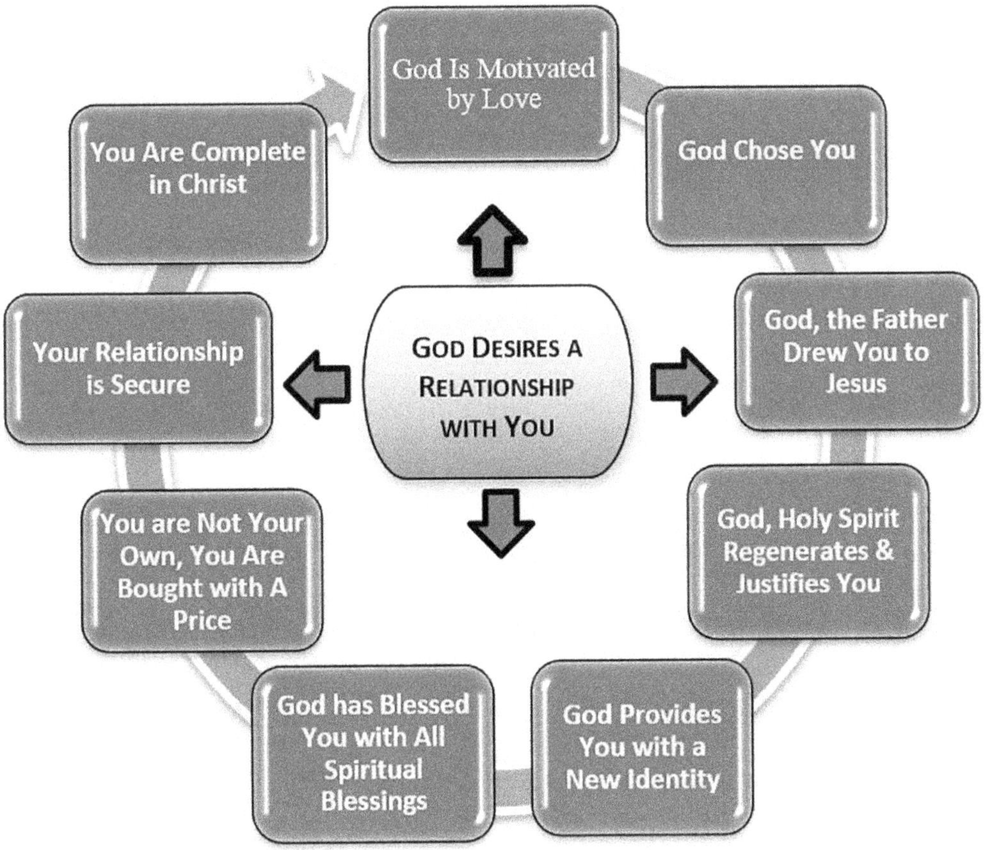

Figure 25: Understanding how God prepared you for a relationship with Him

God is a holy God and could not compromise His holiness by entering into a relationship with an unholy people. God had to make some drastic spiritual changes in mankind in order for them to enter into the household of faith in fellowship with Him through Jesus Christ.

> The purpose of the incarnation was to give "life," which constitutes the basis, or necessary prerequisite, of fellowship between regenerated sinners and God the Father and the Son.
>
> —Merrill F. Unger

You need to understand several significant facts about your relationship with God. These facts will enable you to personalize your relationship with God. Personalizing your relationship will allow you to experience the great love that God has already demonstrated toward you and will enable you to express and convey that indwelling love through fellowshipping with God.

God Chose You

Ye have not chosen me, but I have chosen you, and ordained you, that ye should go and bring forth fruit, and *that* your fruit should remain: that whatsoever ye shall ask of the Father in my name, he may give it you. (John 15:16)

According as he hath chosen us in him before the foundation of the world, that we should be holy and without blame before him in love (Ephesians 1:4)

- ☐ You must learn that God chose you personally to enter into a relationship with Him to have fellowship with Him.
- ☐ God initiated the relationship process with you long before you were even aware that He chose you.

God the Father Drew You to Jesus

No man can come to me, except the Father which hath sent me draw him: and I will raise him up at the last day. (John 6:44)

And he said, "Therefore said I unto you, *that no man can come unto me, except it were given unto him of my Father.*" (John 6:65)

- ☐ God the Father personally drew you to His Son, Jesus, in order that you could be saved and enter into a relationship with Him.
- ☐ God's drawing you to Jesus was the only way you could come to Him; there is no other way.

God Prepared You for Your Relationship with Him

But after that the kindness and love of God our Savior toward man appeared, not by works of righteousness which we have done, *but according to his mercy he saved us, by the washing of regeneration, and renewing of the Holy Ghost;* Which he shed on us abundantly through Jesus Christ our Savior; *That being justified by his grace,* we should be made heirs according to the hope of eternal life. (Titus 3:4–7)

- ☐ God saved you by the power of His Spirit through spiritual regeneration (the new birth, born-again).
- ☐ You are justified and brought into a relational right standing with God, through the blood of His Son.

God Provides You with a New Identity

Therefore, if any man *be* in Christ, *he is a new creature: old things are passed away;* behold, *all things are become new.* (2 Corinthians 5:17)

- ☐ You received a new identity through spiritual rebirth, you are no longer the same individual due to spiritual change.
- ☐ Your old identity is finished; it no longer exists.

- ☐ With your new identity, you have the potential for change in every area of your life.

A *new heart also will I give you*, and a *new spirit will I put within you*: and *I will take away the stony heart* out of your flesh, and I will give you a heart of flesh. And I will *put my spirit within you*, and cause you to walk in my statutes, and ye shall keep my judgments, *and do them.* (Ezekiel 36:26–27)

God Has Blessed You with All You Need for a Relationship with Him

Blessed *be* the God and Father of our Lord Jesus Christ, *who hath blessed us with all spiritual blessings in heavenly places in Christ.* (Ephesians 1:3)

- ☐ God has provided you with everything you need for a vibrant relationship with Him through salvation in Christ.

You Are Not Your Own, You Are Bought with a Price

What? Know ye not that your body is the temple of the Holy Ghost *which is* in you, which ye have of God, *and ye are not your own? For ye are bought with a price*: therefore, glorify God in your body, and in your spirit, which are God's. (1 Corinthians 6:19–20)

For he that is called in the Lord, *being* a servant, is the Lord's freeman: *likewise, also he that is called, being free, is Christ's servant. Ye are bought with a price*; be not ye the servants of men. Brethren, let every man, *wherein he is called, therein abide with God.* (1 Corinthians 7:22–24)

- ☐ God paid the price so that you would have the opportunity to enter into a relationship with Him. He bought you back from the slave market of sin with the precious blood of Jesus.
- ☐ You now belong to God as His friend; you no longer have a life of your own because it belongs to God.

Your Relationship Is Secure

Let your conversation *be* without covetousness; *and be* content with such things as ye have: for he hath said, *"I will never leave thee, nor forsake thee."* (Hebrews 13:5)

What shall we then say to these things? If God be for us, who can be against us? He that spared not his own Son, but delivered him up for us all, how shall he not with him also freely give us all things? Who shall lay anything to the charge of God's elect? It is God that justifieth. Who is he that condemneth? It is Christ that died, yea rather, that is risen again, who is even at the right hand of God, who also maketh intercession for us. Who shall separate us from the love of Christ? Shall tribulation, or distress, or persecution, or famine, or nakedness, or peril, or sword? As it is written, For thy sake we are killed all the day long; we are accounted as sheep for the slaughter. Nay, in all these things we are more than conquerors through him that loved us. For I am persuaded, that neither death, nor life, nor

> angels, nor principalities, nor powers, nor things present, nor things to come, Nor height, nor depth, nor any other creature, shall be able to separate us from the love of God, which is in Christ Jesus our Lord. (Romans 8:31–39)

- ☐ Your spiritual mentor, the Holy Spirit, will not abandon you; He is always available for you.
- ☐ No one or nothing can separate you from God's love.

You Are Complete in Christ

> For in him dwelleth all the fulness of the Godhead bodily. *And ye are complete in him,* which is the head of all principality and power. (Colossians 2:9–10)

- ☐ You must understand and have faith in that you are complete in Christ, just underdeveloped; so now you must grow up and learn to walk in that completeness.

> In whom also ye are circumcised with the circumcision made without hands, *in putting off the body of the sins of the flesh* by the circumcision of Christ: Buried with him in baptism, wherein also ye are risen with *him* through the faith of the operation of God, who hath raised him from the dead. And you, being dead in your sins and the uncircumcision of your flesh, *hath he quickened together with him, having forgiven you all trespasses*; Blotting out the handwriting of ordinances that was against us, which was contrary to us, and took it out of the way, nailing it to his cross; *And having spoiled principalities and powers, he made a shew of them openly, triumphing over them in it.* (Colossians 2:11–15)

Your completeness includes:

- ☐ Being able to overcome your old sinful nature (v. 11).
- ☐ Being born again, spiritually regenerated (vv. 12–13).
- ☐ Being forgiven of sins (v. 13).
- ☐ Being free from the man-made requirements regarding your relationship with God (v. 14).
- ☐ Being victorious over evil spirits (v. 15).

THE MOST SIGNIFICANT FACTORS IN RELAPSE PREVENTION FELLOWSHIP WITH GOD

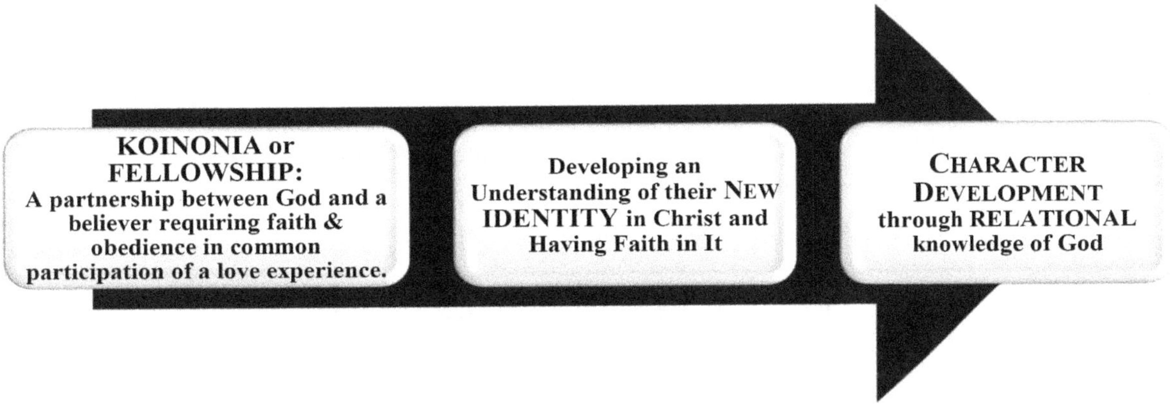

Figure 26: Three Key Factors in Relapse Prevention

> That which we have seen and heard declare we unto you, that ye also may have *fellowship with us: and truly our fellowship is with the Father, and with his Son Jesus Christ.* (1 John 1:3)

Koinonia, or fellowship is a *partnership* between *God* and *you* in common participation of a love experience *requiring your obedience.*

- ☐ Fellowship is the vehicle by which you are able to develop a full, accurate, and personal (relational) knowledge of God through the teaching ministry of the Holy Spirit.
- ☐ Your understanding of and faith in your position in Christ will determine your level of fellowship with God.
- ☐ Fellowship with God and other believers allows you the opportunity for a union between God's Word and life's experiences.

Three Key Factors of Fellowship: Faith, Love, and Obedience

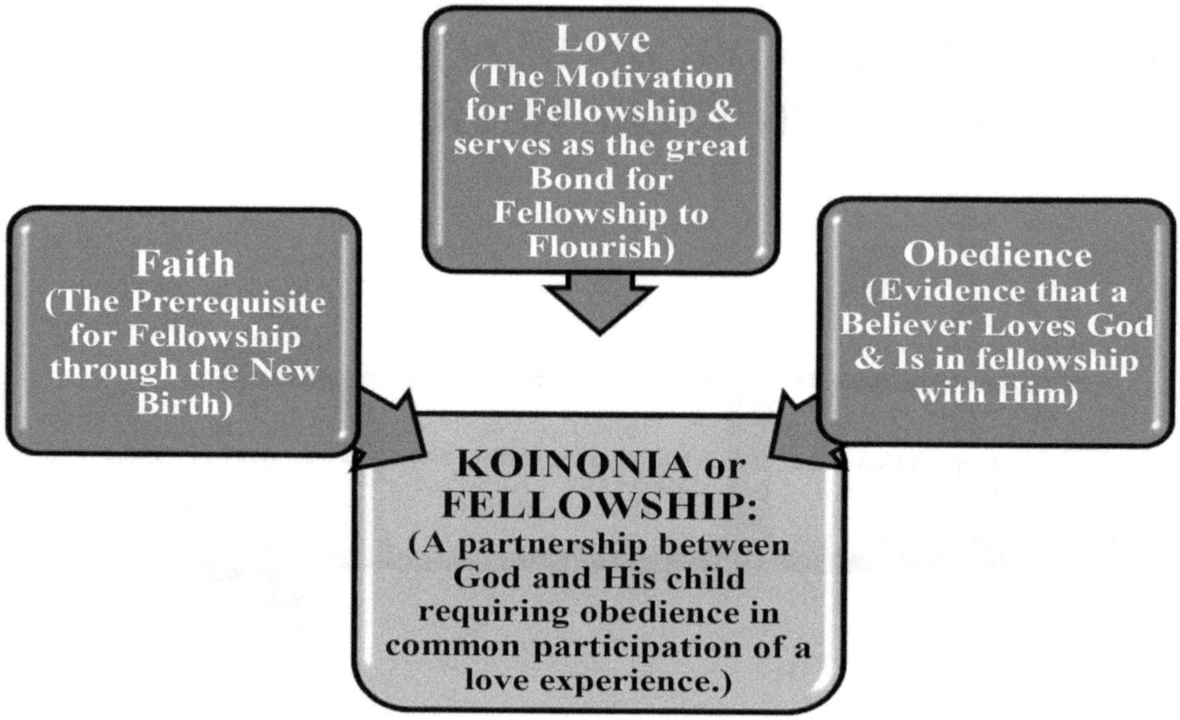

Figure 27: Three Key Factors of Fellowship

Fellowship is a necessity for God's purpose or plans to be accomplished in your life. Faith, love, and obedience are three requirements of fellowship that you must meet in order to develop relational knowledge of God, and of Jesus our Lord. It is through relational knowledge (fellowship) that you will receive the grace and peace necessary to mature in Christ and keep you from relapsing.

> *Whosoever believeth that Jesus is the Christ is born of God*: and every one that loveth him that begat loveth him also that is begotten of him. By this we know that *we love the children of God, when we love God*, and *keep his commandments*. For this is the love of God, *that we keep his commandments*: and his commandments are not grievous. For whatsoever is born of God overcometh the world: and this is the victory that overcometh the world, *even our faith*. Who is he that overcometh the world, *but he that believeth that Jesus is the Son of God?* (1 John 5:1–5)

The Role of Faith in Fellowship

> Now faith is the substance of things hoped for, the evidence of things not seen. (Hebrews 11:1)

This means that faith is the foundation upon which hope is built, and it is considered the "title deed" or assurance of things not seen. Hope is faith relating to the future. To become a Christian, you must have faith in Christ's death, burial, resurrection, and ascension. Likewise, you must have faith in the forgiveness of your sins through Christ's sacrifice on Calvary. *God, the Holy Spirit, has enabled you to believe through the gift of repentance by allowing you to see yourself as you really are—a sinner. Also, He causes you to see Jesus in His full glory through hearing the Gospel.* Now He requires you to act on what He has enabled you to understand.

> Saving faith is God's gift to the repentant sinner that he/she might be saved. It is looking to Christ fully for salvation. This aspect of faith is a passive faith. Here the person trusts Christ and His Word for salvation.
>
> —Kevin J. Conner

Faith Is Belief in Action

Faith is trusting God, His Word, and to have confidence in Him that His Word is true and that He will keep it. It is to totally trust and rely on God and His Word.

Why Is Faith So Important?

- ☐ Faith itself has no power; the power to save comes through faith in Jesus Christ.
- ☐ Therefore, faith gives us access to God's grace and is the source of all other graces.
- ☐ Faith is the foundation on which your relationship is based. You are saved by grace through faith. Grace and faith are also the keys to your continued spiritual growth and development as a Christian.
- ☐ The most important thing to any Christian should be to please God our Father. It is impossible to please God without faith, and faith is obtained through God's Word.

> Therefore, being *justified by faith*, we have peace with God through our Lord Jesus Christ. (Romans 5:1)
>
> For ye are *all the children of God by faith* in Christ Jesus. (Galatians 3:26)
>
> To open their eyes, *and* to turn *them* from darkness to light, and *from* the power of Satan unto God, that they may receive forgiveness of sins, and inheritance among them which are *sanctified by faith* that is in me. (Acts 26:18)
>
> *Who are kept by the power of God through faith unto salvation* ready to be revealed in the last time. (1 Peter 1:5)
>
> And without faith it is impossible to please God, because anyone who comes to him must believe that he exists and that he rewards those who earnestly seek him. (Hebrews 11:6, NIV)

Belief is developed in the mind; faith adds the will. You may believe without using your will (action), but the will is required for faith. Belief focuses on thought; faith focuses on action. Belief is obtained through studying the Bible; faith is demonstrated out in the community, on the job, and in the streets. Faith gives life, reality, and activity to belief. Belief is put into active service by faith. Faith is acting upon what you believe; it is receiving. Faith counts every promise of God to be true and then acts upon those promises.

Looking unto Jesus the author and finisher of our faith; who for the joy that was set before him endured the cross, despising the shame, and is set down at the right hand of the throne of God. (Hebrews 12:2)

- ☐ Faith is the prerequisite for entering into a relationship with God—enabling you to have fellowship with God. Without the Holy Spirit providing faith, enabling a repentant sinner to trust in Christ and His Word to be saved, there can be no relationship with God through fellowship (See Ephesians 2:8).

Who Our Lord Jesus Is to His People

He is the author of their faith; not only the object, but the author. He is the great leader and precedent of our faith, *He trusted God*; He is the *purchaser of the Spirit of faith*, the publisher of the rule of faith, the efficient cause of the grace of faith, and in all respects the author of our faith. He is the *finisher of our faith; He is the fulfiller and the fulfilling of all scripture–promises and prophecies*; He is the perfecter of the canon scripture; *He is the finisher of grace*, and of the work of faith with power in the souls of His people; and He is the *judge and the rewarder of their faith*; He determines who they are that reach the mark, and from Him, and in Him, they have the prize.

—The Matthew Henry Commentary

How Faith is Developed

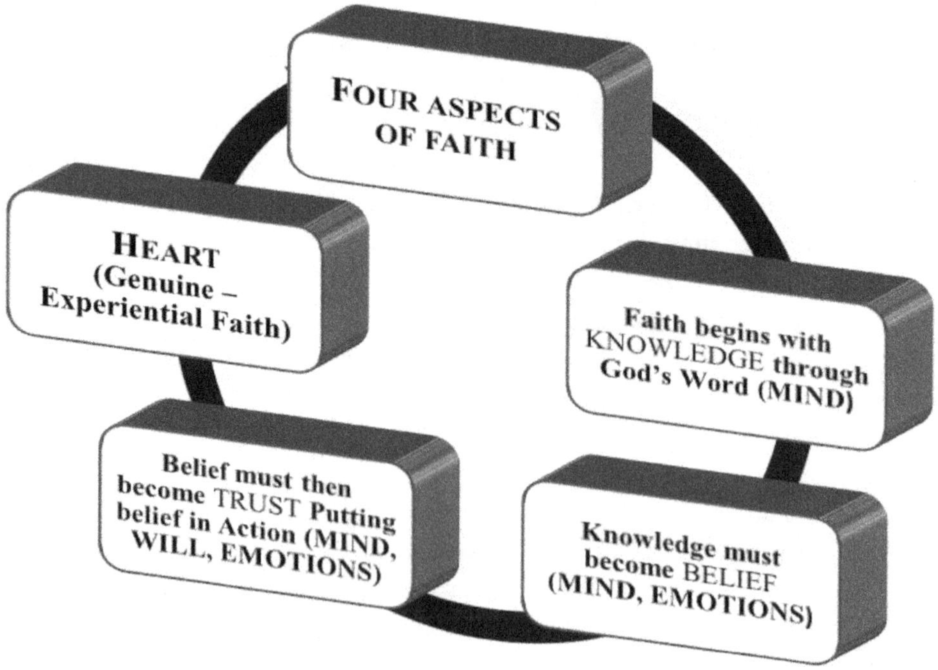

Figure 28: Four Aspects of Faith

God desires that you develop faith in Him because an increase in faith is necessary to grow in fellowship with Him.

- ☐ So God has provided His Word to increase your faith. You must be willing to receive and apply the Word to your life daily to grow in faith.

  So then faith *cometh* by hearing, and hearing by the word of God. (Romans 10:17)

- ☐ God is sought through actively fellowshipping with Him; His Word is the primary tool by which you will learn about God and develop faith in God.

  But faith which worketh by love. (Galatians 5:6)

- ☐ Faith, love, and obedience are inseparable; you cannot have one without the other two components of fellowship.

  Whosoever believeth that Jesus is the Christ is born of God: and every one that loveth him that begat loveth him also that is begotten of him. By this we know that we love the children of God, when we love God, and keep his commandments. For this is the love of God, that we keep his commandments: and his commandments are not grievous. *For whatsoever is born of God overcometh the world: and this is the victory that overcometh the world, even our faith*. Who is he that overcometh the world, *but he that believeth that Jesus is the Son of God?* (1 John 5:1–5)

- ☐ Fellowship with God is based on your faith in Christ, originating in the new birth.
- ☐ Everyone who loves God the Father, loves the children of God (other believers).
- ☐ Your faith is activated or energized by love, which is another essential ingredient necessary for fellowship with God and others. Galatians 5:6b reminds us that faith works by love.

Understanding the Role that Faith Plays in Fellowship

Self-Check

So then faith cometh by hearing, and hearing by the word of God. (Romans 10:17)

How do you rate your *understanding* of the concept of faith? Discuss your answer within your group.

How do you rate your *ability to increase* your faith? Discuss your answer within your group.

Action Steps

List two things you can do to increase your understanding of faith.

1.
2.

List two things you can do to learn to increase your faith.

1.
2.

What scripture in this section has had the greatest impact in your life? Explain.

THE ROLE OF LOVE IN FELLOWSHIP

True love (agape) has its source in God and is a characteristic of every one who has been begotten of God, *those who personally know Him.*

—Merrill F. Unger

God's Love Demonstrated

God finds joy in willfully providing what is best for mankind. This kind of love is unconditional, known as agape love. God has been extremely intentional in drawing you into fellowship with Him through expressing His love—by sacrificing His Most Precious Possession, Jesus Christ. Likewise, He has been intentional about maintaining His fellowship with you by placing His Spirit in you.

- ☐ This love is essential because it serves as the "great bond of fellowship" that unites God to you and you with other Christians in Christ.
- ☐ Love is the key factor in every relationship, and without it, fellowship will not be effective.

> *For God so loved the world, that he gave his only begotten Son, that whosoever believeth in him should not perish, but have everlasting life.* For God sent not his Son into the world to condemn the world; but that the world through him might be saved. (John 3:16–17)
>
> *How great is the love the Father has lavished on us, that we should be called children of God!* And that is what we are! The reason the world does not know us is that it did not know him. (1 John 3:1, NIV)

- ☐ God's greatest expression of love to you has been demonstrated by God in sending His only begotten Son, Jesus, to pay the price for your sins.

> *Greater love hath no man than this, that a man lay down his life for his friends. Ye are my friends, if ye do whatsoever I command you.* Henceforth I call you not servants; for the servant knoweth not what his lord doeth: but I have called you friends; for all things that I have heard of my Father I have made known unto you. (John 15:13–15)
>
> This is how God showed his love among us: He sent his one and only Son into the *world that we might live through him. This is love: not that we loved God, but that he loved us and sent his Son as an atoning sacrifice for our sins.* (1 John 4:9–10, NIV)

- ☐ Jesus's greatest expression of love through obedience has been demonstrated—He made a way for you to enter into fellowship with God.
- ☐ Prior to you becoming saved, you were not capable of loving God.

> Praise be to the God and Father of our Lord Jesus Christ, who has blessed us in the heavenly realms with every spiritual blessing in Christ. *For he chose us in him before the creation of the world to be holy and blameless in his sight.* He predestined us for adoption to sonship through Jesus Christ, in accordance with his pleasure and will. (Ephesians 1:3–5, NIV)

- ☐ God's pleasure and will is to be in fellowship with you, and His love is expressed during His fellowship with you.

God Has Provided Us with His Love

> Therefore, being justified by faith, we have peace with God through our Lord Jesus Christ: By whom also we have access by faith into this grace wherein we stand, and rejoice in hope of the glory of God. And not only *so*, but we glory in tribulations (sufferings) also: knowing that tribulation worketh patience (perseverance); And patience, experience (character); and experience, hope: And hope maketh not ashamed; *because the love of God is shed abroad in our hearts by the Holy Ghost which is given unto you.* (Romans 5:1–5)
>
> *But the fruit of the Spirit is love*, joy, peace, longsuffering, gentleness, goodness, faith, meekness, temperance (self–control): against such there is no law. And they that are Christ's have crucified the flesh with the affections and lusts. (Galatians 5:22–24)
>
> Dear friends, let us love one another, *for love comes from God.* Everyone who loves has been born of God and knows God. *8* Whoever does not love does not know God, *because God is love.* (1 John 4:7–8, NIV)

- ☐ You should be characterized by the love of God (agape). Your love should be demonstrated or expressed in fellowship with God and other Christians.
- ☐ If you are not practicing love through fellowship, it is because you haven't learned to experience the love of God through a personal (relational) knowledge of God.

> But earnestly *desire* and zealously *cultivate the greatest and best gifts and graces* (the *higher gifts and the choice graces*). And yet I will show you a still *more excellent way* [one that is better by far and the highest of them all—*love*]. (1 Corinthians 12:31, AMP)
>
> And so faith, hope, love abide [faith—conviction and belief respecting man's relation to God and divine things; hope—joyful and confident expectation to eternal salvation [*love—true affection for God and man, growing out of God's love for and in us]*; these three; *but the greatest of these is love.* (1 Corinthians 13:13, AMP)
>
> Dear friends, since God so loved us, *we also ought to love one another.* No one has ever seen God; but if we love one another, God lives in us and his love is made complete in us. (1 John 4:11–12, NIV)

- ☐ You are commanded to love one another and in fulfilling that commandment. God's love achieves its purpose; fellowship one with another through Him.

  We know that we live in him and he in us, because he has given us of his Spirit. And we have seen and testify that the Father has sent his Son to be the savior of the world. If anyone acknowledges that Jesus is the Son of God, God lives in him and he in God. *And so we know and rely on the love God has for us God is love. Whoever lives in love lives in God, and God in him.* (1 John 4:13–16, NIV)

- ☐ God, the Holy Spirit, is your spiritual mentor allowing you intimate fellowship with Christ Jesus by providing knowledge of God and your position in Him. If you believe and act upon that love, through understanding that love, it becomes the energizing force in your life, drawing you into a deeper fellowship with God.

  In this way, *love is made complete among us so that we will have confidence on the day of judgment,* because in this world we are like him. There is no fear in love. But perfect love drives out fear, because fear has to do with punishment. The one who fears is not made perfect in love. (1 John 4:17–18, NIV)

  As the Father has loved me, so have I loved you. Now remain in my love. If you obey my commands, you will remain in my love, just as I have obeyed my Father's commands and remain in his love. I have told you this so that my joy may be in you and that your joy may be complete. My command is this: Love each other as I have loved you. Greater love has no one than this, that he lay down his life for his friends. (John 15:9–13, NIV)

- ☐ Love is an indispensable ingredient of fellowship because it provides the proper motivation necessary for fellowship to flourish.
- ☐ Jesus explains how He expressed the same love to them that the Father expressed to Him.
- ☐ Jesus instructs you to follow the example of the fellowship between Him and God the Father, abounding in love that resulted in His obedience.
- ☐ Jesus states His desire is for you to experience His joy through obedience in love.
- ☐ Jesus commands all, including mentors, to express His love in fellowship with one another.

  Hereby perceive we the love *of God*, because he laid down his life for us: and we ought to lay down *our* lives for the brethren. But whoso hath this world's good, and seeth his brother have need, and shutteth up his bowels *of compassion* from him, how dwelleth the love of God in him? My little children, let us not love in word, neither in tongue; but in deed and in truth. (1 John 3:16–18)

God the Son has demonstrated His great love by giving His life that you would have fellowship with the Father that you would experience and transfer that love in relationship with others. God's Word clearly shows love as a verb—an action word to be demonstrated.

> He that saith he is in the light, and hateth his brother, is in darkness even until now. He that loveth his brother abideth in the light, and there is none occasion

of stumbling in him. But he that hateth his brother is in darkness, and walketh in darkness, and knoweth not whither he goeth, because that darkness hath blinded his eyes. (1 John 2:9–11)

- ☐ Love is destroyed by hatred and causes you to break fellowship with both God and others.

A new commandment I give unto you, That ye love one another; as I have loved you, that ye also love one another. By this shall all *men* know that ye are my disciples, if ye have love one to another. (John 13:34–35)

- ☐ Love is evidence of you being in fellowship with God and demonstrated in the human realm by loving others.

Everyone who believes that Jesus is the Christ is born of God, and everyone who loves the father loves his child as well. *This is how we know that we love the children of God: by loving God and carrying out his commands. This is love for God: to obey his commands. And his commands are not burdensome*, for everyone born of God overcomes the world. This is the victory that has overcome the world, even our faith. *Who is it that overcomes the world? Only he who believes that Jesus is the Son of God.* (1 John 5:1–5, NIV)

- ☐ Love for God is the key to overcoming all that is in the world, including bondage to drugs/alcohol. Love for God is developed in every Christian by learning to experience God's love demonstrated on Calvary.
- ☐ Love for God is demonstrated by obedience, and obedience is necessary to prevent you from going back to practicing the works of the flesh or relapsing.
- ☐ Love for God is also demonstrated by your love for other Christians. This is extremely important, because lack of fellowship with other Christians and returning to fellowship with old friends are major factors in relapsing.

Understanding the Role that Love Plays in Fellowship

Self-Check

> *This is how God showed his love among us: He sent his one and only Son into the world that we might live through him.* This is love: not that we loved God, but that he loved us and sent his Son as an atoning sacrifice for our sins. (1 John 4:9–10, NIV)

How do you rate your understanding of God's love? Discuss your answer within your group.

How would you rate the level at which you're experiencing God's love? Discuss your answer within your group.

Action Steps

List two things you can do to increase your understanding of God's love.

1.
2.

List two things you can do to increase the level at which you are experiencing God's love.

1.
2.

What scripture in this section has had the greatest impact in your life? Explain.

Fellowship with the World Excludes You from Loving God

Love not the world, neither the things that are in the world. If any man love the world, the love of the Father is not in him. For all that *is* in the world, the *lust of the flesh,* and the *lust of the eyes,* and the *pride of life, is not of the Father*, but is of the world. And the world passeth away, and the lust thereof: *but he that doeth the will of God abideth forever. (*1 John 2:15–17*)*

During the years you spent separated from God, your worldly experiences thoroughly programmed your brain with thought patterns, memory traces, responses and habits which are alien to God. So even though your old skipper (nature) is gone, your flesh remains in opposition to God as a preprogrammed propensity for sin, which is living independent of God.

—Neil Anderson

Three Channels of Temptation

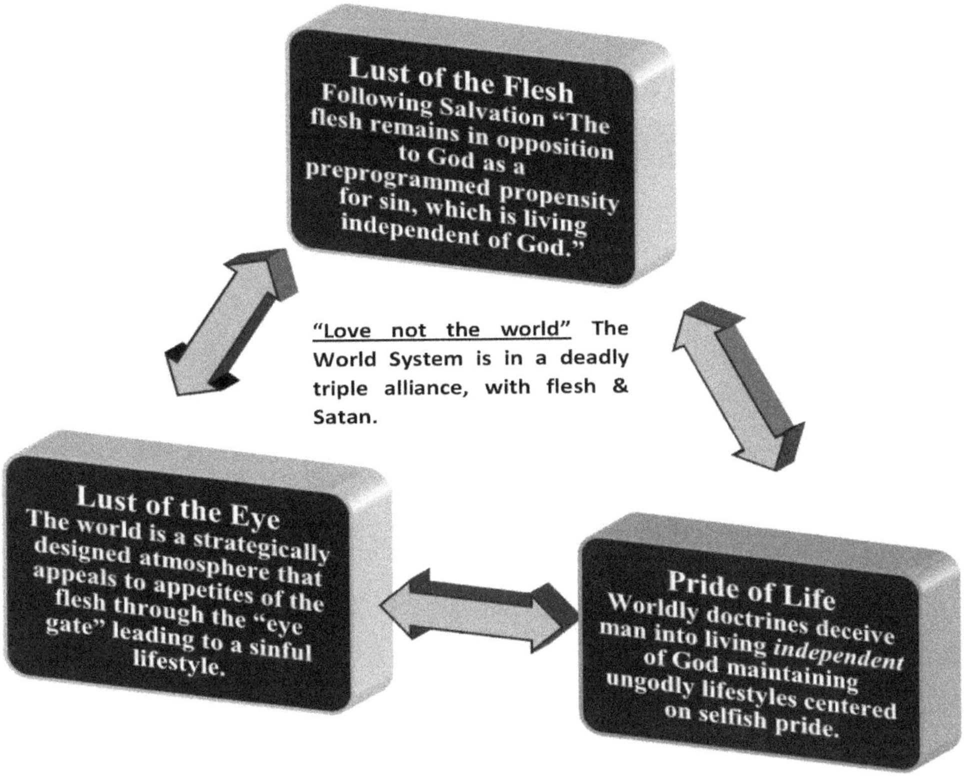

Figure 29: Three Channels of Temptation

The Apostle John provides believers with a two-fold warning regarding Satan's world system. First, he instructs the believer *not to love the world system;* he then includes *the things that are in it* (see Ephesians 2:2 and Matthew 4:8, 9). A Christian should not be deceived into believing that he/she can avoid loving the world but love the things it offers.

Satan is the *"god of this world"* and has set up his kingdom (the world system) to oppose God's plan and purposes for His children (see 2 Corinthians 4:4). This world system is designed to compete for your love for God and to cause you to break fellowship with the Father and your neighbor. You can be saved and out of fellowship with God by practicing a sinful lifestyle.

The world is designed to cater to man's fleshly appetites, passions, and desires. It hinders the fulfillment of the first and second greatest commandments by destroying fellowship with God and others. See Ephesians 2:2,3.

In 1 John 2:16, the Apostle John sums up the "things of the world" by placing them in three channels of temptations used to cater to the flesh and draw you out of fellowship with God. "For all that *is* in the world, the *lust of the flesh,* and the *lust of the eyes,* and the *pride of life,* is *not of the Father,* but is of the world."

Fellowship with the World Hinders You from Loving GOD

Self-Check

How do you rate your *understanding* of the three channels of temptation? Discuss your answer within your group.

Using a scale from 1 to 10, with **#1** being **very high** and **# 10** being **very low**, rank the following channels of temptation according to how they hinder your fellowship with God and others.

1. The lust of the eyes _____
2. The lust of the flesh _____
3. The pride of life _____

Action Steps

List two things you can do to overcome the temptations caused by the lust of the eyes.

1.
2.

List two things that you can do to overcome the temptations caused by the lust of the flesh.

1.
2.

List two things that you can do to overcome the temptations caused by the pride of life.

1.
2.

What scripture in this section has had the greatest impact in your life? Explain.

The Role of Obedience in Fellowship

Obedience is based on the *present work of the Holy Spirit* in your everyday life, while *faith* is based on the *completed work of Christ* on Calvary. *Obedience is a direct measure of your faith energized or activated by love.*

Christ provided you with a position; the Holy Spirit will bring that position into experience through obedience. How much you experience of your salvation is determined by the level of your obedience through submission.

> Do you not know that if you continually *surrender yourselves to anyone to do his will,* you are slaves of him whom you obey, whether that be to sin, which leads to death, or to *obedience which leads to righteousness* [right doing and right standing with God]. (Romans 6:16, AMP)
>
> *By this we know that we love the children of God, when we love God, and keep his commandments. For this is the love of God, that we keep his commandments:* and his commandments are not grievous. (1 John 5:2–3)

- ☐ Obedience and love for other Christians is evidence of being in fellowship with God.

> *We know that we have come to know him if we obey his commands.* The man who says, "I know him," but does not do what he commands is a liar, and the truth is not in him. *But if anyone obeys his word, God's love is truly made complete in him. This is how we know we are in him: Whoever claims to live in him must walk as Jesus did.* (1 John 2:3–6, NIV)

- ☐ Relational knowledge of Christ is inseparable from obedience to Him and loving Him. Obedience is proof of being in fellowship with God and experiencing His love.
- ☐ Through obedience, a Christian's love is made mature and is demonstrated by imitating Christ and by living a godly lifestyle.

> And whatsoever we ask, we receive of him, because we keep his commandments, and do those things that are pleasing in his sight. And this is his commandment, That we should believe on the name of his Son Jesus Christ, and love one another, as he gave us commandment. And he that keepeth his commandments dwelleth in him, and he in him. And hereby we know that he abideth in us, by the Spirit which he hath given us. (1 John 3:22–24)

- ☐ Obedience is pleasing to God and allows a person to remain in fellowship with God. It is assurance that a person is in fellowship with God.

> If ye keep my commandments, ye shall abide in my love; even as I have kept my Father's commandments, and abide in his love. (John 15:10)

Jesus uses His relationship with the Father (He and the Father remained in fellowship through His obedience to the Father) as an example for us to remain in fellowship with the Father through obedience.

Understanding the Role that Obedience Plays in Fellowship

Self–Check

> *We know that we have come to know him if we obey his commands.* The man who says, "I know him," but does not do what he commands is a liar, and the truth is not in him. *But if anyone obeys his word, God's love is truly made complete in him. This is how we know we are in him: Whoever claims to live in him must walk as Jesus did.* (1 John 2:3–6, NIV)

How do you rate your *understanding* of the concept of obedience to God's will? Discuss your answer within your group.

How do you rate your *level of obedience* to God's will in your life? Discuss your answer within your group.

Action Steps

List two things you can do to increase your obedience to God's will for your life.

1.
2.

List two things that are promoting your disobedience to God and His will for you.

1.
2.

What scripture in this section has had the greatest impact in your life? Explain.

FELLOWSHIP OF THE HOLY SPIRIT

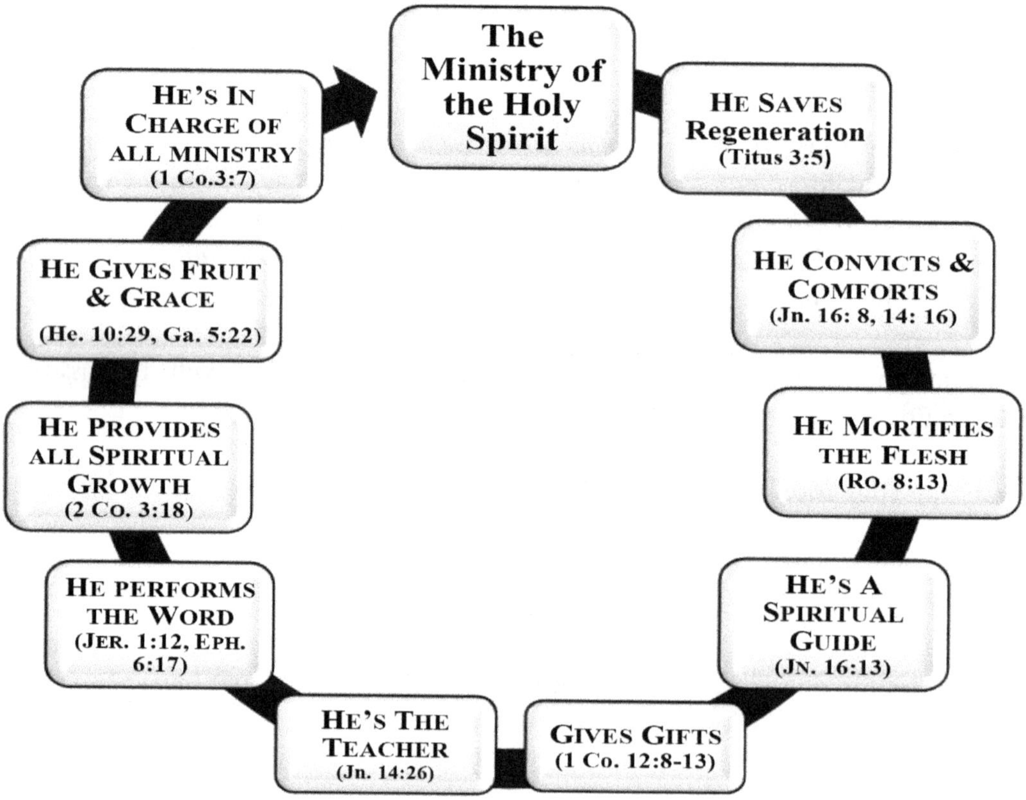

Figure 30: The Ministry of the Holy Spirit

Factors that Hinder Fellowship with the Holy Spirit

Quenching the Holy Spirit

As a believer, you must be aware of certain factors that can hinder the ministry of the Holy Spirit. There are three factors that can hinder the functions of the Holy Spirit and hinder a believer's restoration from drugs/alcohol; these three factors are quenching, grieving, and insulting the Holy Spirit.

> Now we exhort you, brethren, *warn them that are unruly, comfort the feebleminded, support the weak, be patient toward all men. See that none render evil for evil unto any man;* but ever follow that which is good, both among yourselves, and to all *men. Rejoice evermore. Pray without ceasing. In everything give thanks:* for this is the will of

> God in Christ Jesus concerning you. *Quench not the Spirit. Despise not prophesyings.* Prove all things; hold fast that which is good. 22 *Abstain from all appearance of evil.* (1 Thessalonians 5:14–22)

Quenching or suppressing the Holy Spirit is one of three significant factors that hinder a believer's restoration from drugs/alcohol. Quenching the Holy Spirit is centered on the sin of omission, failure of a believer to be responsible to act in a situation or circumstance when they are aware they should. It is the result of a person taking a passive, (complacent) lackadaisical attitude about what he or she knows God requires. Quenching the Holy Spirit is a major factor that sets up a believer for relapse, because it hinders the reception of God's grace, which they need for restoration from their addiction.

A believer can quench the Spirit and hinder their restoration from drugs/alcohol (character development) by:

- ☐ refusing to submit to His will
- ☐ not adhering to His discipline
- ☐ refusing to listen and follow His directions

Grieving the Holy Spirit by Giving Satan an Opportunity

> *Therefore, each of you must put off*, for we are all members of one body. "In your anger do not sin": Do not let the sun go down while you are still angry, *and do not give the devil a foothold.* He who has been *stealing* must *steal no longer*, but must work, doing something useful with his own hands, that he may have something to share with those in need.
>
> Do not let any *unwholesome talk* come out of your mouths, but only what is helpful for building others up according to their needs, that it may benefit those who listen. *And do not grieve the Holy Spirit of God*, with whom you were sealed for the day of redemption. Get rid of all *bitterness, rage and anger, brawling and slander*, along with every form of *malice.* Be kind and compassionate to one another, forgiving each other, just as in Christ God forgave you. (Ephesians 4:25–32, NIV)

Grieving or causing the Holy Spirit sorrow is the second significant factor that can hinder a believer's restoration from drugs/alcohol. Grieving the Holy Spirit is centered on the sin of commission, the resorting back to old addictive behavioral patterns involving the works of the flesh. A believer being restored from drugs/alcohol must understand that they are required by God to begin to develop a new godly lifestyle based on the fruit of the Spirit, through the power of the Holy Spirit.

If a believer doesn't learn to cooperate with the Holy Spirit, he or she will allow Satan a foothold in their life once again, which will eventually lead to returning to their old lifestyle of using/drugs/alcohol (relapsing).

Grieving the Holy Spirit is a major factor that sets up a believer for relapse, because it hinders their relationship with God while also hindering the reception of God's grace, which they need for restoration from their addiction.

A believer can grieve or cause the Spirit sorrow and thus hinder their restoration (character development) from drugs/alcohol by:

- ☐ Indulging in the desires and appetites of the flesh
- ☐ Minding to earthly things
- ☐ Resorting to old attitudes, behaviors, and old character traits

Insulting the Spirit of Grace

> How much worse (sterner and heavier) punishment do you suppose he will be judged to deserve who has spurned and [thus] trampled underfoot the Son of God, and who has considered the covenant blood by which he was consecrated common and unhallowed, thus profaning it and insulting and outraging the [Holy] Spirit [Who imparts] grace (the unmerited favor and blessing of God)? (Hebrews 10:29, AMP)

Insulting the Holy Spirit is the third significant factor that can hinder a believer's restoration from drugs/alcohol. Insulting the Holy Spirit is centered on the sin of rebellion, one's deliberate willful disobedience. This individual is not struggling with overcoming triggers, cravings, or set-up behaviors but is deliberately planning their relapse with full knowledge of what it does to their relationship with God.

Requirements for You to Walk in Fellowship with God (1 John 1:5–10)

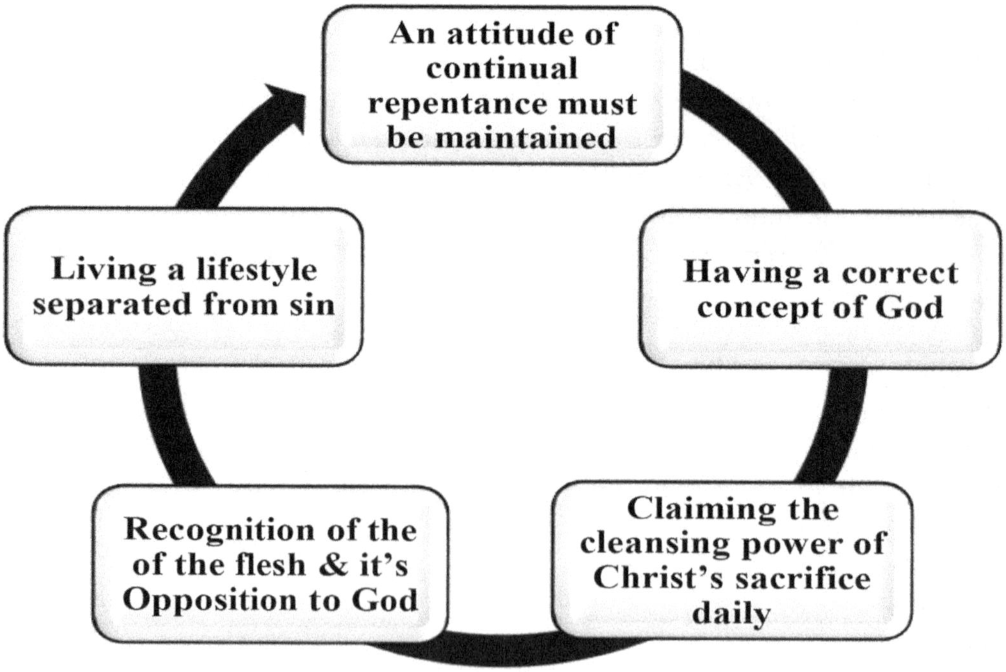

Figure 31: Walk in Fellowship with God

To remain in a position to receive the grace necessary to avoid sowing to the flesh and relapsing, you must continue in fellowship with God by walking in His marvelous light. Faith, love, and obedience are three key foundational ingredients for fellowship; but there are several other requirements necessary for you to continually walk in fellowship with God.

(1) *Having a correct concept of God* (no taint of evil, absolute holiness, and purity is the essence of God's character).

- ☐ There is no compromise in God toward sin. He is holy and demands that you also be holy.

(2) *Living a life separated from sin* (You must not allow your flesh or the world to rule you and develop an indifference to sin).

- ☐ If you claim you have fellowship with God, but you are living in sin, you are living in self-deception.

(3) *Claiming the cleansing power of Christ's sacrifice from daily defilement* (You must recognize sin in your life on a daily basis and look to Christ to address it).

- ☐ An attitude of denial or rejection of the fact that you have to contend with the flesh will cause you to fall from fellowship with God.

(4) *Recognition of the presence of the flesh* (You must be aware of the works of the flesh and understand your own weaknesses to guard against them).

- ☐ You must recognize *when* you have sinned and broken fellowship with an infinitely holy God.

(5) *An attitude of continual repentance must be maintained* (We must acknowledge and confess our sinfulness, and be willing to turn away from sin, in order to be brought back into a proper relational standing with God).

- ☐ If you deny sin in your life, you lose fellowship with God and hinder His purpose for your spiritual growth and character development.

Requirements for Walking in Fellowship with God

Self-Check

How do you rate your *understanding* of the requirements for walking in fellowship with God? Discuss your answer within your group.

How do you rate your fellowship with God? Discuss your answer within your group.

Action Steps

List two things you can do to increase your understanding of the requirements necessary to continue walking in fellowship with God.

1.
2.

List two things that are breaking your fellowship with God.

1.
2.

Using a scale from 1 to 10, with *1* being *very low* and *10* being *very high,* rank the following requirements for walking in fellowship with God according to how they hinder your fellowship.

___Having a correct concept of God.
___Living a life separated from sin.
___Claiming the cleansing power of Christ's sacrifice from daily corruption.
___Recognition of the presence of fleshly desires.
___An attitude of continual repentance must be maintained.

Living Holy: A Necessity for Continual Fellowship with God

Behold, what manner of love the Father hath bestowed upon us, *that we should be called the sons of God*: therefore, the world knoweth us not, because it knew him not. Beloved, now are we the sons of God, and it doth not yet appear what we shall be: but we know that, when he shall appear, *we shall be like him*; for we shall see him as he is. And *every man that hath this hope in him purifieth himself*, even as he is pure. (1 John 3:1–3)

- ☐ By continuing in fellowship with God, you are able to develop a "faith-full" understanding of your new position in Christ, which is the second most significant factor in preventing relapse.

PART TWO

Cultivating Your Relationship with God

In his text, *The Celebration of Discipline,* Richard J. Foster states, "God has given us the Disciplines of the spiritual life as a means of receiving grace. The Disciplines allow us to place ourselves before God so that he can transform us."

He continues by explaining Paul's statement in Galatians 6:8, "He who sows to his own flesh will from the flesh reap corruption; but he who sows to the Spirit will from the Spirit reap eternal life." He further explains the Apostle Paul's analogy:

> A farmer is helpless to grow grain; all he can do is provide the right conditions for the growing of grain. He cultivates the ground, he plants the seed, he waters the plants, and then the natural forces of the earth take over and up comes the grain. This is the way it is with the Spiritual Disciplines, they are the way of sowing to the Spirit. The Disciplines are God's way of getting us into the ground; they put us where he can work within us and transform us. By themselves the Spiritual Disciplines can do nothing; they can only get us to a place where something can be done. They are God's means of grace. The inner righteous we seek is not something that is poured on our heads. God has ordained the Disciplines of the spiritual life as the means by which we place ourselves where he can bless us.
>
> *I am the true vine, and my Father is the gardener.* He cuts off every branch in me that bears no fruit, while every branch that does bear fruit he prunes so that it will be even more fruitful. You are already clean because of the word I have spoken to you. Remain in me, and I will remain in you. No branch can bear fruit by itself; it must remain in the vine. Neither can you bear fruit unless you remain in me. "I am the vine; you are the branches. *If a man remains in me and I in him, he will bear much fruit; apart from me you can do nothing."* (John 15:1–5, NIV)

Messages provide you with *spiritual food*; prayer *restores you*; the study and meditation of God's word *refreshes you*; praise and worship *strengthen you*; fasting provides you with *spiritual focus*, and fellowship provides opportunity for *spiritual growth.* However, the *greatest method God uses to build you up is the discipline of the Holy Spirit.*

Just as in the example of farming, God has provided certain disciplines or ways for you to grow as a Christian. You must actively participate in these disciplines or you will not grow. As a farmer who does not perform his duties will not produce a crop, neither will you if you neglect disciplining. However, as a Christian, you must continually realize your dependence on the Holy Spirit. The spiritual disciplines are only a means of getting to grace. The spiritual disciplines do not work on their own apart from God.

> I planted the seed, Apollos watered it, but *God made it grow.* So neither he who plants nor he who waters is anything, *but only God, who makes things grow.* (1 Corinthians 3:6–7, NIV)

The Divine Law of Sowing and Reaping

> Be not deceived; God is not mocked*: for whatsoever a man soweth, that shall he also reap. For he that soweth to his flesh shall of the flesh reap corruption; but he that soweth to the Spirit shall of the Spirit reap life everlasting.* And let us not be weary in well doing: for in due season we shall reap, if we faint not. As we have therefore opportunity, let us do good unto all *men,* especially unto them who are of the household of faith. (Galatians 6:7–10)
>
> The law of sowing and reaping is just as valid in the spiritual as in the physical and moral realms. The frustration and the hopelessness of humanistic psychology, psychiatry, and counseling can be traced, among other things, to their refusal to consider the immutable spiritual law of sowing and reaping. A person's character cannot be changed until his nature is changed, and that can happen only through the new creation that comes from trust in Jesus Christ.
>
> —John MacArthur Jr.

The Divine Law of Sowing and Reaping not only was key in your understanding how you became addicted, but it also plays an important role in relapse prevention.

In the passage of scripture above, the Apostle Paul warns us not to be deceived into thinking that God does not deal with sin in the lives of His children. There are consequences for the choices we make. The Divine Law of Sowing and Reaping applies to every human being, saved or unsaved.

> *For he that soweth to his flesh shall of the flesh reap corruption.* (Galatians 6:8)

Prior to accepting Christ as Lord, you were involved in a lifestyle of sin, unaware of the consequences, being deceived into believing there are no consequences for your sin. Addiction is one of the numerous consequences you faced when you choose to sow to the flesh.

- ☐ The term *corruption* spoken of here in the first portion of Galatians 6:8 refers to physical death and other earthly consequences (HIV, addictions, lung cancer, disease of liver, incarceration, STD, divorce, financial ruin, etc.).

> *But he that soweth to the Spirit shall of the Spirit reap life everlasting.* (Galatians 6:8)

You need to understand that *the quality of your spiritual life* following salvation will depend on what *field* you chose to sow to. If you chose "to sow to the flesh," the quality of your spiritual life will be *low* and your spiritual growth hindered and you will struggle with the works of the flesh. However, if you *"sow to the Spirit,"* He will produce His fruit in you, and you will prosper spiritually and experience a high quality of spiritual life and grow enormously.

> But the fruit of the Spirit is love, joy, peace, longsuffering, kindness, goodness, faithfulness, gentleness, *self-control.* Against such there is no law. (Galatians 5:22–23)
>
> I say then: *"Walk in the Spirit, and you shall not fulfill the lust (works) of the flesh. For the flesh lusts against the Spirit, and the Spirit against the flesh; and these are contrary to one another, so that you do not do the things that you wish. But if you are led by the Spirit, you are not under the law."* (Galatians 5:16–18)
>
> *And let us not be weary in well doing: for in due season we shall reap, if we faint not.* (Galatians 6:9)

Learning to "walk in the Spirit" which is the same as you "sowing to the Spirit" is extremely important to keep you from relapsing. And notice how you are cautioned not to become weary or tired in doing so. Because it is in God's timing that you will receive the benefits of your sowing if you don't give up (faint).

The Discipline of the Word

The Bible is not an outdated history book or a collection of devotional articles; it is men performing, experiencing, and living out the Word of God. The Bible is a living book, "God-breathed." It is a living book because it is spoken by the living God. The *governing principal* throughout the Bible is *the Word becoming flesh (experiential) in us.*

The Holy Spirit's Primary Tool for Change

> Take the helmet of salvation and the *sword of the Spirit, which is the word of God.* (Ephesians 6:17, NIV)
>
> *All scripture is God-breathed* (inspired) and is useful for *teaching, rebuking, correcting and training* in righteousness, so that the man of God may be thoroughly equipped for every good work. (2 Timothy 3:16–17, NIV)

Jesus is the Word

> In the beginning was the Word, and the Word was with God, and the Word was God. (John 1:1, NIV)
>
> The Word became flesh and made his dwelling among us. We have seen his glory, the glory of the One and Only, who came from the Father, full of grace and truth. (John 1:14, NIV)
>
> For the word of God is *living* and *active.* Sharper than any double–edged sword, it *penetrates even to dividing soul and spirit,* joints and marrow; it *judges the thoughts and attitudes of the heart.* Nothing in all creation is hidden from God's sight. Everything is uncovered and laid bare before the eyes of him to whom we must give account. (Hebrews 4:12–13, NIV)

The Holy Spirit's primary tool for restoring you from bondage to alcohol and other drugs is His Word, the Bible.

- ☐ As a believer, you must understand that the Bible is not an ordinary book or collection of writings. It is powerful, effective, alive, and active in accomplishing God's purpose. You must believe in the authority of God's inspired Word and its ability to penetrate man's inner being (soul/spirit) and change his thoughts and emotions.
- ☐ Through God's Word, the Holy Spirit convicts you of your wrongs by showing you the truth; He corrects that which is wrong in your life and disciplines and chastens you.

THE ROLE & FUNCTIONS OF THE WORD

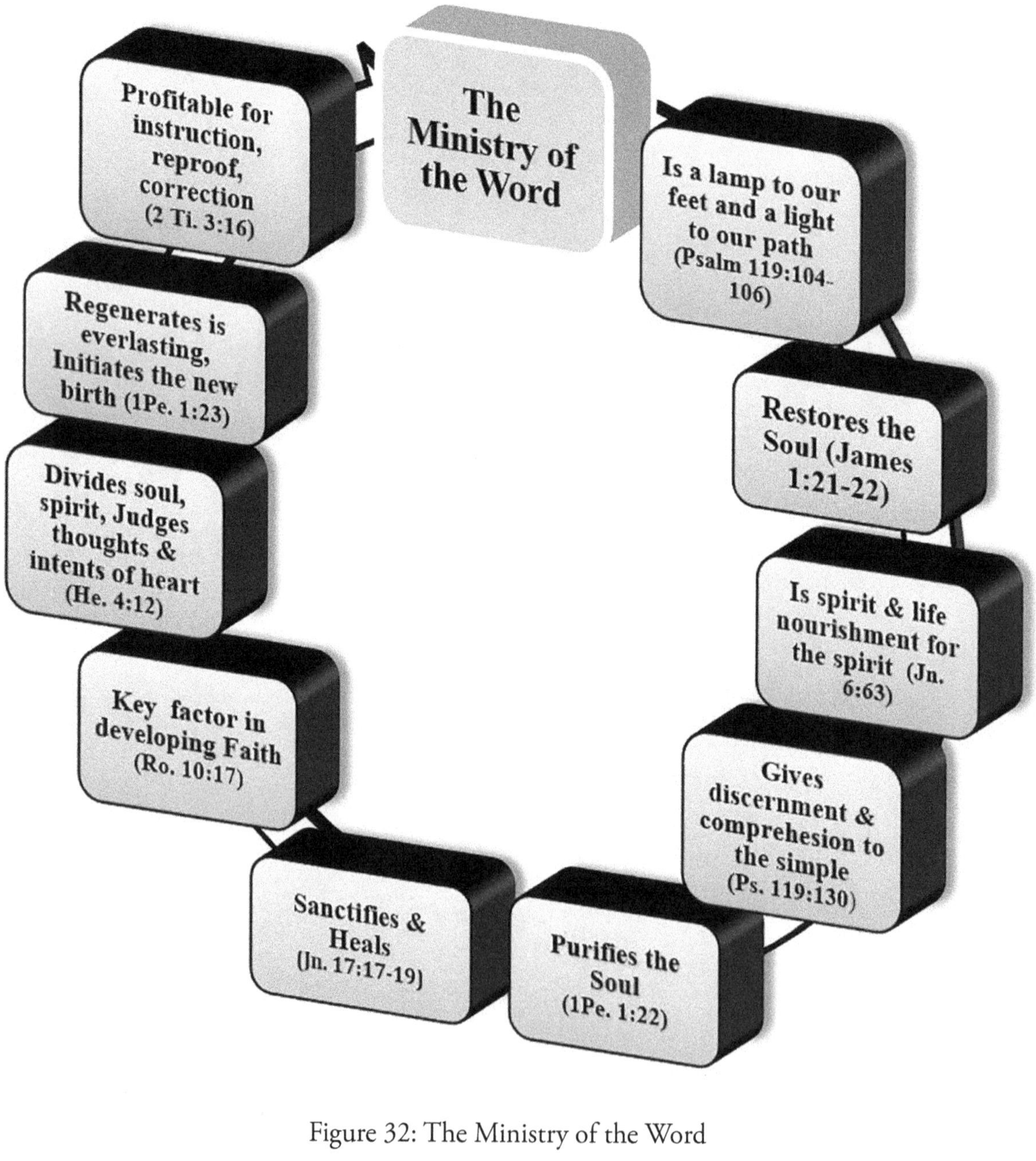

Figure 32: The Ministry of the Word

> Therefore, I urge you, brothers, in view of God's mercy, to offer your bodies as living sacrifices, holy and pleasing to God—this is your spiritual act of worship. Do not conform any longer to the pattern of this world, but be transformed by the renewing of your mind. Then you will be able to test and approve what God's will is—his good, pleasing and perfect will. For by the grace given me I say to every one of you: Do not think of yourself more highly than you ought, but rather think of yourself with sober judgment, in accordance with the measure of faith God has given you. (Romans 12:1–3, NIV)

According to Apostle Paul in Roman 12:1–2, the key to your restoration from alcohol and other drugs is:

- ☐ Developing new biblical views and forming new attitudes about your new life and the world around you.
- ☐ Obtaining biblical knowledge and the willingness to know what to do and how to do it (application).
- ☐ Truth, knowledge, and study are important factors in making your transition into the Christian lifestyle.

The truth of God's Word is powerful and transforms your mind, protecting it from worldly thoughts that produce desires for alcohol and other drugs. Therefore, your mind being renewed through the study of God's Word plays a vital role in His plan for changing you. God's Word is key in your life, because it will provide you with God's view that alters how you view your security and your source of significance.

- ☐ In your past lifestyle, you sought and found your significance in the world through the desires of the flesh (money, sex, alcohol and other drugs, power, prestige, etc.)
- ☐ Now that you have become a child of the King, you must learn to find your significance in your relationship with the Father through Jesus Christ.

In his text, *Winning the War Within,* Charles Stanley makes the following statement regarding the importance of understanding the sense of one's significance:

> As long as men and women seek to gain their sense of significance and self–worth from anything other than God, they will be set up for temptation. Certain people, places, or things always have an inordinate ability to lure them into sin. Until they change their definition of significance and until they transfer their security to Someone who can give them real security, they will never experience lasting victory in their lives.

- ☐ True security and significance are obtained by establishing and maintaining a vibrant relationship with God the Father through His Son Jesus Christ. God's Word teaches you how that is accomplished.

> And without faith it is impossible to please God, because anyone who comes to him must believe that he exists and that he rewards those who earnestly seek him. (Hebrews 11:6, NIV)
>
> Consequently, *faith comes from hearing the message,* and the message is heard *through the word of Christ.* (Romans 10:17, NIV)

Faith gives us access to God's grace. Faith is the foundation on which your relationship is based; you were saved by grace through faith, and both grace and faith are also keys to your continued spiritual growth and development as a Christian.

- ☐ It is through believing God's Word that you learn what God has done for you. His Word informs you of the accomplished works of Christ. Without the Word of God, you cannot place your trust in the works of Christ.
- ☐ You would have no knowledge of Christ's works without God's Word. The most important thing is pleasing God, your heavenly Father.
- ☐ It is impossible to please God without faith, and faith is obtained through God's Word.

> Wherefore lay apart all filthiness and superfluity of naughtiness, *and receive with meekness the engrafted word, which is able to save (restore) your souls.* But be ye doers of the word, and not hearers only, deceiving your own selves. (James 1:21–22)
>
> Sanctify them by the truth; your word is truth. As you sent me into the world, I have sent them into the world. For them I sanctify myself, that they too may be truly sanctified. (John 17:17–19, NIV)

- ☐ The Holy Spirit uses the Scriptures to free you from the power of your addiction (thoughts and desires) in order that it will not rule your life.
- ☐ It is God's Word that separates you for His use by purifying your soul through progressive holiness.

> "For My thoughts are not your thoughts, neither are your ways My ways," says the Lord.
>
> "For as the heavens are higher than the earth, so are *My ways higher than your ways and My thoughts than your thoughts.* For as the rain and snow come down from the heavens, and return not there again, but water the earth and make it bring forth and sprout, that it may give seed to the sower and bread to the eater, So shall My word be that goes forth out of My mouth*: it shall not return to Me void [without producing any effect, useless], but it shall accomplish that which I please and purpose, and it shall prosper in the thing for which I sent it.*" (Isaiah 55:8–11)

Charles Stanley in his text, *Winning the War Within,* states four primary reasons the power of the Word is so effective with regard to combating temptations in the life of the believer. Therefore, you must understand these four reasons.

(1) God's Word expresses the sinfulness of whatever you are being tempted with. *It helps you view the temptation for what it is—a lie.*

(2) God's Word provides you with *God's view* (divine perspective). This will help you understand that your temptation to return to using alcohol and other drugs is something that is happening to you, not a part of you.
(3) God's Word helps you to "short-circuit" sinful thoughts and desires for alcohol and other drugs and to take those thoughts captive. God's Word will help you by *"nipping temptations in the bud"* before they can lead you back to relapse (Philippians 4:8; Colossians 3:2).
(4) Using God's Word against temptation is also effective for you because it is an *expression of faith.* Believing in God's Word during times of temptation will assist you in overcoming cravings and keep you from giving in to your old desires and appetites.

The Sower Sows the Word

The gospel writer Mark provides believers with several important principles (truths) regarding the *ability to receive God's Word.* These principles provide valuable insight into understanding how the *condition of one's heart (garden) can either hinder the effectiveness of the Word or cause it to prosper and be fruitful.*

He gives four examples in this parable, and in each example, the key factor is the condition of the *heart, which is viewed as a garden* and the *Word as seed.* The heart (garden) has the potential to produce either "good" or "bad" fruit depending on what kind of seed is sown. The "poisonous seeds of the flesh" will produce corruption, whereas the Word of God will produce a plentiful harvest of fruit.

> And He said to them, "Do you not discern and understand this parable? How then is it possible for you to discern and understand all the parables? *The sower sows the Word.*
>
> The ones along the path are those who have the Word sown [in their hearts], but when they hear, *Satan comes at once and [by force] takes away the message which is sown in them."*

This first example explains what happens to the Word when a believer continues to operate in the "works of the flesh" and does not guard their heart. This allows the enemy entry into their life through operating in the flesh, and the Word can be taken away by Satan.

> And in the same way the ones sown upon ***stony ground*** [hardened heart] are those who, when they hear the Word, at once receive and accept and welcome it with joy; ***And they have no real root in themselves, and so they endure for a little while; then when trouble or persecution arises on account of the Word, they immediately are offended (become displeased, indignant, resentful) and they stumble and fall away.*** (Mark 4:13–17)

This second example explains what happens to the Word when a believer has allowed their heart to become hardened (stony ground)—willfully living a lifestyle of sin, a lack of perseverance, an unwillingness to stand firm on the truth, and getting caught up in emotionalism can hinder them from prospering from the Word.

> And the ones sown among the thorns are others who hear the Word; *Then the cares and anxieties of the world and distractions of the age, and the pleasure and delight and false glamour and deceitfulness of riches, and the craving and passionate desire for other things creep in and choke and suffocate the Word, and it becomes fruitless.* (Mark 4:18–19)

This third example explains what happens to the Word when a believer has allowed their hearts to be polluted by the carnal mind with its ungodly appetites, desires, and passions (thorns). This causes the Word to be choked out and suffocated—making it fruitless.

> And those sown on the good (well–adapted) soil are the ones who *hear the Word and receive and accept and welcome it and bear fruit—some thirty times as much as was sown, some sixty times as much, and some [even] a hundred times as much.* (Mark 4:20)

This final example explains what happens to the Word when a believer's heart and mind are lined up with God's will (good, well-adapted soil) and they received the engrafted Word of God with meekness: it will result in producing a harvest of fruit. And the more sincere (contrite) their heart is, the greater the harvest.

Biblical Formula for Purifying Your Lifestyle by Keeping God's Word Exercise

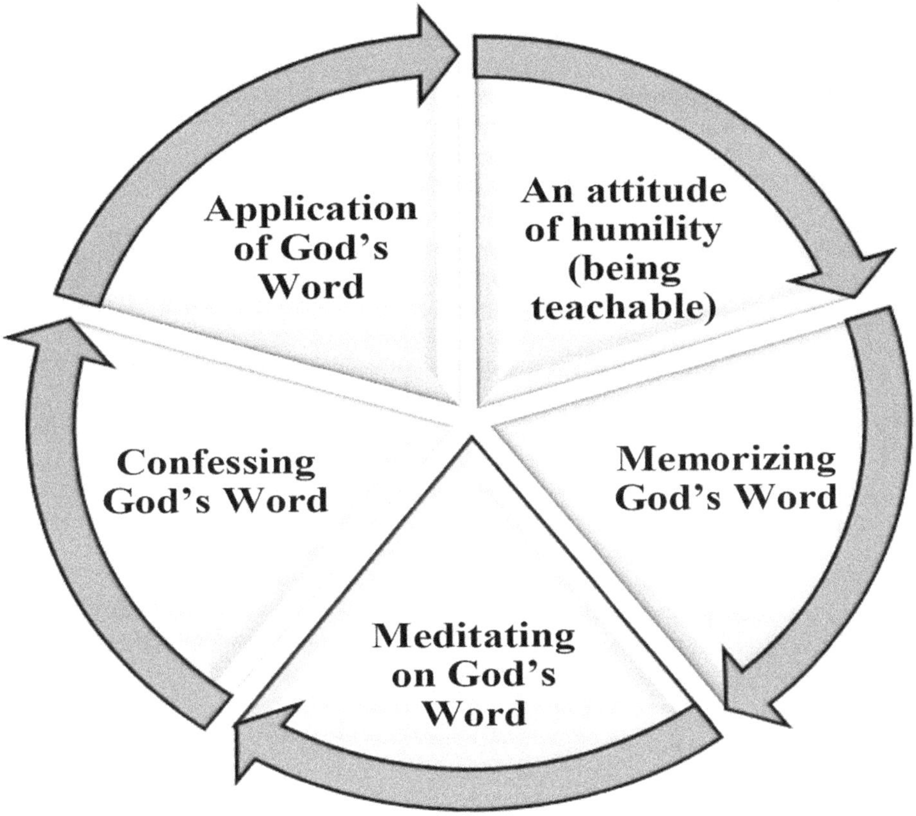

Figure 33: A Biblical Formula within the Word

> How can a young man keep his way pure? By living according to your word. I seek you with all my heart; do not let me stray from your commands. I have hidden your word in my heart that I might not sin against you. Praise be to you, O LORD; teach me your decrees. With my lips I recount all the laws that come from your mouth. I rejoice in following your statutes as one rejoices in great riches. I meditate on your precepts and consider your ways. I delight in your decrees; I will not neglect your word. (Psalm 119:9–16, NIV)

Review the diagram below and answer the following questions.

1. Which step in the biblical formula is the greatest challenge for you? Please discuss this challenge with your group members.

2. Which steps do you find easier for you to practice?

3. How important do you think attitude is in regards to following this biblical formula?

4. What scripture in this section has had the greatest impact in your life? Explain.

The Discipline of Prayer

> To seek aid in time of distress from a supernatural Being is an instinct of human nature. I believe in the truthfulness of this instinct, and that man prays because there is something in prayer. As when the Creator gives His creature the power of thirst, it is because water exists to meet its thirst; and as when He creates hunger there is food to correspond to the appetite; *so when He inclines men to pray it is because prayer has a corresponding blessing connected with it.*
>
> —Charles Spurgeon

You must understand that of all the spiritual disciplines, prayer allows us to be in continual communion with God and is thought of as being the most central of the disciplines.

- ☐ Only through prayer can you seek divine assistance as you surrender your problems completely to God.
- ☐ Prayer is a great mystery, in that you, a human being, can enter into a conversation with the almighty creator of the universe so that change within you and your circumstances can result. Prayer plays a significant role in God changing you.

Richard J. Foster, in his text, *Celebration of Discipline,* states, "To pray is to change. Prayer is the central avenue God uses to transform us. If we are unwilling to change, we will abandon prayer as a noticeable characteristic of our lives."

As a believer, you may be asking why pray? Isn't God all-knowing and all-powerful? He already knows; why must I ask? Why are my prayers needed? Why won't He begin His work before I pray? What is prayer? Jesus calls us to pray, and prayer works.

What Is Prayer?

Prayer is you aligning your will with God's will. Prayer is the union of your thoughts, a child with the will of God, your Father. The true purpose of prayer is for you to pray for the fulfillment of the will of God in your life.

- ☐ Prayer is not you asking God to yield to your request to fulfill your selfish desires.
- ☐ It is not asking God to change His will and to do something He is unwilling to do.
- ☐ Your desires must be changed along with your thoughts; they must conform to the things God desires. As the Holy Spirit teaches you this, you will begin to see things from His point of view.

> In the same way, the Spirit helps us in our weakness. We do not know what we ought to pray for, but the Spirit himself intercedes for us with groans that words cannot express. And he who searches our hearts knows the mind of the Spirit, because the Spirit intercedes for the saints in accordance with God's will. (Romans 8:26–27, NIV)

As a believer, you must realize and accept that developing an effective prayer life is a learning process. Prayer is not a natural function, and therefore, it does not come easy to man. Man's natural tendency is to find excuses not to pray. The carnal mind automatically opposes prayer and will find any reason not to enter into prayer.

Prayer: A Part of the Full Armor of God

> And pray in the Spirit on all occasions with all kinds of prayers and requests. With this in mind, be alert and always keep on praying for all the saints. (Ephesians 6:18. NIV)
>
> Far from being a support activity, prayer is the actual front line of spiritual warfare. It is not optional, but an essential, vital ingredient for success. Prayer is not merely a weapon to be used; it is the heart of the battle. This is why praying is so difficult for most of us. Spiritual warfare without prayer is like Raisin Bran without the raisins. The two are intricately linked together.
>
> —Dr. Terry Wise

Prayer: A Learning Process

In His Word, Jesus teaches us to pray. There are two model prayers that Jesus left for us so that we would learn how to pray. The first and most popular is the "Our Father," (Matthew 6:9–15, 7:7). He also instructs you in praying for others in His intercessory prayer, recorded in John chapter 17.

> One day Jesus was praying in a certain place. When he finished, one of his disciples said to him, "Lord, teach us to pray, just as John taught his disciples." (Luke 11:1, NIV)
>
> *Then Jesus told his disciples a parable to show them that they should always pray and not give up. He said:* "In a certain town there was a judge who neither feared God nor cared about men." And there was a widow in that town who kept coming to him with the plea, "Grant me justice against my adversary." For some time he refused. But finally, he said to himself, "Even though I don't fear God or care about men, yet because this widow keeps bothering me, I will see that she gets justice, so that she won't eventually wear me out with her coming!" (Luke 18:1–5, NIV)
>
> Rejoice evermore. Pray without ceasing. In everything give thanks: for this is the will of God in Christ Jesus concerning you. (1 Thessalonians 5:16–18)
>
> Continue in prayer, and watch in the same with thanksgiving. (Colossians 4:2)
>
> Rejoicing in hope; patient in tribulation; continuing instant in prayer. (Romans 12:12)

I thank God, whom I serve from *my* forefathers with pure conscience, that without ceasing I have remembrance of thee in my prayers night and day. (2 Timothy 1:3)

Hindrances to Prayer

Conscious Sin

If I had cherished sin in my heart, the Lord would not have listened. (Psalm 66:18, NIV)

Surely the arm of the LORD is not too short to save, nor his ear too dull to hear. But your iniquities have separated you from your God; your sins have hidden his face from you, so that he will not hear. (Isaiah 59:1–2, NIV)

We know that God does not listen to sinners. He listens to the godly man who does his will. (John 9:31, NIV)

Therefore, confess your sins to each other and pray for each other so that you may be healed. The prayer of a righteous man is powerful and effective. (James 5:16, NIV)

Willful Disobedience

If anyone turns a deaf ear to the law, even his prayers are detestable. (Proverbs 28:9, NIV)

"But they refused to pay attention; stubbornly they turned their backs and stopped up their ears. They made their hearts as hard as flint and would not listen to the law or to the words that the LORD Almighty had sent by his Spirit through the earlier prophets. So the LORD Almighty was very angry. "When I called, they did not listen; so when they called, I would not listen," says the LORD Almighty. (Zechariah 7:11–13)

Wrong Motives

When you ask, you do not receive, because you ask with wrong motives, that you may spend what you get on your pleasures. (James 4:3, NIV)

This is the confidence we have in approaching God*: that if we ask anything according to his will, he hears us.* And if we know that he hears us—whatever we ask—we know that we have what we asked of him. (1 John 5:14–15, NIV)

"And when you pray, do not be like the hypocrites, for they love to pray standing in the synagogues and on the street corners to be seen by men. I tell you the truth, they have received their reward in full." (Matthew 6:5, NIV)

Doubt

But when he asks, *he must believe and not doubt*, because he who doubts is like a wave of the sea, blown and tossed by the wind. *That man should not think he will receive anything from the Lord;* he is a double–minded man, unstable in all he does. (James 1:6–8, NIV)

And all things, whatsoever ye shall ask in prayer, *believing*, ye shall receive. (Matthew 21:22)

Therefore I say unto you, "What things so ever ye desire, when ye pray, *believe that ye receive them, and ye shall have them*." (Mark 11:24)

Ask and it will be given to you; seek and you will find; knock and the door will be opened to you. For everyone who asks receives; he who seeks finds; and to him who knocks, the door will be opened. (Matthew 7:7–8, NIV)

And without faith it is impossible to please God, because anyone who comes to him must believe that he exists and that he rewards those who earnestly seek him. (Hebrews 11:6, NIV)

Unwillingness to Forgive

And when ye stand praying, *forgive, if ye have ought against any*: that your Father also which is in heaven may forgive you your trespasses. *But if ye do not forgive, neither will your Father which is in heaven forgive your trespasses.* (Mark 11:25–26)

Therefore, if thou bring thy gift to the altar, and there rememberest that thy brother hath ought against thee; Leave there thy gift before the altar, *and go thy way; first be reconciled to thy brother, and then come and offer thy gift.* (Matthew 5:23–24)

Pride

To some who were confident of their own righteousness and looked down on everybody else, Jesus told this parable:

> "Two men went up to the temple to pray, one a Pharisee and the other a tax collector. The Pharisee stood up and prayed about himself: 'God, I thank you that I am not like other men—robbers, evildoers, adulterers—or even like this tax collector. I fast twice a week and give a tenth of all I get."
>
> But the tax collector stood at a distance. He would not even look up to heaven, but beat his breast and said, "God, have mercy on me, a sinner. *I tell you that this man, rather than the other, went home justified before God. For everyone who exalts himself will be humbled, and he who humbles himself will be exalted."* (Luke 18:9–14, NIV)
>
> There they cry, *but none giveth answer, because of the pride of evil men*. Surely God will not hear vanity, neither will the Almighty regard it. (Job 35:12–13)

Unresolved Conflict within the Home

Husbands, in the same way be considerate as you live with your wives, and treat them with respect as the weaker partner and as heirs with you of the gracious gift of life, *so that nothing will hinder your prayers.* (1 Peter 3:7, NIV)

According to scripture, your relationship begins with God the moment you receive Jesus in your life. Anyone can pray to the Father, but to expect prayer to be answered, a Christian must be obedient and be walking in faith with Christ.

Different Types of Prayer

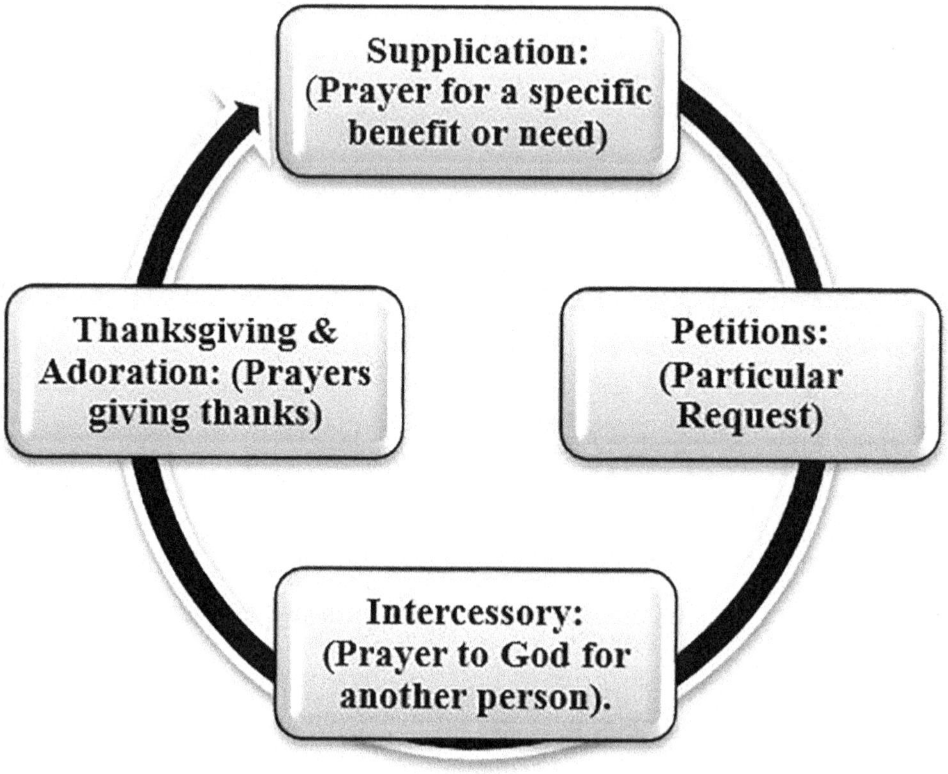

Figure 34: Types of Prayer

And pray in the Spirit on all occasions with all kinds of prayers and requests. With this in mind, be alert and always keep on praying for all the saints. (Ephesians 6:18, NIV)

I exhort therefore, that, first of all, *supplications,* prayers, *intercessions, and giving of thanks,* be made for all men. (1 Timothy 2:1)

Be careful for nothing; but in everything by prayer and *supplication* with *thanksgiving* let your requests be made known unto God. (Philippians 4:6)

And if we know that he hear us, whatsoever we ask, we know that we have the *petitions* that we desired of him. (1 John 5:15)

OBSTACLES TO PRAYER EXERCISE

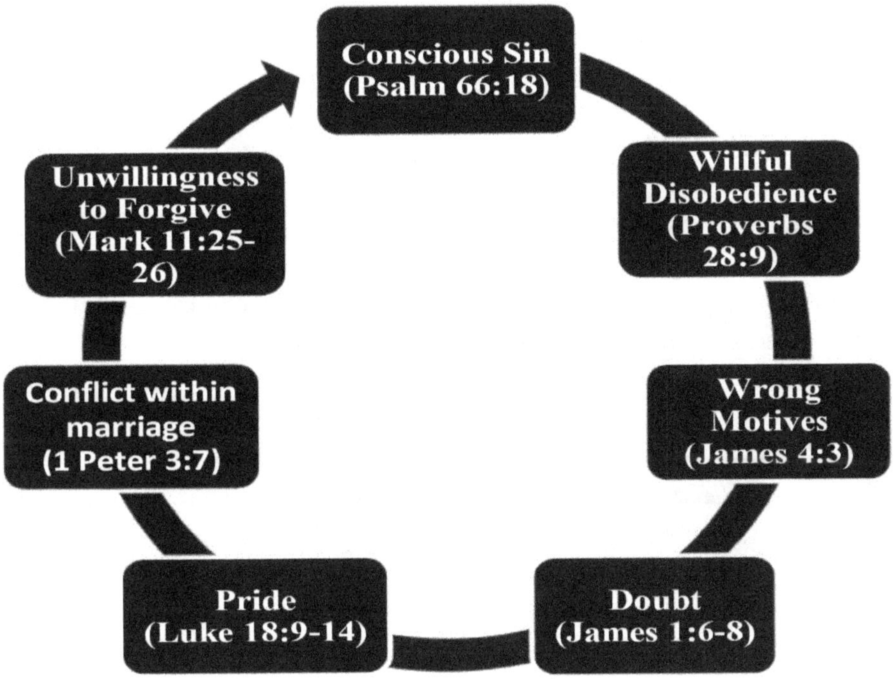

Figure 35: Obstacles to Prayer

EXERCISE:

Review the seven reasons above concerning what hinders prayer from being answered, and answer the following questions.

1. Which one of the seven obstacles to answered prayer do you think will cause your prayers to be hindered?

2. Can you relate to any of the other obstacles to prayer? Please discuss them with your group members.

3. What scripture in this section has had the greatest impact in your life? Explain.

DISCIPLINE OF PRAISE AND THANKSGIVING

Man's primary goal or purpose is to glorify God and to spend eternity with Him. Praise aids man in reaching this goal. Praise is defined as the act of vocal adoration, giving God divine honor, respect, and love. Adoration plays a significant role in our relationship with God because praise allows you, as His child, to acknowledge God as Father.

- ☐ The discipline of praise and thanksgiving are closely related but yet different. Praise focuses on who God is, whereas thanksgiving focuses on what God has done for you.
- ☐ Thanksgiving and praise can be either vocal or mental, and both are vital means of obtaining grace and placing yourself in position to be blessed by God.
- ☐ Therefore, these disciplines are vital tools/weapons in your arsenal for growth and warfare.

> Praise the LORD, O my soul; all my inmost being, praise his holy name. *Praise the LORD, O my soul, and forget not all his benefits*—who forgives all your sins and heals all your diseases, who redeems your life from the pit and crowns you with love and compassion, who satisfies your desires with good things so that your youth is renewed like the eagle's. The LORD works righteousness and justice for all the oppressed. He made known his ways to Moses, his deeds to the people of Israel: The LORD is compassionate and gracious, slow to anger, abounding in love. He will not always accuse, nor will he harbor his anger forever; he does not treat us as our sins deserve or repay us according to our iniquities. For as high as the heavens are above the earth, so great is his love for those who fear him; as far as the east is from the west, so far has he removed our transgressions from us. As a father has compassion on his children, so the LORD has compassion on those who fear him; for he knows how we are formed, he remembers that we are dust. As for man, his days are like grass, he flourishes like a flower of the field; the wind blows over it and it is gone, and its place remembers it no more. But from everlasting to everlasting the LORD's love is with those who fear him, and his righteousness with their children's children—with those who keep his covenant and remember to obey his precepts. The LORD has established his throne in heaven, and his kingdom rules over all. Praise the LORD, you his angels, you mighty ones who do his bidding, who obey his word. Praise the LORD, all his heavenly hosts, you his servants who do his will. Praise the LORD, all his works everywhere in his dominion. Praise the LORD, O my soul. (Psalm 103:1–22, NIV)
>
> A psalm. For giving thanks. Shout for joy to the LORD, all the earth. Worship the LORD with gladness; come before him with joyful songs. Know that the LORD is God. It is he who made us, and we are his; we are his people, the sheep of his pasture. Enter his gates with thanksgiving and his courts with praise; give

> thanks to him and praise his name. For the LORD is good and his love endures forever; his faithfulness continues through all generations. (Psalm 100:1–5, NIV)
>
> And be not drunk with wine, wherein is excess; but be filled with the Spirit; Speaking to yourselves in psalms and hymns and spiritual songs, singing and making melody in your heart to the Lord; Giving thanks always for all things unto God and the Father in the name of our Lord Jesus Christ. (Ephesians 5:18–20)
>
> *Give thanks in all circumstances,* for this is God's will for you in Christ Jesus. (1 Thessalonians 5:18, NIV)

As a believer, you must learn the value of giving thanks to God for what He has already done and is doing in your life. As a believer, there are numerous blessings that you can learn to thank God for:

- ☐ Specific spiritual (e.g., salvation), physical (e.g., health), and material (e.g., employment) blessings, both past and present.
- ☐ Future blessings you expect to receive "in advance."
- ☐ Any special favors you may have forgotten about or never thanked Him for.

As a believer, you must learn that developing and maintaining an attitude of thanksgiving is extremely important, because it is your special gift to God for His kindness. Likewise, you must also learn to praise and worship God for who He is. The Old Testament names of God tell us who and what God is to us. They are foundational for the Christian faith and lifestyle.

- ☐ Jehovah—Nissi (The Lord who protects)
- ☐ Jehovah—Rapha (The Lord who heals)
- ☐ Jehovah—Jirh (The Lord who provides)
- ☐ Jehovah—Shammah (The Lord who is forever present)
- ☐ Jehovah—Shalom (The Lord of peace and contentment)

Harold Lindsell is quoted in the text, *The Hour That Changes the World,* as stating, "Since adoration brings man into immediate and direct contact with God, in the role of servant to Master, or the created to the Creator, it is foundational to all other kinds of prayer." As a believer, there are several important reasons for making praise and worship a part of your daily devotion to God.

In that same text, Phil Billheimer states, "Here is one of the greatest values of praise: it decentralizes self. The worship and praise of God demands a shift of center from self to God. One cannot praise God without relinquishing occupation with self. Praise produces forgetfulness of self–and forgetfulness of self is health."

- ☐ Selfish pride and how you view circumstances are two major issues that hinder spiritual growth.
- ☐ Praise and worship allow you the freedom to overcome these two obstacles. As you enter into the presence of God with thanksgiving and praise, you begin to realize that God is all-powerful and in charge of all circumstances.

Praise and worship are also extremely effective weapons of spiritual warfare. The Word states that, "God inhabits the praises of the saints." Therefore, praise and worship of God cause Satanic forces to flee; they free a believer from satanic oppression.

Paul Billheimer states, "Satan is allergic to praise, so where there is massive triumphant praise, Satan is paralyzed, bound, and banished." The Scriptures identify several patterns of praise:

- ☐ Psalm 33:2, 57:8, 150:3–5 (with music)
- ☐ Rev. 19; Eph. 5;19; Psalm 71:8 (with mouth)
- ☐ Psalm 63:4, 134:2, 141:2, 47:1 (the hands)
- ☐ Psalm 95:6; Eph. 3:14 (by bowing & kneeling)
- ☐ Acts 3:8; 2 Sam. 6:16 (by walking & leaping)
- ☐ Psalm 150:4; 2 Sam. 6:14 (by dancing)

Results of Praise:

- ☐ Psalm 149:1–4 (delights God)
- ☐ Psalm 50:23 (glorifies God)
- ☐ Jude 1:20 (edifies those involved in praise)

As a believer, you must understand when honor, respect, and thanksgiving are given, then honor and respect are received. When you minister to God with thanksgiving and praise, God will minister to you in return.

> Through Jesus, therefore, let us continually offer to God a sacrifice of praise—the fruit of lips that confess his name. (Hebrews 13:15, NIV)
>
> Wherefore the LORD God of Israel saith, I said indeed *that* thy house, and the house of thy father, should walk before me forever*: but now the LORD saith, "Be it far from me; for them that honor me I will honor, and they that despise me shall be lightly esteemed."* (1 Samuel 2:30)

Discipline of Praise and Thanksgiving Exercise

> And be not drunk with wine, wherein is excess; but be filled with the Spirit; Speaking to yourselves in psalms and hymns and spiritual songs, singing and making melody in your heart to the Lord; Giving thanks always for all things unto God and the Father in the name of our Lord Jesus Christ. (Ephesians 5:18–20)

1. What are you instructed to be filled with instead of using alcohol and other drugs?
2. Who are you to give thanks to, and when are you supposed to do it?
3. In whose name are you to give thanks?
4. What are some of the reasons why you should praise and give thanks to God?

THE DISCIPLINE OF FELLOWSHIP

Koinonia: A Major Component in God's Plan for the New Believer

> That which we have seen and heard declare we unto you, that ye also may have fellowship with us: and truly our fellowship is with the Father, and with his Son Jesus Christ. (1 John 1:3)

You must realize that *Koinonia,* or fellowship, plays a key role in the restoration process in every new believer's life. For individuals who were once in bondage to alcohol and other drugs, fellowship is extremely important because of their past lifestyle. They need high levels of accountability and support.

- ☐ *Koinonia,* or fellowship, is a partnership between God and believers in a common participation of a love experience requiring obedience. This process is extended into the human realm from one believer to another through a relational learning process known as mentoring/discipleship.

  > Fellowship with other Christians is not optional, but essential to successful Christian living. One cannot be out of fellowship with other believers and experience fellowship with God. In the mind and teaching of Jesus, a church is a vital, living dynamic fellowship of believers.
  >
  > —Transition of Prisoners, Inc.

- ☐ Friendships and associations were centered on drug/alcohol use prior to their conversion. Without Christian fellowship to develop new friends within the Body of Christ, new converts will eventually return to interacting with old friends and associates, and this most likely will lead them back to a lifestyle of crime and/or relapsing (returning to the works of the flesh.)
- ☐ The responsibility of providing acceptance through genuine Christian fellowship rests on the Body of Christ (local church). Spiritual union through Christian fellowship is a necessity for those who have been entangled in the snares of crime and drug addiction to make a successful transition into the Body of Christ.
- ☐ Spiritual power is gained through fellowship with other Christians. This power is needed to overcome the desires to return to hanging out with old friends and associates of a former lifestyle of crime.

In an essay, "Strong Mentoring Relationships," in the *Seven Promises of a Promise Keeper*, Glen Wagner clearly states, "In strong mentoring relationships, we obey what God commands us to do within the Body of Christ. All issues of spiritual growth and maturity are framed in the context of relationships." This concept is clearly expressed in the many "one another" passages of the New Testament.

Obey the "One Another" Commands

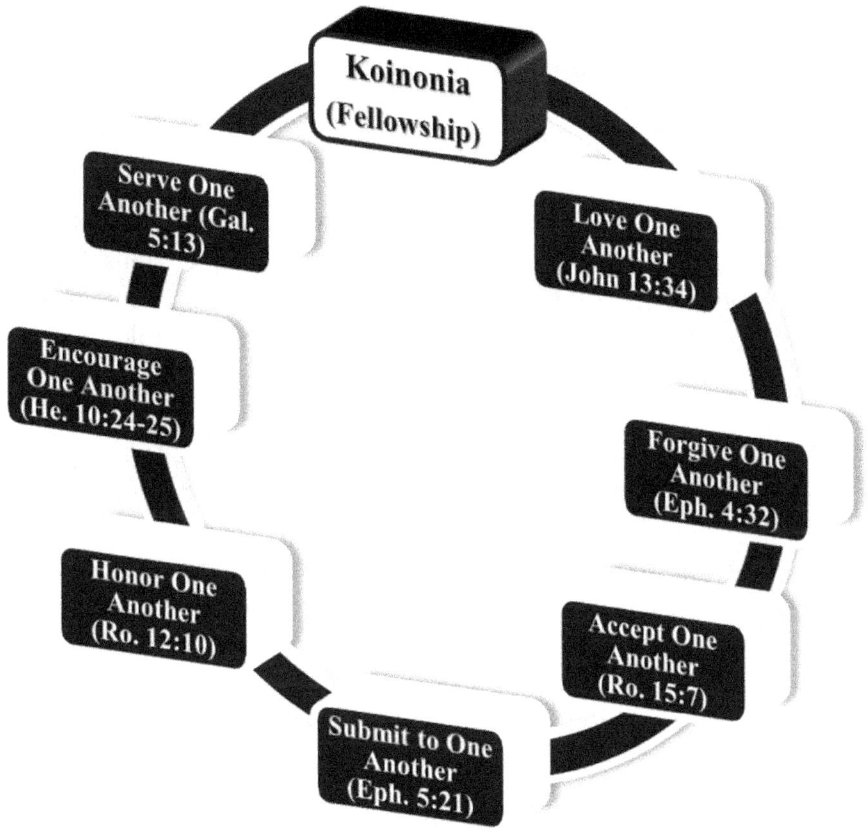

Figure 36: One Another Commands

> *As we have therefore opportunity, let us do good unto all men, especially unto them who are of the household of faith.* (Galatians 6:10)

- ☐ The term *opportunity* literally refers to a fixed and distinct period of time. The phrase *"as we have"* or *"while we have"* does not refer to occasional opportunities that may arise in a believer's life; it refers to the total opportunity of his present earthly existence. The meaning of thought is, "As we have opportunity during our life on earth, let us do good…"
- ☐ A believer's entire life is his/her *unique but limited opportunity* to serve others in the Lord's name. The idea is also implied of seeking for and even making particular opportunities within the broader opportunity of our time on earth *(being intentional)*. "Let us do" *means to be active*—to work effectively and diligently, a call to great effort in taking opportunity to sow into the lives of others through mentoring/discipleship for God's glory.
- ☐ Paul is speaking of a particular *good;* it is the goodness of moral and spiritual excellence—a fruit of the Spirit. It is not simply a goodness that is limited to physical and temporal things.

It is the internal goodness produced by the Spirit in the hearts of obedient believers, which then finds its expression in external goodness expressed in the relational learning process of mentoring/discipleship.

- ☐ Loving concern within a relationship will do more to win a nonbeliever to Christ than the most carefully articulated argument. Sowing into the lives of believers through a mentoring/discipleship is a priority for Christians as Paul emphasizes, *"especially unto them who are of the household of faith."*
- ☐ As important as doing good to unbelievers is, it is especially to be demonstrated to those who are of the household of faith. *The first test of our love for God is our love for His other children, our brothers and sisters in Christ.*

Fellowship means to have something in common with someone else, a community of interest; it also means companionship, to participate in, or to cultivate a loving relationship.

Learning to fellowship on a regular basis with other Christians and avoiding fellowship with former unsaved friends/associates from your past lifestyle plays a key role in preventing you from relapsing.

- ☐ Learning to establish and maintain new relationships is going to be a major task due to the many years you have spent in negative relationships within the world, centered on an addictive lifestyle.
- ☐ You must be willing to put forth the effort necessary to enter into new relationships within the Body of Christ (local church), and God will provide you with the necessary grace to do so.

> Consequently, you are no longer foreigners and aliens, *but fellow citizens with God's people and members of God's household,* built on the foundation of the apostles and prophets, with Christ Jesus himself as the chief cornerstone. In him the whole building is joined together and rises to become a holy temple in the Lord. *And in him you too are being built together to become a dwelling in which God lives by his Spirit.* ((Ephesians 2:19–22, NIV)
>
> Just as each of us has one body with many members, and these members do not all have the same function, so in Christ we who are many form one body, *and each member belongs to all the others. We have different gifts, according to the grace given us.* If a man's gift is prophesying, let him use it in proportion to his faith. If it is serving, let him serve; if it is teaching, let him teach; if it is encouraging, let him encourage; if it is contributing to the needs of others, let him give generously; if it is leadership, let him govern diligently; if it is showing mercy, let him do it cheerfully. (Romans 12:4–8, NIV)
>
> We proclaim to you what we have seen and heard, so that you also may have fellowship with us. And our fellowship is with the Father and with his Son, Jesus Christ. (1 John 1:3, NIV)

- ☐ You must accept that God's greatest desire for you is to have continual fellowship with Him, through Jesus Christ. He wishes that you develop the same desire for Him.

> If we claim to have fellowship with him yet walk in the darkness, we lie and do not live by the truth. But if we walk in the light, as he is in the light, we have fellowship with one another, and the blood of Jesus, his Son, purifies us from all sin. (1 John 1:6–7, NIV)

- ☐ If you return to hanging out with your former ungodly friends and associates and become involved in worldly activities and think you still are in fellowship with God, you are deceiving yourself.
- ☐ True fellowship is accomplished through interacting with others, and it allows Christians to grow in Christ together.

> And let us consider how we may *spur one another on toward love and good deeds. Let us not give up meeting together, as some are in the habit of doing, but let us encourage one another*—and all the more as you see the Day approaching. (Hebrews 10:24–25, NIV)

- ☐ True Christian fellowship is a necessity, because it provides opportunities for you to encourage others who are walking with the Lord. It will allow you to interact with mature brothers/sisters in the Lord who can share their experiences in the Lord.
- ☐ When you make yourself available for fellowship, God can bring individuals into your life that have been restored from bondage to alcohol and other drugs to share valuable insight in preventing you from relapsing.

> Then they that gladly received his word were baptized: and the same day there were added *unto them* about three thousand souls. And they continued steadfastly in the apostles' doctrine and fellowship, and in breaking of bread, and in prayers. (Acts 2:41–42)

- ☐ Paul expresses the need for new converts in the early church to stay in close fellowship with other Christians within the Body of Christ (the local church).

> For as the body is one, and hath many members, and all the members of that one body, being many, are one body: so also *is* Christ. For by one Spirit are we all baptized into one body, whether *we be* Jews or Gentiles, whether *we be* bond or free; and have been all made to drink into one Spirit. For the body is not one member, but many. (1 Corinthians 12:12–14)

- ☐ Every Christian is a member of the Body of Christ and God requires us to be joined together through fellowship for His common purpose for our lives.

The Body of Christ (Church): The Major Support System for Believers in Restoration from Addiction?

Many churches view addiction as a *social problem* instead of a spiritual issue. This causes a major problem within the Body of Christ when it comes to addressing drug/alcohol addiction. Because of this *faulty view* of addiction, many churches have *adopted and adapted* to the World's Recovery System, which is a limited approach designed to address the *bio/psycho/social* aspects of addiction without addressing the root of the problem, which is spiritual. This system is designed to assist unbelievers in *managing sin* through *behavior modification* and *arresting addiction.*

As a result, most churches are *not thoroughly equipped* to minister to individuals entering the church from a lifestyle of *drug/alco*hol addictions. Also, due to the faulty perception that most churches have, many haven't taken time to develop biblically based curriculums for addressing the practical aspect of addiction and the effects (trigger, cravings, and set-up behavior).

Due to the ineffectiveness within the Body of Christ to address the issue of drugs/alcohol addiction, God has raised up many *para-church organizations* to assist believers in their restoration from addiction. These ministries, which God has blessed with *biblical insight in the field of addiction/relapse prevention,* have an obligation as members within the Body of Christ to equip local churches to better serve the addicted population; but on a whole, they *have failed to do so.*

Many believers being restored from drug/alcohol addiction are better equipped for transitioning into recovery groups within the Worlds Recovery System than they are to enter into the Body of Christ, local churches where they really belong.

Because of not understanding the addicted population, many churches have been taken advantage of and are *not receptive* to individuals coming from a lifestyle of addiction. Likewise, churches are *no*t viewed by the recovery population as a *primary support system* when transitioning from a lifestyle of crime/addiction.

Not understanding and having faith in their identity in Christ causes one of the greatest challenges to believers in restoration from addiction; it is *learning to "fit in" and feel accepted into a local church.* There is no room for "lone rangers" operating outside the Body of Christ. Jesus is the Head and the Church is the Body of Christ; thus, every believer is a vital part of that membership.

How intentional they are about entering into the relational learning process (mentoring) will play a significant role in them overcoming the feeling of not being accepted in a local church.

Benefits of Fellowship

Why You Need to Be in Constant Fellowship with Other Christians

> Iron sharpeneth iron; so a man sharpeneth the countenance (character) of his friend. (Proverbs 27:17)

- ☐ God uses relationships to strengthen members within the Body of Christ (local church).
- ☐ Every Christian needs a mature brother/sister in Christ pouring into their life so that they can grow and reach their full potential in Christ.
- ☐ Relationships have a duo purpose in God's plan for your life; they provide opportunities for spiritual growth and maturity in your personal life. They provide opportunities for you to assist others in furthering their spiritual growth and development.

> Confess your faults one to another, and pray one for another, that ye may be healed. The effectual fervent prayer of a righteous man availeth much. (James 5:16)
>
> Two are better than one, because they have a good return for their work: *If one falls down, his friend can help him up.* But pity the man who falls and has no one to

> help him up! Though one may be overpowered, two can defend themselves. *A cord of three strands is not quickly broken.* (Ecclesiastes 4:9–12, NIV)
>
> Again, I say unto you, "That if two of you shall agree on earth as touching anything that they shall ask, it shall be done for them of my Father which is in heaven. *For where two or three are gathered together in my name, there am I in the midst of them.*" (Matthew 18:19–20)

Jesus clearly states how He honors fellowship with His presence and that fellowship also allows Christians the opportunity to have prayers answered through agreement with each other.

> A Song of degrees of David. Behold, how good and how pleasant *it is* for brethren to dwell together in unity! (Psalm 133:1)

- ☐ God uses fellowship between Christian brothers/sisters as an opportunity to develop unity within the Body of Christ.

BENEFITS OF FELLOWSHIP EXERCISE

1. How can you benefit from developing relationships with other Christians and becoming open about your life?
2. How important is it for you to pray for other Christians and for them to pray for you?
3. What are three benefits you can gain from developing new friends within the church?
4. How does Jesus honor those Christians who come together in His name and pray in agreement with one another through fellowship?
5. What scripture in this section has had the greatest impact in your life? Explain.

Fellowship with God and Other Christians

Self-Check

Jesus said unto him, "*Thou shalt love the Lord thy God with all thy heart, and with all thy soul, and with all thy mind.* This is the first and great commandment. And the second *is* like unto it, "*Thou shalt love thy neighbor as thyself.*" (Matthew 22:37–39)

Check [√] the box that answers the questions listed below.

1. Have you made a commitment to become a member of a local church?
   [ ] yes [ ] no
2. Do you attend a weekly worship service?
   [ ] yes [ ] no
3. Do you attend a weekly Bible study class?
   [ ] yes [ ] no
4. Are you attending a Biblically based relapse prevention class?
   [ ] yes [ ] no
5. Do you have a Christian mentor (sponsor)?
   [ ] yes [ ] no
6. Since being saved, have you developed new Christian friends?
   [ ] yes [ ] no
7. Do you have a daily devotion time (prayer, studying the Word, etc.)?
   [ ] yes [ ] no
8. Since being saved, has your time alone with God increased?
   [ ] yes [ ] no
9. Since becoming saved, has your understanding of God increased?
   [ ] yes [ ] no
10. Has your faith (trust) in God increased since you were saved?
   [ ] yes [ ] no

If your answer to three or more of these was "no," you need to examine if you have been serious about your relationship with God and other Christians (fulfilling God's plan for your life).

Self-Rating

How do you rate your fellowship with other Christians? Discuss your answer within your group.

Action Steps

List three things you are willing to do to increase your fellowship with other Christians?

1.
2.
3.

The Discipline of Fasting

Fasting literally means to abstain or go without food for spiritual purposes. People can also fast for physical benefits, such as for health reasons. To fast means to do without something or to practice self-denial. Fasting, in the general sense, does not necessarily mean food and drink only, but from anything that hinders our relationship with God. A good example of this is a fast from television, sports, or some other hobby that has become a hindrance to a believer's fellowship with God.

> Where for forty days he was tempted by the devil. He ate nothing during those days, and at the end of them he was hungry. The devil said to him, "If you are the Son of God, tell this stone to become bread." (Luke 4:2–3, NIV)
>
> In scripture the normal means of fasting involves abstaining from all food, solid or liquid, but not from water. In the forty day fast of Jesus, we are told that 'he ate nothing' and that toward the end of the fast 'he was hungry' and Satan tempted him to eat, indicating that the abstaining was from food but not from water. From a physical standpoint, this is what is usually involved in a fast.
>
> —Richard J. Foster

Types of Fast

> After fasting forty days and forty nights, he was hungry. (Matthew 4:2, NIV)

I. *Normal:* going without all foods both liquid and solid, but not water.

> I ate no choice food; no meat or wine touched my lips; and I used no lotions at all until the three weeks were over. (Daniel 10:3, NIV)

II. *Partial:* choosing to restrict your diet to certain foods or liquids.

> For three days he was blind, and did not eat or drink anything. (Acts 9:9, NIV)

III. *Absolute:* choosing to abstain from all food and drink including water.

Caution: The absolute fast should never be engaged in unless God clearly instructs one to do so, and then it should not last longer than three days.

What Did Jesus Say About Fasting?

> *So when you give to the needy*, do not announce it with trumpets, as the hypocrites do in the synagogues and on the streets, to be honored by men. I tell you the truth, they have received their reward in full. (Matthew 6:2, NIV)
>
> *And when you pray*, do not be like the hypocrites, for they love to pray standing in the synagogues and on the street corners to be seen by men. I tell you the truth, they have received their reward in full. (Matthew 6:5, NIV)
>
> *When you fast*, do not look somber as the hypocrites do, for they disfigure their faces to show men they are fasting. I tell you the truth, they have received their reward in full. *But when you fast, put oil on your head and wash your face, so that it will not be obvious to men that you are fasting*, but only to your Father, who is unseen; and your Father, who sees what is done in secret, will reward you. (Matthew 6:16–18, NIV)
>
> Although many passages of scripture deal with this subject, two stand out in importance. The first is Jesus's startling teaching about fasting in the Sermon on the Mount. Two factors bear directly on the issue at hand. His teaching on fasting is directly in the context of his teaching on giving and praying. It is as if there is an almost unconscious assumption that giving, prayer, and fasting are all part of Christian devotion.
>
> —Richard J. Foster

Therefore, fasting is an important discipline in developing and maintaining your Christian lifestyle. Jesus does not say if you fast, but "when you fast." Jesus is assuming that you will fast just as you are to pray and to give to the needy.

> Then John's disciples came and asked him, "How is it that we and the Pharisees fast, but your disciples do not fast?" Jesus answered, "How can the guests of the bridegroom mourn while he is with them? The time will come when the bridegroom will be taken from them; then they will fast." (Matthew 9:14–15, NIV)

WHAT IS THE PURPOSE FOR FASTING? THE GUIDEPOST LIST

The Following Benefits of Fasting

Many of us think of fasting as a spiritual duty to God, depriving ourselves of food and drink for a period of time in order to prove our love for Him. While longsuffering is a part of being human and certainly a part of being Christian, fasting should not be included when we think about "suffering for Christ."

On the contrary, fasting is less about what we're giving up and much more about what we're making room for. When we fast, we exchange what we need to survive for what we need to live—more of God. Here are five spiritual benefits to fasting:

1. *A soul cleansing.* How often we forget that our bodies are the temple of the Lord, especially when deciding what to eat! Fasting is a great time to remember the spiritual connection we have to our physical bodies. Without the toxins we put in our bodies, we not only give our bodies a break from the digestive process, but we also allow our spirits to be detoxed. Fasting is a faith-move, an expectation we have that God will fill us with His Holy Spirit, just as He promised. But as Christ told His disciples, "No one pours new wine into old wineskins. Otherwise, the wine will burst the skins, and both the wine and the wineskins will be ruined. No, they pour new wine into new wineskins." By fasting, we meditate and it cleanses the soul and makes it new so we can receive the Holy Spirit and become empowered to live for Christ in a new way.
2. *A new desire for God.* When we acknowledge through fasting that we need God to *live* and to live more abundantly, we can begin to desire God in a new way. When we realize we need God more than we need food, we can start to understand what the Psalmist meant when he wrote, "Like the deer that pants after water, my soul longs for You." God, the sustainer of all life, wants nothing more than a closer connection with us, and through fasting, we can quench that new desire for more of Him in our lives.
3. *A deeper praise.* Because the body does not have to do the work of digestion, it has more energy to focus on other things. In the same vein, since we are not consumed by what we are going to eat next and when we have more energy to devote to God. While we're experiencing a new desire for Him through fasting, we should also emit a deeper praise as we think about everything God is to us and all He has done. Once we get caught up in our desire for God and our praise for His mighty acts, we won't have time to be hungry or count down the hours until our fast is over. We'll be celebrating the whole time!
4. *A sensitivity to God's voice.* The New Testament prophetess, Anna, is praised in the book of Luke for being a devoted servant to God and His temple. Because she regularly fasted and prayed, she was able to hear the voice of God speak clearly to her the day that Baby Jesus was brought into her

temple to be dedicated. She knew He was the Christ and told everyone who would listen about His arrival. When we detox the spirit and become consumed with desire and praise for God, we become sensitive to His voice. Like Anna, when God speaks to us in the midst of chaos, we'll still be able to pick out His voice and know what He wants us to do, because we have trained our ear to hear Him through fasting, prayer, study, and praise.

5. *A new satisfaction.* When you finish your fast, renewed, full of energy, detoxed, with a new desire, a new praise, and a sensitivity to God's voice, you'll find that the absence of food was small in comparison to what you gained. When Christ's disciples noticed that He hadn't eaten all day and tried to get Him to slow down to eat, Christ said, "I have food to eat that you know nothing about…my food is to do the will of Him who sent me and to finish His work."

> Ask all the people of the land and the priests, "When you fasted and mourned in the fifth and seventh months for the past seventy years, was it really for me that you fasted?" (Zechariah 7:5, NIV)
>
> While they were worshiping the Lord and fasting, the Holy Spirit said, "Set apart for me Barnabas and Saul for the work to which I have called them." (Acts 13:2)
>
> When I humbled my soul with fasting. (Psalm 69:10, NRSV)
>
> So we fasted and petitioned our God for this, and he listened to our entreaty. (Ezra 8:23, NRSV)

God's Word clearly states that every individual enters into a spiritual crisis the moment they accept Jesus as Lord and savior. The spirit being is awakened and desires to follow God; the "works of the flesh" still remain, and the flesh desires to continue fulfilling its ungodly desires and appetites.

Fasting allows a believer to bring those natural desire (sex, sweets, television) and "works of the flesh" under control; and in doing so, automatically they allow the spirit-man to be fed, making God's directions and will clear. Fasting is valuable in addressing emotional strongholds such as anger, loneliness, self-pity, etc.

Dr. Don Colbert, MD, in his text, *TOXIC Relief,* makes the following statement regarding fasting, "This process of crucifying the flesh must be accomplished daily through prayer, renewing the mind by regularly reading the Word of God, and by watching every word that comes out of our mouths. All of these things are hammers, pickaxes, drills, and machinery that operate at the rock quarry of your hardened flesh. In this effort, fasting is the dynamite that makes all of the other efforts easier and more effective."

PRACTICING THE SPIRITUAL DISCIPLINES EXERCISE

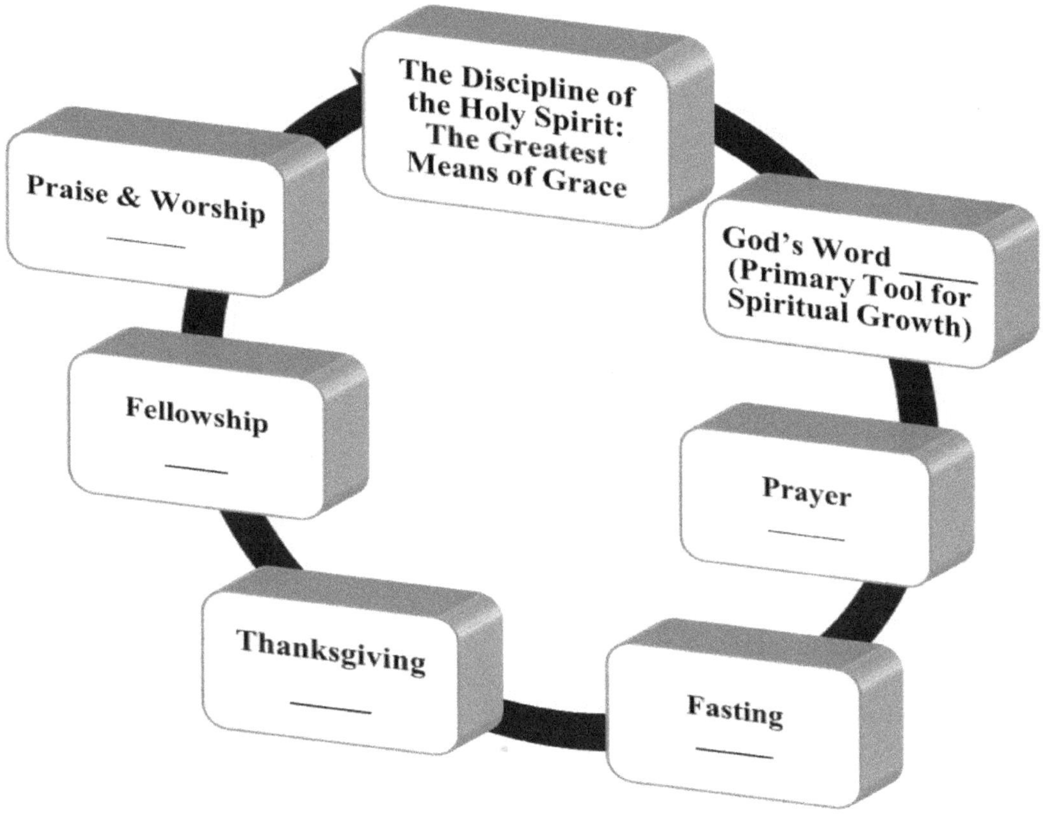

Figure 37: Six Basic Spiritual Disciples

Review the above diagram, Practicing the Spiritual Disciplines, and rank the spiritual disciplines according to how much time you spend practicing them.

1. Place *1* in the slot of the spiritual discipline where you spend the *greatest amount* of time.
2. Place *6* in the slot of the spiritual discipline where you spend the *least amount* of time.
3. Continue ranking the spiritual disciplines according to the amount of time you spend, practicing them until each discipline has a number in the slot provided.
4. Discuss with your group members how you can *increase* the time you spend in certain spiritual disciplines so you can have a more balanced approach.

Prayer for Increasing Fellowship with God

Dear heavenly Father, help me to understand and experience Your great love for me so I can express that love to You and others. Help me to understand and be willing to increase my faith in You and to become more obedient to You. I thank You for placing Your Spirit in me so that I can have continual fellowship with You. Help me to understand that the key to me avoiding my old lifestyle is in staying in fellowship with You.

In Jesus name I pray. Amen!

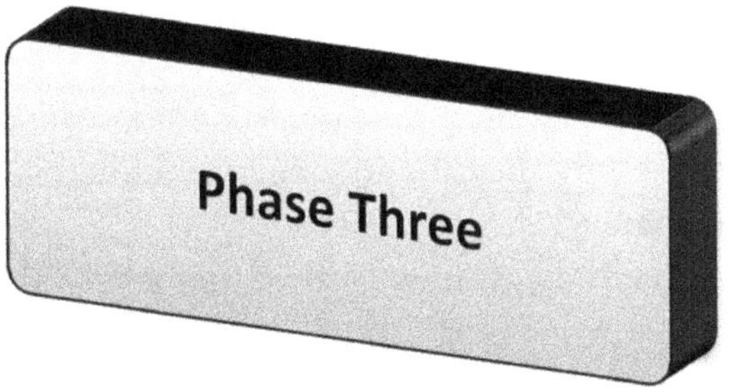

THE SECOND SIGNIFICANT FACTOR IN RELAPSE PREVENTION

Understanding and Having Faith in Your Identity in Christ

Therefore, if anyone is in Christ, he is a new creation; the old has gone, the new has come!

—2 Corinthians 5:17, NIV

Learning Objectives

For the workshop participant to be able to:

- Identify the six benefits of being in a right relational standing with God (justified).
  - ☐ Describe in biblical terms why they are no longer an addict/alcoholic.
- Recognize how/when God changed their identity.
  - ☐ Identify the scriptures that indicate how God views them in their new identity.
  - ☐ Describe what they receive from God during adoption (inheritance).

Key Biblical Concepts and Definitions

(1) *Right Relational Standing (Justification):* is a legal term meaning your guilt has been removed. God's acquittal of your charges for sin and to make you righteous.

(2) *Repentance:* is to have a *change of mind/attitude* in how you view God and to make a conscious decision to turn away from your old lifestyle of sin and turn to Jesus; then *God changes your heart.*

(3) *Position of Holiness*: is to be *made holy, separated unto the Lord and for His service*; it is an activity of the Holy Spirit, setting you apart for God for salvation and also enabling you to be holy (dedicated to the Lord) as God is holy.

(4) *Adoption*: After becoming a born-again child of God through the agencies of the Holy Spirit and the Word of God (John 3:5,8 and 1 Peter 1:23), you are placed into a position as a mature son/daughter through these two agencies and given *full privileges and rights of inheritance* (study Galatians 4:1–7 and Romans 8:14–17).

(5) *Rebirth (Regeneration)*: is to be "born again," receiving a *new nature* and a new life in God, being placed in the "Body of Christ."

(6) *Inner Man*: Through man's *spirit,* his new nature created in God's image and likeness, located in man's heart, where the Holy Spirit resides, is how man interact with God (Genesis 1:27; 1 Corinthians 6:19,20; Ephesians 2:22; Hebrews 9:14).

(7) *Outer Man*: Man's *soul* which consists of his mental, (mind), volitional (will), and emotional (emotions) capacity to interact with others (Gen. 2:7).

SPIRITUAL (CHANGE) TRANSFORMATION HOW GOD GAVE YOU A NEW IDENTITY

Repentance: The Prerequisite for Divine Change

Repentance means to have a *change of mind/attitude* in how one views God and to make a conscious decision to turn away from their old lifestyle of sin and turn to Jesus, then *God changes their heart.*

God, the Holy Spirit, enabled you to believe through the gift of repentance by allowing you to see yourself as you really are—a sinner—and to see Jesus in His full glory through hearing the Gospel. Then He required that you act on what He had enabled you to understand.

> Saving faith is God's gift to the repentant sinner that he/she might be saved. It is looking to Christ fully for salvation. This aspect of faith is a passive faith. Here the person trusts Christ and His Word for salvation.
>
> —Kevin J. Conner

Repentance: A Gift from God

> Repentance is not something which one can originate within himself, or pump up within himself as one would pump water out of a well. *It is a divine gift.* How then is a man responsible for not having it? We are called upon to repent in order that we may feel our own inability to do so, and consequently be thrown upon God and petition Him to perform this work of grace in our hearts.
>
> —William Evans

> *Godly sorrow brings repentance that leads to salvation and leaves no regret, but worldly sorrow brings death.* (2 Corinthians 7:10, NIV)
>
> When they heard these things, they held their peace, and glorified God, saying, *"Then hath God also to the Gentiles granted repentance unto life."* (Acts 11:18)
>
> In meekness instructing those that oppose themselves; *if God peradventure will give them repentance to the acknowledging of the truth.* (2 Timothy 2:25)
>
> *The God of our fathers raised up Jesus, whom ye slew and hanged on a tree.* Him hath God exalted with his right hand *to be* a Prince and a Savior, *for to give repentance to Israel, and forgiveness of sins.* (Acts 5:30–31)

☐ Divine change is initiated by God and begins with repentance.

> *No man can come to me, except the Father which hath sent me draw him*: and I will raise him up at the last day. (John 6:44)
>
> And he said, *"Therefore said I unto you, that no man can come unto me, except it were given unto him of my Father."* (John 6:65)
>
> Now when they heard *this*, they were pricked in their heart, and said unto Peter and to the rest of the apostles, Men *and* brethren, what shall we do? Then Peter said unto them, "*Repent*, and be baptized every one of you in the name of Jesus Christ for the remission of sins, and ye shall receive the gift of the Holy Ghost."
>
> *Then they that gladly received his word* were baptized: and the same day there were added *unto them* about three thousand souls. (Acts 2:37–38,41)

You must acknowledge your lifestyle of sin and recognize you have sinned first and foremost against God. Then you must be willing to turn away from that lifestyle of sin and accept God's sacrifice for sin, Jesus Christ, as your savior. If not, you will never undergo the most significant form of change, *divine change*, being born again. It is the *rebirth* that provides you with the *power* and *potential* for all other forms of significant change.

> I will give you a new heart and put a new spirit in you; I will remove from you your heart of stone and give you a heart of flesh. And I will put my Spirit in you and move you to follow my decrees and be careful to keep my laws. (Ezekiel 36:26–27, NIV)

What Means Does God Use to Bring about Repentance?

> *Because our gospel came to you not simply with words, but also with power, with the Holy Spirit and with deep conviction.* You know how we lived among you for your sake. You became imitators of us and of the Lord; in spite of severe suffering, you welcomed the message with the joy given by the Holy Spirit. And so you became a model to all the believers in Macedonia and Achaia. (1 Thessalonians 1:5–7)
>
> *I am not ashamed of the gospel, because it is the power of God for the salvation of everyone who believes:* first for the Jew, then for the Gentile. (Romans 1:16, NIV)

Repentance by Way of the Gospel

What is the gospel? The gospel literally means "good news." So what is the "good news?" The good news is that Christ came down from heaven in the form of man, walked this earth, was crucified, died, and was buried, and on the third day, God, the Father raised Jesus from the grave and seated Him in heaven at His right hand. The death He died on Calvary was for all the sins of mankind, and He took our place, and the shedding of His blood (Jesus) washes away our sins. When we believe and confess this, the Bible tells that we are saved.

> For God so loved the world that he gave his one and only Son, that whoever believes in him shall not perish but have eternal life. *For God did not send his Son into the world to condemn the world, but to save the world through him.* Whoever believes in him is not condemned, but whoever does not believe stands condemned

already because he has not believed in the name of God's one and only Son. (John 3:16–18, NIV)

- ☐ The Gospel is the only message that God uses to lead an individual into salvation.
- ☐ Not only does the Gospel call for you to repent, but it also causes you to turn to Jesus.

But if our gospel be hid, it is hid to them that are lost: *In whom the god of this world hath blinded the minds of them which believe not,* lest the light of the glorious gospel of Christ, who is the image of God, should shine unto them. (2 Corinthians 3:3–4)

What Takes Place During Repentance?

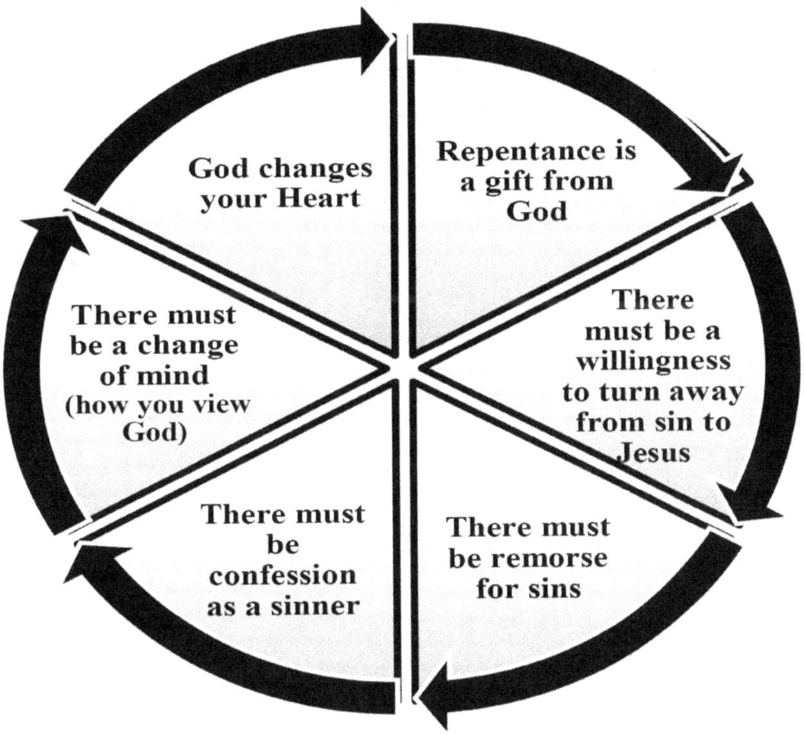

Figure 38: True Repentance

Exercise: Testimony
Repentance Leading to Salvation or Rededication

If you haven't repented and invited Jesus into your life, are you ready now?

If you are a born-again believer, take a few minutes to write down a few notes to guide you through your testimony. Be honest and sincere in your testimony and include the following information and be specific.

- ☐ What events led you to repent (change your mind about your past lifestyle)?
- ☐ If you had already accepted Jesus as Lord before, what led you away from Him?
- ☐ What brought you back to Him?
- ☐ What was going on with you emotionally? Share with group what happened.
- ☐ Where had your addiction led you?
- ☐ What type of criminal behavior were you involved in?
- ☐ How had your lifestyle affected your family, health, and finances?
- ☐ Where were you when God came to get you?
- ☐ When and where did you make your confession of faith in Jesus Christ?

POSITIONAL CHANGE

Sanctification means to be made holy, separated unto the Lord and for His service. It is an activity of the Holy Spirit setting you apart for God, for salvation, and also enabling you to be holy, dedicated to the Lord, as God is holy.

God has spiritually changed you and this is the *first phase* of change in your life. Now you must advance in your Christian walk with Christ through the grace provided by the Holy Spirit. Holiness in your *conduct,* and *character* will be a result of your cooperation with the Holy Spirit. Your *role was passive* with regard to your *positional holiness*; however, you are required by God to play *an active role in progressive holiness.*

Positional Holiness: God's Method of Change

PAST ASPECT OF HOLINESS	PRESENT ASPECT OF HOLINESS	FUTURE ASPECT OF HOLINESS
POSITIONAL. (1Cor 1:2,30) *All* believers have been set aside and made holy for God's service as saints, regardless of age, or spiritual growth.	PROGRESSIVE. Depends upon our knowledge of and faith in our position in Christ (Rom. 6:1-11), changing position into experience.	Final. When you see the Lord and are made like Him-sinless, without illness, deathless (1 Cor. 4;15:54; 1Jn. 3:2
Your position is final, unchangeable, inseparable from your right relational standing, and the result solely of our union with Christ.	Progressive, changeable, depends upon submitting to God's will (Rom. 6:13) and conforming to God's Word (Rom. 12:2).	Eternal. Will result in your final state in eternity (Phil 3:21).
As God sees you in Christ (1 Cor. 1:2, 30, with Phil. 1:1, etc).	As you are in your conduct (2 Thess. 2:13).	As you shall be in glory (Rom. 8:29, 1 Cor. 15:49).

—Unger's Bible Book (modified)

Figure 39: Positional Holiness

The very moment you accepted Christ as savior, you were sanctified. This means you have been separated from sin and set aside for God's purpose and service by salvation. Your being delivered from evil for God's service can be viewed in three different time frames—the past, present, and future.

Because you have been separated from sin and set apart for God, you are now a saint. Every Christian is a saint because God begins processing them through sanctification at the moment of salvation. Your act of faith in Jesus Christ places you into a right relationship with God, and that relationship admitted you immediately into the process of holiness.

- ☐ Now that you are being sanctified by the Holy Spirit and the Word of God (2 Thessalonians 2:13; (John 17:17; Ephesians 5:23–25; 1 Thessalonians 5:23), you are expected by God to grow up and reach your full potential in Christ.
- ☐ You must learn to view your position in Christ as God views it, fixed and unchangeable.

> *And the very God of peace sanctify you wholly;* and *I pray God* your whole spirit and soul and body be preserved blameless unto the coming of our Lord Jesus Christ. Faithful *is* he that calleth you, who also will do *it.* (1 Thessalonians 5:23–24)
>
> But we ought always to thank God for you, brothers loved by the Lord, *because from the beginning God chose you to be saved through the sanctifying work of the Spirit and through belief in the truth. He called you to this through our gospel,* that you might share in the glory of our Lord Jesus Christ. (2 Thessalonians 2:13–14, NIV)
>
> Who have been chosen according to the foreknowledge of God the Father, *through the sanctifying work of the Spirit,* for obedience to Jesus Christ and sprinkling by his blood: Grace and peace be yours in abundance. (1 Peter 1:2, NIV)

No believer, including yourself, could ever become holy by their own effort; however, you can yield to God, and holiness will be accomplished through His grace. God Himself did a work in you, and as a result, you have received a position of holiness.

How Were You Made Holy?

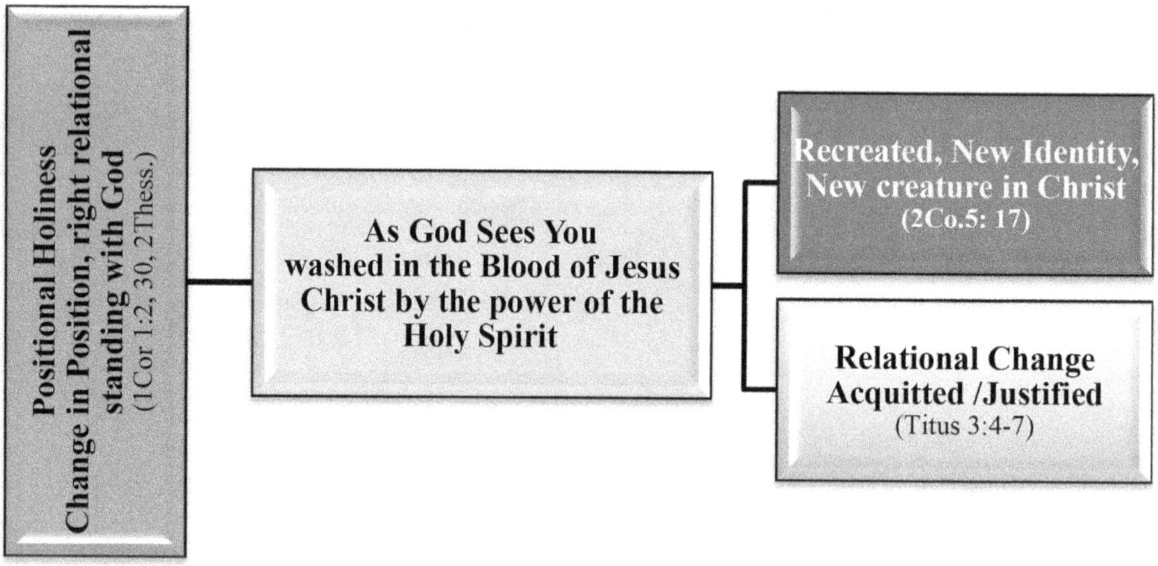

Figure 40: How Were You Made Holy?

The Blood of Jesus Christ

And so Jesus also suffered outside the city gate to make the people holy through his own blood. (Hebrews 13:12, NIV)

And by that will, we have been made holy through the sacrifice of the body of Jesus Christ once for all. (Hebrews 10:10, NIV)

Both the one who makes men holy and those who are made holy are of the same family. So Jesus is not ashamed to call them brothers. (Hebrews 2:11, NIV)

But if we walk in the light, as he is in the light, we have fellowship one with another, and the blood of Jesus Christ his Son cleanseth us from all sin. (1 John 1:7)

By the Holy Spirit

To be a minister of Christ Jesus to the Gentiles with the priestly duty of proclaiming the gospel of God, so that the Gentiles might become an offering acceptable to God, *sanctified by the Holy Spirit.* (Romans 15:16, NIV)

He saved us, not because of righteous things we had done, but because of his mercy. *He saved us through the washing of rebirth and renewal by the Holy Spirit.* (Titus 3:5, NIV)

Who have been chosen according to the foreknowledge of God the Father, through the sanctifying work of the Spirit, for obedience to Jesus Christ and sprinkling by his blood: Grace and peace be yours in abundance. (1 Peter 1:2, NIV)

For in him dwelleth all the fulness of the Godhead bodily. *And ye are complete in him,* which is the head of all principality and power. (Colossians 2:9–10)

- ☐ Your identity in Christ is the foundation on which your Christian walk is based. You must understand that you are complete in Christ but underdeveloped.
- ☐ You must understand that at one time, you were darkened in your understanding and separated from the life of God because of your ignorance due to the hardening of your heart (Ephesians 4:18).
- ☐ God changed your heart at the moment of conversion, and you must be willing to offer your body as a living sacrifice, holy and pleasing to God, not conforming any longer to the patterns of this world.
- ☐ This means not submitting your body to a sinful lifestyle. You must become committed to being changed by the renewing of your mind (Romans 12:1, 2) by submitting yourself to God's Word through Bible study, church attendance, and a willingness to apply what you learn to your daily life.
- ☐ You must understand that you need not fear the changes taking place in your life. You can't get caught up in your past, how you used to be, or what your old friends say and think about you.
- ☐ You must learn to experience your freedom in Christ who has set you free, and you must stand firm and not allow yourself to get caught up again in your old sinful lifestyle (Galatians 5:1). You must learn to please God, not people, so that you will not return to your old lifestyle and habits.

- ☐ Once you understand, believe, and receive by faith your new identity in Christ, you have a solid foundation on which to enter the next phase of change, progressive holiness, the restoring of your soul.

To the church of God in Corinth, *to those sanctified in Christ Jesus and called to be holy,* together with all those everywhere who call on the name of our Lord Jesus Christ—their Lord and ours. (1 Corinthians 1:2, NIV)

And such were some of you: *but ye are washed, but ye are sanctified, but ye are justified in the name of the Lord Jesus, and by the Spirit of our God.* (1 Corinthians 6:11)

By the which will *we are sanctified through the offering of the body of Jesus Christ once for all.* (Hebrews 10:10)

Positional Change Exercise

Review the section on Positional Holiness in the diagram above and share with your group members the following information.

1. What have you been set aside for?
2. What can change your position in Christ?
3. What is your relationship with God based on?
4. Position of holiness is based on whose view of you?

What scripture in this section has had the greatest impact in your life? Explain that experience with your group.

UNDERSTANDING HOW GOD PROVIDED YOU A NEW IDENTITY IN CHRIST

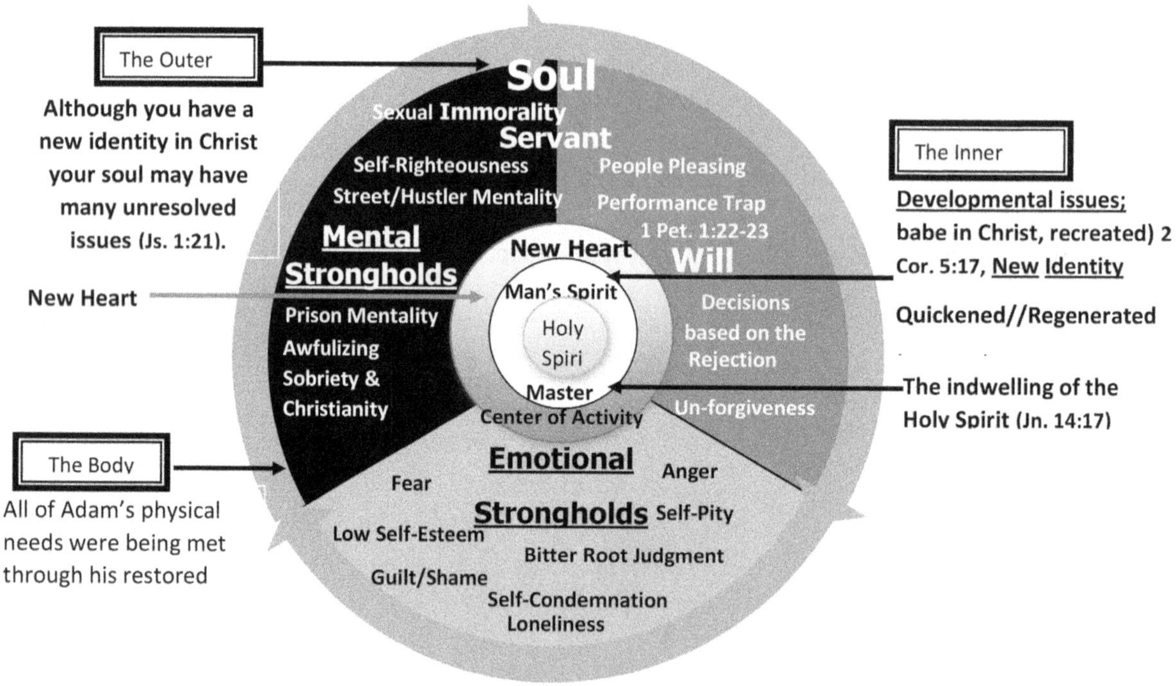

Figure 41: New Identity with unrestored soul

This diagram represents the condition of an individual's soul (outer man) and spirit (inner man-new identity) who was in bondage to drug/alcohol addiction.

You have been regenerated (born again), not from a mortal *(corruptible seed)* origin (seed, sperm), but from one that is immortal *(incorruptible seed)* by the ever-living and lasting Word of God.

Salvation is the only way that *spiritual order can be restored*; and with salvation, God has provided you with a new identity in Christ, which provides you entrance into a relationship with Him. *Through your new identity, God has provided the solution to the origin of all your problems including your addiction* (1 Peter 1:23).

There are several important biblical truths you must understand in order to have faith in your new identity:

1. That you have been born again from *God's seed*, providing you *with His nature* and *a new heart* (spiritual transformation of the inner man).
2. Your *identity* is determined by *God's seed, not* by what has taken place in the *outer man.*

3. You must remember that *your identity is not based* on *what has happened to you* during your addiction or *what you have done to others,* but rather, it is based *on the miraculous work Christ has done in the inner man.*

If you look into the circular diagram on the previous page, you will see that the outer man has numerous mental and emotional strongholds that were developed during addiction. The outer man does not determine a person's identity.

Most Christians are taught in recovery to identify with what has taken place in the outer man instead of the inner man. They refer to themselves as "addicts, alcoholics, criminals"—identifying with their old behaviors, thereby reinforcing their old identities.

Relational Change: Acceptance by God (Right Relational Standing)

Justification is a legal term meaning your guilt has been removed (acquittal of charges) to make you righteous.

Acceptability

> If I am to become *psychologically* whole and *spiritually mature*, I must understand clearly that my acceptability to God is not based on my behavior but rather on Jesus's behavior (Titus 3:5). He was (and is) perfect. Because He never sinned, He never deserved to die. *But He voluntarily went to the cross. His death was the punishment which my sins deserved. In His love, He provided for an exchange. When I give my sins, He pays for them in order to justly forgive me, then He gives me the gift of His righteousness. God declares me to be righteous on the basis of what Jesus has done for me.* I have been declared just. I am justified. It is a gift which God does not put in me but which He declares is now mine. I cannot lose. *I am accepted as I am because my acceptability has nothing to do with how I am or how I was yesterday or how I will be tomorrow.* It depends on Jesus's perfection alone.
>
> —Dr. Larry Crabb

> *Therefore, being justified by faith*, we have *peace* with God through our Lord Jesus Christ: By whom also we have *access by faith into this grace* wherein we stand, and rejoice in hope of the glory of God. (Romans 5:1–2)
>
> But when the kindness and love of God our savior appeared, he saved us, not because of righteous things we had done, but because of his mercy. He saved us through the washing of rebirth and renewal by the Holy Spirit, whom he poured out on us generously through Jesus Christ our savior, so that, having been justified by his grace, we might become heirs having the hope of eternal life. (Titus 3:4–7, NIV)

In his text, *Effective Biblical Counseling*, Dr. Larry Crabb continues, stating, "The foundation of the entire Christian life then is a proper understanding of justification." As a babe in Christ, you must understand how crucial it is that you have a clear awareness of your acceptability through justification.

- ☐ Your acceptance by God serves as the basis for all future motivation, and your behavior depends on your awareness of God's acceptance of you. God has blessed you with a position of acceptance; now He instructs you to grow up in your position.

- ☐ The Holy Spirit guides you in how to live and enables you to live a godly lifestyle. The motivating factor for your obedience and the basis for your continual psychological and spiritual growth is receiving God's love through His acceptance.
- ☐ Your awareness and willingness to receive God's unconditional acceptance will determine how you view your two basic needs, *significance* and *security*. Only then will you understand that true significance depends on who you are in Christ and that you are secure because you are unconditionally accepted and cared for, both now and forever.

Dr. Larry Crabb states, "God has seen me at my worst and still loved me to the point of giving His life for me. That kind of love I can never lose. I am completely acceptable to Him, regardless of my behavior. I am under no pressure to earn or keep His love. My acceptability to God depends only on Jesus's acceptability to God and on the fact that Jesus's death was counted as full payment for my sins."

God is aware of your past lifestyle and all the events leading up to your acceptance. Nothing you have done in the past is so terrible that He would not accept you. You are accepted based on Jesus's behavior alone. The moment you believe in Him and surrender all to Him, God takes control of your welfare. You can avoid living in the past, questioning if God will forgive those terrible deeds you possibly committed, or striving for self-acceptance by attempting to perform to a certain standard and striving to please others to be accepted.

Accountability

> I beseech you therefore, brethren, by the mercies of God, that *you present your bodies a living sacrifice*, holy, acceptable to God, *which is* your reasonable service. *And do not be conformed to this world*, but *be transformed by the renewing of your mind*, that you may prove what *is* that good and acceptable and perfect will of God. (Romans 12:1–2)

As a child of God, you must understand God's unconditional acceptance of you as His child. Likewise, and equally important, you must understand how God holds His children accountable. To teach acceptability without teaching accountability would be offering you a license to sin. Similarly, to teach accountability without teaching acceptability would lead you into legalism.

God transformed (spiritually changed) you, providing you with a new nature and identity; with that new identity comes the potential to be changed into the "image and likeness" of Christ in conduct and character.

> For those God foreknew he also predestined *to be conformed to the likeness of his Son*, that he might be the firstborn among many brothers. (Romans 8:29, NIV)
>
> Behold, what manner of love the Father hath bestowed upon us, *that we should be called the sons of God*: therefore, the world knoweth us not, because it knew him not. Beloved, now are we the sons of God, and it doth not yet appear what we shall be: but we know that, when he shall appear, *we shall be like him*; for we shall see him as he is. And *every man that hath this hope in him purifieth himself*, even as he is pure. (1 John 3:1–3)
>
> What? Know ye not that your body is the temple of the Holy Ghost *which is* in you, which ye have of God, *and ye are not your own*? *For ye are bought with a*

> *price*: therefore, glorify God in your body, and in your spirit, which are God's. (1 Corinthians 6:19–20)
>
> For he that is called in the Lord, *being* a servant, is the Lord's freeman: *likewise, also he that is called, being free, is Christ's servant. Ye are bought with a price*; be not ye the servants of men. Brethren, let every man, *wherein he is called, therein abide with God.* (1 Corinthians 7:22–24)

The moment you received the "new birth," you were also justified. Not only did God change your nature, but He also changed your relational standing with Him. You once lived under the guilt and condemnation of sin. Justification is God's acquittal and acceptance. God's attitude has changed toward you when you were washed in the blood of Jesus, and your attitude has likewise changed toward God. Being in a right relational standing with God plays a vital role in your future, because both your *conduct* and *character* are *controlled* and *conditioned* by your new relationship.

> For all have sinned and fall short of the glory of God, *and are justified freely by his grace through the redemption that came by Christ Jesus. 25 God presented him as a sacrifice of atonement, through faith in his blood.*

He did this to demonstrate his justice, because in his forbearance he had left the sins committed beforehand unpunished.

> *He did it to demonstrate his justice at the present time, so as to be just and the one who justifies those who have faith in Jesus.* Where, then, is boasting? It is excluded. On what principle? On that of observing the law? No, but on that of faith. For we maintain that a man is justified by faith apart from observing the law. (Romans 3:23–28, NIV)
>
> At the moment of your conversion, you were *justified completely in God's sight.* Your old sinful self was destroyed forever. You were made a partaker of the divine nature, the nature of Christ. You became a new person in Christ and you were declared by God to be a saint. This was a one–time transformation. *There is nothing you can do to improve upon God's activity in transforming you and justifying you.* He intends merely that you believe what He's done and accept your identity as His child.
>
> —Neil T. Anderson

> But God demonstrates his own love for us in this: *While we were still sinners, Christ died for us. Since we have now been justified by his blood,* how much more shall we be saved from God's wrath through him! (Romans 5:8–9, NIV)

Justification is a divine task provided by Christ Jesus's blood that was shed on Calvary. You are justified by faith. The Holy Spirit produced the faith in you by which you have been declared not guilty. As a born-again Christian, you must understand that your Christian experience begins with justification, the act of you being declared acceptable by God.

For if by one man's (Adam) offence (sin) death reigned by one; much more they which receive abundance of grace and of the gift of righteousness shall reign in life by one, Jesus Christ.) Therefore, as by the offence of one *judgment came* upon all men to condemnation; *even so by the righteousness of one the free gift came upon all men unto justification of life.* For as by one man's disobedience many were made sinners, *so by the obedience of one shall many be made righteous.* (Romans 5:17–19)

But the one whom God raised from the dead did not see decay. "Therefore, my brothers, *I want you to know that through Jesus the forgiveness of sins is proclaimed to you. Through him everyone who believes is justified from everything you could not be justified from by the law of Moses."* (Acts 13:37–39, NIV)

Six Results/Benefits of Being Justified by Faith

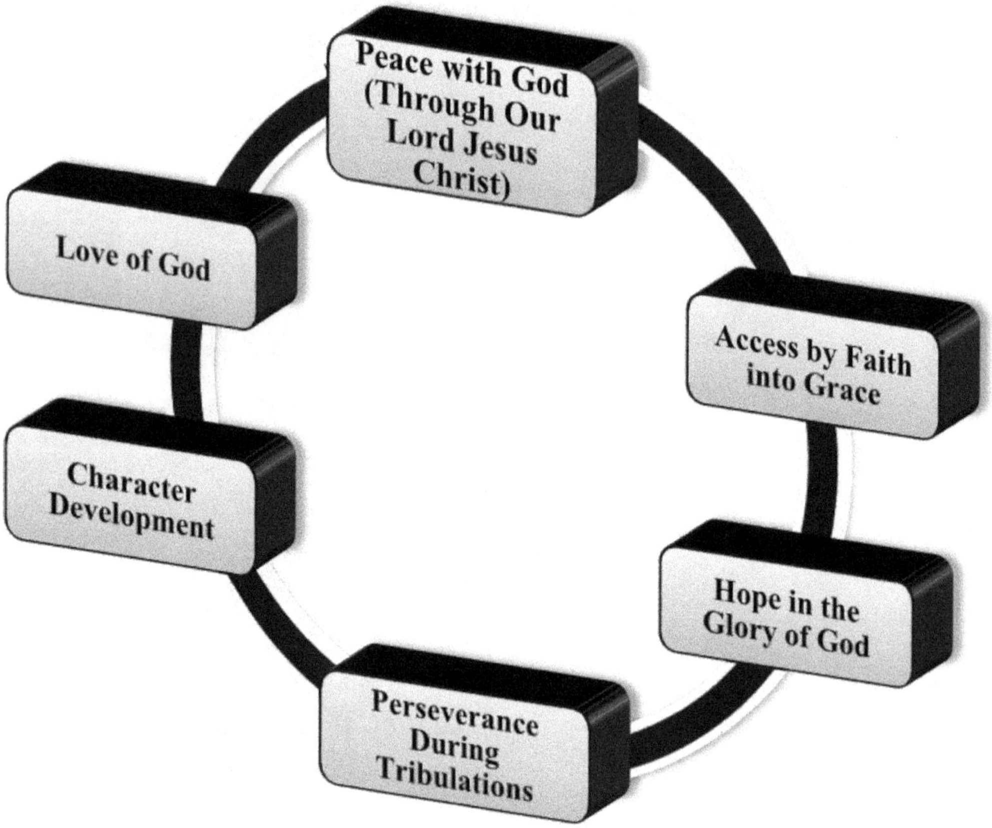

Figure 42: Right Relational Standing with God

a) Peace
b) Access by faith to God
c) Hope in the glory of God
d) Able to withstand tribulations (trials)
e) Character development
f) Hope, love of God by the Holy Spirit

EXPERIENCING THE BENEFITS OF YOUR NEW IDENTITY IN CHRIST

Self-Check

> *Therefore, being justified by faith*, we have *peace* with God through our Lord Jesus Christ: By whom also we have *access by faith into this grace* wherein we stand, and rejoice in hope of the glory of God. And not only *so*, but *we glory in tribulations (sufferings)* also: knowing that *tribulation worketh patience (perseverance);* And patience, *experience (character);* and experience, hope: And hope maketh not ashamed; *because the love of God is shed abroad in our hearts by the Holy Ghost which is given unto us. (*Romans 5:1–5)

*Using a scale from 1 to 10, with **1** being **very high** and **10** being very low, rank the following benefits of being in a relationship with Christ according to how you are experiencing each.*

1. What level of peace are you experiencing in your relationship with God? _____
2. How aware are you that you have access to God's resources by faith? _____
3. What is the level of your hope in God's plan for your life? _____
4. What is the level of your endurance during trials? _____
5. What level of character development are you experiencing? _____
6. What level of God's love are you experiencing? _____

Total _____

Self-Rating

How do you rate your understanding of being forgiven and accepted by God and a member of His family (justified) by faith? Discuss your answer with your group.

How do you rate your acceptance of being forgiven and accepted by God and a member of His family (justified) by faith? Discuss your answer with your group.

Action Steps

List two things you can do to increase your understanding of being forgiven and accepted by God.

1.
2.

List two things you can do to learn to experience your acceptance by God more fully in your life.

1.
2.

What scripture in this section has had the greatest impact in your life? Explain that experience with your group.

ADOPTION (INHERITANCE)

A Child of God

As a born-again child of God, you are placed into a position as a son/daughter and through your adherence to the Word of God and the Holy Spirit, and thereby given full privileges and rights of inheritance.

> For he chose us in him before the creation of the world to be holy and blameless in his sight. In love he predestined us to be adopted as his sons through Jesus Christ, in accordance with his pleasure and will. (Ephesians 1:4–5, NIV)
>
> So the law was put in charge to lead us to Christ that we might be justified by faith. Now that faith has come, we are no longer under the supervision of the law. You are all sons of God through faith in Christ Jesus. (Galatians 3:24–26, NIV)
>
> Even so we, *when we were children, were in bondage under the elements of the world*: But when the fullness of the time was come, *God sent forth his Son,* made of a woman, made under the law, *To redeem them that were under the law, that we might receive the adoption of sons.* (Galatians 4:3–5)
>
> For he chose us in him before the creation of the world to be holy and blameless in his sight. In love he predestined us to be adopted as his sons through Jesus Christ, in accordance with his pleasure and will. (Ephesians 1:4–5, NIV)

- ☐ God has chosen you to become His son through adoption long before you realized you needed to establish a relationship with Him—by believing in Jesus as your personal savior.
- ☐ God's act of love toward you began before the foundation of the world. God, as a parent, had made provision for you before the beginning of time.
- ☐ If you were to adopt a child, it would be an act of grace on your part; it would have nothing to do with the child. Your adoption into the family of God had nothing to do with anything you have done and was strictly an act of God's undeserved favor due to Christ's work in you.
- ☐ You are adopted as a son/daughter by grace; Christ is God's Son by nature.

> *For as many as are led by the Spirit of God, they are the sons of God.* For ye have not received the spirit of bondage again to fear*; but ye have received the Spirit of adoption, whereby we cry, Abba, Father. The Spirit itself beareth witness with our spirit, that we are the children of God.* (Romans 8:14–16)

Receiving the Spirit of adoption is a great privilege belonging only to those who are in Christ. You have become God's property owned and loved by Him.

- ☐ The Holy Spirit has become your new Guardian through your adoption into the family of God. The Holy Spirit now lives in you for the purpose of developing you as a child of the Father into a mature spiritual adult.
- ☐ The Spirit endeavors to lead you; therefore, you have to learn to submit to His guidance through obedience of the Scriptures. During regeneration (new birth), you became a "babe" in Christ, a minor. You must mature into receiving the full adoption of sons.
- ☐ Your adoption provides you with a change in position. Immediately, the moment you believed in Jesus Christ, you received your inheritance and went from the slave market of sin to son/daughter of the King.
- ☐ Because of your new position as a son in the family of God, you now have the privilege and honor of calling God your Father.
- ☐ The Spirit of adoption has developed a childlike love in you, thereby weaning you from the breasts of your mother to be drawn now toward your father, resulting in you being able to learn to depend on God and view Him as your Father.

> But as many as received him, to them gave he power to become the sons of God, *even* to them that believe on his name. (John 1:12)
>
> Behold, *what manner of love the Father hath bestowed upon us, that we should be called the sons of God*: therefore, *the world knoweth us not, because it knew him not.* Beloved, now are we the sons of God, and it doth not yet appear what we shall be: but we know that, when he shall appear, we shall be like him; for we shall see him as he is. (1 John 3:1–2)
>
> And if children, *then heirs; heirs of God, and joint–heirs with Christ;* if so be that we suffer with *him*, that we may be also glorified together. (Romans 8:17)

- ☐ Unbelievers around you and those who knew you prior to your salvation experience will not understand your new position.
- ☐ You must not only understand your adoption, but believe in it and learn to act accordingly. It is through your adoption that you receive the rights to all the privileges and to the inheritance of God.

The inheritance belongs to Christ, but by the grace of God, you now are able to share in that inheritance.

- ☐ You now have a down payment of your inheritance, the gift of the Holy Spirit who dwells in you—guiding, comforting, and making you holy.

God's plan of adoption is far superior to man's plan for adoption. When a son/daughter is adopted as a child and heir by parents according to man's plan, they are not able to become like their parents. However, when you accepted Jesus as your savior, God made you His son/daughter through your spiritual rebirth. You became a partaker of the nature of God, your Father. You were not born His child, but now He has accepted you into His family with full rights and privileges as His child.

Result of Adoption

As His Child, You Have an Inheritance

Praise be to the God and Father of our Lord Jesus Christ! In his great mercy he has given us new birth into a living hope through the resurrection of Jesus Christ from the dead, *and into an inheritance that can never perish, spoil or fade—kept in heaven for you,* who through faith are shielded by God's power until the coming of the salvation that is ready to be revealed in the last time. (1 Peter 1:3–5, NIV)

As His Child, You Inherit the Family Name

For this cause, I bow my knees unto the Father of our Lord Jesus Christ, *Of whom the whole family in heaven and earth is named.* (Ephesians 3:14–15)

Behold, *what manner of love the Father hath bestowed upon us, that we should be called the sons of God*: therefore *the world knoweth us not, because it knew him not.* (1 John 3:1–2)

As His child, you inherit your Father's nature

Whereby are given unto us exceeding great and precious promises*: that by these ye might be partakers of the divine nature*, having escaped the corruption that is in the world through lust. (2 Peter 1:4)

And have put on *the new man*, which is renewed in knowledge after the *image of him that created him. (*Colossians 3:10*)*

For whom he did foreknow, he also did predestinate *to be conformed to the image of his Son,* that he might be the firstborn among many brethren. (Romans 8:29)

But we all, with open face beholding as in a glass the glory of the Lord, *are changed into the same image from glory to glory, even as by the Spirit of the Lord.* (2 Corinthians 3:18)

As His Child, You Inherit A Family Love

He that saith he is in the light, and hateth his brother, is in darkness even until now. *He that loveth his brother abideth in the light,* and there is none occasion of stumbling in him. But he that hateth his brother is in darkness, and walketh in darkness, and knoweth not whither he goeth, because that darkness hath blinded his eyes. (1 John 2:9–11)

We know that we have passed from death unto life, *because we love the brethren.* He that loveth not *his* brother abideth in death. Whosoever hateth his brother is a murderer: and ye know that no murderer hath eternal life abiding in him. *Hereby perceive we the love of God, because he laid down his life for us: and we ought to lay down our lives for the brethren.* But whoso hath this world's good, and seeth his brother have need, and shutteth up his bowels *of compassion* from him, how dwelleth the love of God in him? My little children, let us not love in word, neither in tongue; but in deed and in truth. (1 John 3:14–18)

Whosoever believeth that Jesus is the Christ is born of God*: and every one that loveth him that begat loveth him also that is begotten of him.* (1 John 5:1)

As His Child, He Will Comfort You

Blessed *be* God, even the Father of our Lord Jesus Christ, the Father of mercies, and the *God of all comfort; Who comforteth us in all our tribulation,* that we may be able to comfort them which are in any trouble, *by the comfort wherewith we ourselves are comforted of God.* (2 Corinthians 1:3–4)

As His Child, He Will Discipline You

Because the Lord disciplines those he loves, and he punishes everyone he accepts as a son. Endure hardship as discipline; God is treating you as sons. *For what son is not disciplined by his father? If you are not disciplined (and everyone undergoes discipline),* then you are illegitimate children and not true sons. Moreover, we have all had human fathers who disciplined us and we respected them for it. *How much more should we submit to the Father of our spirits and live! Our fathers disciplined us for a little while as they thought best; but God disciplines us for our good, that we may share in his holiness.* No discipline seems pleasant at the time, but painful. Later on, however, it produces a harvest of righteousness and peace for those who have been trained by it. (Hebrews 12:6–11, NIV)

As His Child, He Places His Spirit in You

Having believed, you were marked in him with a seal, *the promised Holy Spirit, who is a deposit guaranteeing our inheritance until the redemption of those who are God's possession*—to the praise of his glory. (Ephesians 1:11, NIV)

And I will ask the Father, and he will give you another *Counselor* to be with you forever—*the Spirit of truth.* The world cannot accept him, because it neither sees him nor knows him. But you know him, *for he lives with you and will be in you.* (John 14:16–17, NIV)

As His Child, You Have Victory Over Your enemy, World, Flesh, and Satan

O give thanks unto the LORD, for *he is* good: for his mercy *endureth* forever. Let the redeemed of the LORD say *so, whom he hath redeemed from the hand of the enemy. (*Psalm 107:1–2*)*

And having *disarmed the powers and authorities,* he made a public spectacle of them, triumphing over them by the cross. (Colossians 2:15, NIV)

He that committeth sin is of the devil; for the devil sinneth from the beginning. For this purpose, the Son of God was manifested, *that he might destroy the works of the devil.* (1 John 3:8)

For whatsoever is born of God overcometh the world: and this is the victory that overcometh the world, *even our faith. Who is he that overcometh the world, but he that believeth that Jesus is the Son of God?* (1 John 5:4–5)

Knowing this, that *our old man (flesh) is crucified with him*, that the body of sin might be destroyed, that henceforth we should not serve sin. For he that is dead is freed from sin. (Romans 6:6–7)

EXERCISE: ADOPTION

How You Benefit from Being Adopted by God

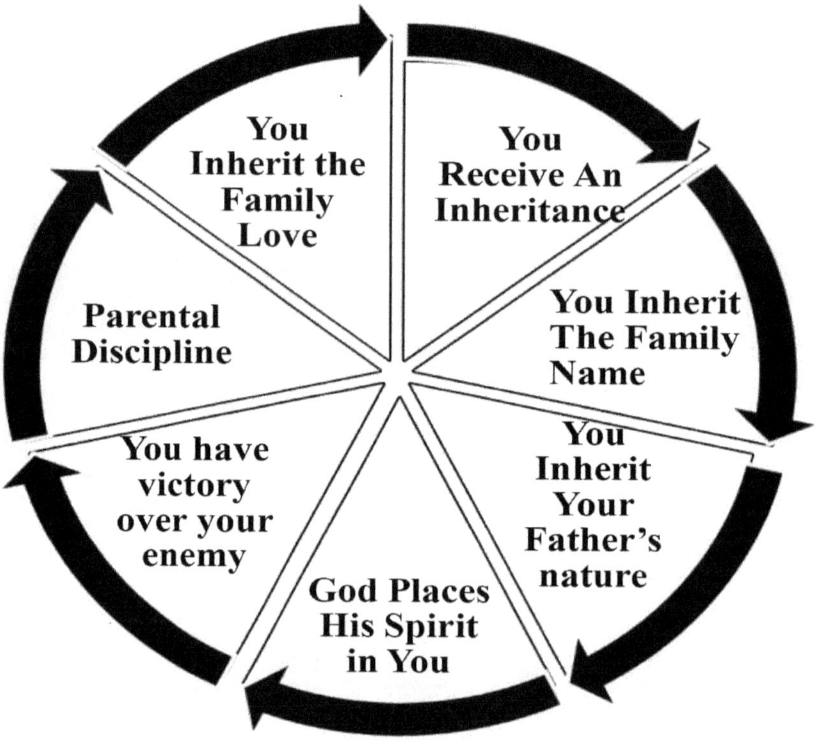

Figure 43: Benefits of Being Adopted

Review the diagram above on Benefits of Being Adopted and share with your group members the following information:

1. Which benefit of being adopted into God's family are you *experiencing the most*?
2. Which benefit of being adopted into God's family are you *experiencing the* least? Explain your answer to your group.
3. Which benefit of being adopted into God's family do you *find most challenging*?
4. Which benefit of being adopted into God's family do you *find most difficult to understand*? Explain your answer to your group.
5. What benefits do you find *most difficult for you to accept?* Discuss the reasons why you find it so difficult to accept with your group members.

6. What benefits *touch your heart* the most and *inspire your walk* with God? Explain your answer to your group.

What scripture in this section has had the greatest impact in your life? Explain that experience with your group.

Part Two

Avoiding the Identity Crisis

Regeneration (Rebirth)
Having Faith in Your New Position in Christ

To be "born again," receiving a *new nature* and a new life in God, being placed in the "Body of Christ."

At the moment of your conversion, you were justified completely in God's sight. Your old sinful self was destroyed forever. You were made a *partaker of the divine nature,* the nature of Christ. You became *a new person in Christ* and you were declared by God to be a saint. This was a one–time transformation. There is nothing you can do to improve upon God's activity in transforming you and justifying you. He intends merely that you believe what He's done and accept your identity as His child.

—Neil T. Anderson

Therefore, if anyone is in Christ, *he is a new creation; the old has gone, the new has come!* (2 Corinthians 5:17, NIV)

For we know that our old self was crucified with him so that the body of sin might be done away with, that we should no longer be slaves to sin. (Romans 6:6, NIV)

Do you not know that the wicked will not inherit the kingdom of God? Do not be deceived: Neither the *sexually immoral* nor *idolaters* nor *adulterers* nor *male prostitutes* nor *homosexual offenders* nor *thieves* nor the *greedy* nor *drunkards* nor *slanderers* nor *swindlers* will inherit the kingdom of God. *And that is what some of you were.* But you were *washed,* you were *sanctified,* you were *justified* in the name of the Lord Jesus Christ and *by the Spirit of our God.* (1 Corinthians 6:9–11, NIV)

During the years you spent separated from God, your worldly experiences thoroughly programmed your brain with thought patterns, memory traces, responses and habits which are alien to God. So even though your old skipper (nature) is gone, your flesh remains in opposition to God as a preprogrammed propensity for sin, which is living independent of God.

—Neil Anderson

You could have been an addict, prostitute, murderer, thief, or homosexual; but the moment you were regenerated, you became a new creature because you were given a new nature, and your old nature was crucified with Christ. Yes, you may still have some of your old desires, appetites, passions, and you may still experience some of your old behaviors, attitudes, and thoughts, but you are still a new creature. You're a new creature because the Holy Spirit has performed a miraculous work in you.

> *For as he thinketh in his heart, so is he...* (Proverbs 23:7)
>
> Those who belong to Christ Jesus *have crucified the sinful nature with its passions and desires.* (Galatians 5:24, NIV)

- ☐ You must believe in the victory Christ has given you over your old sinful nature and the thoughts and desires that accompanied it and live accordingly.

> I have been crucified with Christ and I no longer live, but Christ lives in me. The life I live in the body, I live by faith in the Son of God, who loved me and gave himself for me. (Galatians 2:20, NIV)

- ☐ You must learn to acknowledge the death of your old (addicted) self and experience the power of Christ living in your new person.
- ☐ You may have been an addict and lived a criminal lifestyle involving addiction, violence, abuse—disregarding the life and property of self and others—but that was prior to your relationship with Christ.
- ☐ If you were a Christian living this type of lifestyle, it was because you never had faith in your identity in Christ and really weren't living according to biblical standards.
- ☐ Without a thorough understanding of your new identity in Christ, you will not only struggle with your past, but you will fail to live a life of holiness in the future and most likely return to a lifestyle of addiction.

UNDERSTANDING THE DYNAMICS OF ADDICTION

What Makes a Person an Addict/Alcoholic?

As for you, you were dead in your transgressions and sins, *in which you used to live when you followed the ways of this world and of the ruler of the kingdom of the air (Satan),* the spirit who is now at work in those who are disobedient. All of us also lived among them at one time, *gratifying the cravings of our sinful nature and following its desires and thoughts (alcohol and other drugs).* Like the rest, we were by nature objects of wrath. (Ephesians 2:1–3, NIV)

The Old Man

Figure 44: The Old Man

You were separated from God due to spiritual death at birth and the seeds of addiction were planted in your heart and once you began "sowing to the flesh" strongholds were developed in your soul, resulting in your bondage to alcohol and other drugs. An addict/alcoholic is an individual, which is spiritually dead, separated from God in bondage to alcohol and other drugs.

Note: If you were ever involved in the 12-Step Movement, attended NA, AA, or CA, you were taught that once an addict/alcoholic always an addict/alcoholic. You probably were required to make a statement that you were an addict/alcoholic prior to speaking in meetings.

What determines your identity in God's eyes is if you are born again or not. If a person is saved, they have a new nature and identity. The world bases a person's identity on their behavior (conduct/character and their past), while *God bases a person's identity on their relationship with Him through accepting Jesus as their Lord and savior.*

Why a Christian Isn't an Addict/Alcoholic?

> Remember that at that time you were separate from Christ, excluded from citizenship in Israel and foreigners to the covenants of the promise, *without hope and without God in the world. But now in Christ Jesus you who once were far away have been brought near through the blood of Christ.* For he himself is our peace, who has made the two one and has destroyed the barrier, the dividing wall of hostility, (Ephesians 2:12–14, NIV).

New Creature in Christ

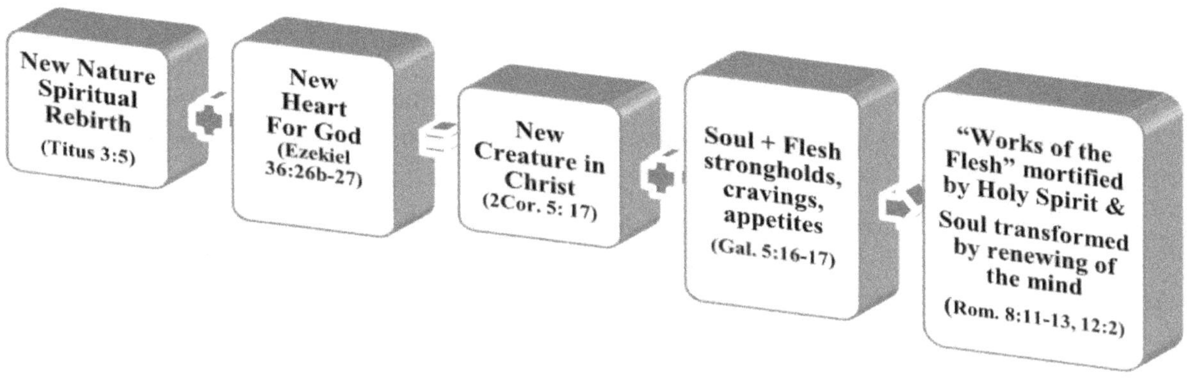

Figure 45: The New Man

> Do you not know that the wicked will not inherit the kingdom of God? Do not be deceived: Neither the sexually immoral nor idolaters nor adulterers nor male prostitutes nor homosexual offenders nor thieves nor the greedy nor drunkards nor slanderers nor swindlers will inherit the kingdom of God. *And that is what some of you were.* But you were washed, you were sanctified, you were justified in the name of the Lord Jesus Christ and by the Spirit of our God. (1 Corinthians: 6:9–11, NIV)

Bondage (addiction) to alcohol and other drugs has its origin in your old nature due to spiritual death with a hardened heart. These two factors determined whether you are an addict/alcoholic or not. Only God's plan of salvation could have changed your nature and addressed the root cause of addiction. You have been born again with a new nature (heart and spirit). Yes, you may continue in old behaviors, but your identity has changed forever. Now you must learn to follow God's plan for your life by allowing Him to restore your soul from the effects of addiction.

- ☐ You must understand that God has spiritually changed you during salvation, and you must develop faith in your position in Christ:

a) This is one of the most important factors in preventing you from returning to your old lifestyle of "sowing to the flesh" (relapse). This is the biblical foundation on which your spiritual restoration (recovery) is based; if you don't learn to identify with your savior, Jesus Christ, you will automatically identify with your old self, the fallen Adam.

> I will give you a new heart and put a new spirit in you; I will remove from you your heart of stone and give you a heart of flesh. And I will put my Spirit in you and move you to follow my decrees and be careful to keep my laws. (Ezekiel 36:26–27, NIV)

- ☐ You must understand you have received a new heart and spirit, and your old nature was crucified with Christ. You have a new nature and are under new management by the Holy Spirit who dwells in you. Now you must learn to cooperate with Him.
- ☐ The enemy will try to trick you into accepting an identity based on where you have been and what you have done in your past lifestyle of addiction. God, however, bases your identity on what He has done to you through accepting Jesus Christ as Lord and savior (salvation).

Because of your new birth, you are now God's own workmanship, and He is preparing you to enter into service for Him. He has a purpose for saving you. Many new converts who have been in bondage to drugs/alcohol, once they have been delivered from street-life, experience an identity crisis following salvation. This crisis is a result of not clearly understanding their position in Christ.

- ☐ You may think that you are less than other Christians or that you will not fit in a local body of believers because of your past, or that you can't measure up to the Christian standard of living.

> But when the kindness and love of God our savior appeared, he saved us, not because of righteous things we had done, but because of his mercy. He saved us through the washing of rebirth and renewal by the Holy Spirit, whom he poured out on us generously through Jesus Christ our savior, so that, having been justified by his grace, we might become heirs having the hope of eternal life. (Titus 3:4–7, NIV)

You must learn that at the same time you received the "new birth," you were also justified. Not only did God change your nature, but He also changed your relational standing with Him. You once lived under the guilt and condemnation of sin. Justification is God's acquittal and acceptance. God's attitude has changed toward you due to you being washed in the blood of Jesus. Your attitude has also changed toward God because of your repentance.

- ☐ Being in a right relational standing with God plays a vital role in your future, because both your *conduct* and *character* are *controlled* and *conditioned by your new relationship.*
- ☐ Understanding and having faith in your relationship with God will provide you with the *proper motivation* (love of God) to avoid returning to your old lifestyle of "sowing to the flesh (relapsing)."

> For in Christ Jesus, neither circumcision nor uncircumcision has any value. *The only thing that counts is faith expressing itself through love.* (Galatians 5:6, NIV)

If you are experiencing an identity crisis as a born-again believer, there are several important spiritual truths you must understand regarding your new identity.

> Know ye not, that so many of us as were baptized into Jesus Christ were baptized into his death? *Therefore, we are buried with him by baptism into death: that like as Christ was raised up from the dead by the glory of the Father, even so we also should walk in newness of life.* For if we have been planted together in the likeness of his death, we shall be also *in the likeness* of *his* resurrection. (Romans 6:3–5)

In your acceptance of Jesus Christ:

- ☐ You must have faith in what God has done to you through spiritual rebirth, providing you with a new heart and new spiritual birth, making you a new creature.
- ☐ You are no longer an addict or alcoholic but a new creature in Christ. Even though you may still be experiencing some of effects of your bondage to drugs/alcohol, appetites, thoughts, cravings, memories, old addictive behaviors, and attitudes, you are a new person.

> Knowing this, that our old man is crucified with *him*, that the body of sin might be destroyed, that henceforth we should not serve sin. For he that is dead is freed from sin. Now if we be dead with Christ, we believe that we shall also live with him: Knowing that Christ being raised from the dead dieth no more; death hath no more dominion over him. (Romans 6:6–9)

- ☐ You must have faith in the salvation process and know that your old (addictive) nature was crucified with Christ so that addiction (sin) would be destroyed along with all forms of sin in your life.
- ☐ You must accept the truth that you were buried with Christ by baptism into His death, and you have been raised up in a new life by the Father and in a new likeness of Christ.
- ☐ Your old person (addict/alcoholic) was crucified with Christ and buried with Him, and your new person is resurrected with Him.
- ☐ You have been freed from addiction, because sin is no longer your master; you no longer have to serve sin (addiction).

A Comparison of the New Man to the Old Man

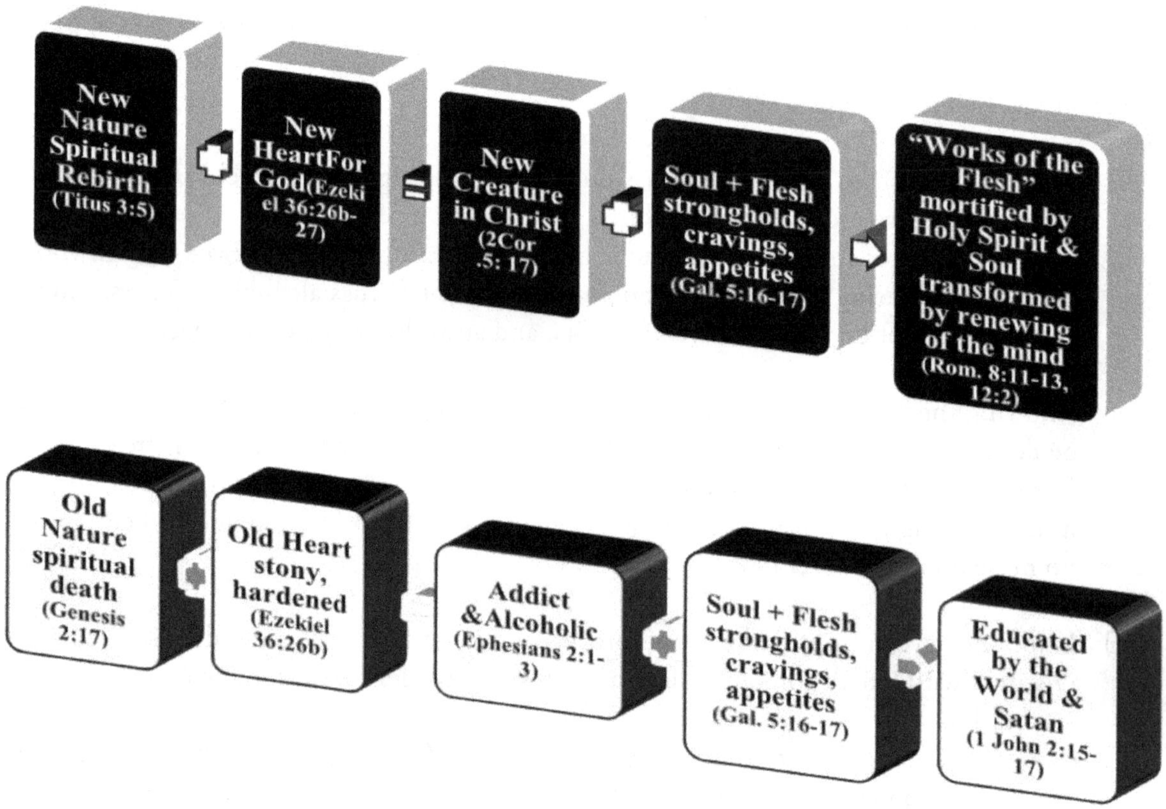

Figure 46: Old Man in Comparison to the New Man

The Reckoning

> For in that he died, he died unto sin once: but in that he liveth, he liveth unto God. *Likewise reckon ye also yourselves to be dead indeed unto sin, but alive unto God through Jesus Christ our Lord.* Let not sin therefore reign in your mortal body, that ye should obey it in the lusts thereof. (Romans 6:10–12)

- ☐ You must learn to reckon (believe) your old (addictive) sinful nature is dead, and live daily as though it were making your daily decisions according to the truth that you are a new creation in God, not having to live in sin like you did in your past lifestyle.

> *Neither yield ye your members as instruments of unrighteousness unto sin: but yield yourselves unto God, as those that are alive from the dead, and your members as instruments of righteousness unto God.* For sin shall not have dominion over you: for ye are not under the law, but under grace. (Romans 6:13–14)

- ☐ You must stop allowing your body, soul (mind, will, emotions) to be tools of unrighteousness. You need to be conscious of your language, how you dress, who you fellowship with, what you read, watch on TV, listen to on the radio, etc.
- ☐ Your bondage to drugs/alcohol (addiction) has been destroyed; you now must learn to cooperate with the Holy Spirit and walk in Christ's victory and experience your freedom from addiction.
- ☐ If you don't develop an understanding of faith in your position in Christ, you most likely will experience one of the following states of mind: hopelessness, loneliness, worthlessness, and self-pity, which lead to "sowing to the flesh," or relapsing.

Who Am I Now that I Believe in Jesus Christ?

I am Christ's friend. John 15:15
I am part of the true vine, a branch of Christ's life. John 15:1–5
I am a child of God (part of His family). Rom. 8:16; John 1: 12
I am chosen and appointed by Christ to bear His fruit. John 15:16
I am a son of God (God is my Spiritual Father) Gal. 3:26, 4:6; Rom. 8:14–15
I am a joint–heir with Christ sharing His inheritance with Him. Rom. 8:17
I am a temple (home) of God. His Spirit (His life) lives in me.1 Cor. 3:16, 6:19
I am joined (united) to the Lord and am one spirit with Him. 1 Cor. 6:17
I am a member (part) of Christ's body. see Eph.5:30; 1 Cor. 12:27
I am God's workmanship (handiwork) created (born anew) in Christ to do His work that He planned beforehand that I should do. Eph. 2:10
I am a fellow citizen with the rest of God's people in His family. Eph. 2:19
I am a prisoner of Christ. Eph. 3:1; 4:1
I am righteous and holy. Eph. 4:24
I am hidden with Christ in God. Col. 3:3
I am one of God's living stones and am being built up in Christ as a spiritual house. 1 Pet. 2:5
I am a chosen race, a royal priesthood, a holy nation a people for God's own possession to proclaim the excellences of Him. 1 Pet. 2:9–10
I am an alien and stranger to this world I temporarily live in. 1 Pet. 2:11

Figure 47: Who Am Now That I Believe in Christ?

EXERCISE

1. What three passages of scriptures above do you find touch you the most regarding how God has changed your life?

2. What three passages of scriptures do you find most difficult to understand and accept regarding how God has changed your life?

3. Memorize the one scripture that touches you most, and the one that you find most difficult to understand and accept regarding how God has changed your life from the list above.

By the Grace of God I...

have been justified (completely forgiven and made righteous). Rom. 5:1
died with Christ and died to the power of sin's rule over my life. Rom. 6:1–6
am free from condemnation. Rom. 8:1
have received the Spirit of God into my life that I might know the things freely given to me by God. 1 Cor. 2:12
have been given the mind of Christ. 1 Cor. 2:16
have been bought and paid for with a price. I am not my own. I belong to God.1 Cor. 6:19–20
have been given the Holy Spirit as a pledge (a deposit/down payment), guaranteeing my inheritance to come. Eph. 1:13, 14
since I have died, I no longer live for myself, but for Him (Christ). 2 Cor. 5:14–15
have been crucified with Christ and it is no longer I who live, but Christ lives in me. (The life I am now living is Christ's life). Gal. 2:20
have been blessed with every spiritual blessing. Eph. 1:3
have been redeemed, forgiven, and am the recipient of His lavish grace. Eph. 1:7,8
have direct access to God through the Spirit. Eph. 2:18
may approach God with boldness, freedom, and confidence. Eph. 3:12
have been delivered from the domain of darkness (Satan's rule) and transferred to the kingdom of Christ. Col. 1:13
Christ Himself is in me. Col. 1:27
have been given a spirit of power, love, and self–discipline. 2 Tim. 1:7
have been saved and called (set apart) according to God's doing. 2 Tim. 1:9; Titus 3:5
have the right to come boldly before the throne of God (the throne of grace) to find mercy and find grace in time of need. Heb. 4:16

Figure 48: By the Grace of God I...

EXERCISE

1. What three passages of scriptures above do you find touch you the most about your new identity?
2. What three passages of scriptures do you find most difficult to understand and accept regarding your new identity?
3. Memorize the scripture that most inspires you and the one you find most difficult to understand and accept regarding your new identity from the list above.

HEAVEN'S GROCERY STORE

I was walking down life's highway, a long time ago,
One day I saw a sign that read: "Heavens Grocery Store"
As I got a little closer the door came open wide,
And when I came to myself, I was standing inside.
I saw a host of angels, they were standing everywhere;
One handed me a basket and said, "My child shop with care."
Everything a Christian needed was in that grocery store,
And all you couldn't carry, you could come back for more.
First, I got some **PATIENCE**, **LOVE** was in the same row.
Further down was **UNDERSTANDING**, you need that everywhere you go.
I got a box or two of **WISDOM**, a bag or two of **FAITH**,
I just couldn't miss the **HOLY GHOST** for He was all over the place.
I stopped to get some **STRENGTH** and **COURAGE** to help me run this race,
By then, my basket was getting full, but I remembered I needed some **GRACE**.
I didn't forget **SALVATION**, for salvation, that was free.
So, I tried to get enough of that to save both you and me.
Then I started up to the counter to pay my grocery bill,
For I thought I had everything to do my Master's will.
As I went up the aisle, I saw **PRAYER** and I just had to put that in,
For I knew when I stepped outside, I would run right into sin.
PEACE and **JOY** were plentiful, they were on the last shelf,
SONG and **PRAISES** were hanging near, so I just helped myself.
Then I said to the angel, "How much do I owe?"
He just smiled and said, just take them everywhere you go.
Again, I smiled at him and said, "How much do I really owe?"
He smiled at him and said, **"MY CHILD, JESUS PAID YOUR BILL A LONG TIME AGO."**

—Author Unknown

UNDERSTANDING YOUR POSITION IN CHRIST

PRINCIPLE	SOURCE	ORIGINATED	RESULTS
REPENTANCE (Acts 11:18, 5:30-31, 2 Cor. 7:9-10)	Divine Gift presented through the Gospel	When God touched your heart through the gospel, you experienced a change in mind, acknowledged and turned away from sin, turned to God	Pardon and the forgiveness of sin Saving faith
SAVING FAITH (Eph. 2:8, Rom. 5:1, 10:9-10)	Divine Gift of God's grace & through belief and application of God's Word	When you believed & received the gospel by accepting Jesus as Savior	Salvation (rebirth, justification, adoption, sanctification
REBIRTH (Titus 3-5, Ez. 36:26-27, Jn. 3:3-7)	Divine Gift of God through acceptance of Jesus Christ	The moment you believed in Jesus Christ	Change in nature, new creation, "babe in Christ," new life (life of God)
JUSTIFICATION (Titus 3:4-7,Rom. 5:8-9)	By God's grace through the Blood of Jesus Christ	The moment you believed in Jesus Christ	Change in relational standing, God's attitude towards you changed (found not guilty of sins)
ADOPTION (Eph. 1: 4-5, Rom. 8:14-17)	By God's grace through faith in Jesus Christ	Before the foundation of the world (you were chosen) The moment you believed in Jesus Christ it happened	Change in position, legal status as a son/daughter full rights of inheritance
POSITIONAL HOLINESS (1 Pet. 1:2, 2 Thess. 2:13-14, 1 Cor. 1:2)	By God's grace through faith in Jesus Christ	The moment you believed in Jesus Christ	Separated for God's purpose, service
PROGRESSIVE HOLINESS (Col. 2:6-10, Rom. 12:1-2) 2 Cor. 3:18)	By God's grace through faith in Jesus Christ	Began at the moment you believed in Jesus Christ and is Presently occurring on a daily basis	The potential to grow in character and conduct in your position in Christ (process)

Figure 49: Understanding Your Position in Christ

God has been extremely intentional in bringing you into a relationship with Him and providing you with a position in Christ. Your understanding and faith in that position is the foundation for your new lifestyle in Christ.

UNDERSTANDING YOUR IDENTITY IN CHRIST

Self-Check

Therefore, if any man *be* in Christ, *he is* a *new creature*: *old things are passed away*; behold, *all things are become new*. (2 Corinthians 5:17)

Do you not know that the wicked will not inherit the kingdom of God? Do not be deceived: Neither the *sexually immoral* nor *idolaters* nor *adulterers* nor *male prostitutes* nor *homosexual offenders* nor *thieves* nor the *greedy* nor *drunkards* nor *slanderers* nor *swindlers* will inherit the kingdom of God. *And that is what some of you were.* But you were *washed*, you were *sanctified*, you were *justified* in the name of the Lord Jesus Christ and *by the Spirit of our God*. (1 Corinthians 6:9–11, NIV)

Check [√] the box that best indicates how well you <u>*understand*</u> *the seven principles listed below.*

1. Repentance	[ ] very little	[ ] somewhat	[ ] good
2. Saving Faith	[ ] very little	[ ] somewhat	[ ] good
3. Rebirth	[ ] very little	[ ] somewhat	[ ] good
4. Justified (God's acceptance)	[ ] very little	[ ] somewhat	[ ] good
5. Adoption	[ ] very little	[ ] somewhat	[ ] good
6. Holiness (Position)	[ ] very little	[ ] somewhat	[ ] good
7. Holiness (Progressive)	[ ] very little	[ ] somewhat	[ ] good

If you answered most of the questions *"very little"* or *"somewhat"*, you need to review the chart, *Understanding Your Position in Christ* (next page) and read and study the scriptures listed under each of these principles.

Self–Rating

How well do you understand that you are a *new creature* in Christ? Discuss your answer with your group.

How well do you understand that you have been given a *new heart* and *new spirit*? Discuss your answer with your group.

Action Steps

List three things you are willing to do to increase your understanding of your identity in Christ.

1.
2.
3.

What scripture in this section has had the greatest impact in your life? Explain that experience with your group.

Charles Stanley, in his text, *Winning the War Within,* makes the following statement regarding the importance of understanding the sense of one's significance:

> As long as men and women seek to gain their sense of significance and self–worth from anything other than God, they will be set up for temptation. Certain people, places, or things will always have an inordinate ability to lure them into sin. Until they change their definition of significance and until they transfer their security to Someone who can give them real security, they will never experience lasting victory in their lives.

Prayer for Understanding and Having Faith in New Identity

Dear heavenly Father, I thank you for changing me so I could become Your child. I thank You for accepting me and not holding my past lifestyle of drugs/alcohol against me and for making me a new person with a new identity. Help me to understand my new identity and to have faith in my identity in Christ. I thank You for no longer seeing me as an alcoholic/addict but as Your child. Help me see myself as You see me and look to You for my future.

In Jesus name I pray. Amen!

Phase Four

THE THIRD SIGNIFICANT FACTOR IN RELAPSE PREVENTION

Character Development

And we know that all things work together for good to those who love God, to those who are the called according to His purpose. For whom He foreknew, He also predestined to be conformed (molded) to the image (likeness)of His Son, that He might be the firstborn among many brethren.

—Romans 8:28–29

The law of sowing and reaping is just as valid in the spiritual as in the physical and moral realms. The frustration and the hopelessness of humanistic psychology, psychiatry, and counseling can be traced, among other things, to their refusal to consider the immutable spiritual law of sowing and reaping. A person's character cannot be changed until his nature is changed, and that can happen only through the new creation that comes from trust in Jesus Christ.

—John MacArthur Jr.

LEARNING OBJECTIVES

For the workshop participant to be able to:

- ➢ Distinguish between "positional holiness" and "progressive holiness."
- ➢ Identify the five fundamental attitudes necessary for spiritual growth and development.
- ➢ Recognize how grace and peace is multiplied in their life.
- ☐ Identify the six basic spiritual disciplines that position them to receive God's grace.

Key Biblical Concepts and Definitions

(1) ***Past Aspect of Holiness***: Your position in Christ as God sees you, resulting solely from your union with Christ, *unchangeable*, inseparable from a right relational standing. You have been set aside and made holy for God's service as a saint, regardless of age, or spiritual growth (1 Corinthians 1:2, 30 with Philippians 1:1).

(2) *Present Aspect of Holiness*: As you are in conduct and character (2 Thessalonians 2:13). It is a *progressive state, changeable* depending on your knowledge of and faith in your position in Christ and upon you *submitting* to God's will (Romans 6:13) and *conforming* to God's Word (Romans 12:2). You willfully change your position into experience (Romans 6:1–11).

(3) *Relational Knowledge:* Your clear, personal and exact knowledge as a result of being actively involved in a relational learning process with God. This enhances your spiritual growth and development because it provides you with the additional grace and peace.

PART ONE: THE BIBLICAL PRINCIPLE OF HOLINESS (SANCTIFICATION)

The second reason God created man was to reproduce His nature and character. God the Father wanted His children to look like Him on the inside. He wanted them to bear the family *"image and likeness"* (Genesis 1:26). Character is one of the main thoughts in the meaning of the word "image." In Hebrew 1:13, Jesus is described as being "the express image" of His father's person.

The Greek word translated *image* in that verse is from where we get the English word *character*. God wants man to partake of His divine nature (2 Peter 1:4–7) to be conformed to the image of His Son (Romans 8:28, 29), *and to be changed into His image by the Spirit* (2 Corinthians 3:18; 4:4). Since it was a corruption of character (disobedience) that broke man's relationship with God, *it is necessary that man's character be changed, restored, and made just like God's own nature.* The sinful, self-centered element in man's nature must be replaced by the holy, loving and self–giving nature of God.

Sanctification means to be made holy, separated unto God. It is an activity of the Holy Spirit setting a believer apart for the Lord, and then for His service, enabling him to be holy, as God is holy.

God Himself has spiritually transformed you and this is the first phase of change in your life. Now you must advance in your Christian walk with Christ through the grace provided by the Holy Spirit. Holiness in your conduct and character will be a result of your cooperation with the Holy Spirit. Your role was passive with regard to your positional holiness; however, you are required by God to play an active role in your progressive holiness.

How *Were* You Made Holy?

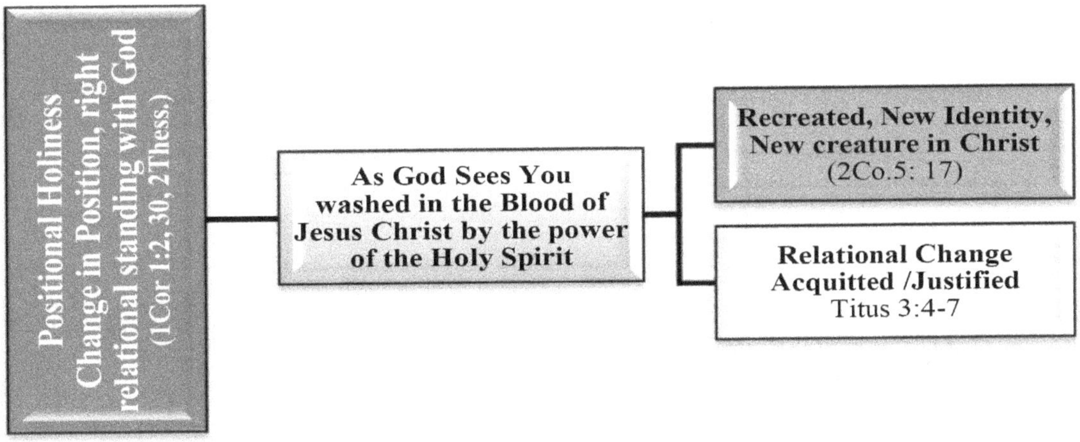

Figure 50: Positional Holiness

The Blood of Jesus Christ

And so Jesus also suffered outside the city gate to make the people holy through his own blood. (Hebrews 13:12, NIV)

Who have been chosen according to the foreknowledge of God the Father, through the sanctifying work of the Spirit, *for obedience to Jesus Christ and sprinkling by his blood:* Grace and peace be yours in abundance. (1 Peter 1:2, NIV)

He saved us, not because of righteous things we had done, but because of his mercy. *He saved us through the washing of rebirth and renewal by the Holy Spirit.* (Titus 3:5, NIV)

And by that will, we have been made holy through the sacrifice of the body of Jesus Christ once for all. (Hebrews 10:10, NIV)

Both the one who makes men holy and those who are made holy are of the same family. So Jesus is not ashamed to call them brothers. (Hebrews 2:11, NIV)

But if we walk in the light, as he is in the light, we have fellowship one with another, and the blood of Jesus Christ his Son cleanseth us from all sin. (1 John 1:7)

Character Development: God's Relapse Prevention Plan

PAST ASPECT OF HOLINESS	**PRESENT ASPECT OF HOLINESS**	**FUTURE ASPECT OF HOLINESS**
<u>POSITIONAL.</u> (1 Cor 1:2, 30) *All* believers have been set aside and made holy for God's service as saints, regardless of age, or spiritual growth.	<u>PROGRESSIVE.</u> Depends upon our knowledge of and faith in our position in Christ (Rom. 6:1-11), changing position into experience.	**<u>FINAL.</u>** When you see the Lord and are made like Him—sinless, without illness, deathless (1 Cor. 4; 15:54; 1 Jn 3:2)
Your position is final, unchangeable, inseparable from your right relational standing, and is the result solely of our union with Christ.	Progressive, changeable, depends upon submitting to God's will (Rom. 6:13) and conforming to God's Word (Rom. 12:2).	Eternal. Will result in your final state in eternity (Phil 3:21).
As God sees you in Christ **(1 Cor. 1:2, 30 with Phil. 1:1, etc).**	As you are in your conduct (2 Thess. 2:13).	**As you shall be in glory** (Rom. 8:29, 1 Cor. 15:49).

Unger's Bible Book (modified)

Figure 51: Progressive Holiness

- ☐ Note: Progressive Holiness (how you are in conduct and character) is dependent upon your *knowledge* of and *faith* in your *position in Christ* (obtained through fellowship).
- ☐ Therefore, the key to spiritual restoration (relapse prevention) is the same for every Christian and begins with how you view yourself in Christ (degree of fellowship).

- ☐ An accurate view of your position in Christ through fellowship will provide you with a sincere love for God, *the proper motivation for living the Christian lifestyle* free of drugs/alcohol. Every Christian must find their significance in their position in Christ.

How *Are* You Being Made Holy?

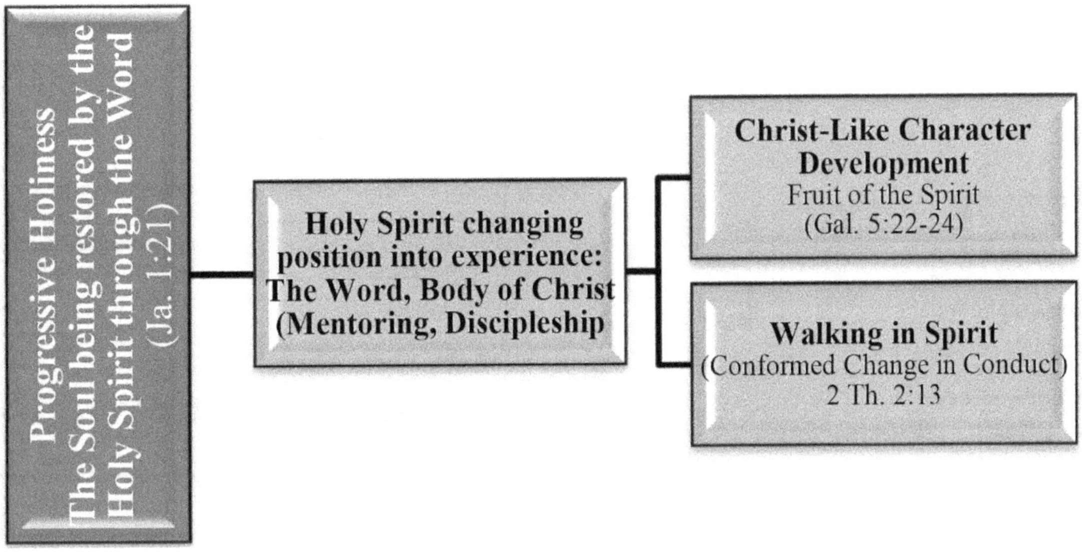

Figure 52: How Are You Being Made Holy?

Wherefore lay apart all filthiness and superfluity of naughtiness, *and receive with meekness the engrafted word, which is able to save your souls.* (James 1:21)

Sanctify them through thy truth: thy word is truth. (John 17:17)

Wherewithal shall a young man cleanse his way*? by taking heed thereto according to thy word.* (Psalm 119:9)

That he might *sanctify* and *cleanse* it with the *washing of water by the word.* (Ephesians 5:26)

By the Holy Spirit

But if the Spirit of him that raised up Jesus from the dead dwell in you, he that raised up Christ from the dead shall also quicken your mortal bodies by his Spirit that dwelleth in you. Therefore, brethren, we are debtors, not to the flesh, to live after the flesh. *For if ye live after the flesh, ye shall die: but if ye through the Spirit do mortify (put to death) the deeds of the body, ye shall live. (*Romans 8:11–13*)*

Cultivating the Fruit of the Spirit

Developing Christ–Like Character

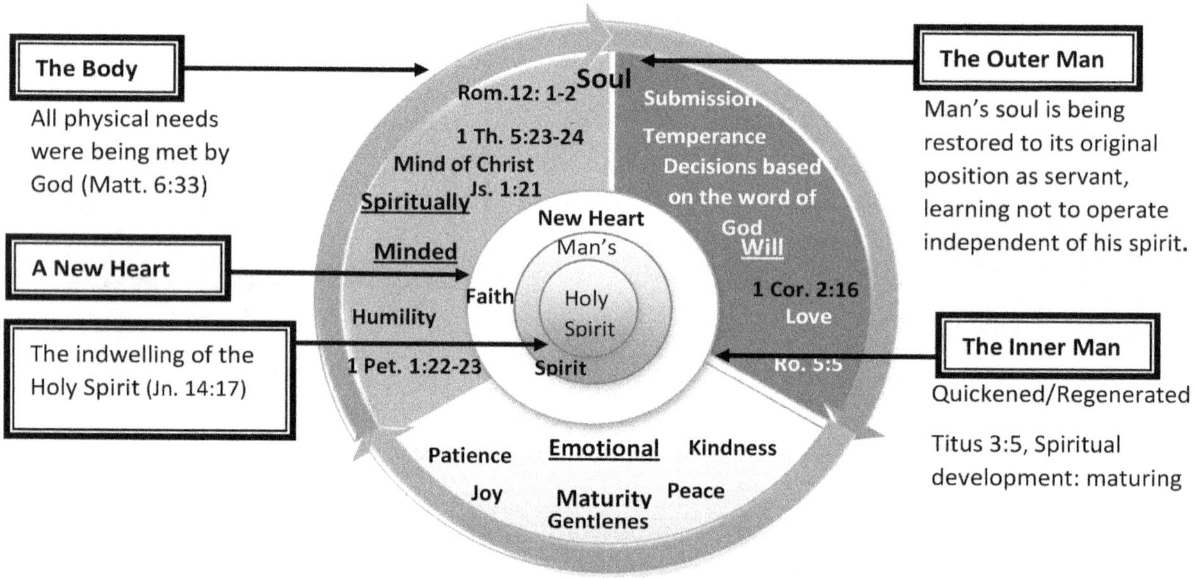

Figure 53: Character Development is based on the Fruit of the Spirit

> But the fruit of the Spirit is love, joy, peace, longsuffering, gentleness, goodness, faith, Meekness, *temperance (self-control):* against such there is no law. *And they that are Christ's have crucified the flesh with the affections and lusts.* (Galatians 5:22–24)

The "works of the flesh" are put to death by "sowing to the Spirit;" because in doing so, you are blessed with the "fruit of the Spirit" which nullifies or takes the strength out of the "works of the flesh."

- ☐ God has provided you with everything you need to avoid relapsing. You have the "fruit of the Spirit" within you that is the key to destroying the "works of the flesh;" but the multi–faceted fruit of the spirit is in seed-form, and therefore requires cultivating to be developed.
- ☐ All of the "fruit of the Spirit" are equally important, but one in particular is of great significance when being restored for addiction—*temperance or self-control.*
- ☐ The world's understanding of self-control is centered totally on abstinence through one's own will power and depends on a person's own strength.
- ☐ The self-control or temperance that is provided by the Holy Spirit for a believer is much different because it is a part of the "fruit of the Spirit"—a quality God provides for His children.

Believers practice abstinence; however, God's type of self-control does not depend on your own personal strength but on your cooperation with the Holy Spirit; and it is a Christlike characteristic developed through an active relationship with God.

- ☐ Christ accomplished victory over the "works of the flesh" on the cross, and that victory is a part of our inheritance. Now you must learn to experience that victory daily in your life by cooperating with the Holy Spirit.

THE KEY TO RELAPSE PREVENTION

Fruit of the Spirit

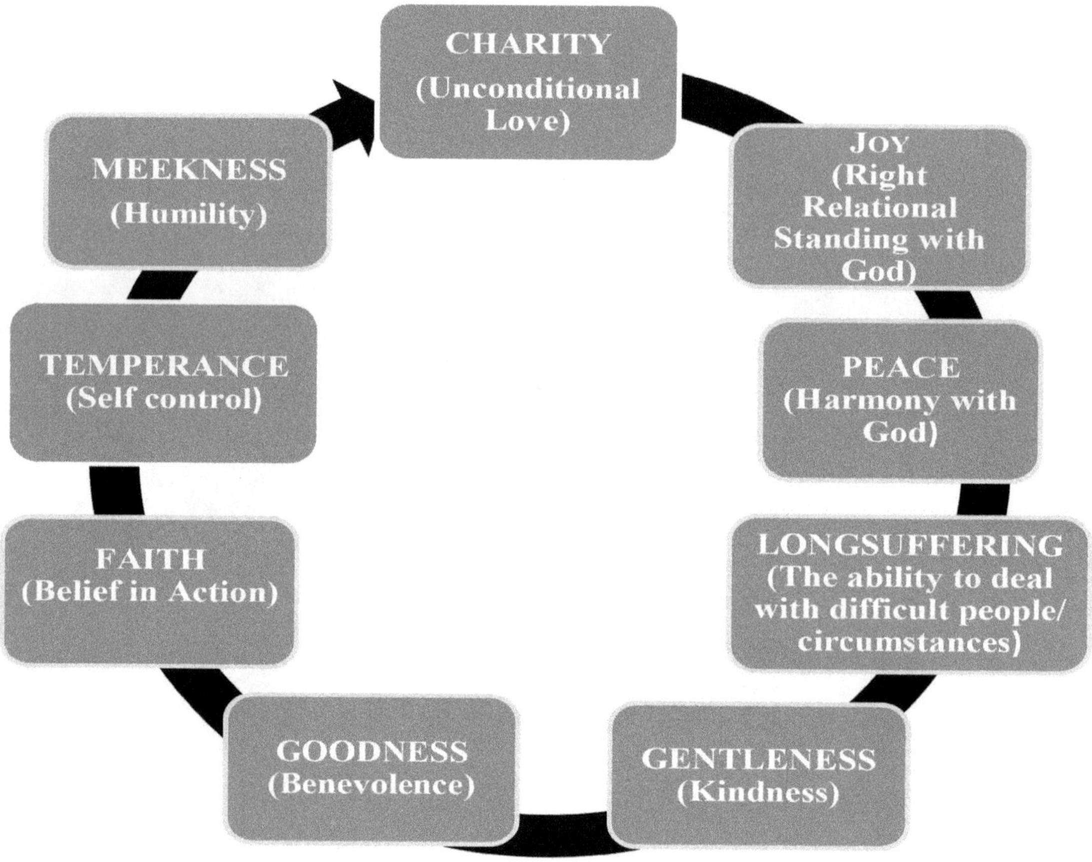

Figure 54: The Fruit of the Spirit

FRUIT OF THE SPIRIT

Self-Check

Using a scale from 1–9 rank the "fruit of the Spirit" in your life according to part of the fruit that you experience the strongest with ***(1 being the weakest) and (9 being the strongest).*** *Begin by placing 1 in the slot of the weakest part of the fruit; next, place the 9 in the slot of the strongest part of the fruit and continue until each slot has a number.*

1. Love ______
2. Joy ______
3. Peace ______
4. Longsuffering ______
5. Gentleness ______
6. Goodness ______
7. Faith ______
8. Meekness ______
9. Self-control ______

What scripture in this section has had the greatest impact in your life? Explain that experience with your group.

CHARACTER DEVELOPMENT

A Benefit of a Right Relational Standing with God

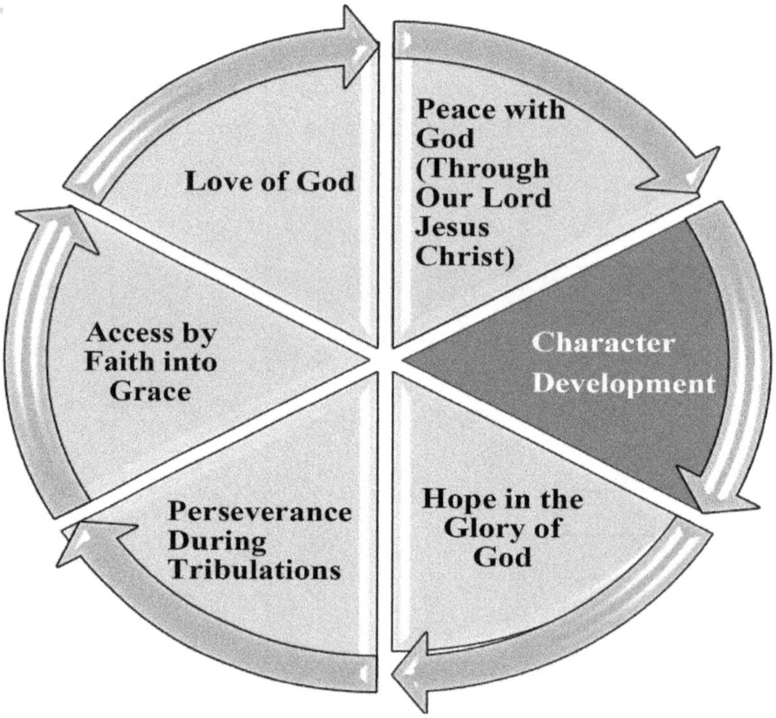

Figure 55: Character Development: A Benefit

Therefore, being justified by faith, we have *peace* with God through our Lord Jesus Christ: By whom also we have *access by faith into this grace* wherein we stand, and rejoice in hope of the glory of God. And not only *so*, but *we glory in tribulations (sufferings)* also: knowing that *tribulation worketh patience (perseverance);* And patience, *experience (character);* and experience, hope: And hope maketh not ashamed; *because the love of God is shed abroad in our hearts by the Holy Ghost which is given unto us.* (Romans 5:1–4)

Grace and *peace be multiplied* unto you *through the knowledge (relational) of God, and of Jesus our Lord.* (2 Peter 1:2)

God's Amazing Grace

Biblical Formula for Spiritual Growth

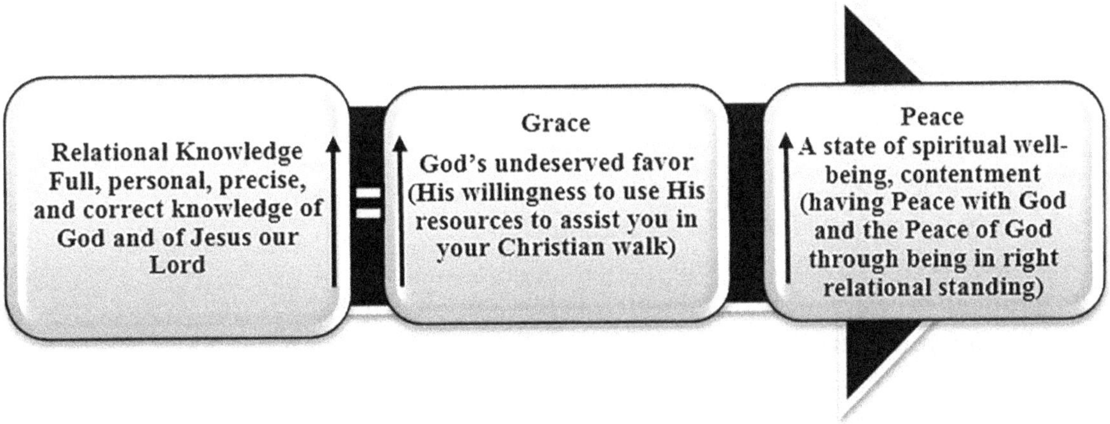

Figure 56: Amazing Grace

Grace is God's undeserved favor. God began blessing you with His gracious and undeserved favor the moment you were saved. God has several different "means of grace," or ways by which you receive His grace. Grace is God's willingness to use His resources to assist you in your new lifestyle of godliness. Prayer, praise, and thanksgiving (worship), fasting, listening to a message, studying, and meditating on God's Word, and fellowshipping are some of God's basic means of grace.

- ☐ Messages provide you with spiritual food; prayer restores you; the study and meditation of God's Word refreshes you; praise and worship strengthen you; fasting provides you with spiritual focus. However, the greatest method God uses to build you up is the discipline of the Holy Spirit.

Richard J. Foster states in his text, *Celebration of Discipline,* "God has given us the Disciplines of the spiritual life as a means of receiving grace. The Disciplines allow us to place ourselves before God so that he can transform us." He continues by explaining how the Apostle Paul stated, "for he who sows to his own flesh will from the flesh reap corruption; but he who sows to the Spirit will from the Spirit reap eternal life" (Gal. 6:8). He further explains the Apostle Paul's analogy.

> Simon Peter, a servant and an apostle of Jesus Christ, to them that have obtained like *precious faith* with us through the righteousness of God and our Savior Jesus Christ: Grace and peace be multiplied unto you through the knowledge of God, and of Jesus our Lord, According as *his divine power hath given unto us all things that pertain unto life and godliness,* through the knowledge of him that hath called us to glory and virtue: Whereby are given unto us exceeding great and precious promises*: that by these ye might be partakers of the divine nature*, having escaped the corruption that is in the world through lust. (Peter 1:1–4)

The Apostle Peter in the passage of scripture above provides us with a basis for Christian growth. Peter first explains how God has provided every Christian with the faith, the foundation for growth "obtained like precious faith." This faith is based on the redemptive work of Christ on Calvary. As a believer, you need to understand that your spiritual mentor, the Holy Spirit, is the source of grace necessary for your growth, and He facilitates your growth as a Christian.

- ☐ God provides "*divine power*" through your spiritual mentor, the Holy Spirit, who supplies us with "all things" necessary for your life of spiritual growth and development.
- ☐ Likewise, through the teaching ministry of your spiritual mentor, it is possible for you to receive grace through full, personal, accurate "*knowledge of Him*" (John 3:13–15).
- ☐ God has given you His "*exceeding great and precious promises,*" His Word to correct, reproof, and instruct you in truth.
- ☐ Through your new birth, and by placing His Spirit in you, God has given you a new nature, allowing you to become a fellow partner, a partaker of the divine nature.
- ☐ You need to understand that you, "*having escaped the corruption that is in the world through lust,*" are a result of God's resources, His divine power, your spiritual mentor, the Holy Spirit, and the administering of His Word.

As a believer, you need to understand that what is needed for God's plan for growth in your life is your participation as "*a partaker of the divine nature.*" You must be willing to cooperate with God in His plan for your growth.

> *Grace* and *peace be multiplied* unto you *through the knowledge (relational) of God, and of Jesus our Lord.* (2 Peter 1:2)

Gaining relational knowledge of God by actively participating with Him, learning to "sow to the Spirit" is the key to you doing the things necessary to keep you from returning to your old lifestyle of practicing the "works of the flesh (using drugs/alcohol)." You must increase two things in your life to keep from returning to your old lifestyle (relapsing).

Peter presents a practical formula for you to multiply *grace* and *peace,* two essentials that are provided by God that are necessary for your *character development* and spiritual well-being.

God provides every Christian with two essential ingredients that are necessary for character development through their active fellowship within their relationship with Him. Without these two necessary ingredients, Christians can fall away from God and return to ungodly lifestyles of sowing to the flesh.

> Wherefore the rather, brethren, give diligence to make your calling and election sure: *for if ye do these things, ye shall never fall (relapse)*. (2 Peter 1:10)

What things are Paul talking about "if you do these things" you will never fall/return to practicing the "works of the flesh (relapse)?" You are responsible for making sure that you truly have a relationship with God through Jesus Christ. There are some requirements, if you don't want to return to "sowing to the flesh (relapse)." By fulfilling these requirements, you will ensure that you have been called by God and are saved.

For this very reason, make every effort to add to your faith goodness; and to goodness, knowledge; and to knowledge, self–control; and to self–control, perseverance; and to perseverance, *godliness; and to godliness,* brotherly kindness; and to brotherly kindness, love. (2 Peter 5–7, NIV)

RELATIONAL KNOWLEDGE PROVIDES CHRISTLIKE QUALITIES

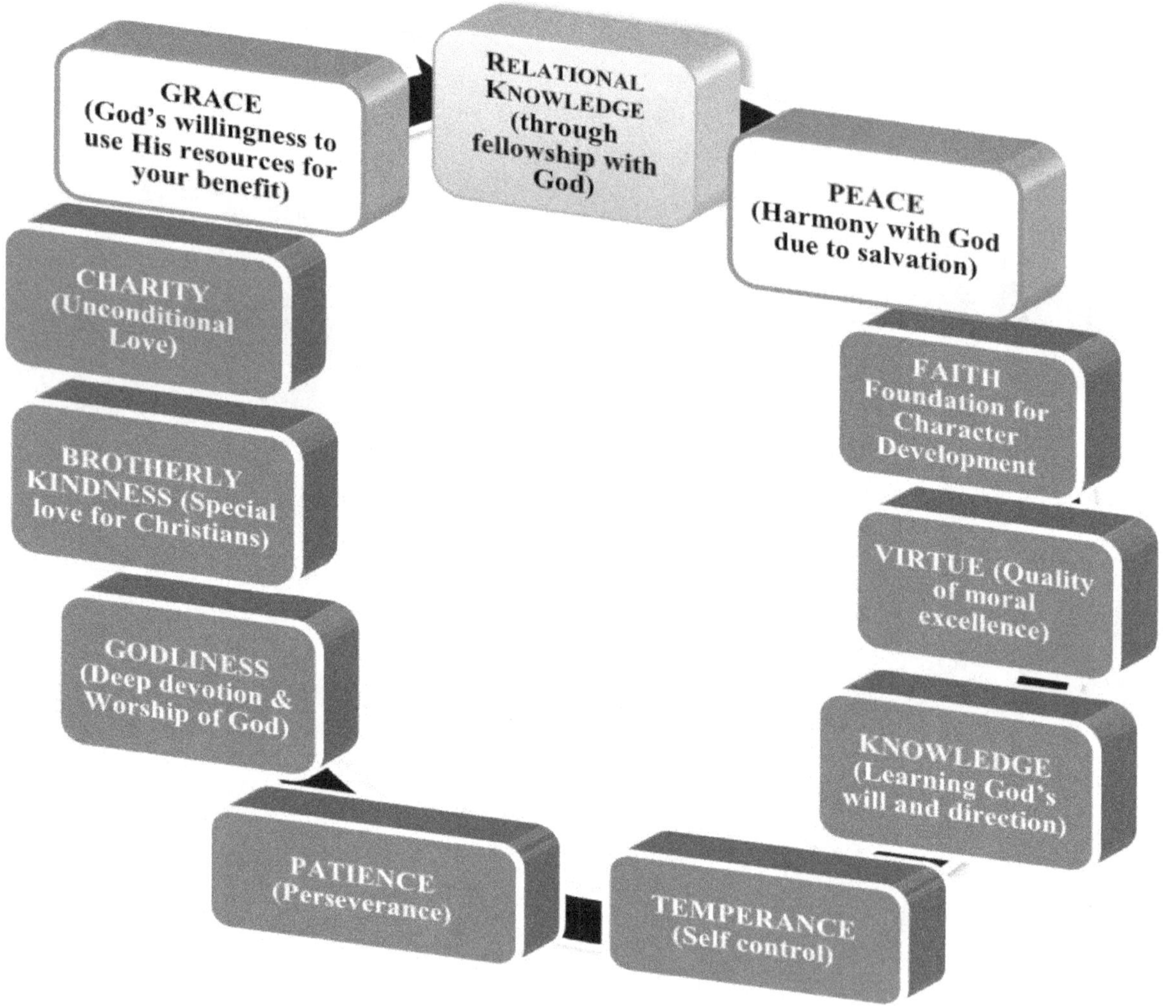

Figure 57: Developing Relational Knowledge of God

Virtue (goodness) is the quality of moral excellence, the ability to stand for and practice what you know is right. It is the quality of character of having the strength and courage to practice your knowledge of God's will for your life, now that you are saved. It is the willingness to do what is necessary so that you don't return to your old lifestyle (relapsing).

Knowledge is the ability to deal with circumstances and people wisely (prudence). You must learn God's will and direction for your life so you can follow it daily. Christian prudence will enable you to establish new friends and avoid your old ungodly associates/friends and environment from the past.

Patience (perseverance) is the ability to endure adverse or difficult situations while remaining calm. It is strength of character developed in the midst of the storm. It is a necessity for adjusting to your new lifestyle that will have numerous trials and tribulations due to the conflict that will be waging inside of you between your new nature and the desires of the flesh.

Temperance or self-control is a much-needed fruit of the Spirit due to your past lifestyle of living out of control. You must learn to be sober and to use moderation in every aspect of your natural living—rest, recreation, diet, finances (spending/credit), work. Temperance is a part of the fruit of the Spirit and is a result of "sowing to the Spirit." Jesus, our savior, exhibited the ultimate example of self-control as He was tempted in every way, yet did not sin (Hebrew 4:15).

- ☐ This relational knowledge is the key factor in leading you into a deeper, more meaningful relationship with both God and your neighbor, and enables you to fulfill the first and second greatest commandments.

Godliness is a quality that God will bless you with as a result of you actively participating with Him, which will result in you entering into an even deeper relationship with Him. Your devotion and worship will become much deeper and your relationship with Him more meaningful. God will honor your desire to love and worship Him with a quality that will increase that desire and love. He will reward you for your faithfulness within your relationship with Him.

Brotherly kindness is a special love that Christians have for one another because of a common spiritual bond. It is a much-needed quality that will enable you to establish meaningful relationships within the Body of Christ. You must learn that you are a member of the household of faith, and developing this Christlike quality will help you feel at home with the other saints in a local church.

Charity is agape or the quality of unconditional love. You need to understand that this fruit of love is a special love that only God can give, an unselfish love. Before you can love God or another person, you must first *receive* (experience) this special love—God's love. You must also remember that to love is not an option but something that God commands every Christian to do, and that it is an act of the will; it is a decision one makes. 2 Peter 1:8 declares, "For if you possess these qualities in increasing measure, they will keep you from being ineffective and unproductive in your knowledge of our Lord Jesus Christ" (NIV).

If you are intentional about developing relational knowledge by actively participating with the Holy Spirit, these qualities will keep you from being unproductive and ineffective in your relationship with God and returning to your old lifestyles.

> But if anyone does not have them, he is nearsighted and blind and has forgotten that he has been cleansed from his past sins. (2 Peter 1:9, NIV)

If you fail to develop relational knowledge by actively participating with the Holy Spirit, grace and peace—the two vital ingredients necessary for spiritual growth and development—are limited, and these qualities are hindered in your life. At this point, returning "to sowing to the flesh" and relapsing is inevitable.

> Wherefore the rather, brethren, give diligence to make your calling and election sure: for if ye do these things, ye shall never fall (relapse). (2 Peter 1:10)

- ☐ Your calling and election are confirmed through your character development as a result of an increase in God's grace and peace through your relational knowledge of Him.
- ☐ It is your relational knowledge (participating with Him) of God that keeps you from relapsing, returning to your old lifestyle of practicing the "works of the flesh (using drugs/alcohol)."
- ☐ If you are actively participating with Him, you will develop the Christlike character that provides you with an increase in grace and peace, allowing you to grow close to God and to continue in your relationship with God. You will receive what you need to continue by participating daily in His plan for you.

CHARACTER DEVELOPMENT THROUGH PARTICIPATING WITH GOD

Self-Check

Wherefore the rather, brethren, give diligence to make your calling and election sure: *for if ye do these things, ye shall never fall (relapse).* (2 Peter 1:10)

Using a scale from 1-10, ***(1 being very little)*** *and* ***(10 being quite a lot)****, place a number on the slot that best indicates how much* ***growth*** *you have* ***experienced*** *in the seven areas listed below.*

1. **Faith** ___
2. **Virtue** ___
3. **Knowledge** ___
4. **Self-control** ___
5. **Patience** ___
6. **Godliness** ___
7. **Brotherly Kindness** ___

*If you answered most of the questions "****very little,****" you need to make a commitment to allow the Holy Spirit to develop the Christ-like qualities in you listed above to prevent you from relapsing.*

Action Steps

List two things you are willing to do to increase your opportunity to develop Christlike qualities.

1.
2.

What scripture in this section has had the greatest impact in your life? Explain that experience with your group.

THE SIX BASIC SPIRITUAL DISCIPLINES

A Means to God's Grace

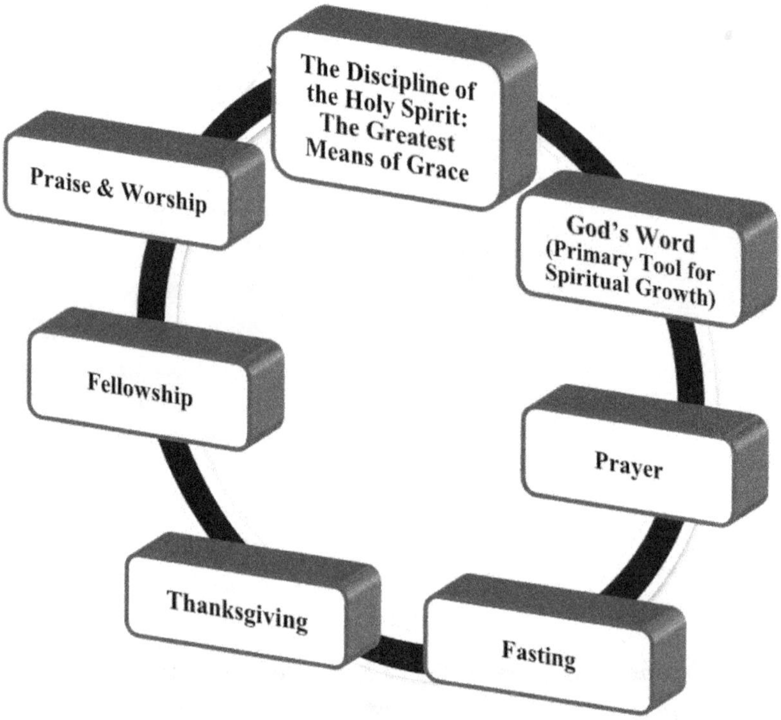

Figure 58: The Spiritual Disciplines

A farmer is helpless to grow grain; all he can do is provide the right conditions for the growing of grain. He cultivates the ground, he plants the seed, he waters the plants, and then the natural forces of the earth take over and up comes the grain. This is the way it is with the Spiritual Disciplines; they are the way of sowing to the Spirit.

The Disciplines are God's way of getting us into the ground; they put us where He can work within us and transform us. By themselves, the Spiritual Disciplines can do nothing; they can only get us to a place where something can be done. They are God's means of grace. The inner righteousness we seek is not something that is poured on our heads. God has ordained the Disciplines of the spiritual life as the means by which we place ourselves where He can bless us.

You Must Do	You Cannot Do
(position to receive grace)	Make yourself grow

Meditate on God's Word
Study God's Word
Praise/Thanksgiving to God
Prayer

Control the conditions of growth

Positioning Yourself to Receive Grace to Grow

Self-Check

> *Grace* and *peace* be multiplied unto you through the knowledge (relational) of God, and of Jesus our Lord. (2 Peter 1:2)

Using a scale from 1-10, ***(1 no time)*** and ***(10 being a lot of time)***, place a number on the slot that best indicates how much ***time*** you spend practicing each of the six basic spiritual disciplines listed below.

1. Meditating (studying) on God's Word ______
2. Fellowshipping with Other Christians ______
3. Praise/Worship ______
4. Prayer ______
5. Fasting ______
6. Thanksgiving ______

Self-Rating

How would you rate your understanding of God's *grace*? Discuss your answer with your group.

How would you rate your understanding of how to *receive God's grace*? Discuss your answer with your group

Action Steps

List three things you are willing to do to increase your understanding of God's grace.

1.
2.
3.

List three things you are willing to do to receive more of God's grace.

1.
2.
3.

What scripture in this section has had the greatest impact in your life? Explain that experience with your group.

UNDERSTANDING PEACE

Peace, the second essential ingredient, is the tranquil condition of the mind, which is a result of you experiencing your relationship with Christ. You can be at ease or rest mentally knowing that your life is in the right order with God. Peace, like joy, is not dependent upon your circumstances but your relationship with God.

- ☐ Jesus is the Prince of Peace and provides peace to all that accept Him as Lord through the Spirit.

  Therefore, since we have been justified through faith, we have *peace with God through our Lord Jesus Christ.* (Romans 5:1, NIV)

- ☐ Peace is a result of entering into a right relational standing with God, being pardoned of your sins by being washed in the blood of Jesus.

  For they that are after the flesh do mind the things of the flesh; but they that are after the Spirit the things of the Spirit. *For to be carnally minded is death; but to be spiritually minded is life and peace.* Because the carnal mind *is* enmity (hostile) against God: for it is not subject to the law of God, neither indeed can be. So then they that are in the flesh cannot please God. But ye are not in the flesh, but in the Spirit, if so be that the Spirit of God dwell in you. Now if any man have not the Spirit of Christ, he is none of His. (Romans 8:5–9)

- ☐ Peace is a product of continuing in your relationship with God by allowing your mind to be restored through the Word and learning to allow the Holy Spirit to lead, guide, and direct your life.

  But the fruit of the Spirit is love, joy, *peace,* longsuffering, gentleness, goodness, faith, meekness, temperance: against such there is no law. (Galatians 5:22–23)

- ☐ Peace is a fruit of the Spirit provided by the Spirit for you as you learn to cooperate with Him by following God's agenda for your life through living a godly lifestyle.

  Do not be anxious about anything, but in everything, by prayer and petition, with thanksgiving, present your requests to God. And the peace of God, which transcends all understanding, will guard your hearts and your minds in Christ Jesus. (Philippians 4:6–7, NIV)

- ☐ You will experience peace as a result of your learning to trust God and submitting all your cares to Him in prayer and by maintaining an attitude of thanksgiving, rather than becoming anxious.

  You will keep in perfect peace him whose mind is steadfast, because he trusts in you. Trust in the LORD forever, for the LORD, the LORD, is the Rock eternal. (Isaiah 26:3–4, NIV)

Both these essentials (grace and peace) are provided *"through the knowledge of God, and of Jesus our Lord."* This is a special knowledge gained in a relational learning process with the Holy Spirit and is the key to Peter's formula to prevent you from returning to your old lifestyle.

- ☐ Relational knowledge means a clear and exact knowledge through being actively involved in a relational learning process with God, resulting in spiritual growth and development.
- ☐ Relational knowledge is more intimate than knowing God at the time of your rebirth, because it expresses a more thorough participation with God.
- ☐ It refers to a relational knowledge that affects your spiritual growth and development, because it provides you with the additional grace and peace necessary for continued relational growth and development.

  His divine power has given us everything we need for life and godliness through our knowledge of him who called us by his own glory and goodness. (2 Peter 1:3, NIV)

Through His power, God has provided all you need to live a godly life; there is no need to return to your old lifestyle. God called you out of your addiction into a relationship with Him.

- ☐ God has transformed you spiritually through your rebirth, bringing you into a right relational standing with Him (justification), adopting you into His family with full rights. He has provided you a position of holiness and every spiritual blessing necessary to grow up in your position (sanctification) in Christ.

  Through these, he has given us his very great and precious promises, so that through them you may participate in the divine nature and escape the corruption in the world caused by evil desires. (2 Peter 1:4, NIV)

Through your new birth and the indwelling of the Holy Spirit, you now are able to escape your addiction and overcome your evil desires to use drugs/alcohol.

The Holy Spirit increases this relational knowledge by your active participation with Him in a relational learning process by allowing Him to confirm the Word of God in your everyday life.

> And beside this, giving all diligence, add to your faith virtue; and to virtue knowledge; And to knowledge temperance (self-control); and to temperance patience; and to patience godliness; And to godliness brotherly kindness; and to brotherly kindness charity. (2 Peter 1:5–7)

You are instructed to put forth great effort (be intentional) to add to your faith several Christlike qualities.

- ☐ Paul is referring to a relational knowledge that powerfully influences the spiritual quality of your life, because it promotes Christlike qualities in you.

Understanding Peace

Self-Rating

How would you rate your understanding of God's *peace*? Discuss your answer with your group.

How would you rate your understanding of how to *receive God's peace*? Discuss your answer with your group.

Action Steps

List three things you are willing to do to increase your understanding of God's peace.

1.
2.
3.

List three things you are willing to do to receive more of God's peace.

1.
2.
3.

What scripture in this section has had the greatest impact in your life? Explain that experience with your group.

THE DISCIPLINE OF THE HOLY SPIRIT: GOD'S GREATEST MEANS OF GRACE

> I planted the seed, Apollos watered it, but *God made it grow.* So neither he who plants nor he who waters is anything, *but only God, who makes things grow.* (1 Corinthians 3:6–7, NIV)

> I am the vine; you are the branches. If a man remains in me and I in him, he will bear much fruit; *apart from me you can do.* (John 15:5, NIV)

Just as in the example of farming, God has provided certain disciplines or ways that are necessary in order for you to grow and overcome your addiction. You must learn to actively participate in these disciplines or they will not grow, just as a farmer who does not perform his duties will not produce a crop.

Most farmers place their confidence in their duties. You must not make the same mistake; you must not place your confidence in God's spiritual disciplines by themselves (prayer, meditation, etc.), but realize they are means to an end but *not the end* themselves. You must continually realize your dependence on God. The spiritual disciplines do not work on their own apart from God. You must understand and not neglect the *greatest means of all grace, which is the discipline of the Holy Spirit.* This is God's most important means of grace.

> And I will ask the Father, and he will give you another Counselor to be with you forever—*the Spirit of truth.* The world cannot accept him, because it neither sees him nor knows him. But you know him, *for he lives with you and will be in you.* (John 14:16–17, NIV)
>
> But I tell you the truth: It is for your good that I am going away. Unless I go away, the Counselor will not come to you; but if I go, I will send him to you. *8 When he comes, he will convict the world of guilt in regard to sin and righteousness and judgment: 9* in regard to sin, because men do not believe in me; (John 16:7–9, NIV)
>
> But the Counselor, the Holy Spirit, whom the Father will send in my name, *will teach you all things and will remind you of everything I have said to you.* (John 14:26, NIV)

A major role of the Holy Spirit is as a teacher, to bring every Christian into the truth and relational knowledge of Christ Jesus.

- ☐ This is accomplished through fellowship by gaining full, accurate, and personal knowledge of God through the teaching ministry of the Holy Spirit.

The primary tool for gaining this relational knowledge (experiencing fellowship) is the Word of God.

> As newborn babes, *desire the pure milk of the word*, that you may grow thereby, if indeed you have tasted that the Lord *is* gracious. Coming to Him *as to* a living stone, rejected indeed by men, but chosen by God *and* precious, you also, *as living stones, are being built up* a spiritual house, a holy priesthood, to offer up spiritual sacrifices acceptable to God through Jesus Christ. (1 Peter 2:2–5)

Relapse prevention begins in the Word. In order for you to overcome the effects of addiction, you must be continually committed to studying and applying the Word in your daily life. God's Word is the foundation on which your spiritual growth is built. The Holy Spirit teaches you through the Word and then provides opportunities through discipline (training) for the Word to become operative in your life. The discipline of the Holy Spirit provides opportunities for construction in your life, an opportunity for you to be "built-up."

> And you have forgotten that word of encouragement that addresses you as sons: "My son, *do not make light of the Lord's discipline*, and do not lose heart when he rebukes you, because the *Lord disciplines those he loves*, and he punishes everyone he accepts as a son." Endure hardship as discipline; God is treating you as sons. For what son is not disciplined by his father? If you are not disciplined (and everyone undergoes discipline), then you are illegitimate children and not true sons. Moreover, we have all had human fathers who disciplined us and we respected them for it. How much more should we *submit to the Father of our spirits and live!* Our fathers disciplined us for a little while as they thought best; but *God disciplines us for our good, that we may share in his holiness*. No discipline seems pleasant at the time, but painful. Later on, however, *it produces a harvest of righteousness* and *peace* for those who have been trained by it. (Hebrews 12:5–11, NIV)

God the Holy Spirit continually allows opportunities to guide you into further spiritual development. When you fail to accept these disciplines as being beneficial for your spiritual growth and development, they quench His working and hinder your preparation for reaching a higher level of maturity. You must learn to submit to the disciplining of the Holy Spirit and view them as positive opportunities for growth and development (character development).

> Consider it pure joy, my brothers, whenever you face trials of many kinds, because you know that the testing of your faith *develops perseverance. Perseverance must finish its work so that you may be mature and complete, not lacking anything.* If any of you lacks wisdom, he should ask God, who gives generously to all without finding fault, and it will be given to him. (James 1:2–5, NIV)

> Blessed is the man who *perseveres under trial*, because when he has stood the test, he will receive the crown of life that God has promised to those who love him. (James 1:12, NIV)
>
> Not only so, but we also rejoice in our sufferings, because we know *that suffering produces perseverance; perseverance, character; and character, hope*. And hope does not disappoint us, because God has poured out his love into our hearts by the Holy Spirit, whom he has given us. (Romans 5:3–5, NIV)
>
> n this you greatly rejoice, though now for a little while you may have had *to suffer grief in all kinds of trials. These have come so that your faith—of greater worth than gold, which perishes even though refined by fire—may be proved genuine* and may result in praise, glory and honor when Jesus Christ is revealed. (1 Peter 1:6–7, NIV)

When believers being restored from addiction encounter difficult people, circumstances, hardship, trials, and tribulations, often they are viewed as negative opportunities and are avoided. Many take the easy way out and miss excellent opportunities for the Holy Spirit to allow the Word to be built-up in their lives and to become operative. How you respond to the disciplining of the Holy Spirit will determine whether you benefit from the opportunity to grow, which will prevent you from relapsing.

> And we know that *all things work together for good to those who love God*, to those who are the *called according to His purpose*. For whom He foreknew, He also predestined *to be conformed (molded) to the image (likeness) of His Son*, that He might be the firstborn among many brethren. (Romans 8:28–29)

God promises to work all things out for the good of His children, but many times we fail to understand and accept the methods God uses and how He works all things out. He uses the disciplining of the Holy Spirit, trials, tribulations, difficult people, and circumstances to provide character development by molding believers into the image and likeness of Christ.

God has already dealt with root causes of all life's issues, (sin) on the cross, including addiction to drugs/alcohol. A major role of the Holy Spirit is as a teacher, to bring every Christian into the truth and knowledge of Christ Jesus in order that His victory on the cross can become a part of a believer's everyday life.

You must understand and not neglect the greatest means of all grace, which is the discipline of the Holy Spirit. This is God's most important means of grace.

DISCIPLINE OF THE HOLY SPIRIT: GOD'S GREATEST MEANS OF GRACE

Self-Rating

How would you rate your understanding of God's *disciplines*? Discuss your answer with your group.

How would you rate your understanding of how to *receive God's disciplines*? Discuss your answer with your group.

Action Steps

List three things you are willing to do to increase your understanding of God's *disciplines*

1.
2.
3.

List three things you are willing to do to submit to more of God's *disciplines.*

1.
2.
3.

What scripture in this section has had the greatest impact in your life? Explain that experience with your group.

PART ONE

Fundamental Attitudes Necessary for Spiritual Maturity

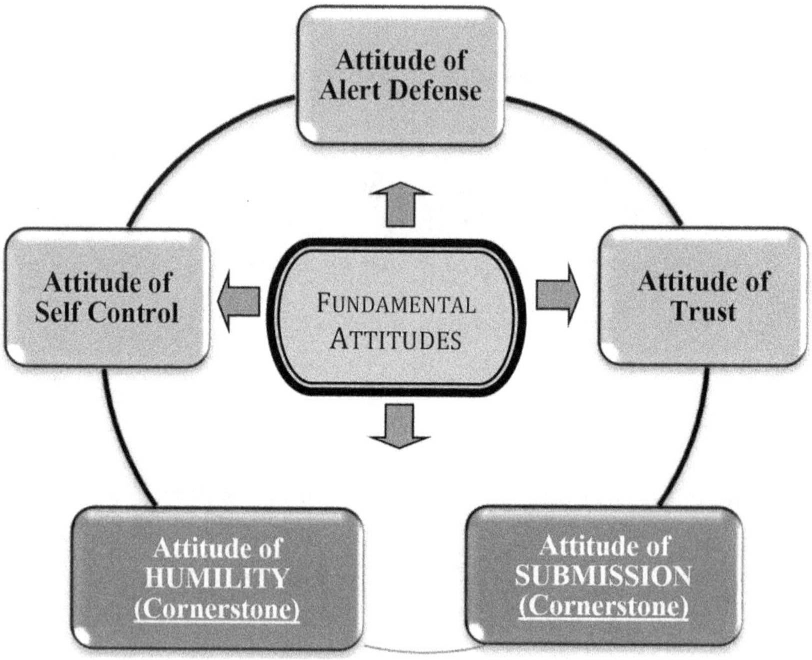

Figure 59: The Fundamental Attitudes

If you don't learn to cooperate with the Holy Spirit, "sowing to the Spirit," you will return to "sowing to the flesh," or relapse (become entangled in your old addictive lifestyles). The Apostle Peter discusses a set of attitudes necessary for spiritual growth leading to change through character development. Dr. John MacArthur Jr. refers to these attitudes as *"the fundamental attitudes for spiritual growth."*

- ☐ Godly wisdom through knowing His Word and practicing it daily in fellowship with Him is the foundation for the basic attitudes necessary for spiritual growth.

Attitude of Submission

For a believer to willingly come under the authority of God and other superiors and assume a dependent position.

> Young men, in the same way *be submissive to* those who are older. All of you, clothe yourselves with humility toward one another, because, "God opposes the proud but gives grace to the humble." Humble yourselves, therefore, under God's mighty hand, that he may lift you up in due time. (1 Peter 5:5–6, NIV)

Peter's theme throughout this passage of scripture is directed toward the basic motives or attitudes needed for character development and spiritual maturity. *Submission* and *humility* are the first two attitudes discussed in this passage of scripture and *are the cornerstones for spiritual maturity.* As a believer, you must understand the significant role these two Christlike qualities play in your spiritual growth through character development.

- ☐ Submission counteracts a familiar tool of the enemy—rebellion caused by selfish pride.
- ☐ An attitude of submission is significant, because either you will submit to the principle of God's authority or the principle of the world's rebellion.
- ☐ You cannot serve two masters. You cannot serve God with a rebellious attitude. Obedience or submission to authority is the first lesson a believer should learn because it plays an important role in character development.
- ☐ As a believer, you must be honest and acknowledge that in the past, you most likely have demonstrated an attitude of rebellion of some degree.

> Obey your leaders and submit to their authority. They keep watch over you as men who must give an account. Obey them so that their work will be a joy, not a burden, for that would be of no advantage to you. (Hebrews 13:17, NIV)
>
> Now we ask you, brothers, to respect those who work hard among you, who are over you in the Lord and who admonish you. Hold them in the highest regard in love because of their work. Live in peace with each other. (1 Thessalonians 5:12–13, NIV)

It is necessary for you to be actively attending a local church body under the authority of a pastor or elder. *A lone ranger mentality* will allow you to stray from the Body of Christ, hindering your character development, and possibly result in you returning to your old lifestyle.

> Submit yourselves for the Lord's sake to every authority instituted among men: whether to the king, as the supreme authority, or to governors, who are sent by him to punish those who do wrong and to commend those who do right. For it is God's will that by doing good you should silence the ignorant talk of foolish men. Live as free men, but do not use your freedom as a cover-up for evil; live as servants of God. (1 Peter 2:13–16, NIV)
>
> Everyone must submit himself to the governing authorities, for there is no authority except that which God has established. The authorities that exist have been established by God. Consequently, he who rebels against the authority is rebelling against what God has instituted, and those who do so will bring judgment on themselves. For rulers hold no terror for those who do right, but for those who do wrong. Do you want to be free from fear of the one in authority? Then do what is right and he will commend you. (Romans 13:1–3, NIV)

- ☐ You must learn to submit to all laws and regulations—federal, state, and local governments.
- ☐ You must be in continuous prayer for the death of your pride, actively involved in the confession of sin, and developing confidence in a caring God to develop an attitude of submission.

1 Samuel 15:23 declares, "*For rebellion is as the sin of witchcraft, and stubbornness is as iniquity and idolatry.* Because thou hast rejected the word of the LORD, he hath also rejected thee from *being* king."

- ☐ You must understand that there is no sin as serious as rebellion and nothing more important than obedience through submission.
- ☐ All authority is established by God and responsible to God for how they use that authority; and you are responsible for how you respond to their authority.

> Submit yourselves, then, to God. Resist the devil, and he will flee from you. (James 4:7, NIV)

- ☐ Submission to God is a necessity for being successful in spiritual warfare.

Attitude of Humility

For a believer to have an accurate view of oneself, realizing total dependence on God, having nothing…receiving everything from God.

> Young men, in the same way be submissive to those who are older. All of you, *clothe yourselves with humility toward one another*, because, *"God opposes the proud but gives grace to the humble." Humble yourselves*, therefore, under God's mighty hand, *that he may lift you up in due time.* (1 Peter 5:5–6, NIV)

- ☐ A prideful attitude will hinder the grace necessary from God for your spiritual growth and character development.

> But he giveth more grace. Wherefore he saith, *"God resisteth the proud, but giveth grace unto the humble."* (James 4:6, NIV)

- ☐ A prideful attitude not only will result in hindering your growth and development, it will also place you in opposition to God.

> *The LORD detests all the proud of heart. Be sure of this: They will not go unpunished.* (Proverbs 16:5, NIV)
>
> *Pride goes before destruction, a haughty spirit before a fall.* Better to be lowly in spirit and among the oppressed than to share plunder with the proud. (Proverbs 16:18–19, NIV)
>
> The fear of the LORD teaches a man wisdom, and *humility comes before honor.* (Proverbs 15:33, NIV)

> Before destruction the heart of man is haughty, and *before honor is humility.* (Proverbs 18:12)
>
> *Humble yourselves in the sight of the Lord, and he shall lift you up.* (James 4:10)

The second and equally significant cornerstone of spiritual growth through character development is *humility.* Just as submission attacks self-pride, humility attacks self-love. As a believer, you must understand and develop a biblical view of servitude that is obtained through an attitude of humility. You must have a biblical view of yourself in God's marvelous plan here on earth. Jesus demonstrated the ultimate act of humility as He left His glory with the Father in heaven and came in the form of a servant to die for mankind.

- ☐ Humility is a key characteristic of Jesus, and the Scriptures instruct every Christian to be like-minded. Humility or meekness is an attitude that is developed through the continual yielding and adhering to the discipline of your spiritual mentor, the Holy Spirit. Through that yielding, you will develop a deep respect or reverence for God.
- ☐ The world has an incorrect view of humility. Humility is not weakness, it is having a true or correct view of yourself and your position in God's family. Learning to be humble is learning to give God His respect. You need to be involved in a daily devotional of prayer, praise, and worship to assist in developing an attitude of humility.
- ☐ You need to be teachable, open to the instruction of the Word and the teaching ministry of the Holy Spirit.

> If you have any encouragement from being united with Christ, if any comfort from his love, if any fellowship with the Spirit, if any tenderness and compassion, then make my joy complete by being like–minded, having the same love, being one in spirit and purpose. Do nothing out of selfish ambition or vain conceit, but in humility consider others better than yourselves. Each of you should look not only to your own interests, but also to the interests of others. Your attitude should be the same as that of Christ Jesus: (Philippians 2:1–5, NIV)

Attitude of Trust

An attitude of trust is to be set free from fear and doubt, having confidence in God, having learned to depend on Him to meet all needs.

> Trust in the LORD with all your heart and lean not on your own understanding; in all your ways acknowledge him, and he will make your paths straight. Do not be wise in your own eyes; fear the LORD and shun evil. (Proverbs 3:5–7, NIV)
>
> It is better to take refuge in the LORD than to trust in man. It is better to take refuge in the LORD than to trust in princes. (Psalm 118:8–9, NIV)
>
> O taste and see that the LORD *is* good: blessed *is* the man *that* trusteth in him. O fear the LORD, ye his saints: for *there is* no want to them that fear him. Young lions do lack, and suffer hunger: but they that seek the LORD shall not want any good *thing.* (Psalm 34:8–10)

> *Trust in him at all times; ye* people, pour out your heart before him: God *is* a refuge for us. Selah.
>
> *Trust not in oppression*, and become not vain in robbery: if riches increase, set not your heart *upon them*. (Psalm 62:8,10)

The third basic attitude of spiritual growth necessary for your character development is an attitude of *trust*. Trust is a must for spiritual growth because it plays a key role in your relationship with God and other Christians.

- ☐ 1 Peter 5:7 says, "Casting all your care upon him; for he careth for you." This particular attitude assists believers in remaining humble. You must trust God with your affairs, issues, and burdens to be free to walk with the Lord.
- ☐ You must learn to view God as your source of significance through your relationship with Christ. Trust is by far the most difficult aspect of faith because it captures the personal application of faith, an act that primarily involves the heart and will but which also includes the mind and emotions.

You must participate in God's plan for developing trust by consenting to the Scriptures, studying the truths of Christian faith, and being willing to act on those truths. You must be a hearer and doer of the Word, involved in Bible study, Christian education, constantly placing yourself in position to be strengthened through the Scriptures. You must understand that without God's Word you cannot learn to trust Him.

Attitude of Self-Control

An attitude of self-control is characterized by being willing to abstain from fleshly appetites, passion, and desires, being forearmed with the understanding of how the world caters to them and Satan's desire to exploit them. It involves being willing to allow the Holy Spirit to guide you in mortifying the flesh.

> Be self-controlled and alert. Your enemy the devil prowls around like a roaring lion looking for someone to devour. Resist him, standing firm in the faith, because you know that your brothers throughout the world are undergoing the same kind of sufferings. (1 Peter 5:8–9, NIV)
>
> The end of all things is near. Therefore, be clear minded and self-controlled so that you can pray. (1 Peter 4:7, IV)
>
> Like a city whose walls are broken down is a man who lacks self-control. (Proverbs 25:28)
>
> It teaches us to say "No" to ungodliness and worldly passions, and to *live self-controlled*, upright and godly lives in this present age, while we wait for the blessed hope—the glorious appearing of our great God and savior, Jesus Christ, who gave himself for us to redeem us from all wickedness and to purify for himself a people that are his very own, eager to do what is good. (Titus 2:12–14, NIV)

> *But the fruit of the Spirit* is love, joy, peace, patience, kindness, goodness, faithfulness, gentleness and *self-control.* Against such things there is no law. (Galatians 5:22–23, NIV)

The fourth fundamental attitude of spiritual maturity is an attitude of *self-control.* Temperance or self-control is listed among the fruit of the Spirit. Your spiritual mentor, the Holy Spirit, provides self-control through your active fellowship with Him, learning to be obedient to the Word (walking in union with the Spirit). You must remember to remain spiritually focused and not to get caught up in the flesh and the affairs of the world.

> Therefore, prepare your minds for action; *be self-controlled*; set your hope fully on the grace to be given you when Jesus Christ is revealed. *As obedient children, do not conform to the evil desires you had when you lived in ignorance.* But just as he who called you is holy, so be holy in all you do. (1 Peter 1:13–15, NIV)

- ☐ A believer is called to prepare his/her mind for self-control by developing a disciplined mind and avoiding worldly attitudes of his/her old lifestyles.

> You must teach what is in accord with sound doctrine. *Teach the older men to be temperate, worthy of respect, self-controlled,* and sound in faith, in love and in endurance. (Titus 2:1–2, NIV)
>
> And do this, understanding the present time. The hour has come for you to wake up from your slumber, because our salvation is nearer now than when we first believed. The night is nearly over; the day is almost here. So let us put aside the deeds of darkness and put on the armor of light. *Let us behave decently, as in the daytime, not in orgies and drunkenness, not in sexual immorality and debauchery, not in dissension and jealousy.* Rather, clothe yourselves with the Lord Jesus Christ, *and do not think about how to gratify the desires of the sinful nature.* (Romans 13:11–14, NIV)

You are called to abstain from alcohol, drugs, sexual activity outside of marriage, to resist the desires and impulses of the world, and to be self-controlled and sound-minded. God's Word clearly explains how you are not to feed the desires of your flesh.

- ☐ This means that you are to avoid anything that excites your flesh, causing you to have ungodly desires. This excitement comes in many different forms: movies, a television program, song or type of music, books or magazines, attending clubs or parties, an old friend or associate, or even a conversation glorifying the world.
- ☐ You must learn to avoid any and all people, places, and things that cause your flesh to become excited.

> *Do not be yoked together with unbelievers.* For what do righteousness and wickedness have in common? Or what fellowship can light have with darkness? What harmony is there between Christ and Belial? What does a believer have in common with an unbeliever? What agreement is there between the temple of God and idols? For we

> are the temple of the living God. As God has said: "I will live with them and walk among them, and I will be their God, and they will be my people. *Therefore, come out from them and be separate, says the Lord. Touch no unclean thing, and I will receive you.* I will be a Father to you, and you will be my sons and daughters," says the Lord Almighty. (2 Corinthians 6:14–18, NIV)

- ☐ You must remember that the Scriptures teach that bad company corrupts good character.
- ☐ Giving into the desires of your flesh will hinder your spiritual growth. Without being self-controlled, you will not be able to develop and maintain an attitude of an *alert defense*, the final basic attitude for spiritual growth.

Attitude of an Alert Defense

Being keenly aware of and prepared for the spiritual warfare designed to hinder your relationship with God and others and to hinder your spiritual growth and development.

> Be self-controlled and alert. Your enemy the devil prowls around like a roaring lion looking for someone to devour. Resist him, standing firm in the faith, because you know that your brothers throughout the world are undergoing the same kind of sufferings. (1 Peter 5:8–9, NIV)
>
> *"Be careful, or your hearts will be weighed down with dissipation, drunkenness and the anxieties of life,* and that day will close on you unexpectedly like a trap. For it will come upon all those who live on the face of the whole earth. *Be always on the watch,* and pray that you may be able to escape all that is about to happen, and that you may be able to stand before the Son of Man." (Luke 21:34–36, NIV)
>
> The end of all things is near. *Therefore, be clear minded and self-controlled so that you can pray.* (1 Peter 4:7, NIV)

Finally, you must be alert, watchful, and cautious, understanding that carelessness will result in you being suddenly overtaken by some destructive action designed by the enemy to hinder your spiritual growth and development.

- ☐ The attitude of self-control works hand in hand with the attitude of an alert defense. You must develop the understanding that the victory has already been won, that your savior has already dealt Satan a defeating blow and has overcome the world and the flesh.
- ☐ You must learn to engage the enemy from a position of victory. You must learn, "For though we walk in the flesh, we do not war after the flesh: for the weapons of our warfare are not carnal but mighty through God to the pulling down of strong holds" (2 Corinthians 10:3,4).
- ☐ You must learn to realize that the soul (mind, will, emotions) is where the war is waged, with the mind as the primary battlefield.
- ☐ You must be alert, watchful, and aware of the schemes and devices of the enemy and must be properly dressed for battle.
- ☐ The attitudes of submission, humility, trust, self-control, and alert defense are all basic attitudes necessary for spiritual growth.

You, however, did not come to know Christ that way. *Surely you heard of him and were taught in him in accordance with the truth that is in Jesus.* You were taught, with regard to your former way of life, *to put off your old self,* which is being corrupted by its deceitful desires; to be made new in the *attitude of your minds.* (Ephesians 4:20–23, NIV)

FUNDAMENTAL ATTITUDES NECESSARY FOR SPIRITUAL MATURITY

Self-Check

Using a scale from 1-5, ***(1 being the attitude you have least problem with)*** *and* ***(5 being the attitude you have greatest problem with)****. Then place a number on the remaining slots that best indicates the degree of difficulty you are experiencing with each of the fundamental attitudes necessary listed below.*

1. Attitude of Submission ______
2. Attitude of Humility ______
3. Attitude of Trust ______
4. Attitude of Self control ______
5. Attitude of Alert Defense ______

Self-Rating

Answer the following questions within your group.

1. How would you rate your understanding of the *attitude of humility*?
2. How would you rate your understanding of the *attitude of submission*?
3. How would you rate your understanding of the *attitude of trust*?
4. How would you rate your understanding of the *attitude of self-control*?
5. How would you rate your understanding of the *attitude of alert defense*?

Action Steps

List two things you are willing to do to increase your understanding of an attitude of submission.

1.
2.

List two things you are willing to do to increase your understanding of an attitude of humility.

1.
2.

List two things you are willing to do to increase your understanding of an attitude of trust.

1.
2.

List two things you are willing to do to increase your understanding of an attitude of self-control.

1.
2.

List two things you are willing to do to increase your understanding of an attitude of alert defense.

1.
2.

What scripture in this section has had the greatest impact in your life? Explain that experience with your group.

THE "PUT OFF PUT ON" PRINCIPLE

Four Steps to Character Development

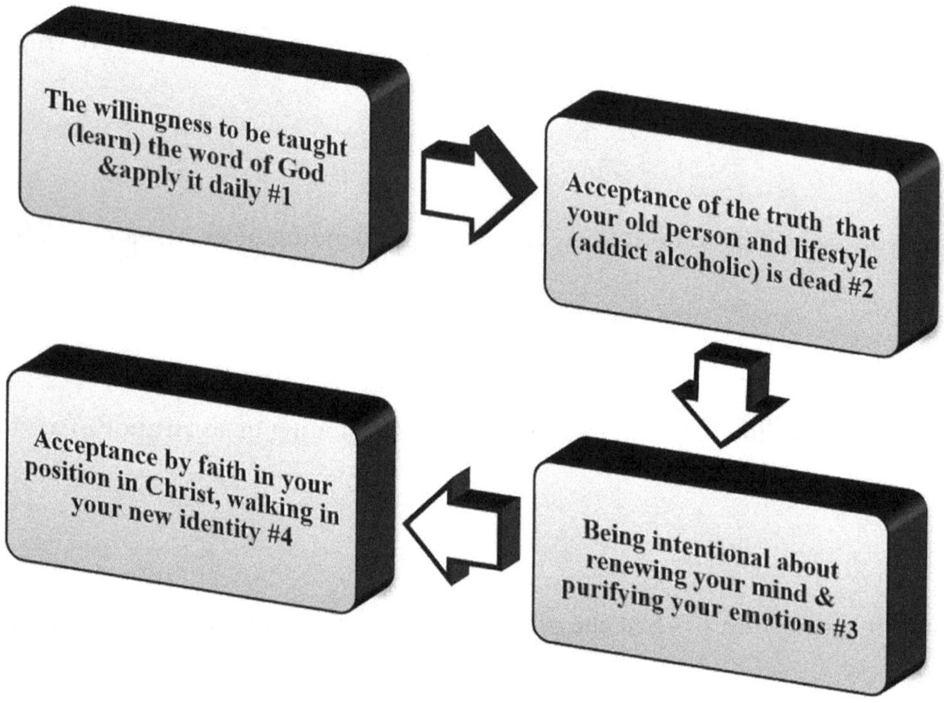

Figure 60: Character Development

Spiritual maturity through character development plays a significant role in you being restored from alcohol and other drugs, relapse prevention (returning to "sowing to the flesh"). scripture cites four crucial steps leading to character development.

> But ye have not so *learned* Christ; If so be that ye have heard him, *and have been taught by him, as the truth is in Jesus.* (Ephesians 4:20–21)

- ☐ You must be willing to learn about the Christian faith. You must be willing to be taught the Word and gain the biblical insight necessary to continue in a lifestyle of holiness and not return to your old addictive lifestyle.
- ☐ You must avail yourself to the Word by attending a local church and actively participate in not only worship service but also Bible studies, Sunday school, biblically based relapse pre-

vention classes, and maintain a daily devotion time with God. You must learn to pursue the Word of God like you did alcohol and other drugs.

- ☐ You must understand that in order to experience Christ's victory in your daily life, you must first be taught about Jesus and the truths of the Christian faith.

That ye *put off concerning the former conversation the old man, which is corrupt according to the deceitful lusts.* (Ephesians 4:22)

- ☐ You must understand and believe that your old person, the addict/alcoholic, is dead; and act accordingly. You must learn to value who God says that you are no longer what the world and everyone else says you are.

What shall we say then? Shall we continue in sin, that grace may abound? God forbid. How shall we, that are dead to sin, live any longer therein? *Know ye not, that so many of us as were baptized into Jesus Christ were baptized into his death? Therefore, we are buried with him by baptism into death: that like as Christ was raised up from the dead by the glory of the Father, even so we also should walk in newness of life.* For if we have been planted together in the likeness of his death, we shall be also *in the likeness* of *his* resurrection: *Knowing this, that our old man is crucified with him, that the body of sin might be destroyed, that henceforth we should not serve sin.* (Romans 6:1–6)

- ☐ You must accept your new life in Christ and accept that the old you have been crucified with Christ and that the "body of sin" which your addiction was a part of has been destroyed.
- ☐ You must be intentional about "putting off" past lifestyles of the old dead person. You must be willing to develop new relationships with the "Body of Christ" and discontinue old relationships from your past that are detrimental to your relationship with God.
- ☐ You must be willing to avoid old neighborhoods and places that could tempt you to return to your old lifestyle. You must be committed to developing a thorough understanding of the Christian lifestyle and walking it daily.

To be made *new in the attitude* of your minds. (Ephesians 4:23, NIV)

Do not conform any longer to the pattern of this world, but *be transformed by the renewing of your mind.* Then you will be able to test and approve what God's will is—his good, pleasing and perfect will. (Romans 12:2, NIV)

- ☐ You must change your entire attitude by renewing your mind through the Word of God. Your mind must be transformed and your emotions purified in order for you to have a new attitude—the attitude of Christ.
- ☐ Without breaking the patterns of your old lifestyle and developing a new Christ-like attitude, you will not be able to know God's will for your life.

And that ye *put on the new man*, which after God is *created in righteousness and true holiness.* (Ephesians 4:24)

- ☐ You must develop an understanding of your new identity and develop faith in your position in Christ and learn to walk it daily.
- ☐ You must learn to view yourself as God sees you and accept the miraculous work the Holy Spirit did to you during salvation and to cooperate with the Holy Spirit in the work He's performing in your conduct and character daily.

  And *grieve not the Holy Spirit of God*, whereby ye are sealed unto the day of redemption. (Ephesians 4:30)

- ☐ God the Holy Spirit is the most important person in your restoration process and is the one who will ultimately keep you from returning to a lifestyle of addiction if you will just learn to cooperate with Him.
- ☐ You must realize that failing to cooperate with God the Holy Spirit as He works in your life to develop a Christlike attitude in you will cause Him *grief*. Failing to cooperate with the Holy Spirit gives Satan an opportunity in your life.

FOUR STEPS TO CHARACTER DEVELOPMENT

Self–Check

To be made *new in the attitude* of your minds. (Eph. 4:23 NIV)

Answer the following questions within your group.

1. How well do you understand *step #1* of character development?
2. At what level are you applying *step #1* to your everyday life?
3. How well do you understand *step #2* of character development?
4. At what level are you applying *step #2* to your everyday life?
5. How well do you understand *step #3* of character development?
6. At what level are you applying *step #3* to your everyday life?
7. How well do you understand *step #4* of character development?
8. At what level are you applying *step #4* to your everyday life?

Action Steps

List three things you are willing to do to become more involved in your character development.

1.
2.
3.

What scripture in this section has had the greatest impact in your life? Explain that experience with your group.

Prayer for Character Development

Dear heavenly Father, I thank you for Your desire to mold and shape me into the image of Your Son, Jesus Christ. I thank You for the "fruit of Your Spirit" that You have placed in me so I can develop a Christlike character. I also thank You for spiritual disciplines—Your Word, prayer, praise and worship, thanksgiving, fellowship, and fasting—that I can use to put myself in position to receive the grace I need to grow. Father, help me to renew my attitude so I can continue to grow in relational knowledge of You and reach my full potential in Christ Jesus.

In Jesus Name I pray; *Amen!*

Phase Five

OVERCOMING THE EFFECTS OF ADDICTION

But each one is tempted when, by his own evil desire, he is dragged away and enticed. Then, after desire has conceived, it gives birth to sin; and sin, when it is full–grown, gives birth to death.

—James 1:14–15, NIV

Learning Objectives

For workshop participants to be able to:

- ☐ Distinguish the difference between "the world's recovery system" and the "biblical approach" to addressing addiction.
- ☐ Define the process of *relapse.*
- ☐ Define what a craving, trigger, and set-up behavior is.
- ☐ Distinguish between the different types of triggers, cravings, and set-up behaviors.
- ☐ Describe the major set-up behavior.

Key biblical Concepts and Definitions

(1) *Cravings:* Temptations in the form of desires, lust, appetites, and passion for drugs, alcohol, and other works of the flesh practiced in the old lifestyle. They may be stimulated by old thoughts, memories, feelings, attitudes, behaviors, environment, or old friends from a past lifestyle.

(2) *Triggers:* Any person, place or thing that activates a desire, lust, appetites, passions, or cravings for drugs, alcohol, and other works of the flesh practiced in the old lifestyle. They may be stimulated by old thoughts, memories, feelings, attitudes, behaviors, environment, or old friends from a past lifestyle.

(3) *Set-Up Behaviors:* Sinful attitudes, mental/emotional strongholds leading to ungodly behaviors from the old lifestyle of "sowing to the flesh" that expose a person to relapsing.

(4) *"Spiritual Short-Circuiting":* Using God's resources, spiritual disciplines (Word, praise/worship, fellowship), and Christ's authority (of rebuking) to interrupt and cancel out cravings before they can become actions.

(5) *"Hustler's Mentality:"* An attitude of being controlled by greed (carnal mind), causing a person to view criminal activities that provide large quantities of money in relatively short periods of time as an acceptable way of life.

(6) *"Prison mentality:"* An attitude (worldly) of not "trusting" others, "expressing feelings," or "communicating" that a person may have unconsciously developed while they were incarcerated.

(7) *"Street mentality:"* An attitude of being controlled by the carnal mind causing a person to continue to accept criminal behaviors, such as the selling of drugs, armed robbery, burglary, prostitution, etc., as an acceptable means of employment.

(8) *"Awfulizing" sobriety:* A negative attitude (worldly), causing a new believer to view a lifestyle of sobriety as being a boring, dull lifestyle, overemphasizing what they view as being the negatives rather than focusing on the positives.

(9) *"Awfulizing" Christianity:* A negative attitude (worldly), causing a new believer to view the Christian walk as a lifestyle of restrictions as being boring, lacking in enjoyment, overemphasizing what they view as being the negatives rather than focusing on the positives.

(10) *Attitude of Rebellion:* A believer's unwillingness to submit to the authority of God, and those authorities established by Him, and assume a dependent (submissive) position.

(11) *Attitude of Pride:* A believer having an unrealistic view of oneself placing total dependence on self, refusing to acknowledge God as being in control, taking credit for what God is doing in their life.

(12) *Attitude of Fear and Doubt:* A believer not understanding and having faith in their position in Christ, lacking trust (confidence) in God and His plan and purpose for their life.

(13) *Undisciplined Attitude:* A believer's unwillingness to abstain from their fleshly appetites, passions, and desires, and their ignorance as to how the world caters to those desires. How Satan *exploits you*, and their unwillingness to cooperate with the Holy Spirit in mortifying (putting to death) the flesh.

(14) *Attitude of Ignorance to Spiritual Danger:* A believer's unawareness of, and being unprepared for, spiritual warfare resulting in their spiritual growth and development being hindered.

(15) *"Re-entrapment":* A form of idolatry that occurs when a believer being restored from the effects of addiction becomes entangled in other activities. Rather than looking to God and His resources to adjust to change, they rely on work, sex, or something else to compensate for their addiction to drugs/alcohol and become dependent on something else.

Part One

Understanding the Difference between God's Plan for Relapse Prevention and The World's Plan

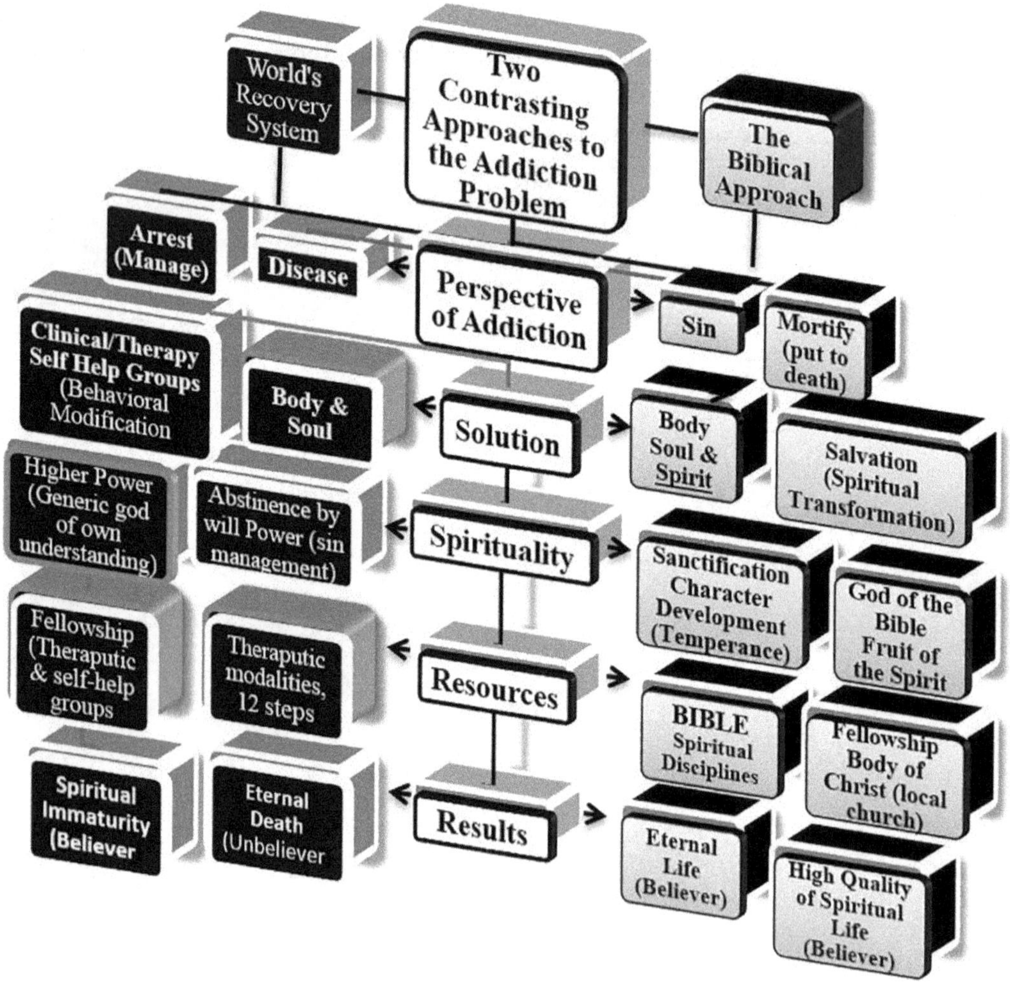

Figure 61: World's Recovery System in Contrast to God's Recovery Plan

Review the above chart, *Understanding the Difference Between God's Plan for Relapse Prevention and The World's Plan,* and answer the following questions:

1. What is the world's perspective of addiction? What is the biblical perspective of addiction? How do they differ?
2. What is the world's solution? What is the biblical solution? Which solution addresses the whole person?
3. What is the major difference in the resources used in the world's approach to addiction and the resources used by the biblical approach to addiction?
4. What are the major differences in the results a person receives from using these two different approaches to addressing their bondage to addiction?
5. Which approach is most effective and why?

Written Goodbye Letter Exercise

(To your drug(s) of choice)

Letter to My Addiction

Find a quiet place and pray, ask the Holy Spirit to guide you, and be as honest as possible about your relationship with drug(s) and alcohol, be specific in writing to your drug(s) choice (crack, cocaine, heroin, alcohol, meth, etc.).

Write the letter to your addiction, not to the group or leaders in the group!

Explain to your addiction how it affected you throughout your life as you recall and share both your positive and negative experiences from being in an intimate relationship with your drug(s) of choice:

- Spiritually (God)
- Socially (family & friends)
- Physically (health)
- Mentally/Emotionally
- Financially
- Legally

Explain to your drug(s) of choice why you are discontinuing the relationship with it, what you think of the time (years) you spent in a relationship with it, and tell it, "Goodbye!"

UNDERSTANDING THE CRAVINGS

What is a Craving?

Cravings are temptations in the form of desires, lust, appetites, and passions for drugs, alcohol, and other works of the flesh practiced in the old lifestyle. They may be stimulated by old thoughts, memories, feelings, attitudes, behaviors, environment, or old friends from a past lifestyle.

Different Types of Cravings and Their Origins

Figure 62: Cravings and Their Origin

Where Do Cravings Come From?

> *All of us also lived among you at one time, gratifying the cravings of our sinful nature and following its desires and thoughts.* Like the rest, we were by nature objects of wrath (Ephesians 2:3, NIV).
>
> but each one is tempted when, by his own evil desire, he is dragged away and enticed. *Then, after desire has conceived, it gives birth to sin; and sin,* when it is full-grown, gives birth to death (James 1:14–15, NIV).

☐ You need to understand that prior to your salvation, the cravings of your old sinful nature mostly controlled how lived. You acted on the thoughts of your carnal mind and fulfilled lusts and desires of the flesh in your past lifestyle. As a result, you became a slave of drugs/alcohol.

> Dear friends, I urge you, as aliens and strangers in the world, *to abstain from sinful desires, which war against your soul* (1 Peter 2:11, NIV).

- ☐ God has brought you out of the world, but your old sinful desires remain, and there is a battle for control of your soul (mind, will, emotions).

Prayer for a Believer

Dear heavenly Father,

I understand that I need a godly person in my life who has spent some time with You and understands You. I need someone to keep me accountable, to walk with me through difficult times, to challenge me to grow and reach my full potential in Christ Jesus. Father, help me to find such a person as You restore me from the effects of addiction.

> *Teaching us that, denying ungodliness and worldly lusts*, we should live soberly, righteously, and godly, in this present world. (Titus 2:12)

- ☐ You must learn through the direction of God's Word, under the guidance of the Holy Spirit, *not* to allow cravings to control you. You must live a godly life of self-control, accepting the fact that you should never return to using drugs/alcohol: it is detrimental to your relationship with God.

> For everything in the world—the cravings of sinful man, the lust of his eyes and the boasting of what he has and does—*comes not from the Father, but from the world* (1 John 2:16, NIV).

- ☐ You must recognize that the world is designed by Satan to create an atmosphere that stimulates the cravings of your old sinful nature, to lure you into practicing the "works of the flesh," which will result in you returning to your old lifestyle (relapsing).

> *Those who belong to Christ Jesus have crucified the sinful nature with its passions and desires* (Galatians 5:24, NIV).

- ☐ You must understand and have faith in your position in Christ, knowing that you have the victory over the cravings of your old sinful nature, and learn to experience that victory daily.

Understanding Cravings

Self-Check

1. How well do you understand what cravings are? Please discuss your answer with your group.

2. Was there a scripture(s) in this section that impacted your life? Discuss that experience with your group.

Action Steps

List two things you are willing to do to increase your understanding of cravings.

1.
2.

What Can Cause A Physical Craving (Physiological)?

Authorities in the field of substance abuse cite three physical factors leading to physical cravings:

(1) Brain damage due to chronic alcohol and drug poisoning
(2) Poor diet
(3) Lack of exercise

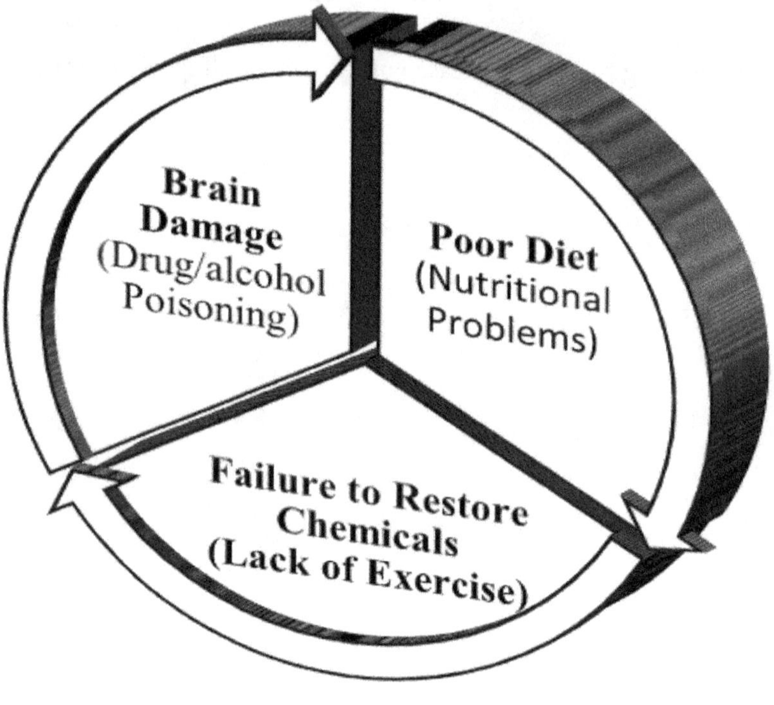

Figure 63: Physical Cravings

Brain Damage (Reduced Chemicals)

Alcohol and other drugs such as cocaine and heroin interfere with the chemical balance of the brain by depleting its neurotransmitters and eventually damaging the brain's regulatory system. Once the neurotransmitters are reduced during addiction to a level lower than the brain's normal functioning capacity, the brain experiences withdrawals, causing depression and physical pain (craving).

Not only did God create man to be relational, He also provided us with a "pleasure center" that enables us to derive a sense of enjoyment and pleasure from those relationships. He ordained. Some scientists refer to this "pleasure center" as the dopamine system.

Dopamine is a neurotransmitter within the brain that directly affects our ability to experience joy and pleasure. Normally, when we experience something pleasurable—a hug, a smile from a friend or loved one, or eat our favorite meal—our dopamine system pumps the chemical into gaps between us and related brain cells. This dopamine system helps us to recognize pleasurable experiences and acts as a reinforcement that motivates us do or to repeat that which brings us pleasure.

God's way of keeping this "pleasure center" in check is that shortly after the brain releases dopamine, the chemical is recycled back into the transmitting neuron by a specialized protein called the dopamine transporter. This recycling process regulates the intensity of the pleasure one derives from a particular experience.

You see, it was not God's intention that we derive such an intense pleasure from a particular experience that it would cause us to ignore or neglect those relationships that were ordained by Him. When we use drugs, we disrupt the "pleasure center" of the brain. The use of drugs causes the brain to release large amounts of dopamine and prevents dopamine from being recycled back into the transmitting neuron, thereby causing dopamine to build up. This build-up of dopamine causes continuous stimulation or what is better known as the intense "high" that drug users experience.

This overstimulation of the "pleasure center" causes brain damage in that it depletes the brain of dopamine, causing depression and intense cravings for drugs. Suddenly, the pleasure derived from a hug, a smile from a friend or loved one can hardly compete with the intense pleasure derived from the use of drugs. The drug user gradually begins to ignore or neglect the very relationships ordained by God and becomes totally preoccupied with their relationship with drugs. Because of the chemical imbalance caused by the use of drugs, some chronic drug users have to be placed on antidepressant drugs long after they have stopped using.

BRAIN DAMAGE EXERCISE (DEPLETION OF CHEMICALS)

Self-Check

1. How well do you understand how *a reduction of chemicals in the brain* can cause physical cravings? Please discuss your answer with your group.

2. Have you ever witnessed a person experiencing a craving due to "*a reduction of chemicals in the brain?*" Please discuss your answer with your group.

Action Steps

List two things you are willing to do to keep increasing your understanding of how "*a reduction of chemicals in the brain*" can cause physical cravings.

1.
2.

Lack of Exercise (Failure to Restore Chemicals)

God has placed within each of us the biological chemistry to produce a sense of physical well-being. Endorphins, neurotransmitters, or chemicals produced in the brain have been called the "messengers of paradise." These are the same neurotransmitters that are depleted during alcohol/drug addiction.

Exercise is probably the single most unused, unacknowledged, and least understood benefit of believers being restored from addiction. Regular aerobic exercise is believed to reduce physical cravings by promoting the replenishment of chemicals (endorphins) in the brain deleted during addiction and to be a great asset during the first few months of restoration from drugs/alcohol.

Endorphins, the "messengers of paradise," are biologically the right way to come to the peace and freedom from pain that individuals seek through drugs/alcohol. Raising endorphin levels, thereby reducing pain and cravings while elevating peace, are within every believer's reach through their natural internal relief of endorphins.

Lack of Exercise (Failure to Restore Chemical)

Self-Check

1. How well do you understand how the *"lack of exercise"* causes physical cravings? Please discuss your answer with your group.

Poor Diet (Nutritional Problems)

Physical cravings are activated by chemical imbalances in the body; therefore, proper nutrition and maintaining a correct diet is necessary to prevent cravings. The overuse of food and drink containing excessive amounts of caffeine and sugar can activate a physical craving. Caffeine is a low-grade nervous system stimulant; but taken in large quantities, it can produce similar effects of cocaine, a high-grade central nervous system stimulant.

Excessive amounts of sugar can also cause high elevations of blood sugar levels, or "pseudo highs," followed by rapid declines, causing effects similar to coming down off drugs. This often results in physical cravings for drugs/alcohol. Therefore, junk food and some energy drinks can be harmful for believers being restored from the effects of addiction if they consumed large quantities.

Just How Bad Are Energy Drinks for Recovering People?

Written by Stephanie Torres, September 29, 2014:

For those recovering from alcohol and drug addictions, the urge to find a fix seems to be never-ending. To replace their drug of choice, the recovering addict will find other means to soothe their minds and souls. *A replacement "high"* that has become common among recovering people is the use of energy drinks.

Energy drinks combinations of caffeine, vitamins, and herbs can provide the kick they need, and it's legal and can be found at any corner store. Energy drinks can be a healthier alternative to *drugs and alcohol*, but what most don't know is that the very things that make energy drinks so popular can also lead to active addiction.

How Bad Are Energy Drinks for Those in Recovery?

What may come as a shock is that caffeine is classified as a drug. Caffeine crosses the blood/brain barrier and stimulates the nervous system causing increased alertness and insomnia. Those who use caffeine build a tolerance and experience withdrawals. While caffeine is an effective diuretic and is useful in the treatment of asthma, people who consume excessive amounts can experience caffeine intoxication which can include increased agitation and irritability. Other complications from caffeine intoxication can include heart issues, seizures, psychosis, and even death.

Many energy drinks also include the amino acid *taurine*. Commonly found in meat, fish, and eggs, taurine is used in energy drinks to help increase mental clarity and physical performance. However, excessive amounts of taurine, along with caffeine and sugar, has unnatural effects on the central nervous system. One of the functions that can be impaired is in the way stress is handled. If the ways stress is handled are impaired, any new coping skills that were learned in *treatment* can also be impaired. Therefore, the old ways in which we dealt with stress (drugs and alcohol) resurface.

In a posting on the *Alternatives for Alcohol* website, the following point was made: *"When you consume caffeine in any form, it stimulates the liver to dump large doses of glycogen (sugar) reserves into the bloodstream. This results in a sugar high, and then insulin is released to control the blood sugar levels and the blood sugar drops very rapidly to below–normal levels and symptoms such as depression, anxiety, irritability, fatigue, and then cravings for sugar, alcohol or your substance of choice may appear."*

Caffeine addiction, and namely the use of energy drinks, can be a major pitfall for the recovering addict. While the use of energy drinks in moderation is not harmful if done in moderation, caffeine is a mood-altering drug and its use needs to be monitored closely. If you or a loved one is experiencing symptoms of caffeine addiction, it is best to consult with a doctor or *addiction specialist*.

POOR DIET (NUTRITIONAL PROBLEMS)

Self-Check

1. How well do you understand how *"poor diet"* causes physical cravings? Please discuss your answer with your group.

2. How well do you understand how *"caffeine"* causes physical cravings? Please discuss your answer with your group.

Action Steps

List three things you are willing to do to that will assist you in not experiencing cravings caused by *"poor diet."*

1.
2.
3.

UNDERSTANDING PHYSICAL CRAVINGS

Self-Check

Rank the following factors according to how well you understand they can cause cravings. Place the #1 on the slot of the factor that you *least understand that causes cravings* and the #3 on the slot of the factor that you most understand causes *cravings;* and rank the last factor #2.

1. Drug/alcohol poisoning _____
2. Lack of exercise _____
3. Poor diet _____

What Can Activate or Trigger a Psychological Craving?

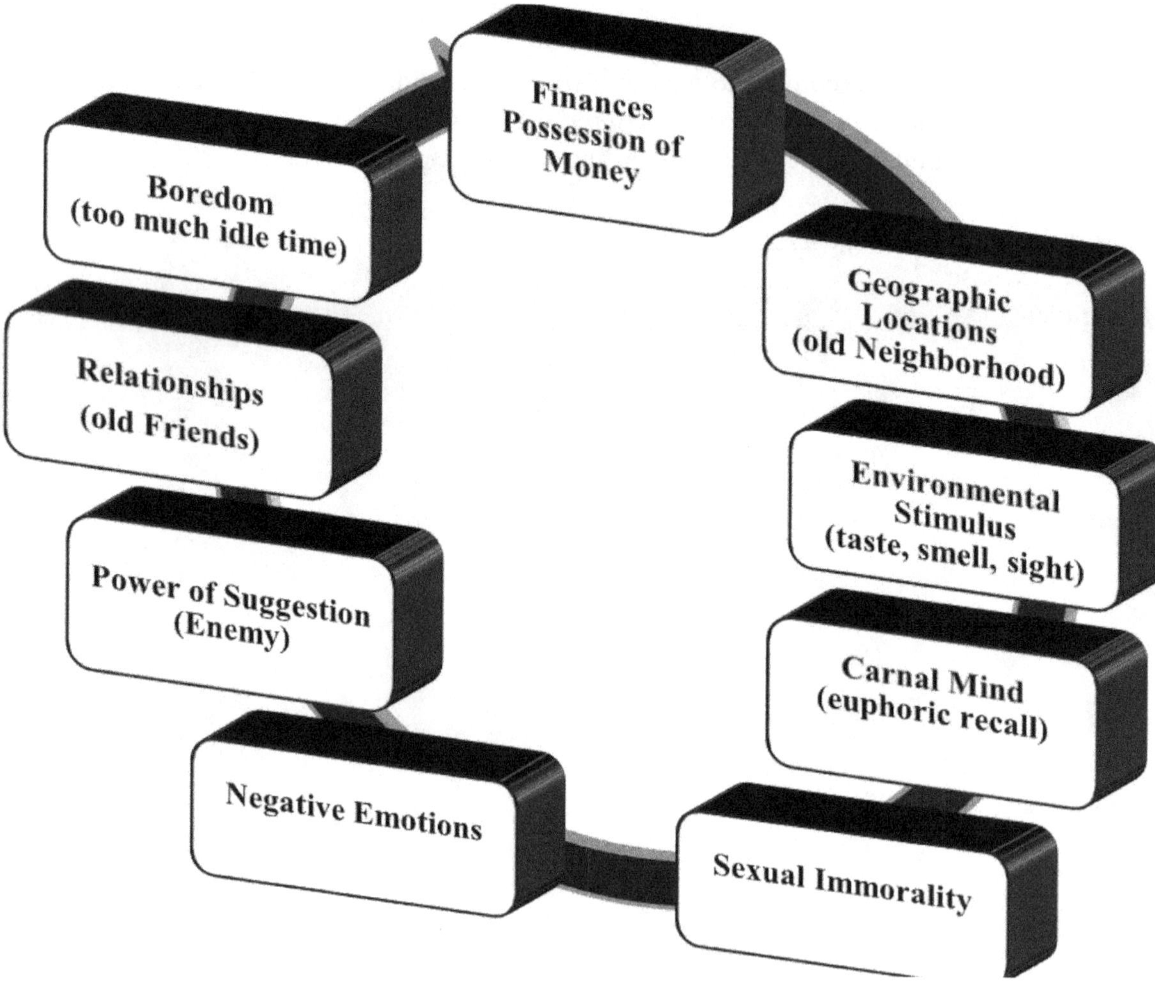

Figure 64: What Can Trigger a Psychological Craving?

Negative Emotions: A Serious Problem

As a believer being restored from an addiction, you must learn to develop a proper understanding of your new identity (position) in Christ and have faith to walk in that new identity. The lack of a proper understanding of your position in Christ and failing to walk in the faith of your new identity places you in serious emotional danger.

- ☐ Without experiencing God's unconditional love and forgiveness, you cannot express unconditional love, grace, and forgiveness toward others.

Low Self-Esteem: Satan's Deadliest Psychological Weapon

David Seamands, in his text, *Healing for Damaged Emotions*, makes the following comment regarding Satan's deadliest weapon, low self-esteem.

> Some of the most powerful weapons in Satan's arsenal are psychological. Fear is one of these. Doubt is another. Anger, hostility, worry and of course, guilt. Long–standing guilt is hard to shake off; it seems to hang on even after Christian claims forgiveness and accepts pardoning grace. Satan's greatest psychological weapon (low self-esteem) is a gut-level feeling of inferiority, inadequacy, and low self-worth.

He states how Satan uses his most deadly of all his emotional and psychological weapons of low self-esteem in four ways to defeat the children of God causing you to fail in their Christian walk:

1. To paralyze your potential for spiritual growth and development.
2. To hinder you from fulfilling your God given purpose for your life.
3. To ruin your relationships with yourself, God and others.
4. To hinder your service for God within the "Body of Christ."

> Jesus said unto him, "*Thou shalt love the Lord thy God with all thy heart, and with all thy soul, and with all thy mind.*" This is the first and great commandment. And the second *is* like unto it, "*Thou shalt love thy neighbor as thyself.*" (Matthew 22:37–39)

Your "self-esteem" has to be viewed in a proper vision of your "God esteem." The first greatest commandment is to "*love the Lord thy God with all thy heart, and with all thy soul, and with all thy mind*" and the second greatest commandment is to "*love thy neighbor as thyself.*"

- ☐ scripture implies that when you learn to love God, "the first greatest commandment," that then and only then are you able to love your neighbor as you love yourself.
- ☐ Somewhere in between learning to love God, "the first greatest commandment," and learning to love thy neighbor, "the second greatest commandment" you learn to love "thyself."
- ☐ Therefore, as you understand who you are in Christ in light of Who God is in your life and develop faith in your position (identity) in Christ, you will be able to love your neighbor because you love yourself, "godly self-esteem," because of your "God esteem."

Your carnal mind with its worldly attitudes leads to negative emotions that become major strongholds during a lifestyle of addiction. Some of these emotional strongholds may have been developed in early childhood. The enemy will continue to take advantage of you throughout a person's entire life, if allowed. If not addressed, these emotions could set you up for relapse.

Emotional Triggers

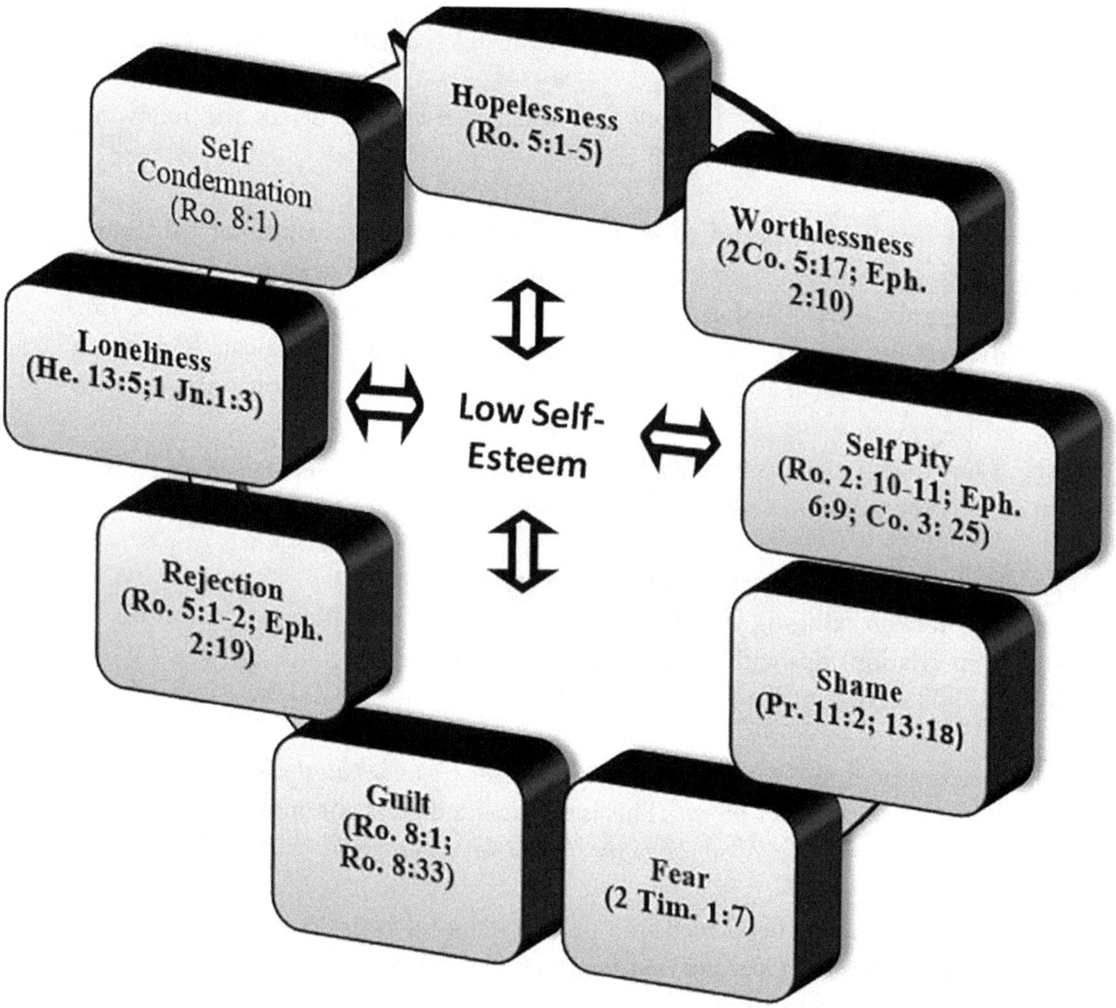

Figure 65: Emotional Triggers

Loneliness: A negative feeling of being separated or isolated from others. It is a feeling of not belonging or fitting in with others. This feeling comes from not knowing that you, as a believer in Christ Jesus, are a fellow citizen with the rest of God's people in His family (Eph. 2:19).

Hopelessness: A negative feeling of despair, being discouraged, depressed, lack of faith, trust, or confidence in your future. This feeling comes from not knowing that you were created in Christ to do His work that He planned beforehand that you should do (Eph.2:10).

Worthlessness: A negative feeling of having no value, of being inadequate, having no ability. This feeling comes from not knowing that you are a member of a chosen race, a royal priesthood, a holy nation, a people for God's own possession, and that you are complete in Christ (1 Pet. 2:9,10; Col. 2:9,10).

Rejection: A negative feeling of not being accepted by others, having a desire to belong, but feeling that others don't approve of you being a part of you. This feeling comes from not understanding that God chose you and drew you to Jesus (Jn. 15:16, 6:44,65).

Self--pity: A negative feeling that you are always a victim being picked on, singled out, that you are destined for bad things to happen to you, feeling sorry for yourself. This feeling comes from not understanding that you are a joint heir with Christ, sharing His inheritance, and have been blessed with every spiritual blessing in Christ (Ro. 8:17; Eph. 1:3).

Guilt: A negative feeling stemming from past behaviors, a feeling of being condemned for past actions during your lifestyle of addiction. This feeling comes from not understanding that you have been justified, completely forgiven, and made righteous (Ro. 5:1).

Shame: A negative emotion caused by believing something is wrong with you, a feeling of being inadequate, and a feeling of humiliation. This feeling comes from not understanding that you have a new identity, that you are a new creature in Christ, have been given a new spirit and heart (2 Co. 5:17; Eke. 36:26,27).

Fear: A feeling of being afraid, a lack of faith, being insecure, nervous. This feeling comes from not understanding that your relationship is secure with God, that He will never leave you or forsake you. It is realizing that God did not give you a spirit of fear, but power, love, and a sound mind (Heb. 13:5; 2 Tim. 1:7).

IDENTIFYING NEGATIVE EMOTIONS

Self-Check

To be made *new in the attitude* of your minds. (Ephesians 4:23, NIV)

Rank the following negative emotions according to how they have caused you to experience cravings in your life. Place the #1 on the slot of the negative emotion that causes you the *least number of cravings* and the #12 on the slot of the negative emotion that causes you the *greatest number of cravings* and rank the remaining negative emotions accordingly.

1. Hopelessness	_____	7. Loneliness	_____
2. Worthlessness	_____	8. Rejection	_____
3. Self–Pity	_____	9. Guilt	_____
4. Fear	_____	10. Shame	_____
5. Anger	_____	11. Bitterness	_____
6. Resentments	_____	12. Rage	_____
Other	_____		

Self-Check

How well do you understand that your *"negative emotions"* cause cravings? Discuss your answer with your group.

Has your *"negative emotions"* ever caused you to have cravings?

Action Steps

List three things you are willing to do that will keep you from allowing your *"negative emotions"* from causing cravings. Discuss your answer with your group.

1.
2.
3.

Was there a scripture(s) in this section that impacted your life? Discuss that experience with your group.

Unforgiveness Leads to Negative Emotions

To whom ye forgive anything, I *forgive* also: for if I forgave anything, to whom I forgave *it*, for your sakes *forgave I it* in the person of Christ; *Lest Satan should get an advantage of us: for we are not ignorant of his devices.* (2 Corinthians 2:10–11)

Lack of Forgiveness to Self & Others

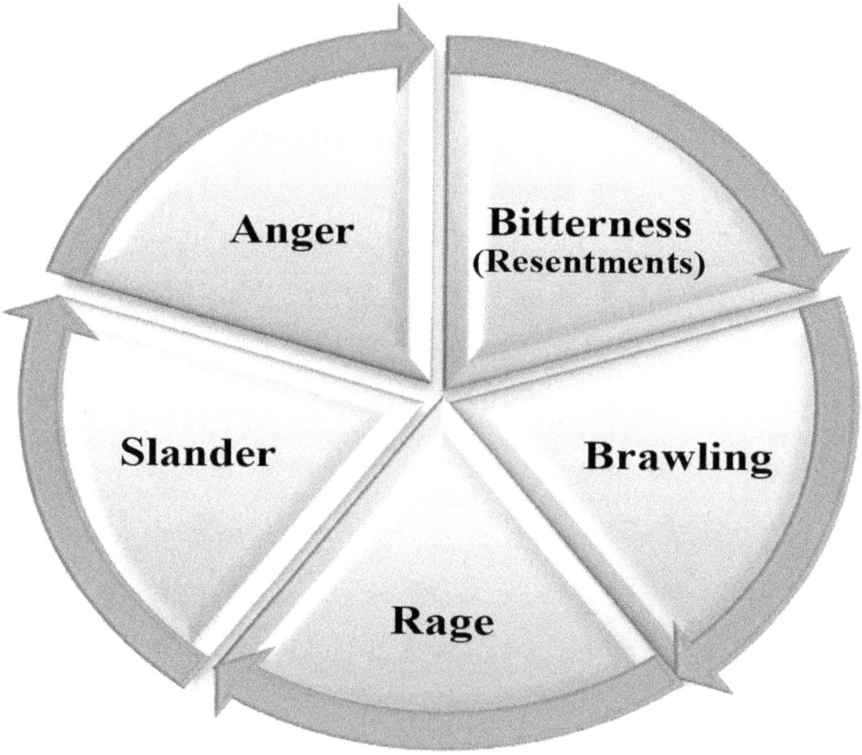

Figure 66: Unwillingness to Forgive Others

An unwillingness to forgive yourself and others is another familiar strategy the enemy will attempt to use to hinder your relationship with your heavenly Father. Satan knows that having an unforgiving spirit is in opposition to God and will hinder God's grace in your life and set the stage for your relapse.

> Get rid of all *bitterness*, *rage* and *anger*, *brawling* and *slander*, along with every form of malice. Be kind and compassionate to one another, *forgiving each other, just as in Christ God forgave you.* (Ephesians 4:31–32, NIV)

Bitterness: A continued feeling of harshness toward another person due to resentments caused by holding a grudge for something that took place in the past (Col. 4:12–13).
Anger: A feeling of hostility, dislike, and displeasure toward another person.
Brawling: Becoming involved in heated verbal and physical confrontations with another person.
Rage: Violent uncontrollable outbursts of anger.
Slander: Falsely attacking another person's character or reputation through lying on you (Col.3 8–9).

Learning to forgive Others

> Therefore, I tell you, whatever you ask for in prayer, believe that you have received it, and it will be yours. And when you stand praying, *if you hold anything against anyone, forgive him, so that your Father in heaven may forgive you your sins."* (Mark 11:24–26, NIV).

- ☐ An unwillingness to forgive others not only hinders your prayers, but hinders your relationship with God as well. You do not have the luxury of not forgiving others if you want to be forgiven by your Father in heaven.

> *But if ye do not forgive, neither will your Father which is in heaven forgive your trespasses.* (Mark 11:26)
>
> Then Peter came to Jesus and asked, "Lord, *how many times shall I forgive my brother when he sins against me?* Up to seven times?" Jesus answered, *"I tell you, not seven times, but seventy-seven times.* (Matthew 18:21–35, NIV)
>
> "Therefore, if you are offering your gift at the altar and there remember that your *brother has something against you*, leave your gift there in front of the altar. First go and be reconciled to your brother; then come and offer your gift. (Matthew 5:23–24, NIV)

- ☐ Likewise, God requires that you make amends with those who have something against you. Your unwillingness to seek forgiveness of others for your wrong doings will hinder your relationship with your heavenly Father.
- ☐ In asking for others forgiveness, you release yourself from the harm and the circumstance that had you in bondage; whether they forgive you or not, you have done your part.
- ☐ You may not be able to make direct amends to everyone you harmed during your addiction, but some individuals you will be able to ask for forgiveness when given an opportunity.
- ☐ You need to seek God's direction throughout your restoration, and as you encounter individuals you have harmed, prayerfully ask their forgiveness. Of course, approaching some individuals too early in your restoration could cause problems.
- ☐ Remember when you ask for forgiveness from others, you are not responsible for them forgiving you. Don't expect everyone, even close family members, to forgive you immediately, and some individuals may never forgive you.

Learning to Forgive Others

Self-Check

How well do you understand that being unwilling to *forgive others* causes negative emotions? Discuss your answer with your group.

Has your unwillingness to *forgive others* caused you to experience negative emotions? Discuss your answer with your group.

Action Steps

List anyone you know that you must decide to forgive to free yourself from negative emotions. You must be willing to look as far back as your childhood.

1.
2.
3.

Was there a scripture(s) in this section that impacted your life? Discuss that experience with your group.

Learning to Forgive Others Exercise

List both the person(s) and the sins Christ forgave you for that *you committed against others.*	List both the person(s) and the sins committed by others *against you* that you are *now* unwilling to forgive you for.
1.	1.
2.	2.
3.	3.
4.	4.
5.	5.
6.	6.
7.	7.
8.	8.
9.	9.
10.	10.

Figure 67: Learning to Forgive Others

LEARNING TO FORGIVE YOURSELF

John 1:29
29 The next day John saw Jesus coming toward him and said, *"Look, the Lamb of God, who takes away the sin of the world!* (NIV)

David A. Seamands, in his text, *Healing Damaged Emotions*, makes an extremely significant statement regarding forgiveness that applies to believers in restoration from addiction, "There is no forgiveness from God unless you freely forgive your brother from your heart. And I wonder if we have been too narrow in thinking that *brother* only applies to someone else. What if *you* are the brother or sister who needs to be forgiven, and *you* need to forgive *yourself*? Does it not apply to *you* too? The Lord says to forgive your enemies. What if you are the worst enemy? Does that exclude *you*?"

NOTE: Until you learn to forgive yourself, you cannot experience the forgiveness of God.

Learning to Forgive Yourself

Self-Check

How well do you understand that being unwilling to *forgive yourself* causes negative emotions? Discuss your answer with your group.

Has your unwillingness to *forgive yourself* caused you to experience negative emotions? Discuss your answer with your group.

Action Steps

List some of the things you know you must decide to *forgive yourself* for so you can be free from negative emotions.

PART TWO

Three Critical Areas Leading back to an Old Lifestyle of "Sowing to the Flesh" (Relapse)

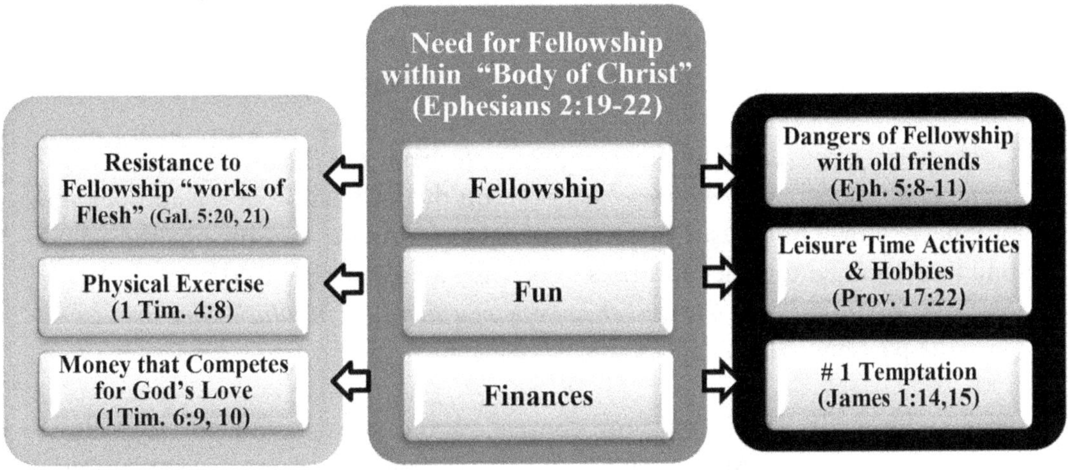

Figure 68: Three Critical Areas Leading to Sowing to the Flesh

Resistance to Fellowship

The third group of sin listed among the works of the flesh is that which corrupts human relationships and hinders the believer from fulfilling the second greatest commandment.

- ☐ You must realize that the "works of the flesh" are in every human being and will destroy your chances of developing new friends and restoring damaged relationships with loved ones if you don't allow God to put those works to death.

(1) Hatred refers to hateful attitudes, resulting in hostility, and reason for opposition to others.
(2) Discord is a direct result of hatred and results in serious conflicts.
(3) Envy refers to a desire to have what belongs to another, resulting in anger and resentment caused by coveting.
(4) Sudden outburst of anger toward others for little or no apparent reason indicates an uncontrollable temper.
(5) Selfishness ambitions and being self-willed.
(6) Divisions,
(7) Quarreling,
(8) Disagreements,
(9) Jealousy: these four sins represent long term disagreements among individuals after original conflict has occurred.
(10) Murder,
(11) Drunkenness,
(12) Reveling or carousing referring to the behavior that results from living a lifestyle out of control, drinking, partying, orgies, etc.

A Need for Change in Fellowship

> Consequently, you are no longer foreigners and aliens, *but fellow citizens with God's people and members of God's household,* built on the foundation of the apostles and prophets, with Christ Jesus himself as the chief cornerstone. In him the whole building is joined together and rises to become a holy temple in the Lord. *And in him you too are being built together to become a dwelling in which God lives by his Spirit.* (Ephesians 2:19–22, NIV)

I recall how lonely I felt following my conversion and my decision not to return to my old lifestyle of using drugs/alcohol. All my relationships were centered on purchasing, selling, and using drugs/alcohol. My so-called friends were still caught up in that same lifestyle, and I found myself at home with a wife I didn't really know (because of being time-consumed with my drug and alcohol addiction). The most difficult fact to come to grips with was now after only being sober for a short period of time, I really didn't know myself. This new person who had committed his life to Christ and to living an entirely different lifestyle of sobriety was a stranger to me.

Developing relationships were relatively easy in my old lifestyle, because we had one thing in common—using drugs/alcohol. *I had yet to realize that I was a part of a new family, the household of God. I had to learn that together, all Christians make up God's household (church), in which He lives by His Spirit.*

> I vividly remember my very first attempt at establishing new relationships. I had been attending church for a few weeks and a group of men were gathering at the home one of the ministers from the church we attended to watch an NFL playoff game and I was invited. I accepted the invitation but in the back of my mind I really didn't want to attend because I figured it wouldn't be much fun hanging with a bunch of "square" boring Christians. I accepted the invitation because I didn't want to offend you. But to my surprise, I found the event very enjoyable and for

> the first time, I realized I could enjoy myself without using drugs/alcohol and that there was enjoyment in the Christian lifestyle. I thank God for the courage and desire to take a chance at venturing out into the unknown because, that proved to be the beginning of a key component in my restoration, fellowship.
>
> —Bob Vann

You must learn to fellowship on a regular basis with other Christians and avoid fellowshipping with old unsaved friends/associates from your past lifestyle. This plays a key role in preventing you from relapsing.

- ☐ Learning to establish and maintain new relationships is going to be a major task because of the numerous years you have spent in negative relationships within the world, centered on an addictive lifestyle.
- ☐ You must be willing to put forth the effort necessary to enter into new relationships within the Body of Christ (local church), and God will provide you with the necessary grace to do so.

> Just as each of us has one body with many members, and these members do not all have the same function, so in Christ we who are many form one body, *and each member belongs to all the others. We have different gifts, according to the grace given us*. If a man's gift is prophesying, let him use it in proportion to his faith. If it is serving, let him serve; if it is teaching, let him teach; if it is encouraging, let him encourage; if it is contributing to the needs of others, let him give generously; if it is leadership, let him govern diligently; if it is showing mercy, let him do it cheerfully. (Romans 12:4–8, NIV)
>
> We proclaim to you what we have seen and heard, so that you also may have fellowship with us. And our fellowship is with the Father and with his Son, Jesus Christ. (1 John 1:3, NIV)
>
> If we claim to have fellowship with him yet walk in the darkness, we lie and do not live by the truth. But if we walk in the light, as he is in the light, we have fellowship with one another, and the blood of Jesus, his Son, purifies us from all sin. (1 John 1:6–7, NIV)

- ☐ If you return to hanging out with your former ungodly associates and become involved in worldly activities (and think you still are in fellowship with God), you are deceiving yourself and are untruthful.
- ☐ True fellowship accomplished by interacting with other Christians allows Christians to grow in Christ together.

> And let us consider how we may spur one another on toward love and good deeds. *Let us not give up meeting together, as some are in the habit of doing*, but let us encourage one another—and all the more as you see the Day approaching. (Hebrews 10:24–25, NIV)

- ☐ True Christian fellowship is a necessity because it provides opportunities for believers to encourage each other in their walk with the Lord. It allows you to interact with mature brothers/sisters in the Lord who can share their experiences in the Lord.
- ☐ When you make yourself available for fellowship, God can bring individuals into your life that have been restored from drugs/alcohol and can share invaluable insight for preventing you from relapsing.

> A Song of degrees of David. Behold, how good and how pleasant *it is* for brethren to dwell together in unity! (Psalm 133:1)

- ☐ God uses fellowship between Christian brothers/sisters as an opportunity to develop unity within the Body of Christ.

> Then they that gladly received his word were baptized: and the same day there were added *unto you* about three thousand souls. And they continued steadfastly in the apostles' doctrine and fellowship, and in breaking of bread, and in prayers. (Acts 2:41–42)

- ☐ Paul expresses the need for new converts in the early church to stay in close fellowship with other Christians within the Body of Christ (church).

> Again, I say unto you, that if two of you shall agree on earth as touching anything that they shall ask, it shall be done for you of my Father which is in heaven. *For where two or three are gathered together in my name, there am I in the midst of you.* (Matthew 18:19–20)

Jesus clearly states how He honors fellowship in His presence and that fellowship also allows Christians the opportunity to have prayers answered through agreement with one other.

> For as the body is one, and hath many members, and all the members of that one body, being many, are one body: so also *is* Christ. For by one Spirit are we all baptized into one body, whether *we be* Jews or Gentiles, whether *we be* bond or free; and have been all made to drink into one Spirit. For the body is not one member, but many. (1 Corinthians 12:12–14)

- ☐ Because you are a member of the Body of Christ, God requires you to be joined together through fellowship with other Christians for the fulfillment of His purpose in your life.

IDENTIFYING YOUR RESISTANCE TO FELLOWSHIP

Self-Check

> The acts of the flesh are obvious: sexual immorality, impurity and debauchery. (Galatians 5:19)

Rank the following *"works of the flesh"* according to the problems they have caused in your relationship with others. Place the *#1* on the slot of the *"works of the flesh"* that caused you the *least amount of problems in relationships* and the *#10* on the slot of the *"works of the flesh"* that causes you the *greatest amount of problems in relationships,* then rank the remaining "works of the flesh" accordingly.

1. Hatred	_____	7. Discord	_____
2. Envy	_____	8. Outburst of Anger	_____
3. Quarreling	_____	9. Selfish Ambitions	_____
4. Jealousy	_____	10. Drunkenness	_____
5. Carousing	_____	11. Murder	_____
6. Resentments	_____	12. Rage	_____

Self-Rating

How well do you understand that the *"works of the flesh"* causes problems in relationships with others? Discuss your answer with your group.

Has the *"works of the flesh"* caused you problems in your relationship with others? Discuss your answer with your group.

Action Steps

List two things you are willing to do that will keep the *"works of the flesh"* from causing you problems in your relationships with others?

1.
2.

Was there a scripture(s) in this section that impacted your life? Discuss that experience with your group.

THE DANGERS OF OLD RELATIONSHIPS

For ye were sometimes darkness, but now are ye light in the Lord: walk as children of light: (For the fruit of the Spirit *is* in all goodness and righteousness and truth;) Proving what is acceptable unto the Lord. *And have no fellowship with the unfruitful works of darkness, but rather reprove you.* (Ephesians 5:8–11)

- ☐ You must realize that you no longer have anything in common with former unsaved friends because you have become a new creature in Christ, and because you are a "babe" lacking spiritual strength, you can't hang around old friends without falling under their worldly influences.

  Do not be misled: *"Bad company corrupts good character."* (1 Corinthians 15:33, NIV)

- ☐ It will be easy for your flesh to lead you back if you are not aware of the dangers of hanging around former unsaved acquaintances.
- ☐ Many of your relationships may date back to childhood, and many may include relatives that are caught up in ungodly lifestyles. Therefore, you must remember that the most important relationship you have now is with your heavenly Father.

  Do not be yoked together with unbelievers. For what do righteousness and wickedness have in common? *Or what fellowship can light have with darkness?* (2 Corinthians 6:14, NIV)

- ☐ Your old friends that still use are in bondage to and controlled by your enemies, the world, flesh, and Satan. You have nothing in common with you any longer, because God has separated you from the world for His service.
- ☐ God may very well use a you as a witness to draw old friends and family members to Him once you have matured spiritually. But until that time comes, you should hold you up in prayer.

  What does a believer have in common with an unbeliever? What agreement is there between the temple of God and idols? For we are the temple of the living God. As God has said: "I will live with you and walk among you, and I will be their God, and they will be my people. *Therefore, come out from you and be separate, says the Lord. Touch no unclean thing, and I will receive you."* (2 Corinthians 6:15–17, NIV)

- ☐ You must understand that you are in the process of being spiritually restored from the very things your old friends are in bondage to. Exposing yourself to those conditions will only hinder your growth process and eventually lead you back into bondage by "sowing to the flesh (relapsing)."

The Dangers of Old Relationships

Self-Check

How well do you understand that hanging out with *"old friends"* can cause cravings? Discuss your answer with your group.

Has hanging out with *"old friends"* caused you to have cravings? Discuss your answer with your group.

Action Steps

List two things you are willing to do that will keep you from hanging out with *"old friends"* so you don't experience cravings?

1.
2.

Self-Rating

How well do you understand that returning to the *"old locations,"* where you used to use drugs/alcohol, causes cravings? Discuss your answer with your group.

Has returning to former *"get high locations"* ever caused you to have cravings? Discuss your answer with your group.

Action Steps

List two things you are willing to do to keep former *"get high locations"* from causing you cravings.

1.
2.

Was there a scripture(s) in this section that impacted your life? Discuss that experience with your group.

Boredom

Counselor Michael D. Vann continues as he shares his thoughts on boredom.

> One of the very reasons that so many individuals, both Christian and non-Christians, relapse is because restoration/recovery is painful and can be very boring. What in restoration/recovery can compare to the way cocaine affects the pleasure center of the brain? A close comparison would be multiple dependencies such as sex, work, and shopping. Ultimately, they must choose the pain of restoration/recovery, or the pain that their active dependency causes. One gets progressively better, and the other gets progressively worse. Many of you who stop using alcohol and other drugs still have a deep, and wide void that longs to be filled and we often will not discriminate when it comes to picking something to fill the void with.
>
> My void was not filled until I accepted Christ and I would not accept Christ until I was broken. I had literally tried all the various dependencies that were available to me, and I even tried some of you twice. I can honestly say that I don't know of anything more powerful than addiction besides the power of God.

BOREDOM

Self-Check

How well do you understand that *"boredom"* causes cravings? Discuss your answer with your group.

Has *"boredom"* ever caused you to have cravings? Discuss your answer with your group.

Action Steps

List two things you are willing to do to keep *"boredom"* from causing cravings in your restoration.

1.
2.

FUN: PHYSICAL EXERCISE/ LEISURE TIME ACTIVITIES

> *For physical training is of some value,* but godliness has value for all things, holding promise for both the present life and the life to come. (1 Timothy 4:8, NIV)

> *A cheerful heart is good medicine,* but a crushed spirit dries up the bones. (Proverbs 17:22, NIV)

God clearly informs us that there is some value to physical exercise and for believers in restoration from drugs/alcohol. There are some distinct advantages. Kathleen W. FitzGerald, PhD, in her article "Endorphins: Feeling Better the Natural Way," states, "Perhaps the single most unused, unacknowledged, and least understood ally of recovering people is their natural internal relief, their endorphins. They have been called the 'messengers of paradise.' They are biologically the right way to peace and freedom from pain that the alcoholic first sought through alcohol."

Raising endorphin levels, thereby reducing pain and elevating peace, is within everyone's reach. The results are immediate:

1. Recovering people are able to cope better with emotions that have been buried.
2. There is less stress experienced when making the changes that recovery demands.

God has placed within each of us the biological chemistry to produce a sense of physical well–being. Physical activity (exercise) can play a significant role in your physical and emotional restoration from drugs/alcohol in the following ways, by:

a) Assisting you in *coping better with negative emotions* from the past.
b) Assisting you in *handling the stress* that accompanies the changes they have to make to adjust to developing a new lifestyle.
c) Assisting you in *addressing boredom,* a major factor that could lead to relapse if not addressed.
d) Provides you with a means of *developing new relationships* with individuals who aren't caught up in their old lifestyle.
e) Assisting you in *controlling weight gain* that, many times, results from changing from an addictive lifestyle to a lifestyle of sobriety.
f) Assisting you in *restoring your physical health.*

God designed believers with an internal means for feeling good about themselves through endorphins (chemical) located within the natural chemistry of the brain. Such minor things as pleasant experiences, laughter, and exercise can elevate endorphin levels. Listening to gospel music, laughing, taking a walk or a swim, playing a game of basketball, chess, or checkers, jogging, fishing, fellowshipping with a friend, watching a movie, attending a Bible study, reading a meditation or psalm can elevate endorphin levels. Those activities that demand the greatest amount of energy provide the most benefits to physical and emotional restoration.

- ☐ Authorities in the field of substance abuse cite three physical factors leading to physical cravings: *damage to the brain due to chronic alcohol and drug poisoning, poor diet,* and a *lack of exercise.*
- ☐ Regular aerobic exercise is believed to reduce physical cravings by replenishing the chemicals in the brain that are depleted during addiction. It is also believed to be a great asset during the first few months of restoration from drugs/alcohol.

PHYSICAL EXERCISE/LEISURE TIME ACTIVITIES

Self-Check

How well do you understand that *"physical exercise"* can reduce cravings? Discuss your answer with your group.

Have you used *"physical exercise"* in the past to reduce cravings? Discuss your answer with your group.

Action Steps

List two things you are willing to do regarding "physical exercise" to reduce cravings during your restoration.

1.
2.

Money, a Major Stimulant of the Flesh

Why Did Our Lord Say So Much About Money?

It surprised me to learn just how much the Bible says about money. There are approximately 500 verses on prayer, fewer than 500 on faith, but more than 2,350 verses on how to handle money. Moreover, Jesus Christ said more about money than any other subject.

—Crown Ministries

Dishonest money dwindles away, but he who gathers money little by little makes it grow. (Proverbs 13:11, NIV)

So if you have not been trustworthy in handling *worldly wealth*, who will trust you with true riches? (Luke 16:11, NIV)

- ☐ If you don't learn to handle your money according to biblical principles, the quality of your spiritual life will be low, which could eventually lead you to relapse.

His master replied, "Well done, good and faithful servant! You have been faithful with a few things; I will put you in charge of many things. Come and share your master's happiness!" (Matthew 25:21, NIV)

- ☐ When they learn to apply the biblical principles in managing their finances, they will experience a deep sense of joy in their relationship with God.

No man can serve two masters: for either he will hate the one, and love the other; or else he will hold to the one, and despise the other. *Ye cannot serve God and mammon. (*Matthew 6:24*)*

- ☐ Understand that money and material possessions can compete with your love for the Lord and His priorities for your life.
- ☐ The greatest stronghold in our American culture is materialism; and now that you are no longer a part of the world, you must realize that your view of money and handling money must be changed. If your view of money doesn't change, it will interfere with your relationship with God and possibly lead you back to practicing the "works of the flesh (relapse)."

People who want to get rich fall into temptation and a trap and into many foolish and harmful desires that plunge men into ruin and destruction. *For the love of money is a root of all kinds of evil.* Some people, eager for money, have wandered from the faith and pierced yourselves with many grieves. (1 Timothy 6:9–10, NIV)

And the *cares of this world*, and the *deceitfulness of riches*, and the *lusts of other things* entering in, *choke the word*, and it becometh unfruitful. (Mark 4:19)

Whoever *loves money never has money enough*; whoever loves wealth is never satisfied with his income. This too is meaningless. (Ecclesiastes 5:10, NIV)

- ☐ Your improper handling of money in your past lifestyle has caused you a considerable amount of pain and grief as a result of your addiction. If you don't allow God to change your view of money and how to handle it, money can lead you to relapse.
- ☐ During your past lifestyle of living in bondage to alcohol and other drugs, money was a key factor in fulfilling the lust of the flesh. Satan may have even exploited your desire for riches and wealth by recruiting you to sell drugs, and thereby assisted him in bringing others into bondage to drugs.
- ☐ Now having become a child of the king and separated from the world for His purpose and service, your old worldly view of money must be changed so you can honor your heavenly Father.
- ☐ For most new converts to the faith who were in bondage to drugs/alcohol (especially drugs), possession of money early in your restoration will excite the flesh, causing intense cravings for drugs/alcohol.
- ☐ If you don't have an alternative for handling money in your relapse prevention plan, paydays could become extremely stressful and eventually lead to your relapse (returning to fulfilling the "works of the flesh").
- ☐ Possession of money early in your restoration from being in bondage to drugs/alcohol most likely will cause intense warfare within your soul (creating cravings) because of how you previously handled money.

Money, A Major Stimulant of the Flesh

Self-Check

How well do you understand that having *"money in your possession"* too early in your restoration can cause cravings? Discuss your answer with your group.

Has having *"money in your possession"* ever caused you to have cravings? Discuss your answer with your group.

Action Steps

List two things you are willing to do to keep from allowing money to cause cravings during your restoration.

1.
2.

Was there a scripture(s) in this section that impacted your life? Discuss that experience with your group.

Sex: A Major Cause of Relapse?

> And do this, understanding the present time. The hour has come for you to wake up from your slumber, because our salvation is nearer now than when we first believed. The night is nearly over; the day is almost here. So let us put aside the deeds of darkness and put on the armor of light. *Let us behave decently, as in the daytime, not in orgies and drunkenness, not in sexual immorality and debauchery, not in dissension and jealousy.* Rather, clothe yourselves with the Lord Jesus Christ, *and do not think about how to gratify the desires of the sinful nature.* (Romans 13:11–14, NIV)

Michael D. Vann, a Certified Alcohol/Drug Counselor III, Director of Men's Services, alcohol and other drug abuse, Asha Family Services, Milwaukee, Wisconsin, states, "A group of males in bondage to alcohol and other drugs consisting of non-Christians, Christians active in the faith, Christians in a backslidden state reported the following information regarding your relapse.

"They stated that when they were engaged in the process of recovery and were experiencing stability, and success, they relapsed when they sought to relive a dope date. These men in bondage to addiction report that though they were in relationships wherein they were readily having sex, they suddenly began to crave the kind of sex they had experienced during a dope date. They reported that this started with a thought (a trigger) of how lascivious cocaine prostitutes were and how enjoyable (euphoric recall) the experience of having sex with a woman who was under the influence of cocaine was. These men in bondage to addiction reported that they became so preoccupied with the thought of reliving a dope date that they soon began to plot and plan how and when to make their connection. They admitted that they weren't looking for just a plain prostitute but a special kind of prostitute, a cocaine-using prostitute. These men said they wanted these women to perform oral sex on them or engage in sexual acts that their wives and girlfriends would not engage in. Clearly, any prostitute could have obliged; however, the agreement was that the woman performing these acts had to be under the influence of cocaine.

"These men indicated that they took the cocaine prostitute to purchase cocaine and that they waited in the other room while she smoked it. Most of these men said that though they became nervous and uncomfortable being in such close proximity to someone smoking cocaine, they gave no consideration to the dangers of doing so prior to the initiation of their transaction. Moreover, all these men said that they rationalized their behavior by saying to themselves that they were not doing anything wrong because they weren't using cocaine and that they had no intentions on using. Invariably, every one of these men said that he eventually relapsed and attributed their relapse to his sexual encounters with a cocaine prostitute.

"We know that the ingestion of alcohol and other drugs affects the pleasure center of the brain, which has much to do with hunger, thirst, and sex. We also know that some individuals in restoration from addiction develop eating disorders (obesity) and that others become oversexed. Though I am not cognizant of research on which individuals in restoration from addiction develop sexual disorders, I have provided counseling to many who said that when they stopped using alcohol and other drugs, sex became their drug of choice. Many of these individuals report that they found themselves being powerless over sex and they said that because of their insatiable sexual appetite, their lives became unmanageable."

SEX: A MAJOR CAUSE OF RELAPSE?

Self-Check

Are you currently involved in the following sexual activities?

Please Check [√] the box of the activity you are currently involved in.

1. Fornication (sex outside of marriage) [ ]
2. Adultery (sex outside of your marriage) [ ]
3. Homosexuality [ ]
4. Pornography [ ]
5. Masturbation [ ]

Discuss the answers to the following questions with your group

1. How well do you understand how *sexual desires* can causes cravings? Discuss your answer with your group.

2. Have your *sexual desires* ever caused you to have cravings for drugs/alcohol? Discuss your answer with your group.

3. Have your *sexual desires* ever caused you to relapse? Discuss your answer with your group.

Action Steps

List two things you are willing to do to keep *sexual desires* from causing cravings.

1.
2.

Environmental Stimulus

A believer needs to understand that environmental stimulus refers to anything that activates a craving through the five senses—taste, smell, sight, hearing, and touch. Usually the power of environmental stimuli to activate cravings diminishes over time. Thus, you are most dangerous during the early stage of restoration.

The sight of liquor bottles, drug paraphernalia (syringes, cookers, crack pipes, bongs, rolling papers, dollar bills rolled up, straws), and seeing others using drugs/alcohol can activate cravings. Seeing newly fallen snow or other powdered substance during early restoration can activate a heroin or cocaine craving. Watching alcohol commercials on television, walking past a beer cooler in a market and glancing inside can activate a craving. An aroma that reminds a person of the familiar odor of free-basing, smoking crack cocaine, or an odor that smells like a favorite mixed drink can activate a craving. Something that appears as harmless as a movie could cause a craving if it has graphic drugs/alcohol scenes that excite the flesh. As harmless as listening to the radio or tapes might seem, you could activate a craving if the songs are associated with drug/alcohol use. The taste of certain foods and medications could remind a person of alcohol or drugs and cause cravings.

ENVIRONMENTAL STIMULUS

Self-Check

1. How well do you understand how *"environmental stimulus"* causes cravings? Discuss your answer with your group.

2. Has *"environmental stimulus"* ever caused you to have cravings? Discuss your answer with your group.

Action Steps

List three things you are willing to do to keep *"environmental stimulus"* from causing you to have cravings.

1.
2.
3.

Understanding Environmental Stimulus Self-Check

Rank the following factors according to how they have led you to experience craving. Place the *#1* on the slot of the sense that causes you the *least number of cravings* and the *#5* on the slot of the sense that causes you the *greatest number of cravings* and rank the remaining senses accordingly.

1. Touch _____
2. Taste _____
3. Sight _____
4. Smell _____
5. Hearing _____

Power of Suggestion

Several scriptures clearly illustrate how Satan specializes in controlling an individual's mind by placing his thoughts inside your minds through the power of suggestion.

> *But your minds were blinded*: for until this day remaineth the same vail untaken away in the reading of the old testament; which *vail* is done away in Christ. (2 Corinthians 3:14)
>
> And even if our gospel is veiled, it is veiled to those who are perishing. *The god of this age has blinded the minds of unbelievers,* so that they cannot see the light of the gospel of the glory of Christ, who is the image of God. (2 Corinthians 4:3–4, NIV)

- ☐ Demonic forces are responsible for blinding your mind when you were an unbeliever, just as he has exploited your passions and desires of the flesh to use alcohol and other drugs.
- ☐ Due to demonic forces' exploitation through the power of suggestion, you continued in a sinful lifestyle of using alcohol and other drugs until you developed a major stronghold in your life, resulting in bondage to witchcraft.

> But I am afraid that just as Eve was deceived by the serpent's cunning, *your minds may somehow be led astray from your sincere and pure devotion to Christ.* (2 Corinthians 11:3, NIV)

- ☐ Demonic forces, through the power of suggestion, will continue attempting to draw you out of fellowship with God, back into a lifestyle of addiction, deceiving you into returning to sowing to the flesh (relapsing).

> The evening meal was being served, and the devil had already prompted Judas Iscariot, son of Simon, to betray Jesus. (John 13:2, NIV)
>
> But a certain man named Ananias, with Sapphira his wife, sold a possession, and kept back *part* of the price, his wife also being privy *to it*, and brought a certain part, and laid *it* at the apostles' feet. But Peter said, "Ananias, why hath Satan filled thine heart to lie to the Holy Ghost, and to keep back part of the price of the land?" (Acts 5:1–3)

- ☐ Not only will demonic forces place thoughts in your mind, but he will also attempt to trick you into believing that his thoughts are your thoughts.

- ☐ The enemy will attempt to achieve this by making his suggestions, using the first-person pronoun "I." He will inject thoughts into your mind, such as, "I sure would like a cold beer;" "I can handle smoking just one rock (cocaine);" "No one will know if I have just one."
- ☐ Demonic forces depend on their power of suggestion to reactivate the stronghold of addiction they had developed in your life from many years of "sowing to the flesh."
- ☐ Your thinking (mind) plays a major role in preventing relapse. The only way to counter Satan's strategic power of suggestion is to learn "to take thoughts captive."

POWER OF SUGGESTION

Self-Check

How well do you understand how the enemy's *"power of suggestion"* causes cravings? Discuss your answer with your group.

Has the enemy's *"power of suggestion"* ever caused you to have cravings? Discuss your answer with your group.

Action Steps

List two things you are willing to do to break the enemy's *"power of suggestion"* in your life.

1.
2.

Was there a scripture(s) in this section that impacted your life? Discuss that experience with your group.

THE CARNAL MIND (EUPHORIC RECALL)

The world under satanic influence provides an atmosphere (opportunity) for your carnal desires to be fulfilled. Alcohol and tobacco are legally sold across our counters; communities are overrun with illicit drugs. Prescription drugs are misused daily as our society seeks "quick fix" solutions for every imagined illness and condition.

Mood change occurs in those recovering from substance abuse, thereby causing a euphoric state or "high," which provides a temporary relief of emotional and mental anguish; these lead to a false sense of reality. Demonic forces have flooded the illegal drug market with mood-altering drugs, such as crack, cocaine, ecstasy, ice, and other designer drugs that offer users an extremely pleasurable sensation that parents abandon your families and children rebel, willing to go to any length to obtain these substances.

Over a relatively short period of time, you most likely began depending on your newly gained experience (euphoric state), which becomes an escape from reality and the pressures of life, temporarily meeting some legitimate need that only God can successfully meet. If you had infirmities (inabilities to bear temptations in a particular area of your life) in the flesh for alcohol or other drugs, you raced to quickly become addicted.

In the spiritual realm, demonic forces observe a person's passion (desire for alcohol and other drugs) and move in quickly to take advantage of your fleshly desires (sin). You, through your choice to "sow to the flesh" (sin), gave the enemy an "opportunity" or foothold in your life. Through the power of suggestion, the enemy maintains their control over your life by taking advantage of your fleshly desires and maintaining the stronghold of addiction in your soul.

Drawing a person into a lifestyle of addiction is a primary strategy of the enemy; however, the enemy's ultimate goal is to destroy any chance of you entering into or maintaining a relationship with God the Father, or friends and family. Demonic forces desires are to hinder the fulfillment of the first and second greatest commandments.

Even if you established a relationship with God and relapse and choose to partake of alcohol or other drugs, there can be a "transfer of faith." Your relationship with God and others can be quickly replaced with alcohol and other drugs. Your faith in God and fellowship with other Christians will diminish rapidly at the hands of the world, flesh, and demonic forces as your faith is replaced by your focus on a euphoric state known as a "high."

You can cause a craving by "glorifying" your old lifestyle of using drugs/alcohol. Discussing the actions and events that took place during your addiction can cause you to experience "euphoric recall," remembering the "rush" and pleasurable experiences while choosing to ignore the negatives you experienced when getting high. It is important for you to remember that euphoric recall can cause cravings.

Even as Christian, you could find yourself unable to fulfill God's two greatest commandments because of your love for a substance. You could end up being controlled by a thought/feeling (euphoric recall) under the influence of the enemy that drives you further and further away from God's plan for your life. The enemy's attempt was to steal your soul when you were an unbeliever, and now it's to hinder your spiritual development to prevent you from growing in Christ and fulfilling God's purpose.

The Carnal Mind

Self-Check

How well do you understand that *"euphoric recall* (remembering the pleasure)" of getting high causes cravings? Discuss your answer with your group?

Has *"euphoric recall"* ever caused you to have cravings? Discuss your answer with your group.

Action Steps

List three things you are willing to do to prevent *"euphoric recall"* from causing you to have cravings.

1.
2.
3.

IDENTIFYING WHAT CAUSES YOUR CRAVINGS

Self-Check

> *Teaching us that, denying ungodliness and worldly lusts*, we should live soberly, righteously, and godly, in this present world. (Titus 2:12)

Rank the following common causes of cravings according to how they have led to you experience cravings. Place the #1 on the slot of the cause that presents the least amount of craving, and the #10 on the slot of the cause that presents you the greatest amounts of cravings then rank the remaining causes accordingly.

1. Money	_____	6. Boredom	_____
2. Old Friends	_____	7. Old Neighborhoods	_____
3. Power of Suggestion	_____	8. Taste, Smell, Sight	_____
4. Sexual Desires	_____	9. Euphoric Recall	_____
5. Negative Emotions	_____	10. ____________________	

PART THREE

How to Address A Craving Biblically

For though we walk in the flesh (live in the flesh), we do not war after the flesh (we do not wage war using mere human weapons): For the *weapons* of our warfare *are* not carnal (physical of flesh and blood), *but mighty through God to the pulling down (overthrow and destruction) of strongholds; Casting down imaginations (reasoning and theories),* and every high thing that exalteth itself against the knowledge of God, *and bringing into captivity every thought to the obedience of Christ.* (2 Corinthians 10:3–5)

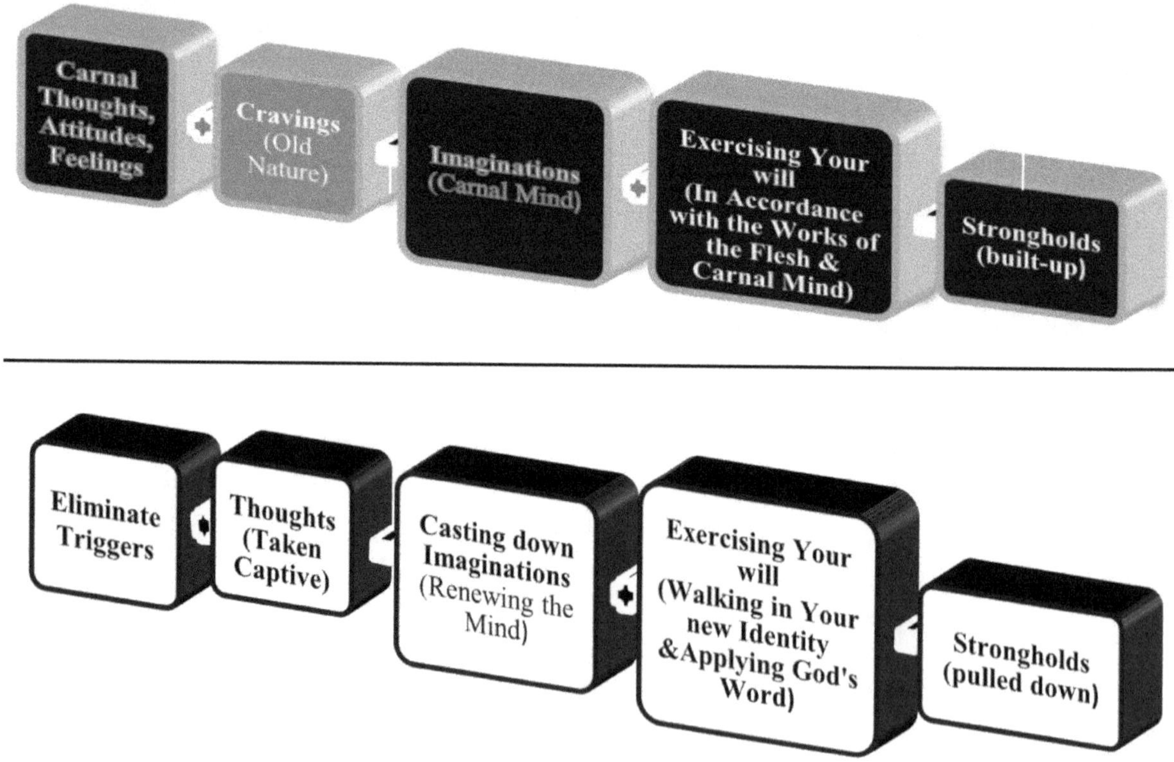

Figure 69: Understanding the Dynamics of the Cravings

No temptation has seized you except what is common to man. And God is faithful; he will not let you be tempted beyond what you can bear. But when you

> are tempted, he will also provide a way out so that you can stand up under it. Therefore, my dear friends, flee from idolatry. (1 Corinthians 10:13–14, NIV)
>
> *Knowing this, that our old man is crucified with him*, that the body of sin might be destroyed, that henceforth *we should not serve sin*. For he that is dead is freed from sin. In the same way, *count (consider) yourselves dead to sin but alive to God in Christ Jesus.* (Romans 6:6–7)

If you continue to relapse as a born-again believer, this indicates several important spiritual truths you are failing to understand regarding your new identity. In your acceptance of Jesus Christ, you must understand four significant facts:

1. The old person was buried with Christ by baptism into His death.
2. You have been raised up in a new life by the Father and in a new likeness of Christ.
3. Your old person was crucified with Christ and buried with Him, and you are a new person resurrected with Him.
4. You have been freed from (addiction) sin and no longer have to serve sin (addiction). Your bondage to drugs/alcohol (addiction) has been destroyed, and now you must learn to experience that victory.

> During the years you spent separated from God, your worldly experiences thoroughly programmed your brain with thought patterns, memory traces, responses, and habits which are alien to God. So even though your old skipper (nature) is gone, your flesh remains in opposition to God as a preprogrammed propensity for sin, which is living independent of God.
>
> —Neil Anderson

> You were taught, with regard to your former way of life, *to put off your old self,* which is being *corrupted by its deceitful desires*; to *be made new in the attitude of your minds;* and to put on the *new self, created to be like God* in *true righteousness and holiness. (*Ephesians 4:22–24)

☐ You must have a change in attitude regarding *how you view yourselves and the cravings* you may continue to experience, *realizing where the cravings come from, and who you are in Christ.*

> For though we walk in the flesh (live in the flesh), we do not war after the flesh (we do not wage war using mere human weapons): For the *weapons* of our warfare *are* not carnal (physical of flesh and blood), *but mighty through God to the pulling down (overthrow and destruction) of strongholds; Casting down imaginations (reasoning and theories)*, and every high thing that exalteth itself against the knowledge of God, *and bringing into captivity every thought to the obedience of Christ.* (2 Corinthians 10:3–5)
>
> Finally, my brethren, be strong in the Lord, and in the power of his might. Put on *the whole armor of God*, that ye maybe able to stand against the wiles of the devil. For we wrestle not against flesh and blood, but against principalities, against powers, against rulers of the darkness of this world, against spiritual wick-

> edness in high places. Wherefore take unto you the whole armor of God, that ye maybe be able to withstand in the evil day, and having done all, to stand. Stand therefore, having your loins girt about with *truth*, and having on the *breastplate of righteousness*; And your feet shod with the *preparation of the gospel of pace.* Above all, taking the *shield of faith*, where with ye shall be able to quench all the fiery darts of the wicked. And take the *helmet of salvation*, and the *sword of the Spirit, which is the word of God*: *Praying* always with all prayer and supplication in the Spirit, and watching thereunto with all perseverance and supplication for all the saints. (Ephesians 6:10–18)

Ready to Battle "the Craving"

Paul instructs us to "put on" the whole armor of God. Each piece of armor is necessary and important for spiritual protection. You must suit yourself up with each piece of armor cited in this passage, never to remove it. If we fail to remain continually dressed for battle, using each piece of armor, we would allow the enemy ample opportunity to access and gain control over some aspect of our lives. Suited with the full armor of God, you are ready to battle your cravings.

Truth

You must be a person of honor, standing and walking in truth. Having your "loins girded about with truth" is your first essential piece of armor. Jesus is the truth (John 14:6), and the Scriptures are true; you must be convinced of the power and reliability of the Word of God (Hebrews 4:12). You must gird the loins of your mind with the truth, having confidence as you battle your cravings.

John 17:17 gives great insight into the power of the truth. Jesus is praying for His mentored disciples, asking the father to "sanctify them by the truth; your word is truth;" and James 1:21 tells believers to "humbly accept the word planted in you, which can save you."

The truth, the Word of God, is the weapon that will break the power of deception, the enemy's primary form of warfare. As a believer, you must be committed to modeling the truth in your everyday affairs. "So if the Son [who is the Truth] sets you free, you will be free indeed" (John 8:36). Are you founding your life on the truth—the Bread of Life—receiving a steady diet through daily devotions, Bible study, and so forth?

Righteousness

The second piece of armor described by Paul is one of the most critical: "the breastplate of righteousness." This piece of armor was vital to the Roman soldiers, and is to you also as you battle your cravings.

In Jewish tradition, the heart represents the mind; the bowels were symbolic of emotions, two primary targets of the enemy. Your full-body "breastplate" protects the mind and emotions from the enemy's accusations (a major form of deception, causing feelings of guilt and condemnation). You must have faith in your right relational standing with God, remembering "to put on the *new self, created to be like God* in *true righteousness and holiness"* (Ephesians 4:24).

You must understand the spiritual importance of confession and repentance. You must apply these principles daily to receive the Father's forgiveness. "If we confess our sins, he is faithful and just and will forgive us our sins and purify us from all unrighteousness" (1 John 1:9). As you are restored from your addiction, you must learn to demonstrate righteous living in order to defeat your cravings.

The Gospel of Peace

The third piece of armor is having one's "feet shod with the preparation of the gospel of peace." This represents "sure footing"—a firm foundation on which to engage the enemy. You must have an assurance of your salvation and be ready to share the Gospel with others. Having made peace with God, you have been given the peace of God (Romans 5:1). This allows you to be at peace with your past and during the most intense cravings.

Faith

You must, above all, take "the shield of faith, wherewith ye shall be able to quench all the fiery darts of the wicked."

In ancient times, flaming darts or arrows (dipped in flammable pitch) were used to set clothing or roofs ablaze. Today, you must use a shield of faith for protection from spiritual darts or arrows, such as emotional triggers (anger, loneliness, self-pity, rejection, etc.) and unforgiveness, bitterness, resentments, condemnation, and pride.

The enemy will try to use these spiritual darts to tempt you to sin and disrupt your relationships with both God and others. The shield of faith can be strengthened as you participate in Bible studies, listen to sermons, and memorize scripture. As you increase your knowledge of God, the shield of faith is enlarged (Romans 10:17). Through faith, you are able to model unwavering confidence in God's promises (Romans 4:20–21).

The Helmet of Salvation

Paul cites another piece of armor, the "helmet of salvation." This provides covering for the most critical part of your anatomy: the mind and battlefield for spiritual warfare.

The Roman foot soldier wore the helmet to protect him from the large swords swung by the cavalry. As a believer, you need the same protection from an enemy who desires to decapitate us through deception, attempting to control our actions by controlling our minds.

Should the "shield of faith" prove to be somewhat small at times, you must be confident that your helmet of salvation guarantees your eternal victory (Romans 8:37–39). This confidence in eternal salvation dispels two major tactics of the enemy: fear and doubt. You must be ready to confirm the assurance of your salvation through God's Word.

The Word of God

Paul continues with "the sword of the Spirit which is the word of God." The Roman soldier's sword was his principal weapon in hand-to-hand combat. Likewise, the Word of God serves as your primary weapon, a spiritual sword for close encounters with the enemy. It serves as both an offensive and defensive weapon. You must acknowledge the Bible not only as the only inspired handbook on spiritual warfare, but also as spiritual medicine, nourishment, and vitamins for all spiritual ills.

Memorize scripture. Meditate on scripture and declare scripture (power of the spoken Word). This three-fold use of the "sword" is the most important weapon against cravings (Satan, flesh, and the world).

Prayer

Prayer is the final piece of armor—the ultimate weapon. Through prayer, you are able to maintain a vibrant relationship with your heavenly Father, demonstrating your dependence on Him. You must recognize prayer as an act of humility, a living out of your faith. Prayer is more than mere "support." It is truly the heart of the battle, the frontline of spiritual warfare (1 Peter 4:7).

As a believer being restored from addiction, you must be actively involved in prayer against the enemy's strongholds in your life and be willing to begin to pray immediately when cravings are triggered. God's Word calls you to be persistent in prayer and to pray for "general requests" as well as "specific petitions (Luke 18:1–8)." You must believe that "the effective fervent prayer of a righteous man availeth much" (James 5:16).

Understanding How to Break the Craving Cycle

> Thou therefore *endure hardness*, as a *good soldier of Jesus Christ.* No man that warreth entangleth himself with the affairs of *this* life; that he may please him who hath chosen him to be a soldier. And if a man also strive for masteries, *yet* is he not crowned, except he strive lawfully. (2 Timothy 2:3–5)

You must understand that gaining biblical understanding into cravings and how they work is extremely important in God's plan for restoring your soul from addiction. Your journey to addiction *began with spiritual warfare* as you listened to (the enemy) the carnal mind, giving in to your fleshly desires and appetite for drugs/alcohol. You must understand that now you are saved, every *craving cycle* is an excellent opportunity to begin tearing down strongholds of addiction. Every time you break the craving cycle, you defeat your enemy, the stronghold of addiction is weakened, and God is glorified. However, every time you give in to the craving, the stronghold of addiction is strengthened and Satan gets the glory.

The Craving Cycle

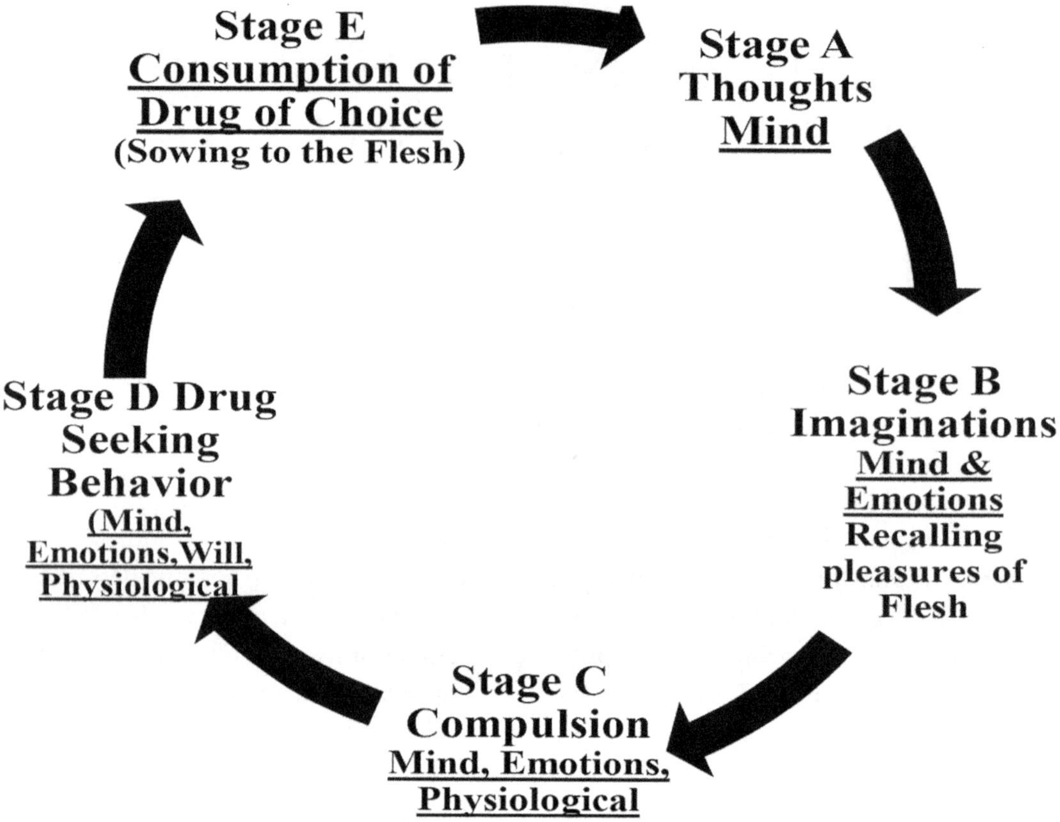

Figure 70: The Craving Cycle

The Role that Triggers Play in Cravings

As you have already learned in the previous section on cravings, thoughts and desires for drugs/alcohol can be activated by various triggers ranging from external factors in your environment, such as money and music to relational and emotional triggers caused by negative emotions. By far, the easiest triggers to eliminate are the external ones. You should avoid having large sums of money in your possession, visiting places where drugs/alcohol are sold and used, and hanging with old associates who are still using drugs/alcohol. However, anger, loneliness, bitterness, resentments, and unforgiveness are more difficult to cope with or eliminate. The emotional and mental triggers are overcome through spiritual maturity, growing up in Christ, which takes time.

Cocaine Cravings

Many individuals continue to crave and/or use cocaine, even though using it no longer provides them with the pleasurable experience they once derived from its use. Instead of pleasure, these individuals who are usually experienced cocaine users consistently experience unreasonable fears, vivid auditory and/or visual hallucinations, and other bizarre behaviors. Yet, these individuals continue to crave and use cocaine only because they ignore these negative experiences. They are motivated to continue using cocaine, because they recall the intense pleasure they once derived from its use. This phenomenon is called *euphoric recall.*

Euphoric recall seems to be more powerful than a thousand negative experiences obtained from using cocaine. Simply put, because the use of cocaine was once so pleasurable to the user, the user cannot and will not view negative experiences from its use as being negative; instead, they are motivated by how cocaine once made you feel.

Stage A

The Role the Carnal Mind Plays in Cravings

> For they that are after the flesh do mind the things of the flesh; but they that are after the Spirit the things of the Spirit. *For to be carnally minded is death; but to be spiritually minded is life and peace.* Because the carnal mind *is* enmity (hostile) against God: for it is not subject to the law of God, neither indeed can be. So then you that are in the flesh cannot please God. But ye are not in the flesh, but in the Spirit, if so be that the Spirit of God dwell in you. Now if any man have not the Spirit of Christ, he is none of His. (Romans 8:5–9)

The key to reducing cravings is for you to *identify* your personal triggers—both external and internal—and reduce as many as possible.

> *All of us also lived among them at one time, gratifying the cravings of our sinful nature and following its desires and thoughts.* Like the rest, we were by nature objects of wrath. (Ephesians 2:3, NIV)

You must understand that the carnal mind is an ally of the flesh (your enemy) and will continuously strive to feed fleshly desires that keep you in bondage to drugs/alcohol. Therefore, the carnal mind wars against your "new identity" in Christ. The carnal mind exploits cravings to rejuvenate fleshly desires and feed your imagination.

Stage A is the *first stage* in a craving. The key to breaking the craving cycle in Stage A is for the believer to take the following steps:

(1) *Take your thoughts captive by recognizing* that the sinful thoughts and desires are coming from your carnal mind. Therefore, you must *disown and separate yourself* from them.
(2) *Recognize* and accept that cravings involve spiritual warfare and that you have victory over cravings. Therefore, you must be willing to walk in the faith of Christ to experience His victory over temptation. *Conclude* that even though you are experiencing thoughts and desires to use drugs/alcohol, these are *not a part of your new identity in Christ.*
(3) *Understand* that *Stage A* is the *easiest stage in which to break* the *craving cycle* before it progresses to the next level, your *imagination, Stage B.*

- ☐ You must realize that your cravings for drugs/alcohol come from carnal mind (flesh), *your old person,* the person you were before you were saved, and is not a part of the new person you are in Christ. Although you are a new creature in Christ, your flesh (carnal mind) wants to continue to respond according to the old person, seeking the pleasures of your old nature, which *must be crucified.*

- ☐ You must realize that because of your involvement with the things of the world (and your past lifestyle), you allowed the enemy to develop certain *strongholds* in your soul. Your mind is your control center; therefore, it plays a key role in these strongholds being destroyed.
- ☐ These strongholds can only be destroyed *by learning to take every thought captive unto the obedience of Christ* by knowing His Word and using it to combat your cravings, desires, and appetites for drugs/alcohol.
- ☐ When you first experience a craving for drugs/alcohol, you must take those ungodly thoughts captive unto the obedience of Christ. You must learn to acknowledge those thoughts at the initial stage of cravings as being a message from the enemy (carnal mind) and a threat to your relationship with God and your restoration.

Stage B

The Role Your Imagination Plays in Cravings

Taking every thought captive is the primary solution to *"casting down imaginations"* or short-circuiting the carnal mind by not allowing it time to dwell on its desires and appetites. This prevents the craving from progressing to *Stage B*, the next level of intensity involving your *emotions.*

Your *imagination* is centered on the *recalling of past experiences ("euphoric recall")* when you viewed using drugs/alcohol as pleasurable. The carnal mind will continue to feed your imagination, if allowed. This will result in strengthening your stronghold of addiction. This stage is more intense because not only are *your current thoughts* involved, but now your carnal mind begins to *recall past experiences* regarding your use of drugs/alcohol, while failing *to recall the guilt, condemnation, and negative consequences.* The key to breaking the craving cycle in Stage B is to:

(1) *Identify* and accept your past experience with drugs/alcohol in *honesty* as sin against God, and not as pleasurable experiences.

(2) You must experience a *change in attitude* regarding how you view your use of drugs/alcohol. *If a believer still views the use of alcohol/drugs as enjoyable, he/she is in trouble.* If so, this reveals that the believer has not experienced a change in attitude, and therefore will not be able to *cast down imaginations.* As pleasurable as your use of drugs/alcohol might have seemed, the new you must recognize that it was sin, an offense against God, your Father.

(3) *Stage B* is a more difficult *stage* to break during the *craving cycle* than Stage A. However, the craving cycle is more easily broken in *Stage B* than it is when the cycle reaches *Stage C—compulsion, where physical desires are aroused.*

Stage C

The Role that Physical Impulses Play in Cravings

Cravings begin with a believer having *thoughts* of using drugs/alcohol and then *imaginations.* These last for only a short period of time; but if not "short-circuited" or addressed, the cravings reach a higher strength and become *compulsions* (of physical desires) in Stage C.

Stage C is a very difficult stage during which to break the craving cycle, because not only is the believer's *mind and emotions* involved in the craving, but the *body* (biological) becomes involved, and now you begin experiences physical impulses, physiological changes (sweating, stomach churning, need to go to bathroom, etc.)

- ☐ An unchallenged thought will result in you experiencing an even stronger desire to use, because now your *thoughts* have caused your *imagination* to run wild, leading to *compulsion* for using drugs/alcohol. Your desire to use increases in strength, eventually leading to alcohol and other drug seeking behaviors. You will be influenced by these desires, and you can cause you to make a conscious decision to use.

Stage D

Stage D is by far the *most difficult stage* in the *craving cycle* to interrupt because your *entire soul, mind, will, and emotions,* plus your *body* have become involved. Now you have made a *conscious decision* to use and you have become involved in *"drug/alcohol seeking behaviors."* You have *exercised your will* to agree with your carnal mind and become involved in sowing to your fleshly desires. The key to breaking the *craving cycle* during Stage D is to:

Have a *change of mind* and *exercise your will* according to God's Word and who you are in Christ. The only way you can stop the *craving cycle* is to *reverse your decision* and stop your drug-seeking behavior.

Stage E

Stage E is the final stage of the *craving cycle,* and when a you reach this stage, you have lost a battle, but not the war. You have allowed your enemy—the world, flesh, and Satan—to *lure* you back to "sowing to the flesh" by using drugs/alcohol. You have missed an excellent opportunity to begin tearing down the stronghold of addiction by not breaking the *craving cycle.* You chose not to take God's way out. *You chose not to exercise your will* according to God's Word. *You failed to realize who you are in Christ* and to disown the craving by taking the *thoughts and desires captive.* You let your *imagination* lead you down a path back to your besetting sin, which you did not have to travel. Still there will be more opportunities for you to combat your cravings, but you will have to learn to deal with it God's way.

Understanding How to Break the Craving Cycle

Self-Check

> For though we walk in the flesh (live in the world), we do not war after the flesh (we do not wage war as the world does): For the weapons of our warfare *are* not carnal (worldly), *but mighty through God to the pulling down of strong holds; Casting down imaginations*, and every high thing that exalteth itself against the knowledge of God, *and bringing into captivity every thought to the obedience of Christ.* (2 Corinthians 10:3–5)

Rank the following stages in the craving cycle according to the difficulty you have in breaking the cycle when you experienced cravings in the past. Place the *#1* on the slot of the *stage you had the most difficulty breaking the cycle, and the #2, etc., until each stage has a number on the slot.*

1. Stage #1 (taking thought captive) _____
2. Stage # 2 (casting down imaginations) _____
3. Stage # 3 (physical desires or impulses) _____
4. Stage # 4 (stopping drug–seeking behavior) _____

Self-Rating

Answer the following questions within your group.

1. How well do you understand the idea of *"taking your thoughts captive"* in stage A of the craving cycle?

2. How well do you understand the idea of *"casting down your imagination"* in stage B of the craving cycle?

3. How well do you understand the idea of "*resisting the physical desire*" (compulsion) in stage C of the craving cycle?

4. How well do you understand that when the craving cycle reaches stage D and you have made "a conscious decision" to use that breaking the craving cycle is most difficult?

Action Steps

Do you have any strategies that you used in the past that were successful in breaking the craving cycle? If your answer is yes, please list them.

List any other strategies you plan to use to break the craving cycle.

1.
2.
3.

"SPIRITUAL SHORT-CIRCUITING"

Using God's resources, spiritual disciplines (Word, praise/worship, and fellowship) and Christ's authority (rebuking) to interrupt, cancel out, and overcome cravings before you can lead to relapse.

"Spiritual short-circuiting" is a term coined by the author during his own restoration from being in bondage to drugs/alcohol. I can vividly remember how early in that process I experienced intense cravings to return to using drugs/alcohol. I had only been attending church for a short period of time, but I had been there long enough to hear my pastor say, "God inhabits the praises of the saints." I hadn't memorized an entire song yet, and I only knew a few phrases to sing from memory. So as I searched for assistance in dealing with my intense craving, I was led of God to begin singing praises, sometimes verbally and other times quietly. To my surprise, in a few quick minutes, the cravings would subside and cease. Sometimes, I would begin repeating that saving and delivering name, Jesus, and as I called His name, expecting His assistance in the craving, in minutes, it would cease altogether.

Excellent ways of nipping cravings in the bud is "short-circuiting" the initial thoughts by:

a) Praising/prayer to God verbally aloud or mentally.
b) Quoting scripture verbally aloud or mentally.
c) Reading/meditating on scripture.
d) Openly sharing your craving with another brother/sister in the Lord (by phone or in person) to break the power of the enemy's deception.
e) Taking thoughts captive by verbally rebuking the craving aloud or rebuking it mentally.

> Seek the Lord while he may be found; call on him while he is near. *Let the wicked forsake his way and the evil man his thoughts.* Let him turn to the Lord, and he will have mercy on him, and to our God, for he will freely pardon. *For my thoughts are not your thoughts, neither are your ways my ways, declares the Lord.* As the heavens are higher than the earth, *so are my ways higher than your ways and my thoughts than your thoughts.* As the rain and the snow come down from heaven, and do not return to it without watering the earth and making it bud and flourish, so that it yields seed for the sower and bread for the eater, *so is my word that goes out from my mouth: it will not return to me empty, but will accomplish what I desire and achieve the purpose for which I sent it.* (Isaiah 55: 6–11, *NIV*)

STRATEGIES FOR "SPIRITUAL SHORT-CIRCUITING" CRAVINGS

Figure 71: Short-Circuiting Cravings

Charles Stanley in his text, *Winning the War Within*, states four primary reasons the power of the Word is so effective with regard to combating cravings (temptations) in the life of the believer and why you need to understand these four reasons.

(1) God's Word expresses the sinfulness of whatever a you are being tempted with. *It helps you view the craving (temptation) for what it is—a lie.*
(2) God's Word provides you with *God's view* (divine perspective). This will help you understand that your cravings (temptations) to return to using alcohol and other drugs is something that is happening to you but is not a part of you and your new nature.
(3) God's Word helps you to "short-circuit" sinful thoughts and desires for alcohol and other drugs and to take those thoughts captive. God's Word will help you by *"nipping cravings (temptations)*

in the bud" before you can lead you back to "sowing to the flesh (relapsing)." (Philippians 4:8; Colossians 3:2)

(4) Using God's Word against cravings (temptations) is also effective for you, because it is an *expression of faith*. Believing in God's Word during times of temptation will assist you in overcoming cravings and keep you from giving in to your old desires and appetites.

> But thou *art* holy, *O thou that inhabitest the praises of Israel.* (Psalm 22:3)

- ☐ God's Word tells us that He inhabits the praises of the saints, His people.

> Again, I say unto you, that if two of you shall agree on earth as touching anything that you shall ask, it shall be done for you of my Father which is in heaven. *For where two or three are gathered together in my name, there am I in the midst of you.* (Matthew 18:19–20)
>
> *Confess your faults one to another, and pray one for another, that ye may be healed.* The effectual fervent prayer of a righteous man availeth much. (James 5:16)

- ☐ You should be in close fellowship with other believers so you have another person who is a Christian that you can confide in. By confessing your craving to another person and openly agreeing to your victory over the craving in the name of Jesus, you are able to break the power of the enemy and stop the craving. This is one reason why fellowshipping is so important.

Identifying Strategies for Short-Circuiting Your Cravings

Self-Check

> For though we walk in the flesh (live in the world), we do not war after the flesh (we do not wage war as the world does): For the weapons of our warfare *are* not carnal (worldly), *but mighty through God to the pulling down of strong holds; Casting down imaginations*, and every high thing that exalteth itself against the knowledge of God, *and bringing into captivity every thought to the obedience of Christ.* (2 Corinthians 10:3–5)

Rank the following strategies for short-circuiting cravings according to which one you are willing to use when you experience a craving. Place the *#1* on the slot of the *strategy you plan to use first, second, etc., until each strategy has a number on the slot.*

1. Praying/praising God verbally aloud or mentally. _____
2. Quoting scripture verbally or mentally. _____
3. Using your Bible (if it is available) by reading/meditating on scriptures. _____
4. Openly sharing your craving with another brother/sister in the Lord to break the power of the enemy's deception (by phone or in person). _____
5. Taking the thought captive by verbally rebuking the craving aloud or rebuking it mentally. _____
6. Do you have any *short-circuiting* strategies that you used in the past that were successful? If your answer is yes, please list them. _____

Self-Rating

How well do you understand the strategies for *"short-circuiting"* your cravings? Discuss your answer with your group.

Have you ever used any of the *"short-circuiting"* strategies listed above to stop cravings? Discuss your answer with your group.

Action Steps

List any other strategies you plan to use when you begin to experience a craving.

1.
2.
3.

Was there a scripture(s) in this section that impacted your life? Discuss that experience with your group.

PART FOUR

Set-Up Behaviors

Set-up behaviors can be defined as a believer's sinful attitudes or mental/emotional strongholds leading to previous ungodly behaviors of "sowing to the flesh" that expose you to relapsing.

Mental Strongholds (The Carnal Mind)
Street Mentality

Ephesians 2:2-6

> 2 **Wherein in time past ye walked according to the course of this world, according to the prince of the power of the air, the spirit that now worketh in the children of disobedience:** 3 Among whom also we all had our conversation in times past in the lusts of our flesh, **fulfilling the desires of the flesh and of the mind; and were by nature the children of wrath**, even as others. 4 But God, who is rich in mercy, 5 Even when we were dead in sins, hath quickened us together with Christ, (by grace ye are saved;) 6 And hath raised us up together, and made us sit together in heavenly places in Christ Jesus:

Prior to your conversion, you may have been controlled by your selfish desires, motivated by material gain. The law of the streets, *"do unto others before they do it to you"* or street mentality leads may have led you to believe that criminal behaviors (such as, the selling of drugs, armed robbery, burglary, etc.), are acceptable as long as they provide you with financial gain.

- ☐ Your selfish interest may have caused you to view victimizing and taking advantage of others as being acceptable as long as you received financial gain or "got paid."
- ☐ Your decision making may have been influenced by your corrupt desires. Your decisions most likely were self-centered disregarding the welfare of others. Now that you are saved, if you do not learn to fully submit your will to God by renewing your mind through God's Word, your old selfish ideas will continue to influence your decisions.
- ☐ Your old thought patterns and desires work together to hinder your dependence on God and your relationships within the Body of Christ.

A Hustler's Mentality

1 Timothy 6:6-10

> But godliness with contentment is great gain. For we brought nothing into this world, and it is certain we can carry nothing out. And having food and raiment let us be therewith content. But you that will be rich fall into temptation and a snare, and into many foolish and hurtful lusts, which drown men in destruction and perdition. For the love of money is the root of all evil: which while some coveted after, you have erred from the faith, and pierced yourselves through with many sorrows.

Material gain in the past may have driven you to become involved in criminal activities that provided large quantities of money in relatively short periods of time. Maybe you are accustomed to making what is generally considered to be a weekly salary in just a few hours hustling in the streets. You may have used the fast money to finance an ungodly lifestyle that provided you with power, prestige and fame or to pay for your own habit.

If you've been exposed to hustling and developed a **"hustler's mentality,"** it is very difficult to overcome without developing a biblical view of finances and employment. Working a forty-hour a week job, making eight to ten dollars an hour is extremely difficult to adjust to after being exposed to the fast illegal money making schemes of the streets. A weekly salary may be viewed as being an insignificant income because of your exposure to quick money in your past lifestyle. You have old associates and friends encouraging you to return to your old lifestyle, ready to provide drugs or other illegal schemes to assist you in "getting back on your feet."

You must be aware of the dangers that a **"hustler's mentality"** can cause during your restoration from the effects of addiction. If you are not open and honest and intentional about addressing this old way of thinking, you will set yourself up for relapse. You need to make a decision right now that dealing drugs or criminal activity is not an option, no matter what your financial situation might look like.

Prison Mentality

Ephesians 4:17-19

> So I tell you this, and insist on it in the Lord, that you must no longer live as the Gentiles do, in the futility of your thinking. You are darkened in your understanding and separated from the life of God because of the ignorance that is in you due to Robert F. Vann A Biblical Cognitive Relapse Prevention Support Group Participant Workbook 390 391 the hardening of your hearts. Having lost all sensitivity, you have given yourselves over to sensuality so as to indulge in every kind of impurity, and you are full of greed.

One returning citizen after being released into the community following fifteen years of incarceration explained how he was dehumanized by prison life. He stated how he was stripped of all compassion, love, and warmth for mankind in order to survive. The survival skills developed by the ex-prisoner population are centered on a **closed-mouth secretive** mentality. They learn not to **"trust"**, **"express feeling"** or **"communicate."**

If you are a returning citizen , you may have developed skills necessary for survival while incarcerated that led to you having a, **"prison mentality."** You may have unintentionally developed an attitude of not **"trusting", "expressing feelings"** or **"communicating."** If so, you can clearly understand that because of this mentality, you will have difficulty developing significant relationships, and that being open and honest won't be easy.

Having a **"prison mentality"** hinders you from establishing and maintaining healthy relationships within the Body of Christ. However, the greatest danger during your restoration from the effects of addiction is to your walk with the Lord, it hinders your spiritual healing.

James 5:16

16 Therefore confess your sins to each other and pray for each other so that you may be healed. The prayer of a righteous man is powerful and effective (NIV).

- ☐ God requires you to be open and honest, an individual of truth, because it will assist you in being restored from the effects of your addiction. Having a **"prison mentality"** will set you up for a lifestyle of relapsing.

"Awfulizing" Christianity and Sobriety

There are two identifiable patterns of thought that a believer being restored from addiction might experience after being saved. You need to clearly understand both of you in order to avoid a relapse setup... "Awfulizing" sobriety and Christianity are two similar negative mindsets that a believer may be unconsciously involved in. These mindsets are the result of living a lifestyle independent of God, abusing drugs/alcohol through living an addictive lifestyle.

- ☐ If you have been addicted any length of time, your initial reaction to sobriety is probably that it is a boring, dull lifestyle. Your lifestyle has probably been centered around your consumption of drugs/alcohol and/or the selling of drugs and you probably viewed this as being exciting, entertaining and fun.
- ☐ Drugs and alcohol lowered your resistance allowing the desires of your flesh to control your life. At the onset of being restored from the effects of addiction, you may be over-exaggerating what you believe are the negative aspects of sobriety and under-emphasizing the positives, such as, having good health, positive relationship with God and others, financial gain, etc.

Once you accept Christ, this negative mind set can be extended to Christianity. You may, likewise, view the Christian walk as being a boring lifestyle lacking in enjoyment. As you prepare to enter a new lifestyle viewed from the **"outside looking in,"** you may view the Christian lifestyle as one of restraints and "can't do this' and can't do that." You may not have experienced the power that accompanies your rebirth in Christ that provides you with a newfound freedom from the power of sin.

- ☐ You may be questioning if you can actually sustain a Christian lifestyle. What you need to understand is that no one can live the Christian lifestyle without the assistance of the Holy Spirit. You may not have an accurate view of sobriety or Christianity.

- ☐ Your attitude may be based on misunderstandings from your past and not on God's Word or any type of actual Christian experience. Your attitude and views may be clouded by two previously discussed worldly mind-sets established prior to your conversion which are referred to as a "street culture" and "prison mentality."
- ☐ You must understand the importance of leisure time activities within the community and be committed to engaging in regular activities with other believers to overcome these negative mind-sets. You need to learn to experience fun and enjoyment within the community setting without your old best friend, drugs/alcohol.

You must be clearly aware of the dangers that mental strongholds present in your restoration from the effects of addiction. They hinder spiritual growth in four key areas of your restoration; employment, finances, relationship and leisure time activities. You must be willing to destroy these old ways of thinking by developing a biblical view in each of these crucial areas or you will be set up to relapse.

- ☐ Following salvation, **the renewing of your mind is key** in preventing you from returning to your old lifestyle. The renewal of your mind is crucial because your old way of thinking will continue to oppose God's will for your life.

Your mind must be renewed through God's Word and be restored to agree with your spirit providing spiritual well-being and peace by being lead of the Holy Spirit. If your old thinking patterns are not changed, they will eventually lead you back to practicing the "works of the flesh" and will keep you from pleasing God. Your old thinking patterns are focused on fulfilling the appetites, passions, and desires that are contrary to God's will.

Romans 12:1-2

I beseech you therefore, brethren, by the mercies of God, that ye present your bodies a living sacrifice, holy, acceptable unto God, *which is* your reasonable service. 2 **And be not conformed to this world: but be ye transformed by the renewing of your mind,** that ye may prove what is that good, and acceptable, and perfect, will of God. God provides you with the guidelines for knowing His will:

a) Paul states first that you must present your bodies as living sacrifices, by not defiling His temple (ingesting alcohol and other drugs).
b) Next, you have to stop conforming to worldly patterns (hanging around old friends/associates and frequenting old establishments).
c) Finally, he says how you are to accomplish these tasks. He states you are to be changed (transformed) by renewing your mind because your mind must become God's ally.

James 1:21

21 Wherefore lay apart all filthiness and superfluity of naughtiness, **and receive with meekness the engrafted word, which is able to save your souls (restore your mind, will, emotions).**

- ☐ You must humbly receive God's Word and be willing to apply it to your daily life and the Holy Spirit will restore your soul (mind, will, emotions) bringing it under the control of your spirit, making it God's ally.Negative Attitudes Leading to Set-Up Behaviors

Hebrews 4:12

12 **<u>For the word of God is living and active.</u>** Sharper than any double-edged sword, **<u>it penetrates even to dividing soul and spirit,</u>** joints and marrow; **<u>it judges the thoughts and attitudes of the heart</u>** (NIV).

- ☐ The only tool designed by God that has the power and ability to reach an un-restored soul and destroy the strongholds established there is the Word of God.
- ☐ God's Word has the power to destroy those old thoughts and attitudes of the heart that could lead you back to your old lifestyle and at the same time, provide you with new biblical insights and understanding to guard your heart from worldly teachings.

Ephesians 4:20-24

20 But ye have not so learned Christ; 21 If so be that ye have heard him, and have been taught by him, as the truth is in Jesus: 22 **That ye put off concerning the former conversation (lifestyle) the old man, which is corrupt according to the deceitful lusts; 23 <u>And be renewed in the spirit of your mind;</u> 24 And that ye put on the new man, which after God is created in righteousness and true holiness.**

- ☐ You must understand that your mind is key in learning how to stop conforming to the patterns of your old lifestyle of using alcohol and other drugs, and must be renewed to become an ally to your spirit rather than an enemy.

Identifying Your Mental Strongholds Leading to Set-up Behaviors

Self – Check

*Rank the following mental strongholds leading to set-up behaviors according to how they have led you to relapse. Place the **<u>(#1)</u>** on the slot of the **<u>"mental stronghold"</u>** you think is **<u>most dangerous</u>** for you and the **<u>(#2)</u>** on the slot of the **<u>"mental stronghold"</u>** you think is the 2nd **<u>most dangerous</u>** for you until each **<u>"mental stronghold"</u>** has a # on the slot.*

1. Hustler's Mentality _____
2. Street Mentality _____
3. Prison Mentality _____
4. Awfulizing Sobriety _____
5. Awfulizing Christianity _____

Self-Rating

How well do you understand that <u>"mental strongholds"</u> leading to relapse? Discuss your answer with your group.

Has a <u>"mental stronghold"</u> set you up to relapse? Discuss your answer with your group.

Action Steps

List three things you are willing to do that will keep <u>mental strongholds</u> from setting you up to relapse.

1.
2.
3.

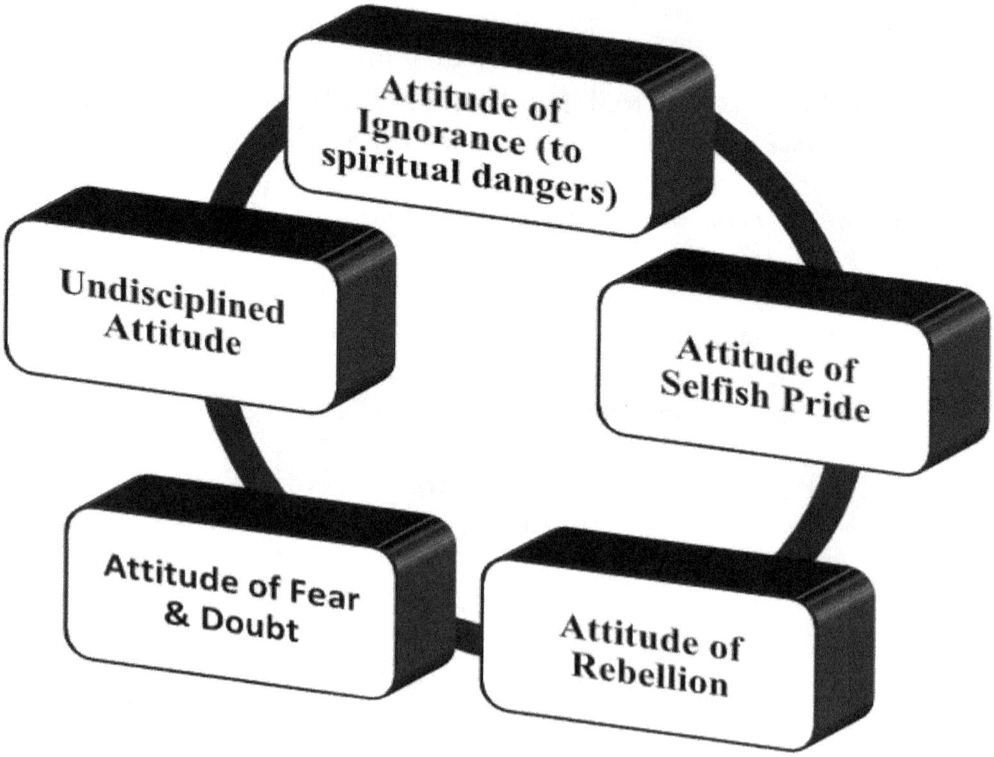

Figure 72: Set-up Behaviors

Attitude of Pride

A prideful attitude is characterized by having an unrealistic view of oneself, placing total dependence on self, refusing to acknowledge God as being in control and by taking credit for what God is doing in your life.

> All of you, *clothe yourselves with humility toward one another*, because *"God opposes the proud but gives grace to the humble." Humble yourselves*, therefore, under God's mighty hand, *that he may lift you up in due time.* (1 Peter 5:5–6, NIV)

PRIDE

My name is Pride. I am a cheater.
I cheat you of your God-given destiny…
Because you demand your own way.
I cheat you of contentment…
Because you "deserve better than this."
I cheat you of knowledge … because you already know it all.
I cheat you of healing … because you're too full of me to forgive.
I cheat you of holiness…
Because you refuse to admit when you're wrong.
I cheat you of vision …
Because you'd rather look in the mirror than out a window.
I cheat you of genuine friendship …
Because nobody's going to know the real you.
I cheat you of love …
Because real romance demands sacrifice.
I cheat you of greatness in heaven …
Because you refuse to wash another's feet on earth.
I cheat you of God's glory …
Because I convince you to seek your own.
My name is Pride. I am a cheater.
You like me because you think I'm always looking out for you.
Untrue.
I'm looking to make a fool of you.
God has so much for you, I admit, but don't worry …
If you stick with me,
You'll never know!
Beth Moore (Living Free)

Pride, the #1 Set-Up Behavior

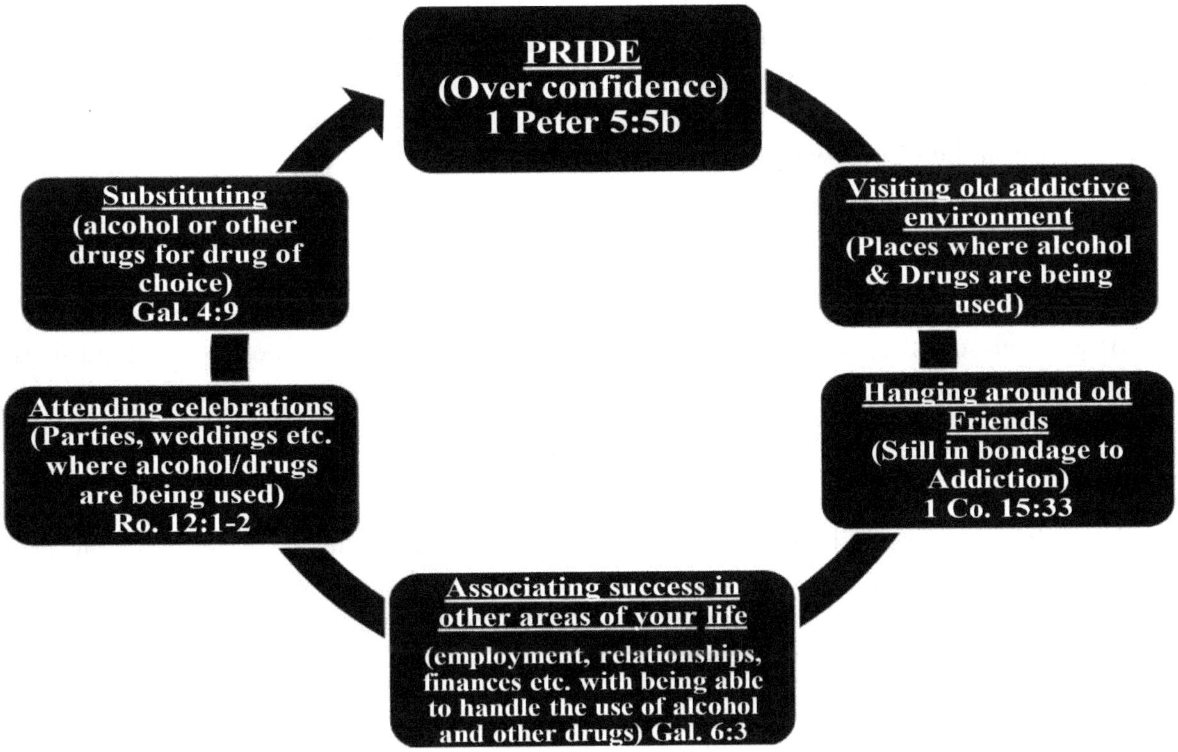

Figure 73: Pride, #1 Set-Up Behavior

Attitude of Rebellion

An attitude of rebellion is revealed and characterized by an unwillingness to submit to the authority of God, those authorities established by Him, and by being resistant to assuming a dependent position.

> Young men, in the same way *be submissive to* those who are older. All of you, clothe yourselves with humility toward one another, because "God opposes the proud but gives grace to the humble." Humble yourselves, therefore, under God's mighty hand, that he may lift you up in due time. (1 Peter 5:5–6, NIV)

Submission and *humility* are the first two attitudes discussed in this passage of scripture and *are the cornerstones for spiritual maturity*. Believers must understand the significant role these two Christlike qualities play in your spiritual growth as well as in the believer's life through character development. Satan is depending on the two opposing attitudes of *rebellion* and *pride* to cause you to relapse. Prior to or during your addiction, you may have developed attitudes (or strongholds) of rebellion and pride; now that you have become a believer, these two major attitudes must be addressed or you will set you up for failure and become a downfall leading to relapse.

Attitude of Fear and Doubt

When a believer doesn't understand what Christ's death, burial, and resurrection afforded you, it is impossible to have the proper faith in your position in Christ, which therefore reveals also your lack of trust or confidence in God and His plan for your life.

> Trust in the LORD with all your heart and lean not on your own understanding; in all your ways acknowledge him, and he will make your paths straight. Do not be wise in your own eyes; fear the LORD and shun evil. (Proverbs 3:5–7, NIV)

The third dangerous attitude harmful to the believer's spiritual growth is an *attitude of doubt and fear*. Trust is a must in the lives of believers; an attitude of distrust/doubt opposes trust. Trust is also a must for spiritual growth, because it is an important key in your relapse prevention process.

Undisciplined Attitude

An undisciplined attitude is characterized by a believer's unwillingness to abstain from fleshly appetites, passions, desires, and ignorance. It shows little regard for how the world caters to those desires, how Satan *exploits you,* and your unwillingness to cooperate with the Holy Spirit in mortifying (or putting to death) the deeds of the flesh.

> It teaches us to say "No" to ungodliness and worldly passions, and to live self–controlled, upright and godly lives in this present age, while we wait for the blessed hope the glorious appearing of our great God and savior, Jesus Christ, who gave himself for us to redeem us from all wickedness and to purify for himself a people that are his very own, eager to do what is good. (Titus 2:12–14, NIV)

The fourth dangerous attitude detrimental to a believer's spiritual maturity that could set you up for relapse is an *undisciplined attitude. An undisciplined attitude opposes temperance or self-control listed among the fruit of the Spirit.* The Holy Spirit provides you with self-control through your active fellowship with Christ as you learn to obey the Word ("walk in the spirit"). You must remember to remain spiritually focused and not get caught up in the flesh and the affairs of the world. You must understand that God's plan for you is to live a balanced lifestyle; Satan deals in extremes and desires to get you caught up in an unbalanced lifestyle.

- ☐ Making provisions for the flesh will hinder your spiritual growth and set you up for a possible relapse. Without self-control, you will develop an *attitude of ignorance to the enemy's spiritual battle plans arrayed against you,* the final dangerous attitude detrimental to your restoration from the effects of addiction.

Attitude of Ignorance to Spiritual Danger

An attitude of ignorance to spiritual danger describes the believer's ignorance and unpreparedness for spiritual warfare, thusly hindering your spiritual growth and development.

> Be self-controlled and alert. Your enemy the devil prowls around like a roaring lion looking for someone to devour. Resist him, standing firm in the faith, because you know that your brothers throughout the world are undergoing the same kind of sufferings. (1 Peter 5:8–9, NIV)

Finally, a believer must be alert, watchful, and cautious, understanding that carelessness will result in you being suddenly overtaken by some destructive action, designed by the enemy to hinder your spiritual growth and development. It will lead you back into your old addictive lifestyle.

The *attitude of ignorance to spiritual dangers* works hand in hand with an undisciplined attitude. It hinders your development of *an alert defense*. You must develop the understanding that the victory has already been won, that your savior has already dealt Satan a defeating blow and has overcome the world and the flesh.

IDENTIFYING NEGATIVE ATTITUDES LEADING TO SET-UP BEHAVIORS

Self-Check

Rank the following mental strongholds leading to set-up behaviors according to how they have led to you relapse. Place the ***(#1)*** *on the slot of the* ***negative attitude*** *you think is* ***most dangerous for you*** *and the* ***(#2)*** *on the slot of the* ***negative attitude*** *you think is the* ***2nd most dangerous for you*** *until each negative attitude has a # on the slot.*

1. An Attitude of Pride
   - ☐ Substituting another drug for your drug of choice ______
   - ☐ Attending Celebrations (Holidays) ______
   - ☐ Associating success in other areas of life (finance, employment, etc.) with being able to successfully use drugs/alcohol. ______
   - ☐ Hanging around with old associates who are in addiction. ______
   - ☐ Visiting bars and other places where you know drugs/alcohol are being used. ______
2. An Attitude of Rebellion ______
3. An Attitude of Fear & Doubt ______
4. An Undisciplined Attitude ______
5. An Attitude of Ignorance to Spiritual Dangers ______

Self-Rating

How well do you understand "*negative attitudes*" leading to relapse? Discuss your answer with your group/

Has a "*negative attitude*" set you up to relapse in the past? Discuss your answer with your group.

Action Steps

List three things you are willing to do that will keep "*negative attitudes*" from setting you up to relapse.

1.
2.
3.

Was there a scripture(s) in this section that impacted your life? Discuss that experience with your group.

GRIEVING THE HOLY SPIRIT BY GIVING SATAN AN OPPORTUNITY

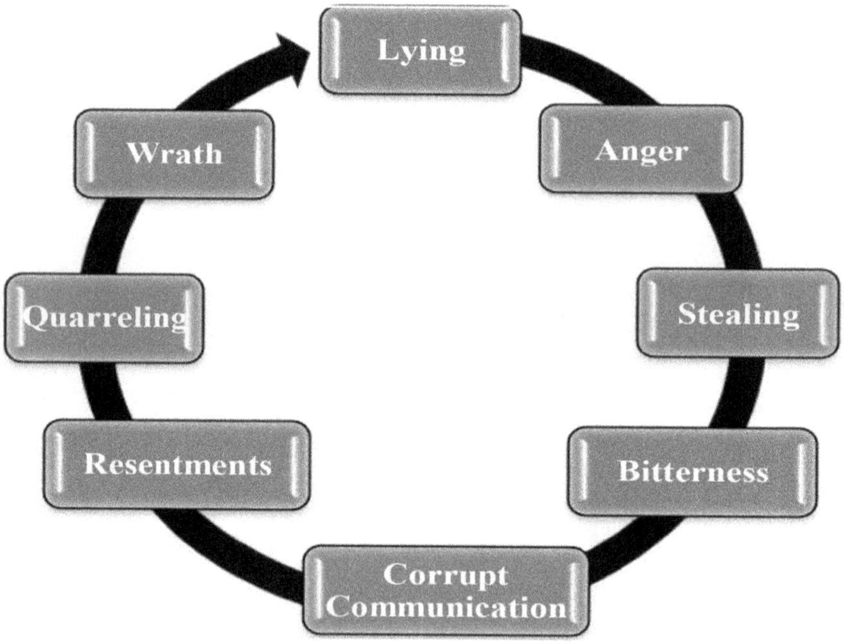

Figure 74: Other Set-up Behaviors

Wherefore *putting away lying*, speak every man truth with his neighbor: for we are members one of another. *Be ye angry, and sin not*: let not the sun go down upon your wrath: *Neither give place to the devil.* Let him that stole steal no more: but rather let him labor, working with *his* hands the thing which is good, that he may have to give to him that needeth. Let no corrupt communication proceed out of your mouth, but that which is good to the use of edifying, that it may minister grace unto the hearers. *And grieve not the Holy Spirit of God,* whereby ye are sealed unto the day of redemption. Let all bitterness, and wrath, and anger, and clamour, and evil speaking, be put away from you, with all malice. (Ephesians 4:25–31)

- ☐ You must understand that you are required by God to begin to develop a godly lifestyle through the power of the Holy Spirit.
- ☐ God spiritually transformed you (has done something to you) at salvation; now He desires to change your conduct through character development (to do something in you).

- ☐ Either you learn to cooperate with the Holy Spirit or you will allow Satan a foothold in your life once again, which will eventually lead to you returning to your old lifestyle of using/drugs/alcohol (relapsing).

God's Plan For Growth	**Satan's set-up behaviors**
God's Plan For Your Growth	*Satan's Schemes For Your Relapse*
Humility (1 Pet. 5-6, Jas. 4:6)	Pride (1 Pet.5:5, 1 Tim. 3:6)
Peace (Gal. 5:22)	Anger Leading To Sin (Eph. 4:26:27)
Edification, Building Up Of Others Through Godly Communication (Eph. 4:29B)	Corrupt Communication (Eph. 4:29A)
Speaking Truth, Honesty Eph. (4:25B)	Lying (Eph. 4:25A, Acts 5:3)
Forgiveness (2 Cor. 2:10)	Lack Of Forgiveness (2 Cor. 2:11)
Confession Of Sin 1Jn. 1:9)	Denial Of Sin (1Jn. 1:8)
God Wants You To Submit Your Will (Jas. 4:7)	Satan Wants To Force His Will On You (2 Tim. 2:26)
To Work And Give To Charity Eph. (4:28B)	Stealing (Eph. 4:28A)
1st Greatest Commandment (Matt. 22:37)	Love Of The World (2 Co. 4:4, 1John 2:15-17)
Living A Sober And Balanced Lifestyle	Living An Undisciplined Lifestyle
(1 Peter 5:8)	(1 Peter 5:8)
2nd Greatest Commandment (Matt. 22:39)	Prejudice & Hatred (1John 2:9-11)
Casting All Your Cares Upon God (1 Peter 5:7-9)	Worry & Anxiety (1 Peter 5:7-9)
Obedience	Rebellion To The Known Will Of God Disobedience, (1 Sam. 15:23)

Figure 75: God's Plan vs. Satan's Plan

Before you were set free from the power of sin, your appetites, passions, and desires (flesh) were united with your old nature, resulting in you fulfilling the "works of the flesh." Now that you have a new nature, your old desires (appetites and passions) continue to seek for many things outside of God. Satan will take full advantage of those desires, appetites, and passions if you give him the opportunity by giving in to them and return to "sowing to the flesh (sinning)."

You must understand that whenever you begin practicing any of your old behaviors that you used to be involved in during your old addictive lifestyle, you are setting yourself up for relapse.

IDENTIFYING YOUR SET-UP BEHAVIORS

Self-Check

All of you, *clothe yourselves with humility toward one another*, because *"God opposes the proud but gives grace to the humble." Humble yourselves*, therefore, under God's mighty hand, *that he may lift you up in due time* (1 Peter 5:5–6, NIV).

*Rank the following common set-up behaviors according to how they have led to your relapse. Place the **(#1)** on the slot of the **set-up behavior you think is most dangerous for you** and the **(#2)** on the slot of the **set-up behavior you think is the 2nd most dangerous for you** until each set-up behavior has a # on the slot.*

1. Unwillingness to forgive others ______
2. Lying ______
3. Anger ______
4. Worry & Anxiety (stress) ______
5. Denial of Sin ______
6. Love for the World (old lifestyle, excitement of street life) ______
7. Living an unbalanced lifestyle (no rest, too much work, no leisure time) ______
8. Rebellion (disobedience to the known will of God) ______
9. Prejudice & Hatred ______
10. Corrupt Communications ______

Self-Rating

How well do you understand "*set-up behaviors*" leading to relapse? Discuss your answer in group.

Has your "*set-up behaviors*" ever caused you to relapse? Discuss your answer in group.

Action Steps

List three things you are willing to do that will keep you from setting yourself up to relapse.

1.
2.
3.

Was there a scripture(s) in this section that impacted your life? Discuss that experience with your group.

Re–Entrapment

It is of the utmost importance that during the process of you being restored from the effects of addiction that you understand when you rely on or use *something* other than *God* (*prayer, praise, worship, fasting, the fellowship of other saints and meditating on His word*) to get through your painful experiences or to provide you with a sense of well-being, you hinder your spiritual growth. When you do, you will often develop a new stronghold (addiction) to that *something.*

You must realize that just because a substance isn't being ingested doesn't mean you aren't using (sowing to the flesh). In order to determine whether you are still using *(re-trapped and feeding a stronghold)* you need to ask yourself, is what you're deriving pleasure from sinful? In other words, is it against God's will? Is what you're doing defiling your body (the temple)? Are you seeking this *something more* than you're seeking God (idolatry)? Are you spending more time with this *something more* than you're spending with God? Is this *something* causing you to neglect your family duties within your home? Is or does this *something* hinder your walk or mar your testimony? Is this *something* allowing you to put on a mask and hide who you really are?

RE–ENTRAPMENT

Self-Rating (Discuss Your Answers with Your Group)

How well do you understand "*re-entrapment*" leading to a new addiction?

Has "*re-entrapment*" ever caused you to trade alcohol/drug addiction for some other addiction?

Identifying Areas of Re-Entrapment Exercise

Check any of the areas below that you consider are areas of possible re–entrapment in your life.

[ ] Sex
[ ] Money
[ ] Work
[ ] Exercise
[ ] Entertainment
[ ] Food
[ ] Other ____________

Action Steps

List three things you are willing to do to that will keep you from setting yourself up for "re–entrapment?"

1.
2.
3.

Jesus Has Provided the Solution to Addiction

- ☐ God provided you with a solution instantaneously the moment you believed on Jesus as Lord. God spiritually transformed (new nature) you, and you became involved in the life-long process of spiritual restoration through sanctification (change in conduct and character).
- ☐ Jesus provided you with the only solution to all sin, including addiction to drugs/alcohol, by giving His life as the ultimate payment required for sin.
- ☐ Therefore, in Him lies the only way to enter into a relationship with God the Father. Without being washed in the Blood of Jesus, there is no forgiveness of sin.
- ☐ There is no solution for addiction to drugs/alcohol without acknowledging Jesus as Lord, only the world's way of managing the sin (addiction) through the self—effort of abstinence. Jesus is the only answer to the sin problem, because only He could have paid the price—and He did.

This I say then, *"Walk in the Spirit, and ye shall not fulfil the lust of the flesh. For the flesh lusteth against the Spirit, and the Spirit against the flesh: and these are contrary the one to the other: so that ye cannot do the things that ye would."* (Galatians 5:16–17)

Prayer for Overcoming the Effect of Addiction

Dear heavenly Father, I thank you for providing victory for me over the cravings and desires of my flesh and for allowing me to understand what causes those cravings. I thank You for changing me by renewing my mind as I read your Word and for giving me a new attitude. I also thank You for the body of believers to fellowship with so I can avoid old friends and associates.

Father, help me to avoid set-up behaviors and old attitudes that lead me away from you and back to my old lifestyle. Father, help me to practice Your methods of short-circuiting any cravings I experience and to be humble enough to admit to another person when I'm struggling with the desire to use drugs/alcohol.

In Jesus's name, Amen!

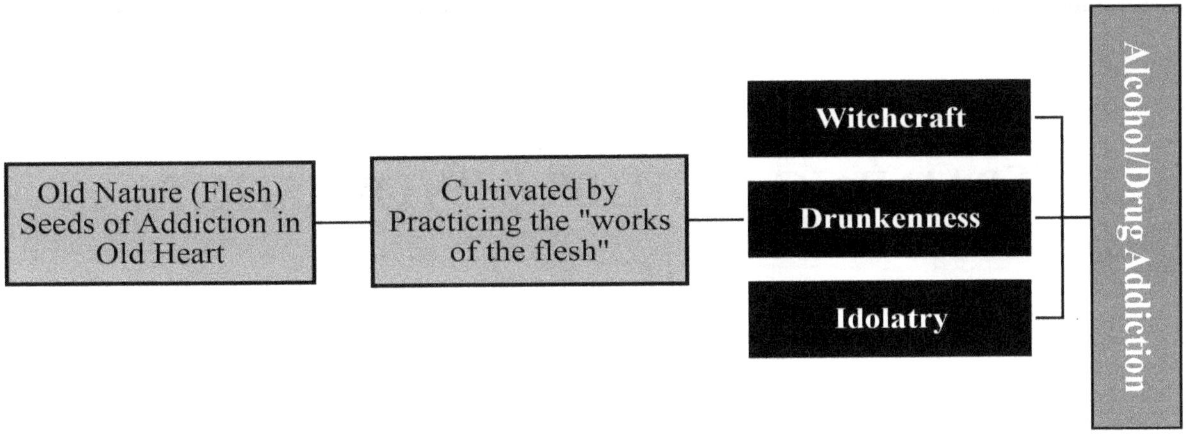

Figure 76: Summarization of a Biblical View of Addiction

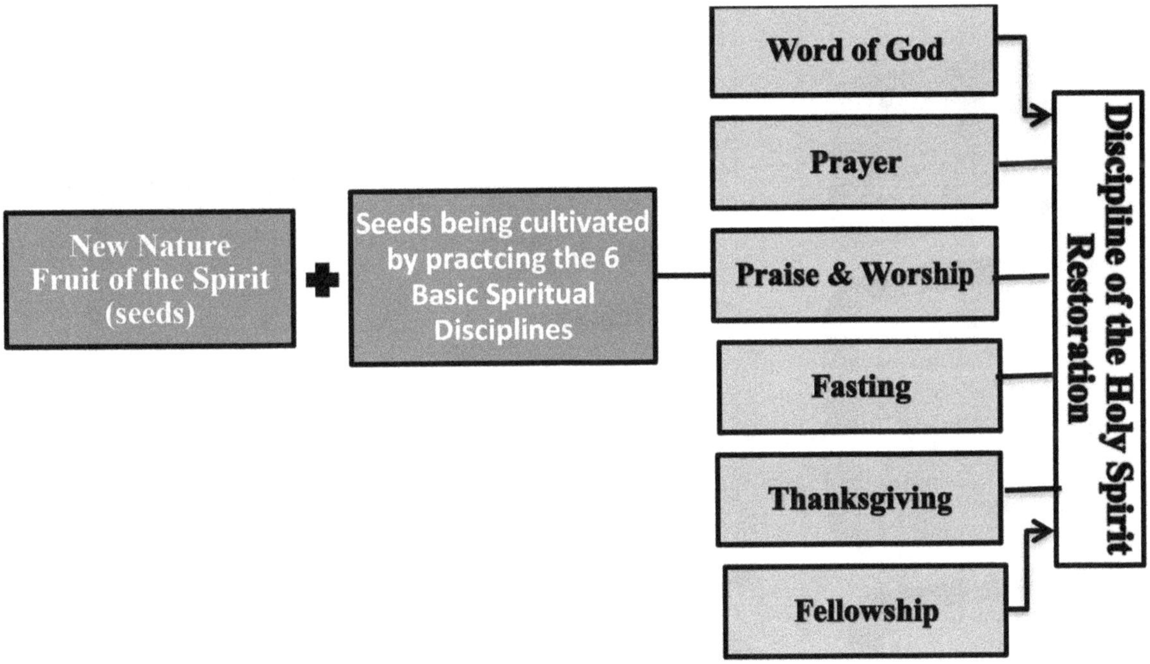

Figure 77: Summarization of a Biblical View of Relapse Prevention

This I say then, "*Walk in the Spirit*, and ye shall not fulfil the lust of the flesh. For the *flesh lusteth against the Spirit, and the Spirit against the flesh:* and these are contrary the one to the other: so that ye cannot do the things that ye would." (Galatians 5:16–17)

TRAINING GUIDES & WORKSHOPS

Presents

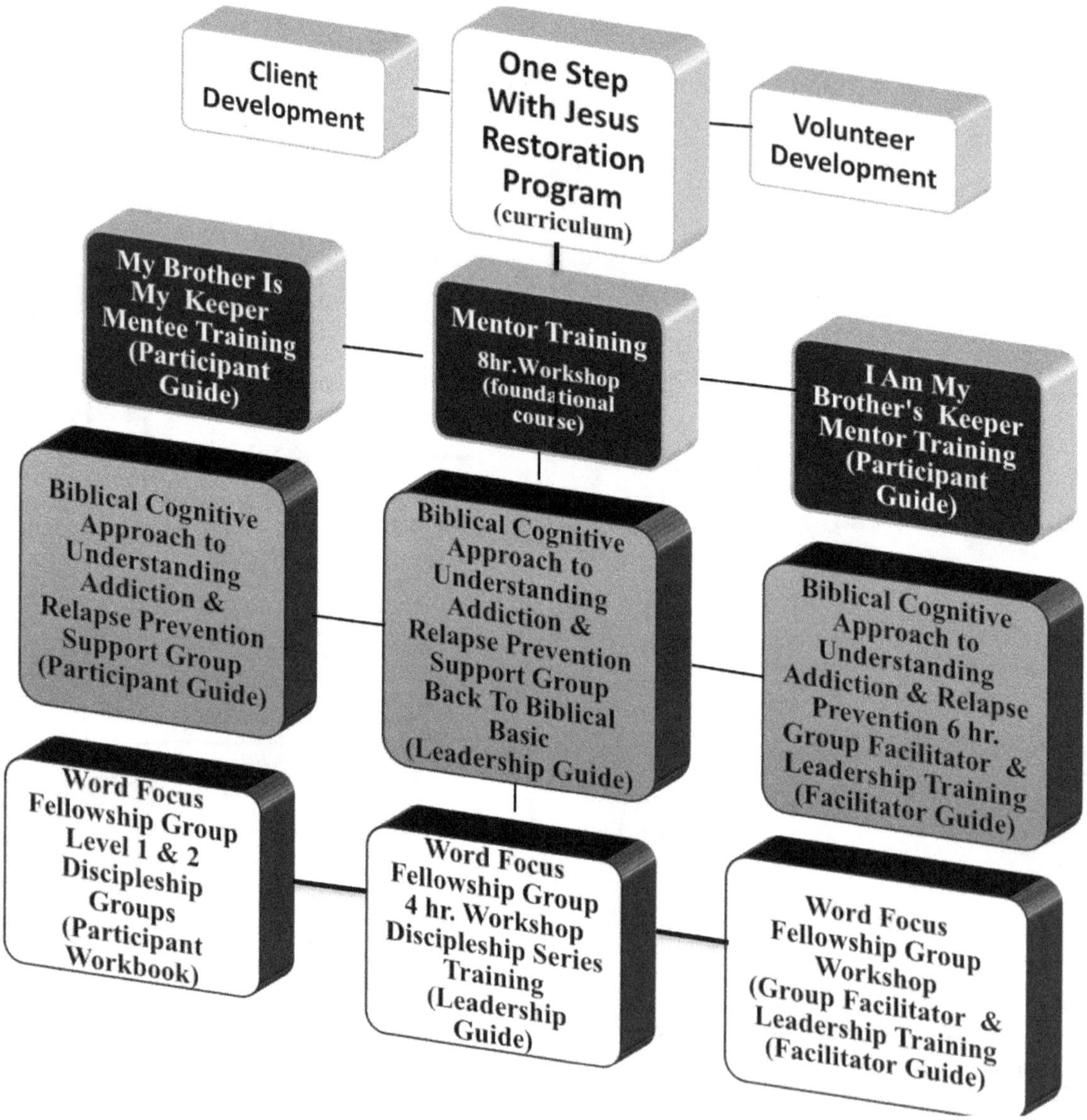

Powerful Training Guides

Ministerial Tools for Pastors, Counselors, Chaplains, and Mentors

Alcohol/Drug Addiction

Back to biblical Basics

A Biblical Cognitive Approach to Understanding Relapse Prevention (Pastors/Counselor Ministry Leaders)

- Facilitator Guide
- Participant Guide
- PowerPoint CD

A Biblical Cognitive Relapse Prevention Plan Workbook

- Facilitator Guide
- Participant Guide
- PowerPoint CD

Word-Focused Fellowship Discipleship Series (Group Study Workbook)

- Facilitator Guide
- Participant Guide (Level I & II)
- PowerPoint CD

Ministerial Tools for Pastors, Counselors, Chaplains, and Mentors

Mentoring

"I Am My Brother's Keeper"

A Biblical Guide for Mentoring Christians who are in Bondage to life controlling issues

- Instructor Guide
- Participant Guide
- PowerPoint CD

"My Brother is My Keeper"

A Biblical Guide for Preparing Christians Who Are in Bondage to Life Controlling Issues for Mentoring Relationship

- Instructor Guide

- Participant Guide
- PowerPoint CD

Equipping Workshops

Mentoring

Course Number MT 101—Mentor Training—Workshop
Course Number MT 102—Mentor Training—Workshop
Course Number MT 103—Mentor Instructor Training—Workshop

Addiction & Relapse Prevention

Course Number AT 101—Addiction & Relapse Prevention Training—Workshop
Course Number AT 102—Biblical Cognitive Relapse Prevention Support Group Facilitator Training Workshop
Course Number AT 103—Addiction & Relapse Prevention Instructor Training—Workshop

Discipleship Series

Course Number AT 104—Facilitator (WFFG) Training Workshop
Course Number AT 103—Facilitator (WFFG) Training Workshop (Level I) & (Level II)

Bibliography

Anderson, T. N. (1990) *Victory Over Darkness*, Regal Publishing, Ventura, California, pg. 80–85, 160,164, 232–239.

Anderson, T. N. (1990) *The Bondage Breaker*, Harvest House Publishers, Eugene, Oregon.

Backgrounder (1995) *The Real Root Cause of Violent Crime: The Breakdown of Marriage, Family, and Community*, Heritage Foundation, Washington, D.C.

Biehl, B., Urquhart, G. (1990) *Believing, Master Planning Group International*, Laguna Niguel, California.

Boehi, D. (1993) *Home Builders Couple Series*, Gospel Light Publishing Co., Ventura, California.

Bishop, J. (1957) *The Day Christ Died*, Harper and Brothers, New York, New York. pg. 290–91.

Bracco, B. (1994) *Called to Counsel*, self-published by Bill Bracco, Detroit, Michigan.

Bubeck, M. (1975) *The Adversary*, Moody Bible Press Publishing Co., Chicago Illinois, pg. 30, 32.

Chambers, O. (1963) *My Utmost for His Highest Journal*, Barbour and Company, Inc. Uhrichsville, Ohio, Feb. 12.

Christian Business Men's Committee of USA (1995) *Operation Timothy Leader's Guide*, CBMC Publications, Chattanooga, Tennessee, pg. 6, 7.

Christian Business Men's Committee of USA (1996) Annual Conference, St. Louis, Missouri, (video tape) Dr. Howard Hendricks.

Clinton R. J. (1992) *The Connection*, NavPress Publishing Company, Colorado, Springs, Colorado.

Conner, K. J. (1980) *The Foundations of Christian Doctrine*, City Bible Publishing, Portland, Oregon. pgs. 129, 130.

Crabb, J. L. (1977) *Effective biblical Counseling*, Zondervan Publishing House, Grand Rapids Michigan, pg. 23–25, 61, 62, 72.

Crown Ministries (1986) Small Group Financial Study, Crown Ministries Inc. Longwood, Florida, pg. 58–60.

Edwards, W. D., Gabel, W. D., Hosmer, F. E. (1986) *On the Physical Death of Jesus Christ*, The Journal of the American Medical Association, pgs. 1457–58

Engstrom, W. T. (1989) *The Fine Art of Believing*, Trinity Press Publishing Co., Newburgh, Indiana, pg. Ix, 49, 40.

Evans, W. (1974) *The Great Doctrines of the Bible*, Moody Press, Chicago, Illinois.

FitzGerald, K. W., PhD (1990) *Addiction & Recovery*, "Endorphins: Feeling Better the Natural Way, pg. 43.

Focus on the Family (1994). *Seven Promises of a Promise Keeper*, Promise Keepers, Navpress Publishing Group, Colorado, Colorado, pgs., 60, 48, 49.

Fortune, Don & Katie (1987) *Discover your God-Given Gifts*. Chosen Books, A Division of Baker Book House Co., Grand Rapids, Michigan, pgs. 14, 26, 27, 37, 39.

Foster, R. J. (1998) *Celebration of Discipline*, Harper Collins Publishers, Inc., San Francisco, California, pg. 7, 52 (prayer fasting).

Gorsuch, G. (1994) Brothers, *Calling Men into Vital Relationships*, Promise Keepers, Navpress Publishing Group, Colorado Springs, Colorado.

Hendricks, H. (1997) *Iron Sharpens Iron,* Moody Press Publishing Company, Chicago, Illinois.

International Bible Society (1985) NIV Study Bible, Zondervan Publishing House, Grand Rapids, Michigan, pg. 1487, 1562.

Jordan, B. (1989) *Believing the Missing Link,* Zoe Ministries Publishing Co., Brooklyn, New York, pg. 31–33.

London: Inter-Varsity (1998) *The Message of Galatians*. pg. 170

Lutzer, E. W. (2001) *Seven Snares of the enemy, Breaking Free from the Devil's Grip,* Moody Press, Chicago, Illinois, pg.64–67.

MacArthur, J. *Fundamental Attitudes Necessary for Spiritual Growth.* (Tape series).

MacArthur, J. (1987) T*he MacArthur New Testament Commentary, Galatians*, Moody Bible Institute, Chicago, Illinois, pg. 183–192, 151, 143, 151, 161, 187

Mains, D. (1992) *Healing the Dysfunctional Church Family*, Victor Books, a division of scripture Press Publications, Inc., USA, Canada, England, and pg. 81.

Mcclung, Jr. F. (1985) *The Father Heart of God,* Harvest House Publishers, Eugene, Oregon.

McGee, Robert (1990) *The Search for Significance*, Rapha Publishing, Houston, Texas. pg. 15.

McReynolds, K., Dr. Luter, B. (1994) "Recovering Through Fully Biblical Recovery," The Christian Research Institute, Rancho Santa Margarita California, pg., 1–2.

Munroe, M. (2001) *Understanding the Purpose and Power of Men,* Whitaker House, New Kensington, PA., pg. 70.

Nee, W. (1968) *The Spiritual Man,* Christian Fellowship Publishers, Inc., New York, New York.

Nee, W. (1965) *The Release of the Spirit,* Sure Foundation Publishers, Indianapolis, Indiana.

Nelson's Electronic Bible Reference Library (1998) Matthew Henry's Commentary. Thomas Nelson, Inc., Nashville, Tennessee.

Rouse, D. (2002) "Breaking Generational Curses" *(audio series)*. Victory World Church, Norcross, Georgia.

Sande, K. (1997) *The Peacemaker,* Baker Books Publishing Co., Grand Rapids, Michigan, pg. 43, 74–79.

Seamands, A. D. (1991) *Healing for Damaged Emotions*, Chariot Victor Publishing, Colorado Springs, Colorado, pg. 13, 31, 32, 39, 134

Stanley, C. (1988) *Winning the War Within*, Thomas Nelson Publishers, Nashville, Tennessee. pg. 50, 69.

Survey of State Prison Inmates (1991) US Department of Justice, Office of Justice Programs, Bureau of Justice Statistics.

Swindoll, C.R. (2001) *A Ministry Anyone Could Trust,* Insight for Living, Anaheim, California, pg. 3, 8, 40, 48, 85.

Swindoll, C.R. (1998) *He Gave Gifts,* Insight for Living, Anaheim, California. Pg. 3.

Swindoll, C.R. (1998, 1999) *The Majesty of God's Son*, Insight for Living, Anaheim, California. pg. 120–124.

The Magazine for Business Today, *CONTACT* (1965), Volume 54, NO.1, CBMC, Chattanooga, Tennessee.

Unger, F. M. Th.D., PhD, (1967). *Unger's Bible Handbook*, Moody Press, Chicago, Illinois. pg. 615, 637, 818–826.

Vann, R. F. (1998) *Principles for Effective Believing Of Ex-Prisoners,* Prison Fellowship Ministries, Reston, Virginia, pgs. 1–78, 93– 112.

White, B. T. (1993) *Breaking Strongholds,* Servant Publications Co., Ann Arbor, Michigan.

Williams, J. (2000) *Program Policy Manual.* Transition of Prisoners, Inc., Detroit, Michigan.

Wise, T. (1997) *The Art of Believing,* (lecture tapes), Trinity Press Publishing Company, Newburgh, Indiana.

Wise, T. (1996) *The Fundamentals of Spiritual Warfare,* (lecture tapes), Trinity Press Publishing Company, Newburgh, Indiana.

Wise, T. (1996) *The Fundamentals of Spiritual Warfare,* Simon & Schuster Custom Publishing, Needham Heights, Massachusetts. pg. 64, 65, 66.

About the Author

Robert Vann is currently the program manager for Soteria CDC Reentry Program in Greenville, South Carolina. He is the executive director and co-founder of "A Strictly Biblical Perspective Ministries (ASBPM)" with his wife, Maria, of thirty-one years.

He has over twenty-seven years of full-time experience in ministry serving as program director for a ninety-two bed Christ-centered transitional housing program, Fuqua Hall, a ministry of the Atlanta Mission as an addiction's counselor, case manager, and program manager at Detroit Rescue Mission Ministries, Prison Fellowship Ministries, and the Atlanta Mission.

He has a Master of the Arts degree from Wane State University in the field of counseling with specialization in substance abuse. He is the author of the *One Step with Jesus Restoration Program with a Cognitive Biblical Approach to Understanding and Addressing Addiction and Relapse Prevention, with Mentoring and Discipleship and Ministry Components*. He has trained over 1,500 mentors throughout the United States and facilitates workshops across the nation and serves as an online professor for the Christian University GlobalNet (CUGN).

Robert has been restored from crack, cocaine, alcohol, and heroin addictions.

CPSIA information can be obtained
at www.ICGtesting.com
Printed in the USA
FSHW020829111020
74598FS